ISLAMIC REVIVALISM IN A CHANGING PEASANT ECONOMY

Scandinavian Institute of Asian Studies

Monograph Series

Southeast Asia:

No. 18	Pensak Chagsuchinda: Nang Loi – the Floating Maiden A recitation from the Ramakien, a Thai epic poem
No. 24	Barend Jan Terwiel: Monks and Magic An analysis of religious ceremonies in central Thailand
No. 25	Thomas Silcock: A Village Ordination The inauguration of a Thai Buddhist monk, bilingual
No. 27	Viggo Brun: Sug, the Trickster who Fooled the Monk A northern Thai tale in the trickster-cycle
No. 30	K.G. Izikowitz & P. Sørensen: The House in East and Southeast Asia Anthropological and architectural aspects
No. 33	Kristina Lindell et al: A Kammu Story-listener's Tales A study of Kammu folklore in Thailand and Laos
No. 40	Kristina Lindell et al: Folk Takes from Kammu – II A story-teller's tales from Thailand and Laos
No. 47	Christine Dobbin: Islamic Revivalism in a Changing Peasant Economy Central Sumatra, 1784-1847

SCANDINAVIAN INSTITUTE OF ASIAN STUDIES
MONOGRAPH SERIES NO. 47

Islamic Revivalism in a Changing Peasant Economy

Central Sumatra, 1784-1847

Christine Dobbin

Curzon Press

Scandinavian Institute of Asian Studies
Kejsergade 2, DK-1155 Copenhagen K.

First published 1983
Reprinted 1987
Curzon Press Ltd: London and Malmö

ISBN 0 7007 0155 9
ISSN 0069 1712

Printed and Bound by Woolnough Bookbinding
of Irthlingborough, Northants.

For Julia

CONTENTS

PREFACE

'The ferment and expansion of Islam was such that in terms of purely religious history, we can best describe the period from 1789 to 1848 as that of a world Islamic revival.'[1]

The revivalist movements which flowered in numerous Islamic societies in the late eighteenth and early nineteenth centuries are still sufficiently unchartered to exhaust a lifetime of scholarly research. One can readily agree with Hugh Seton-Watson, who, when discussing the early nineteenth century Murid movement in the Caucasus, writes: 'Social discontent, hatred of the foreigner, and religious puritanism were combined in the movement, and it is virtually impossible for an historian to disentangle them.'[2] Yet many of the developments apparent in Islamic societies in our own time will remain obscure if historians do not at least attempt the 'disentangling' process, and go on to assess the place of revivalism in the evolution of Islamic societies. Although there have been a number of comparatively recent attempts along these lines, it must be said at the outset that very few studies of the major Islamic revivalist movements of the eighteenth and nineteenth centuries have succeeded in placing these phenomena in anything like an adequate social and economic context.[3]

The decision to attempt to provide this context, to flesh out the bare texts of revivalism, compels the historian to extend his or her investigations deep into the past of the particular community in which an Islamic revivalist movement has manifested itself. In the case of the Padri movement which is the subject of this study, the community involved is that of the Minangkabau of central Sumatra, one of the major communities inhabiting the Indonesian archipelago. Because so little of a scholarly nature has been written on the eighteenth and nineteenth century history of the Indonesian communities, any incursion into the field would appear to present relatively few problems. The historian finds, however, that neglect of these communities by one group of scholars has not been duplicated by other groups, and anthropologists, economists and geographers have been most zealous in their researches. Although their pioneering efforts have been invaluable, it is unfortunate that their categories, applicable, perhaps, to our own time, have so often been imposed upon the past where their validity is somewhat more questionable. The historian involved in reconstructing the past of the Minangkabau must therefore exercise considerable caution when becoming steeped in the work of fellow scholars.

An example might make more comprehensible this need for caution. It soon became apparent to me that to write about the Padri movement involved reconstructing a society in the throes of an agricultural transformation. The necessity arose of collecting information piece by piece on all the major villages of Minangkabau, and in particular on their agricultural history. Yet the historical development of the Indonesian village is still to-day virtually unknown. So far the history of not one village has formed the subject of a scholarly monograph. While keeping in mind studies from the field of European history, where is the historian of Indonesia to turn for possible guidelines if not to the economist specializing in Indonesian affairs? Here, however, the shadow of J.H. Boeke's work lies heavily upon the perceptions. Despite some modern recognition of the Indonesian peasant's willingness to innovate where risk and uncertainty are not too great,[4] with the implication this has for the dynamic of village history, Boeke's argument that 'agricultural production for the market is really alien to the genuine eastern village'[5] must surely have deterred potential historians of the village. More persuasive still as far as historians of Indonesia have been concerned is his view that, where change can be observed in the village economy, 'the movement has never been primarily economic; it is determined not by economic but by social motives . . . The chief characteristic of village life is that such changes as do occur must be sought for in another field, not mainly that of economics.'[6]

The pervasiveness of such a viewpoint gives rise to a temptation to look at social and religious movements in eighteenth and nineteenth century Indonesia in terms of cultural change or in terms of response to direct policy initiatives of the Netherlands Indies colonial government. It is without doubt for this reason that the Padri movement has traditionally been viewed as the product of a clash between the lineage heads of Minangkabau village society and Islamic teachers penetrating the Minangkabau world with new ideas from outside. To try to look at the movement in broader terms, encompassing the economic and social histories of individual villages, has therefore required a willingness both to jettison one's own intellectual preconceptions and to deviate from traditional norms.

Not merely a willingness, but the ability to deviate. Here one is faced with another problem. The source material used in this study has been overwhelmingly Dutch, drawn from official archives and from the published accounts of contemporary Dutch observers of the central Sumatran scene. Only two accounts by Minangkabau participants in the Islamic revivalist movement could be located and used, together with Minangkabau material such as traditional tales, customary sayings and archaeological evidence. Working through the mass of Dutch archival material on this period has required all the skills of the 'historian as archaeologist', for each of the voluminous reports of Dutch campaigns and battles in central Sumatra has had to be sifted for the few sherds of information it contains about the economy of the villages mentioned, their religious persuasion, and any other pertinent details. For the Islamic revivalist movement itself, much of the analysis has had to be based on the earliest accounts jotted down by Netherlands Indies military officers and civilian officials, who made inquiries of Minangkabau with whom they were in contact. Apart from this, the surveys of Dutch scientific investigators and of travellers, invaluable for the study of the village economy, have also proved useful for their references to villages as adherents to or opponents of the Islamic revivalist movement, although careful sifting of the evidence has been required to postulate currents or trends inside a village.

While all works of scholarship represent the credit balance of intellectual debts accumulated over the years, in some works these debts are more immediately apparent than in others. This book falls most heavily into the debtor category, and I hope its appearance will afford some measure of repayment to many people. I should first of all like to thank the late Jim Davidson of the Department of Pacific and Southeast Asian History in the Australian National University for being sufficiently unconventional to award a research fellowship in Indonesian history in his department to a scholar whose previous work had been in another field of historical endeavour. I should also like to thank John Bastin of the School of Oriental and African Studies, University of London, for suggesting that I focus my attention on the Padri movement at a time when I was seeking to encompass the entire nineteenth century history of Islam in Sumatra in my limited grasp; I also owe him thanks for sharing with me his great knowledge of the sources of Sumatran history. Thanks are also owed to Tony Johns of the Department of Indonesian Languages and Literatures at the Australian National University for placing the resources of his department at my disposal and enabling me to learn Indonesian and Dutch, and to both himself and Yohanni for their ready willingness to engage in discussion on Minangkabau and Sumatran Islam. For providing a visiting fellowship and an environment in which I was able to complete this work I owe a debt of gratitude to Gavan Daws and Tony Reid of the Department of Pacific and Southeast Asian History at the Australian National University; I am also grateful to Tony Reid for answering so many questions about Sumatra in general and Aceh in particular, and to Akira Oki for his extreme generosity with his own source material on Minangkabau.

Financial support for my work came from the Australian National University, which made it possible for me to work in archives and libraries in England and the Netherlands, and from the Australian Research Grants Council, which enabled me to visit Sumatra. In the Netherlands my particular thanks are due to the Algemene Rijksarchivaris and staff of the Algemeen Rijksarchief in The Hague, whose willingness to search for material on eighteenth and nineteenth century Minangkabau went far beyond the call of duty, and to the Bibliothecaris and staff of the Koninklijke Bibliotheek in The Hague. Gratitude is also owed to the staffs of the Koninklijk Instituut voor Taal-, Land- en Volkenkunde in Leiden, and of the Algemeen Rijksarchief Hulpdepot in Schaarsbergen. All these institutions have also been most assiduous in answering queries from Australia and in sending photocopied material. In London I was grateful for the assistance of the Librarian and staff of the India Office Library. During my time in Sumatra I was greatly assisted by the kind help of Ir. Muchlis Mochtar of the Fakultas Pertanian, Universitas Andalas, Padang, and by the students and staff of the Deutsches Institut für Entwicklungspolitik of West Berlin, whose time in Bukit Tinggi coincided with my own and who were extremely generous with their transport facilities.

For drawing the maps I should like to thank Theo Baumann of the Department of Human Geography at the Australian National University. The manuscript was prepared for publication by Robyn Walker and the typing staff of the Research School of Pacific Studies, and typed on the Composer by Leona Jorgensen, to whom I am most grateful.

My debts go beyond this, to those whose personal support has enabled me to write anything at all. In this connection I should like to thank my friends Barbara Andaya and Jennifer Terrell; my parents, Harry and Bessie Dobbin, who on numerous occasions shouldered many of my domestic responsibilities; and my daughter, Julia Wright, who since her birth has coped with my infrequent absences and frequent abstraction with equanimity. In the final analysis, it is her judgement of my manuscript – 'very messy and full of mistakes' – which has been a constant inspiration to me.

Canberra C.D.

NOTES TO PREFACE

1 E.J. Hobsbawm, *The Age of Revolution. Europe 1789-1848* (London, 1962), p. 225.
2 H. Seton-Watson, *The Russian Empire 1801-1917* (Oxford, 1967), p. 291.
3 The most successful, in my opinion, is M.A. Khan, *History of the Fara'idi Movement in Bengal (1818-1906)* (Karachi, 1965), which includes a chapter on the geography of the movement.
4 B. Glassburner (ed.), *The Economy of Indonesia* (Ithaca and London, 1971), pp. 162-78.
5 J.H. Boeke, *Economics and Economic Policy of Dual Societies* (New York, 1953), p. 24. Boeke took up the chair of tropical-colonial economics at Leiden in 1929.
6 ibid., p. 30.

ABBREVIATIONS

ANHM	Archief van de Nederlandsche Handel-Maatschappij
ARA	Algemeen Rijksarchief, The Hague
ARAH	Algemeen Rijksarchief Hulpdepot, Schaarsbergen
BKI	*Bijdragen tot de Taal-, Land- en Volkenkunde van Nederlandsch Indië,* uitgegeven door het Koninklijk Instituut voor Taal-, Land- en Volkenkunde
Exh.	Exhibitum
Geh.	Geheim
GM	W.Ph Coolhaas (ed.), *Generale-Missiven van Gouverneurs- Generaal en Raden aan Heren XVII der Verenigde Oostindische Compagnie,* vols 1-6 (The Hague, 1960-1976)
IG	*De Indische Gids*
IM	*Indisch Magazijn*
IOL	The India Office Library, London
JMBRAS	*Journal of the Malayan Branch of the Royal Asiatic Society*
JSAH	*Journal of Southeast Asian History*
JSBRAS	*Journal of the Straits Branch of the Royal Asiatic Society*
KA	Koloniaal Archief
Kab.	Kabinet
KI	Koninklijk Instituut voor Taal-, Land- en Volkenkunde, Leiden
MK	Ministerie van Koloniën
MSS.	Manuscripts
Part.	Particulier
RGP	*Rijks Geschiedkundige Publicatiën. Grote Serie*
SFR	Sumatra Factory Records
SSFR	Straits Settlements Factory Records
TBG	*Tijdschrift voor Indische Taal-, Land- en Volkenkunde,* uitgegeven door het Bataviaasch Genootschap van Kunsten en Wetenschappen
TNGP	*Tijdschrift voor Natuurlijke Geschiedenis en Physiologie*
TNI	*Tijdschrift voor Nederlandsch Indië*
TNNI	*Tijdschrift voor Nijverheid in Nederlandsch Indië*
VBG	*Verhandelingen van het Bataviaasch Genootschap van Kunsten en Wetenschappen*

NOTE ON SPELLING

Wherever possible all Minangkabau place names, titles and nouns have been rendered in their Bahasa Indonesia forms, following the official system of spelling adopted by the Indonesian government in late 1972. Pluralization with the English 's' has been avoided, so that words appear in the same form in both the singular and plural, with the verb providing a sufficient distinguishing guideline. A very few Islamic terms have been retained in their Arabic form, and Batak place names have been spelt in that language. Where Indonesian words appear in quotations, their spelling conforms to the spelling of the original source.

CHAPTER I

INTRODUCTION: THE GEOGRAPHICAL FOUNDATIONS OF CENTRAL SUMATRAN CIVILIZATION

About the turn of the nineteenth century a trader from the highlands of Central Sumatra constructed a map of the island of Sumatra. In the centre he placed Mount Merapi, the highest volcanic peak of his own homeland, and around it in concentric circles he drew the fertile upland valleys with their wet-rice fields characteristic of the area. The rest of Sumatra he depicted as a virtually undifferentiated mass, revolving around this pivot.[1] Observed on a modern map of the Indian Ocean region, however, the island of Sumatra appears to be distinguished from the neighbouring Asian land mass not by the fertile valleys of its central highlands, but by the water which surrounds it. Sumatra through its coastline belongs to the mercantile world of the Indian Ocean; its northernmost shores reach out to the Coromandel coast of India and the trade routes of the Middle East, its eastern shoreline guards the straits leading to the world of the South China Sea and beyond.

Because of its geography, two worlds battle for supremacy in Sumatra. The sober, regular tenor of farming life in the Sumatran highlands is in marked contrast to the bustling, competitive world of the coastal trader. But in the central highlands, which because of certain topographical peculiarities have ample access to the coast, agricultural change and innovation developed side by side with the ability to seize coastal trading opportunities, producing a people of peculiar dynamism and adaptability and necessitating constant readjustment within their society. The inhabitants of the Central Sumatran highlands, the Minangkabau, have become famous throughout the Indonesian world for their agricultural skills, for their commercial adaptability, and for their general willingness to seize new opportunities and adapt to new mental horizons, whether introduced from India, from the Middle East, or from Europe. Hand in hand has gone the capacity to preserve their own particular identity.

The classic homeland of the Minangkabau is the highlands of the central part of Sumatra, on either side of the very spot where the equator passes through the island. Sumatra is an island with an area approximate to that of Sweden (164,000 square miles), stretching out into the Indian Ocean in a north-westerly direction from the South China Sea. It is about 1,100 miles in length and straddles the equator from 6°N to 6°S, its greatest width being about 250 miles, roughly athwart the equator. Its position as one of the major islands in the discontinuous portion of the land bridge between continental Asia and Australia has ensured its importance in the sea communications network between India and China. It fringes the two main straits leading from the Indian Ocean to the South China Sea, its eastern shoreline overlooking the Malacca Straits which are bordered on the opposite side by the Malay peninsula, and its western coastline terminating in the Sunda Strait which separates Sumatra from Java. For this reason the island has long lain open to contact with the outside world, ports on both the east and west coasts of Sumatra being used for centuries by traders and men of culture and religion in search of both commercial and intellectual exchange.

Within the island, however, there are very marked physical divisions, and the physical characteristics of certain areas would seem to militate against outside contact. The outstanding feature of the island, and an apparent barrier to easy communications, is a chain of mountains running parallel to the shore on its western side and known as the Bukit Barisan (*lit.* line of hills). These mountains are very close to the west coast and drop precipitously down to a narrow coastal plain; nowhere is this west coast more than 20 miles wide, and often the mountains descend directly to the sea. To the east the descent is more gradual, the mountain belt giving way to rolling hills of volcanic and sedimentary rocks which then merge into a flat, alluvial lowland, swampy and jungle-covered, extending eastwards for as much as 150 miles and ending in the mangrove-fringed shores of the Straits of Malacca. In the history of the development of the Minangkabau people it is the mountains of the Bukit Barisan which have played the most crucial role. The outcome of a very complex geological evolution, these mountains vary in breadth and appearance at different points in their journey down the western side of the island. For human settlement, however, their most important feature is the longitudinal trough which runs like a groove, with some interruptions, from one end of the chain to the other.

Certain areas of this trough, areas with volcanoes in their midst or around the edge, form saucer-like upland valleys irrigated by mountain streams and covered with fertile volcanic soil far better suited to intensive agriculture and to human settlement than the swamps of the east coast or the monsoon-drenched western coastal strip. These upland valleys are of varying altitudes, but all provide a fairly equable climate for man. They are drained by many rivers, some flowing slowly eastwards into the straits and providing a means of water-borne access to the mountain region and some rushing westwards, breaking through the western mountain wall and forming gorges and canyons which also facilitate approach to the upland valleys. Nowhere along the length of the Bukit Barisan are these mountain valleys more fertile or more accessible than in the region on either side of the equator, the region which is the historic homeland of the Minangkabau people. A pleasantly comfortable altitude, fertile volcanic soil, mountain streams for irrigation, water-borne communication with the outside world, and communications with other uplands communities due to ease of movement in a north-west and south-east direction along the mountain trough have combined over the centuries to make this the most favoured spot for human settlement in the Sumatran world; as a result the Minangkabau today, as they undoubtedly were in the eighteenth century, are the most numerous people in Sumatra, some 25 per cent of the total.

The heartland of Minangkabau settlement consists of four upland basins or valleys, cradled within the Bukit Barisan at a point where it reaches a width of 50 miles and becomes virtually two separate ranges. They form a small region of about 18,000 square miles, representing only 11 per cent of the island's total area. The westernmost valley lies at an altitude of about 3,000 ft. above sea level, while the most easterly basin tips away towards the Straits of Malacca, reaching a height of no more than 1,500 ft. All have damp, swampy or partially lake-filled bottoms, and must at one time have been covered with water which gradually receded, a development recorded in Minangkabau folklore. Each of the four valleys is separated from the others by rugged hills, and each is characterized by proximity to a volcano. At 3,000 ft. above sea level the valley of Agam lies at the foot of Mount Singgalang, a volcano which towers above the valley to a height of 9,400 ft; it lies almost on the equator. To the south-east of the Agam basin lies the valley of Tanah Datar; the two are separated by the huge truncated cone of Mount Merapi, rising to 9,500 ft. and providing the most distinctive point in the Minangkabau landscape. This mountain is the legendary place of first settlement of the Minangkabau people, who gradually descended to the valleys as they became less swampy and waterlogged. Sloping gently away from Mount Merapi, parallel to Tanah Datar but separated from it by low hills, is the Singkarak-Solok valley. On the valley floor lies Lake Singkarak, an elongated oval about 12½ miles long, with a maximum width of 5 miles, which drains towards the east by means of a river which ultimately merges with one of the great rivers of the Sumatran east coast. This valley too has its own volcano, being bounded on the south-west by Mount Talang, which rises to 4,500 ft. above sea level. The fourth valley lies furthest to the east, running roughly parallel to Agam; called Limapuluh Kota, it is the lowest of the four, reaching a height of no more than 1,500 ft. It inclines gently towards the east coast, and is enclosed at its south-eastern extremity by the volcanic Mount Sago, 5,000 ft. above sea level. The girdles of hills which separate each valley have reinforced other geographical differences, permitting each to develop its own social identity. Yet, in spite of certain divisive factors, the four valleys have historically been perceived as a unity by the Minangkabau; they form the *darat,* the land, the Minangkabau homeland and, by extension, the *alam Minangkabau* or Minangkabau world. Everything outside, including other, smaller valleys in the uplands, with their own lakes, rivers and mountains lying both to the north-west and south-east, is the *rantau,* the frontier, areas containing Minangkabau settlements in, but not quite of, the Minangkabau world.

These four valleys have provided the basis for the development of Minangkabau society because of their agricultural potential. To clarify this it should be explained that, in addition to the faulting which produced the upland basins of the longitudinal trough throughout the Bukit Barisan, outpourings of volcanic material have blocked parts of the trough, interrupting and diverting its drainage for a time and often creating temporary lakes which have left fertile alluvial basins. In most of the highlands of the Bukit Barisan the volcanic soils are predominantly acid. However, around the volcanoes where the Minangkabau originally settled, the recent ejecta are mainly neutral-basic, and these have given rise to local patches of much greater fertility than is typical of the uplands as a whole. The eruptions of Mount Merapi have greatly enriched the soil of both Agam and Tanah Datar, and this volcanic soil has enabled a wide variety of crops to be grown. At some period well before the one dealt with in this book, the Minangkabau commenced wet-rice cultivation both on the valley floors and on the lower slopes of the hills and volcanoes; irrigation was facilitated by the plethora of fast-flowing mountain streams.

Equally important, at this altitude the equatorial climate characteristic of Sumatra in general gives way to a more moderate climate, which compounds the geological advantages of the area. While monsoonal rains bring a total annual rainfall of 177 inches to the west coast, the upland valleys lie in the rain shadow of the higher western mountain wall and receive no more than 94 inches per annum, peaking in April and December. Rainfall, as well as relief, facilitate irrigation. Equatorial temperatures, too, drop markedly at this altitude. The average daytime temperature in the valley of Agam, on the equator, is 69°F throughout the year, with virtually no seasonal variation, whilst on the western coastal plain below the mountain valley there is a constant year-round temperature of 79°F and high, enervating humidity. Apart from their agricultural disadvantages, the lowlands on both sides of the mountain chain have become at some stage in their history malarial and parasite-ridden, restricting both the physical and mental activity of the inhabitants and affecting too the animals required for certain types of agriculture.

There is one more attraction for human settlement and development exerted by the Minangkabau highlands, in addition to their good soil and congenial climate. Throughout the whole of Sumatra, metallic minerals are limited to the Bukit Barisan, and in particular to that part of the central highlands around the equator occupied by the Minangkabau. The existence of small but widespread deposits of gold, and the considerable deposits of iron found in these very uplands valleys and hills, unparalleled elsewhere throughout the entire length of the mountain range, further explain the historical development of the Minangkabau people in their homeland. Their iron gave them great advantages in their agricultural endeavours and in their political formation, whilst their gold promoted contact with the outside world to an extent far in advance of any other part of the highlands.

When all has been said about the importance of the upland valleys in the development of the Minangkabau world, more remains to be said about the relationship between this world and other worlds outside. On either side of the Minangkabau mountains lie two other worlds of great significance in Minangkabau life. Both the narrow, monsoon-battered strip of the west coast and the river-coursed swamps of the east coast of Sumatra provide an essential link between the population of the highlands and the rest of mankind. Through them a mountain community, whose very mountains, as exemplified by the swirling mists on Mount Merapi, pierce the clouds, has been brought into contact with the shifting population of the port settlements below and, beyond, with the ocean. Both coasts have, over the centuries, attracted settlement by people of Minangkabau origin, and on both sides of the mountains the Minangkabau have mixed with other, non-Minangkabau groups, and often with individuals coming from a very great distance.

Of the two coasts, the west has historically been less favourable to Minangkabau activities, at least until the sixteenth century. The western flanks of the Bukit Barisan present a steep, highly dissected and jungle-clad face to the ocean. Their precipitous slopes merge into cliffs and headlands, and between these lie mountain foothills and swampy coastal plains. In many places the mountains meet the sea over a considerable distance, and coastal plains, where they do exist, are generally narrow; only in a few exceptional areas is width increased at points where alluvial fans have been built up by the larger rivers rushing down from the mountains to the ocean. The short, swift-flowing rivers for the most part do not break the mountain wall, and this of course impedes easy access to the Minangkabau uplands. Where they do, as where the river Anai cuts a deep, sinuous gorge into relatively soft volcanic debris, Minangkabau settlements with direct access to the interior have sprung up; at points where such rivers enter the ocean, such settlements often grew by the side of port settlements established by traders from other parts of the Malay world, and beyond. These port settlements presented a constant challenge to the classical Minangkabau lifestyle as it had consolidated itself in the uplands. Minangkabau's west coast 'windows on the world' always faced considerable geographical challenges, and not until the twentieth century was there any question of their replacing the uplands as the focus of Minangkabau life.

The Indian Ocean coast of Sumatra is exposed to the full force of monsoon winds, which produce tempestuous seas and heavy surf; as a result, suitable anchorage places are few and far between. The south-east monsoon or dry season begins about May and lasts until September, while the north-west monsoon commences about November, and the heavy rains only cease about March. At the conclusion of each monsoon season dangerous shifting sandbars form anew, posing problems of negotiation for coastal shipping, whilst mouths of rivers shift or silt up, causing disruptions to transportation. The problem is compounded by the prevalence of coastal coral reefs, which make navigation additionally hazardous. Since the rivers tumbling down from the mountains are navigable only for a very short distance from the sea coast, port settlements have been limited historically not only by problems of access to the interior but also by the lack of suitably sheltered bays. Minangkabau port settlements had to be confined to a very small part of the coastline south of modern Padang, and to one or two spots north of Padang where small coral islets offshore provide sheltered anchorage for ocean-going craft.

The physical characteristics of the narrow coastal plains behind the river mouths and their settlements also produced in the past obstacles to permanent human habitation. Near the ocean the plains are characterized by sand dunes, covered with coconut palms or casuarina trees, and between these and the mountain foothills lie swampy lagoons and marshes. Malaria has long been endemic. Often the plain disappears entirely, and where mountain spurs come down to the sea the coast is wild and rocky. Apart from the port settlements, the Minangkabau have confined their settlement on the coast to areas where some of the larger rivers have built extensive alluvial flats, which increase the width of the plain and make agriculture feasible.

Given these difficulties on the west coast, it is hardly surprising that the inhabitants of the Minangkabau uplands should have regarded the east coast of Sumatra as the region most naturally linking them with the outside world. Only periods of political turbulence or interference disrupted the link between the highlands and the east, because it is on this side that the island of Sumatra borders one of the Indonesian archipelago's most sheltered waterways, the straits between Sumatra and the Malay peninsula. The straits provide the shortest sailing route between India and China, are devoid of dangerous coral reefs, liberally studded with islands capable of serving as intermediate ports of call, and well provided with capacious estuaries. To travel from India to the South China Sea by way of the west coast of Sumatra and the Sunda Strait separating Sumatra and Java is indubitably a longer and more hazardous enterprise. Historically, the straits between Sumatra and the Malay peninsula have been the focal point of every important Malay political configuration which, from the days of Srivijaya in the seventh century A.D. to the Johor sultanate in the seventeenth century, have each tried to exert control over both sides of the straits and so dominate the trade route. Known as the Malacca Straits in honour of the greatest of the Malay sultanates, this waterway has also promoted the entry of foreign culture into Sumatra. In this context foreign means largely Indian, and over the centuries Sumatra has received portions of all the great religions which at varying periods struggled for mastery in that complex subcontinent, and has made of them what she could.

The Minangkabau uplands would seem remote from the world of the straits, removed both by distance and by height. However, nearly all the great rivers of eastern Sumatra rise in the Bukit Barisan, and make their way slowly eastwards to the straits through huge, flat alluvial lowlands. It is these rivers, and not the east Sumatran land area itself, which are important to the Minangkabau world. The lowlands, which on the equator extend inland for 125 miles and nowhere reach an elevation of more than 330 ft. above sea level, comprise a vast region of swampy jungle, ending in a coastal belt of mangroves. Settlement on land is only really possible on small, raised patches of dry land lying far inland, generally on the interfluves between the major rivers and on the narrow belt of hills which occur between the Bukit Barisan and the jungle. In this inhospitable, impenetrable landscape the rivers form highways. Rising in the Bukit Barisan, certain rivers originate inside the Minangkabau world itself and, because of their depth and breadth, provide ready access to it. They are navigable by ocean-going ships for considerable distance into the interior, and local vessels can proceed even further inland, meeting the Bukit Barisan as it slopes gradually eastwards. By means of these rivers, meandering interminably, their courses constantly changing, and linked to one another by an intricate network of waterways, the Minangkabau highlands have for centuries communicated with the commercial and intellectual world of the straits. Permanent settlement was less important here than commerce. Some Minangkabau did gradually settle the undulating hill country between the Barisan foothills and the swamps, where movement on land is relatively easy and dry-field (*ladang*) cultivation sustains life. Here too they settled the river banks, but further down the banks become the home of the Sumatran Coast Malays and of a wide variety of other groups attracted to the rivers from as far away as Arabia by their commercial possibilities.

For the Minangkabau world as a whole, Sumatra east of their upland valleys is more important as a land of highways than a land of settlement. There are three rivers which hold the keys to the Minangkabau highlands: the Siak, the Kampar and the Inderagiri. The Siak is the only one which does not actually rise in the Barisan mountains; its tributaries take their source in the belt of hill country between the mountain foothills and the swampy plain. It is navigable for small sea-going vessels for ninety miles upstream, and local craft can travel up its tributaries, the Tapung Kanan and Tapung Kiri, much further into the interior, where trade paths coming from the upland valleys end in Minangkabau settlements dotting the river banks. The Kampar river, though obstructed at its mouth by a tidal bore, is an ancient highway into the Minangkabau interior. Its two tributaries, the Kampar Kanan and Kampar Kiri, are navigable to the foothills of the Barisan ranges, where footpaths descending from the uplands valleys link land-borne and water-borne commerce. Moreover, in the hilly zone between mountain and swamp, footpaths also join the Kampar Kanan to the Siak, the routes watched over by scattered Minangkabau settlements. Similar footpaths connect the Kampar Kiri to the third great water highway into Minangkabau, the Inderagiri, which again can be navigated by local vessels right up to the Minangkabau highlands. Lower down both the Kampar and the Inderagiri, sea-going ships can discharge and pick up cargo at settlements which originally sprang up as staging posts for the safe transfer of goods to and from local craft. Without these rivers the Minangkabau might well have developed in virtual isolation, like many other mountain-dwellers. The low, flat, swampy forest would have been impenetrable, and the mangrove-fringed shores of eastern Sumatra would have isolated the Bukit Barisan from the currents of human development. It is within this geographical framework – this duality of mountain and lowland – that the historical development of the Minangkabau people of Central Sumatra must be observed.

Despite what has been said about the unfavourable characteristics of much of the east coast lowlands of Sumatra, there can be no doubt that these lowlands were for many centuries the home of Malay civilization. Of vital importance in the rhythm of international trade, from at least the seventh century A.D., this civilization far outstripped that of the societies of the Bukit Barisan. The Minangkabau highlands might have remained, as Fernand Braudel has remarked of mountain regions elsewhere, 'a world apart from civilizations, which are an urban and lowland achievement. Their history is to have none, to remain almost always on the fringe of the great waves of civilization . . .'[2] In a certain sense the Minangkabau uplands did remain a world apart; but, nevertheless, they began to develop their own distinctive civilization which came to count for more and more in the Malay world. From about the fourteenth century, these highlands gradually overtook the cultural and political predominance of the lowlands: Minangkabau's climate, fertile soils and mineral wealth slowly built up her reserves of population and commercial importance, whilst the passing centuries saw the lowlands becoming increasingly malarial, unhealthy and enervating.

Nevertheless, even as the balance of power in the Sumatran world shifted in favour of the Minangkabau highlands, and despite the area's accessibility to outside forces, the Minangkabau in their mountains retained a certain characteristic which marks them off as a mountain people. This characteristic concerns their rate of adaptation to cultural penetration. Sumatra as a whole lay athwart the route bringing Hindu, Buddhist and Islamic influences from the Indian subcontinent to the world of Southeast Asia. But the religious geography of mountain areas, as Braudel has pointed out, deserves separate attention.[3] Over the centuries the Minangkabau exhibited towards foreign religions an attitude typical of many mountain-dwellers towards the religions of the civilized world: they remained largely impervious to them, whether they came by way of the eastern or western lowlands. But then, in the late eighteenth century, the mountains were suddenly overtaken by a period of religious enthusiasm and frenzy. It is this period of religious revivalism which is the subject of this book. Investigation centres on how a particular regional variant of Islam, a world religion, which had been introduced into the mountains several centuries earlier with little impact, briefly suffused and transformed an entire society.

To study religious revivalism in the peasant society of the Minangkabau highlands, however, is to study first of all a mountain society in a period of rapid change. Change brings serious destabilization to a society. This was nothing new in Minangkabau; the picture of a traditional, unchanging society negotiating the centuries with the minimum of accommodation is as unrealistic for the Minangkabau world as it is for other Asian societies. But the correlation between change and religious revival in Minangkabau at the end of the eighteenth century is something new. There is one question, therefore, which arises first: what was the magnitude of the change in Minangkabau society which fostered the penetration into that society of a puritanical religious movement generated in the eastern deserts of Arabia?

NOTES TO CHAPTER I

1 S. Müller, *Reizen en Onderzoekingen in Sumatra, gedaan op last der Nederlandsche Indische Regering, tusschen de jaren 1833 en 1838* (The Hague, 1855), p. 123.
2 F. Braudel, *The Mediterranean and the Mediterranean World in the Age of Philip II* (London, 1975), i. 34.
3 ibid., pp. 34-38.

CHAPTER II

VILLAGE AND MARKET IN THE MINANGKABAU DOMESTIC ECONOMY, 1818-1834

Change in the Minangkabau economy

The first Europeans to enter the Minangkabau highlands did so in 1818; it is only from this date that we have available a number of descriptions of Minangkabau society based on first hand observation. The descriptions, of course, lack a historical dimension, and so barely take cognisance of the significant change Minangkabau was experiencing, change initiated at least as early as the 1780s due to the profound alteration in the highlands' external market relations. Nevertheless, these outsiders' analyses are irreplaceable as an aid to the understanding of the world of the Minangkabau highlands. Their picture of the economic life of the society may be somewhat one-dimensional and static, but it is with this picture that a start must be made; the Minangkabau in his village and market-place must first be observed, before the historical path by which he reached them can be followed.[1]

This is not to say that the early observers were unaware of the fluctuations which were taking place in Minangkabau society even in the brief sixteen years dealt with here. Their very presence in the highlands at this period was a concomitant not merely of the dynamism of their own societies, but also of the ready adaptability of the Minangkabau to a new world trading economy far more extensive than anything known before. The approaches made by various Minangkabau to the first European visitor to their highlands indicate this most clearly. In July 1818 an employee of the English East India Company, Sir Thomas Stamford Raffles, visited two of the four Minangkabau valleys, the Singkarak-Solok basin and Tanah Datar. He found two quite different groups of Minangkabau eagerly seeking outside assistance to resolve the crisis brought about in their societies by their respective economic expansion and economic decline.

On 20 July 1818 Raffles signed a treaty at Solok with representatives of thirteen villages lying in the Solok plain and on the surrounding hills.[2] These villages, which seemed willing to sign away coastal land on the western approaches to Minangkabau to the English Company, explained their reasons in a petition to the King of England. They were afraid that the west coast port of Padang, through which they conducted their trade and which had been experiencing an English interregnum for 23 years after having been in Dutch hands for over 100 years, was on the verge of being handed back to the Dutch. This, they declared, would be 'an act of injustice and inhumanity to the Malay nation . . .'[3] The injustice would be to their economic interests; these thirteen villages, particularly those on the hillsides overlooking the Solok plain, had recently discovered that there was international demand for a crop which they could produce with little effort:

. . . since the English have been at Padang the trade has been opened, twenty times the trade is now carried on to what was formerly. We have planted Coffee of our free Will and many trees are not yet in bearing, if the Dutch come they will as formerly shut up the Port, they will fix an inadequate price for the Coffee, they will cheat us as formerly.[4]

Four days later Raffles signed another treaty. Here the circumstances were quite different. The place was Pagarruyung, the seat of one of the Minangkabau royal courts in the rich plains of Tanah Datar, and the signatory claimed to be 'the Rajah of Menancabau'.[5] The Minangkabau royal family had for many centuries owed its survival to its ability to regulate the Minangkabau gold trade with the outside world.[6] By 1818, however, the gold trade of the royal areas was in marked decline, and the royal family was under attack from those elements in Minangkabau society which were profiting from the new export crops. In desperation Minangkabau royalty asked for English military support, in return for cession to the English Company 'in full sovereignty all the Lands of [*sic*] the Westward of the Hills to the Sea including the Islands lying off the same from Indrapora to Natal'.[7] Included in the treaty was a clause permitting English control of the mountain passes between the royal court and the west coast, which was designed to ensure that Minangkabau royalty would no longer be able to keep foreign merchants at arm's length on the coast, as had been the case for several centuries.

Raffles, however, came and went; he had proceeded in advance of English policy, and his actions were disavowed by his masters. The Dutch, representing the Government of the Netherlands Indies, resumed control of the Minangkabau west coast port of Padang. The villages which had participated so long in the gold trade did not abandon their search for outside support, however. The seats of the royal courts were not alone in suffering decline and actual physical attack; all those villages in the interior where gold was produced, or which were strung out along the major gold trade route to the west coast, were experiencing similar vicissitudes. Once again they sought salvation by treaty, but this time in the arms of the Dutch at Padang. The representatives of fifteen villages in the Tanah Datar and Singkarak-Solok valleys, including representatives of the royal seats at Pagarruyung and Suruaso, signed a treaty with the Dutch on 10 February 1821. Far more was now promised to the foreign traders than had been promised in 1818. In exchange for military assistance practically the whole of Tanah Datar, one of the core regions of the Minangkabau world, was offered; the signatories of the 1821 treaty granted ' . . . to the Netherlands Government of the East Indies, formal cession and unconditional surrender of the lands of *Paggar Roeyong, Soengi Tarap* and *Soeroeassoe,* as well as the remaining lands of the State of Maninkabo'.[8] That this treaty was signed at all was as a result of a continuing process of disruption to the internal economy of Minangkabau. New forces had been called into being in the society, and outside forces were summoned to redress the balance. In 1821 the Dutch conquest of the entire Minangkabau world began, slowly at first, intensified after 1833.

It is clear from all three treaties that what was at issue was the consequences of upheaval in the economic life of Minangkabau, caused by changes in the external trade pattern of the highlands. In the Minangkabau world there was no clear dividing line between external or long-distance trade, and the internal trade which was generated by the domestic economy. Gold, for centuries the main item traded internationally, also had the vitally important function of facilitating exchange in the domestic economy; likewise the newer export crops sold to foreign customers involved changes in land use and made new demands for labour, so having an impact on the internal distributive system long before the crops reached coastal export centres. To understand economic change in the longer term, therefore, investigation must first be confined to the Minangkabau domestic economy at a brief period in time: the period between the first European entry into the highlands and the beginning of a very serious European determination to conquer them. An analysis of modes of land use in particular areas, and the market relationships between these areas, will help to clarify the Minangkabau social structure, its points of stability and of potential disintegration. Not only the Minangkabau highlands – the core region of four rice-plains and their surrounding hills – require examination. Equal consideration is merited by those access areas which can be regarded as essential to the economic survival of the highlands, the narrow western coastal strip and the broad, flat riverine plains of the east coast. In this way four major ecological zones impinging upon the economic life of the Minangkabau world can be distinguished, and the economic relationships linking one zone with another will also be seen to be significant for discussion.

The plains village: rice and minerals

The large, saucer-like plains of the four main upland valleys of Minangkabau are excellently suited for wet-rice cultivation, and it was on these valley floors that the classical culture of the Minangkabau people developed. By the 1820s each valley was thickly covered with village communities, each maintaining itself in much the same way, as evinced by the green *sawah* surrounding each settlement and the lush fruit and palm trees hiding the inhabitants and their houses from view. Every European traveller has left an almost identical picture of the valleys of Solok-Singkarak, Tanah Datar, Agam and Limapuluh Kota, and perhaps Raffles can be allowed to speak for them all. Of the Solok plain he noted: 'The whole of the plain, or valley, (I hardly know what to call it) . . . is one sheet of cultivation; in breadth it may be about ten, and in length twenty miles, thickly studded with towns and villages, some of them running in a connected line for several miles . . .'[9] Central Tanah Datar moved him to paint a similar picture: 'The whole country, from Pageruyong, as far as the eye could distinctly trace, was one continued scene of cultivation, interspersed with innumerable towns and villages, shaded by the cocoa-nut and other fruit-trees'.[10]

Despite Raffles' use of the word 'town' to indicate size, the culture which had grown up on these rice plains was essentially one based on the village. Both economically, since the basis of existence of the vast majority of villages was agriculture rather than learning, administration or trade, and politically, since these villages were self-governing communities, the term village is appropriate for virtually all the settlements of the Minangkabau highlands. Even the settlements which housed members of the royal families, about which there might be some conceptual doubt, were in essence trade or market-place villages; they were confined to a small area of Tanah Datar, and had in any case been destroyed by this period. The search for precious minerals and the trade in them which occupied a very few villages on the plains had not developed in these villages the necessary economic versatility for such a village to be regarded as other than a trade village or a market-place village. Towns or cities were yet to develop in the world of the Minangkabau highlands, though, as will be seen, the market-place village played an important role in this world.

The wet-rice villages of the plains had certain characteristics in common. Where possible they were built on the banks of a river, and each occupied a certain well-defined area of land, with boundaries either marked out or well-known in terms of certain natural features, particularly rivers and mountains.[11] Different parts of the village and its land were designated by certain Sanskrit terms, but in essence each village contained a nucleated centre of settlement, called a *kota* and, as the name implies, usually fortified, with numerous dependent out-settlements in the nature of small collections of houses. The group of settlements, together with their land, was called a *negeri* (Minangkabau *nagari*).[12] The out-settlements could straggle off in all directions. Around Solok, the most important village on the Singkarak-Solok plain, out-settlements ran together in a separate line for several miles.[13] Nevertheless, all inhabitants knew the village boundaries, which were either handed down by tradition or even written down in *tambo* (chronicles) which recounted the history of the first establishment. All land, including forests, rivers and fields of *alang-alang* grass (*Imperata cylindrica*) for grazing cattle, was the property of the village within the boundaries of which it lay.[14]

Within the village the most important unit, both of production and social welfare, was represented by a group of large, wooden houses, usually placed close together, with their own rice storage barns and livestock pens, facing away from other groups onto their own common courtyard.[15] These houses were inhabited by members of one lineage, people descended from a common ancestor, and members of this lineage, as well as having access to the village forests and woodlands, would also have their own wet-rice fields, marked off from those of others by dikes and other forms of boundary markers. Surrounding the housing compound, which was enclosed by a hedge or a wall of river stones, would be the lineage members' own groves of fruit trees, fish ponds, vegetable gardens and, in areas where the altitude was not too high, coconut palms.[16]

There were few villages in the 1820s and 30s with less than four of these lineages, and some had double the number. Minangkabau lineages were matrilineal, based on descent from a common female ancestor, and each lineage was divided into large extended branch families, subdivided in turn into family units; the units at each stage traced their descent from a common foremother.[17] Each individual house in the lineage compound represented one of these family units – a woman with her children and grandchildren. The woman's husband, and those of her daughters, were not members of this family, but of that of their own mother and sisters.[18] The group of houses would also contain a building for the lineage *surau,* a gathering-place and sleeping-place for adolescent and adult males, who did not stay overnight in the mother's house and did so infrequently in the wife's.[19] It was the individual house, the *rumah gedang,* which represented the smallest unit in Minangkabau society. Often, according to the size of the family, it seemed to be more like a row of small houses brought under one roof; when one of the daughters or granddaughters married, the mother would allot her a room in which to receive her husband, or, if necessary, rooms would be built on either end. Such a house could contain 60 to 80 people.[20] Its construction was an expensive and important matter, requiring the best quality wood and much labour; many lasted for 80 to 100 years.[21]

Raffles' is the first description we have of such a house, although he admits that this house, at Simawang on Lake Singkarak, was exceptional in being that of a very important personage and containing 150 inhabitants:

> The house in which we were now accommodated was in length about one hundred feet, and from thirty to forty in depth, built in a most substantial manner, and supported along the centre by three large wooden pillars, fit for the masts of a ship: indeed, from the peculiar construction of the house, the gable end of which was raised in tiers like the stern of a vessel, they had very much this appearance. The floor was raised from the ground about ten feet, the lower part being inclosed and appropriated to cattle, etc. The principal entrance is about the centre, but there is a second door at one end. The interior consists of one large room or hall, the height proportioned to the other dimensions; three fire-places, equally distant from each other, were placed on the front side, and at the back were several small chambers, in which we perceived the spinning-wheels and other articles belonging to the women.[22]

The mention of ricefields, rice storage barns, fish ponds, fruit trees and livestock should not be taken to indicate that each lineage in the village was equally blessed with these stores of wealth. In the plains villages wealth was certainly not distributed evenly. However, it would be untrue to say that the uneven distribution of wealth within the village was never challenged or subjected to mutation. In fact, there seems to have been a constant cycle of upward and downward mobility within the village, with community norms and demands ensuring that too great an accumulation of wealth in the hands of any one branch family or lineage was prevented.[23] This wealth-syphoning mechanism will be discussed shortly. What must be said first is that there are no adequate statistics for Minangkabau population at this period, and none whatever for patterns of landholding.[24] The early travellers based their judgement on intelligent observations: it was noted that rice barns (*lombong*) in front of a house were the mark of a prosperous family, as was the breadth, as opposed to length, of the house, and the possession of oxen and buffaloes; horses were the possession of only the wealthiest.[25] But to all families their most important possession was, of course, their rice land. Hence the relationship between the nature of wet-rice cultivation in the Minangkabau uplands and other variables of village life, particularly population growth, is of crucial importance.

The creation and maintenance of a *sawah* (irrigated ricefield) represented considerable labour for a family, and *sawah* was looked on as the family's most valuable property, held in trust for all future generations.[26] It was inherited in the maternal line, and formed the core of what was known as the family's *harta pusaka* or ancestral property, although some *sawah* inherited in the distant past was regarded as belonging to the entire lineage. It was this land which kept the lineage and its branch families in existence.[27] Rice grown on Minangkabau *sawah* produced excellent yields. The seed/yield ratio in the best irrigated parts of Limapuluh Kota and Tanah Datar was 1:50 or 1:60.[28] To obtain such yields by practising wet-rice cultivation, however, required a considerable amount of co-operative labour.[29] Not all localities were amply supplied with water from mountain streams or rivers which could be diverted for irrigation. In many cases, such as the flat valley bottoms of Limapuluh Kota, the drier, dessicated sections of the Agam plain, and parts of Tanah Datar, irrigation was essential. A complex system of irrigation by water-wheels had been constructed by the villagers, and these had to be maintained.[30] Large round wheels constructed of bamboo, with bamboo tubes attached to the circumference, scooped up water from rivers lying below the level of the *sawah* and emptied it into a channel which conducted the water to the level of the fields. To set the wheels in motion and give them impetus, small dam-like structures had to be made in the middle of rivers to direct the current of the water to the edges. Where water had to be conducted over roadways and paths, there operated a system of hollow bamboo tubes leading under the ground from the tanks into which the tubes on the water-wheels emptied their water. Even where water-wheels were not in use, much irrigation had to be done by means of aquaducts, and embankments and raised, narrow ridges protecting the fields had also to be kept in good repair.[31]

The rice-growing year, which began with the rains about November or December and lasted for six or seven months, also required considerable family labour; where *sawah* holdings were extensive, labour had to be drawn from all members of the lineage on a rotational basis.[32] All but the simplest method of preparing the fields by digging the ground with a spade required animals, so that the possession of oxen or buffaloes to draw the iron-tipped plough or to prepare the fields by trampling and churning was a great advantage. The harrows used to break the clods of earth after the initial ploughing could be drawn either by animals or by a man, but obviously those who possessed draught animals were at a great advantage. They had the additional advantage of having cattle to graze on the grass in the *sawah* during the fallow period, ensuring fertilizer for the fields.[33] Though statistics are non-existent, it is known that prosperous areas such as the Solok plain and Limapuluh Kota were 'richly supplied with cattle, buffaloes, goats and horses',[34] though even in this latter area little attention was paid to stockbreeding and improving stock.[35] Certainly not all villagers were equally bountifully supplied with livestock; as late as 1856 a Dutch estimate put at only two-thirds the percentage of *sawah* fields in the uplands which were ploughed, and alleged that in earlier years this percentage had been far smaller due to lack of cattle.[36]

Once the fields had been prepared by the men, family labour continued to be required at all stages of rice-planting and rice-harvesting. Women were important in raising seedlings, transplanting them to the prepared fields when about one month old, and making certain that weeding was done assiduously for the first three months of growing; children's labour was also important here, as it was for looking after the cattle. After this period of four months the fields had to be constantly watered until a few weeks before the harvest. The success of the harvesting itself was dependent on the amount of labour available from within the family unit. Harvesting, like so many other activities in the domestic economy, was again mostly women's work. Shortage of pairs of hands meant that the cut stalks could be left lying in the fields for several days or even weeks before labour was available to husk the rice by means of a wooden pestle and see it stored in the rice barns. During this time the rice suffered from both the weather and the depredations of animals, and the family faced the problem of a bleak year of food-rationing.[37]

Since the *sawah* fields were owned and worked by the family, family size was the most important determinant in the family's ability to maintain and expand its *sawah* holdings. Estimates of Minangkabau population in this period vary greatly, and care must be exercised in basing population estimates for the whole highlands on descriptions which apply only to small areas. In general, however, the earliest European accounts indicate that, as far as the four upland valleys were concerned, population was dense. Raffles' estimate of a population of not less than one million within a range of fifty miles around Pagarruyung in Tanah Datar is certainly exaggerated;[38] Dutch figures for Tanah Datar and the Solok-Singkarak plain in 1824 varied between 200,000 and 600,000.[39] Despite such discrepancies, the first Dutch scientific observers did agree that the valleys were characterized by 'a considerable population'.[40] In 1833 the population of Limapuluh Kota was put at 300,000[41] and that of Agam, which had a dessicated, poorly-watered western part, at 100,000.[42] The villages, too, were more numerous than elsewhere in Minangkabau; closer together, and larger, some even contained a population of several thousands.[43]

This density of population, which had doubtless arisen due to the fertility of the soil, meant that by the early nineteenth century families were required to balance their own population nicely, especially where several generations had escaped the ravages of disease and disability. It was certainly necessary to have the requisite amount of labour to maintain the family's *sawah*. On the other hand, since *sawah* holdings were divided equally among the adult female members of the household, too large a number of children could prove a liability, particularly in years of crop failure, for Minangkabau rice spoiled quickly when stored.[44] By now on the plains the opening up of new *sawah* was a practical proposition only in a few places; instead, abortion seems to have been widely practised as a means of controlling a family's fertility and so assuring future prosperity.[45]

In discussing the landed wealth of the plains villagers, it is important to make a distinction between the lineage (*suku*), and the family (*sebuah perut*) or branch family (*kaum*) in connection with land ownership. While every individual knew to what lineage he belonged and knew his specific lineage name, within the lineage land was brought into cultivation, inherited and apportioned on a family basis, with the exception of land acquired in the distant past by the lineage due to the failure of heirs in a family.[46] It was this system, in addition to certain ritual requirements, which prevented any one lineage dominating the village, just as it was variations in the size of the family which led to changes in the fortunes of respective families within the lineage. In any generation a family might be able to increase its original possessions, only to see the land lost in the next generation due either to lack of ability to work it or to increased expenditure associated with the size of the family.[47] In both cases, although the right to sell land was strictly circumscribed, to meet current requirements the land would have to be alienated by pawning; although this was usually done within the lineage, the situation was such that it was difficult for the descendants of the original owner ever to recover land once pawned.[48] The most important characteristic of the plains village in the 1820s and 1830s, therefore, was the impossibility of permanent concentration of land in a few hands; land seems to have been continually circulating, acquired and alienated as the size of families changed for better or worse.

There was one further important factor influencing the circulation of land within the village; the villagers themselves had established social mechanisms to prevent the concentration of landed wealth in the hands of a few of their fellow villagers. These mechanisms were associated with the system of family and village government, with the nature of the exercise of authority in the society. The branch family was administered by the oldest brother of the oldest woman, the *mamak,* who was the guardian of the family's immovable property. Of this *sawah* ranked first, and it was he who apportioned the family holdings among his sisters.[49] Standing at the head of the lineage, with similar functions, was the *penghulu* (*penghulu suku*), who represented the lineage's interests in all village matters, particularly in questions relating to uncultivated village land, forests and so on. The positions of both *mamak* (often called *penghulu kecil*) and *penghulu* were held by inheritance in the female line, and although in theory claimants to the positions and the titles which went with them had to be men in closest proximity to the founding female of the branch family or the lineage, in practice the relative wealth of the different families concerned very much affected a claimant's success, and wealth by itself tended to produce claimants.[50] A village in the uplands in the 1820s and 1830s would have, according to size, a *penghulu* council (*rapat penghulu*) of between four and twelve members, but the number of *penghulu* in the village, taking into account all the *mamak,* could vary from 50 to 100 or more.[51] Raffles, who asked to confer with the leading men of a group of thirteen villages he passed through in 1818, was confronted with 'some hundreds' assembled in the 'mother village' of the area.[52] At any one time, therefore, there was a large number of titleholders in a village, and titles regularly became vacant.

Competition for these titles could be intense, and there was much jockeying within lineages and families for possession of them; the wealth of the claimant was often a decisive factor in the acquisition of a title. However, the entire process of acquisition and maintenance of the status of titleholder led to extreme fluidity in the social system, because it was necessary for any family which asked for a title to become committed to constant expenditure of surplus wealth. Claimants to titles would give feasts and expensive gifts to win a following. To finance this expenditure the possession of land was essential, and it was very difficult for an impoverished family to claim a *penghulu* title, whatever its relationship to the former titleholder might be.[53] However, upwardly mobile families which did manage to capture a title for one of their male members soon became involved in wide-ranging expenses associated with the installation of the titleholder and the maintenance of his dignity, expenses engendered in particular by the need to reward ostentatiously other members of the family or lineage in various ways. Gradually the need to finance such expenditure would lead them to pawn some of their *sawah* land in an attempt to maintain their status, and slowly the downward spiral into financial difficulties would begin.[54] Hence there was a constant circulation of both land and elite status within individual lineages in the village. Any unit within the lineage which had managed to acquire wealth for itself by being, in the broadest sense of the term, entrepreneurial or 'outwardly oriented' – whether in relation to trade or agricultural ventures – soon found this wealth syphoned off by the ritual demands of village life. An installation followed by one or two marriages, a birth and a funeral could be an excessive strain on even a well-to-do family containing not a single black sheep intent on dissipating family reserves. A succession of expensive ceremonies ultimately resulted in a family pawning land. Conformity to village norms was expensive, and yet Minangkabau literature lays stress on the need to conform for fear of incurring 'public disgrace'.[55] Such conformity acted as a deterrent to 'outward-oriented' forces.

Such a cycle of decline, fall and then rise in a family's fortunes is in fact the subject of the Minangkabau *kaba* (story told in a kind of rhythmic prose) *Rancak diLabueh,* certainly known in its original form before the 1820s. Rancak diLabueh's mother depicts the golden age of her family as it existed in her childhood: ' . . . the family had gold and silver, fine clothes, rice-fields, personal possessions, – sufficient of everything'.[56] The family's wealth is dissipated by ostentatious and careless living; 'caste vanishes when money is gone – '.[57] However, as soon as Rancak diLabueh retrieves the family fortunes both by agricultural enterprise and by trade, his mother at once urges him to improve the family house, buy new clothes, arrange to give a feast and, most important, lay claim to a *penghulu* title vacant in the lineage.[58]

Dutch observations on Minangkabau *penghulu* confirm that display of wealth was essential to the holder of a title. A well-to-do *penghulu* would be sure to have silk cushions in his house for his guests, and silk materials to decorate the seating areas.[59] At the 1824 royal games at Pagarruyung, wealthy titleholders were clearly distinguishable, wearing ceremonial clothes comprising 'black, or red and black striped, turbans, the edges being set with gold spangles or sequins, while they wear clothing made chiefly of red silk woven with gold'.[60] At a feast to mark the installation of a *penghulu* held in 1832 in the coastal foothills there were 600 distinguished guests, wearing sumptuous golden apparel.[61]

Given the importance of family land in plains society, was there much opportunity for individual economic endeavour? There was a category of Minangkabau inheritance entitled *harta pencarian,* indicating that such property had been individually acquired. In general, in addition to *sawah* a well-to-do family would own the family dwelling, the small plantation of fruit trees nearby, a vegetable plot, fish ponds and cattle-pens. All this property was hedged in or surrounded by walls.[62] But where a family was suffering from pressure of numbers, or from possessing too few of these things, individual members would look elsewhere for their livelihood. In most cases this involved undertaking some form of trading venture or performing services for other families. The laying-down of individual *ladang* or dry fields was not very common on the plains, but most family compounds were surrounded by a variety of fruit trees which, as well as supplementing the family diet, also provided items for small-scale trade.[63] In the southern part of Tanah Datar towards Lake Singkarak, for example, it was noted that 'there is no lack of fruit trees and the whole place is a huge orchard of fruit trees and coconut palms, among which the houses nestle'.[64] There are numerous similar descriptions of other rich plains areas.[65] Some localities could specialize to a certain extent: coconuts were particularly prevalent in Tanah Datar and Limapuluh Kota, but were hardly produced at all in Agam because of that valley's height.[66] Limapuluh Kota was so low and marshy that it was noted for its rushes; even in the vicinity of Payakumbuh, the leading village, they were found in the *sawah* and used for basket weaving.[67] *Rameh,* China grass, was cultivated in certain areas and used for making string for fishing nets.[68] Families were also able to breed fish in their own fishponds, which were particularly numerous in Limapuluh Kota and western Tanah Datar.[69] Those who lived near a lake or river could catch fish[70] and, if near Lake Singkarak, burn the lime used for *sirih*-chewing from shells found on the shore.[71] Others prepared lime from limestone where available,[72] or kept poultry and ducks.[73] All these activities were particularly suited to individual enterprise, and gave individuals opportunities to pursue advantage through trade.

However, wealth once acquired in this way tended not to benefit the individual entrepreneur for long. Profits were very quickly turned into land or cattle, which could be sold or pawned when liquid capital was needed. This privately acquired property, *harta pencarian,* in this way very quickly became part of the whole family's *harta pusaka.*[74] It could hardly be otherwise, for the initial trading venture was usually financed by family capital in the first place.

Land, therefore, retained its central importance in society, and with it the *penghulu* as the chief agent of control over its disposal.[75] Since land was in fact the society's circulating capital, and since pawning was the key lubricator, and was very common, the lack of pawn contracts placed all such transactions under *penghulu* control, gave added importance to their position, and led to the elaboration of an intricate customary law code.[76] Disputes over pawning were endless, since no matter how long land had been held in pawn, it was still regarded as the property of the original owner, and often the matter was left to be settled by the heirs.[77] Pawning led to severe quarrels, especially in cases where land was pawned to the owner of an adjacent *sawah,* when all boundary marks could gradually be removed. Despite this, pawning remained a marked characteristic of the villages of the valley floors, and it certainly helped to relieve the pressures caused by overpopulation. Moreover without it, a family suffering temporary difficulties would have been left with the single alternative of turning to trade as a way out of their problems.[78]

Although by far the majority of villages in the upland plains were agriculturally based, there were of course regional variations based on quality of soil, access to water and the availability of other means of livelihood. The greatest deviation from the agricultural pattern lay in what can be called 'mineral villages'. However, regional variations in the agricultural pattern should be noted. The most fertile *sawah* areas in central Minangkabau were, first of all, that part of the Solok valley sloping down to Lake Singkarak around Saningbakar[79] and, on the other side of the lake, the land sloping down from Mount Merapi around Batipuh to Sumpur on the lakeside.[80] In Tanah Datar it was the western part of the valley, in the foothills of Mount Merapi around Sungai Tarab and Gurun, which was particularly fertile, having the advantages of both volcanic soils and the streams of the mountain for irrigation.[81] Such villages were 'rich, prosperous and well-built . . .'[82] In the eastern part of the valley, the greatest fertility was to be found in the side valley of

Andalas, thrusting eastwards and having the advantage of proximity to Mount Marapalam. Such an area was able to sustain villages of more than usually large size.[83] In Agam, by far the most fertile, prosperous and highly populated areas were those surrounding Padang Tarab, Kota Tua and Batutebal in the south-east and east, nestling near the Merapi and watered by its streams, and around Tilatang in the northern part of the plain.[84] Elsewhere on the Agam plain there was much less good land than in the other valleys; limestone hills, rocky soils and deep ravines made only a few favoured areas suitable for *sawah* cultivation, and towards the west and south-west of Bukit Tinggi there was much dry, poor, uncultivated land or land on which maize, potatoes and other dry-field crops were grown. Even the character of settlement was different. The large villages with their family houses gave way to settlements of small huts surrounded by banana trees.[85] In Limapuluh Kota again it was the eastern part of the valley, adjacent to Mount Sago, which possessed rich volcanic soil and exhibited a 'gentle green carpet of rice-fields . . .'[86] Payakumbuh and Taram were the main villages of this prosperous area.[87] In addition to *sawah*-cultivation, some villages lying on the very richest plains also engaged in domestic industry to a certain extent. Such villages were largely those lying on important trade routes through which silk could be imported, or with access to dyestuffs. Sumpur and Pitala, for example, on the Batipuh plain sloping down to Lake Singkarak, were known for dyeing silk red and weaving it.[88]

However, the most important divergence from the classic plains *sawah* pattern was not to be found in domestic industry, but in those villages which had access to mineral deposits. By far the greatest number of such villages in the upland valleys were found in Tanah Datar, where the great bulk of Minangkabau's mineral wealth was located. Mineral deposits, like land, were the property of the village community if found on uncultivated land or in streams, and of a particular family if found on family land.[89] Certain Tanah Datar villages were located near either iron or gold mines and, in addition, gold could be panned in certain fast-flowing streams. It was the gold mining villages of Tanah Datar which developed the only Minangkabau political system worthy of the name, due to their participation in a trade in gold extending as far as southern India.[90]

Raffles was the first outsider to notice the difference between agriculturally based and mining villages; accompanied by a group of coastal merchants involved in the gold trade, he first passed through the rice villages of the Solok plain: 'These towns I found had little to do with commerce; the inhabitants are almost exclusively devoted to agriculture, and to this cause the native merchants who were with me attributed the want of civilization among them. "The people of those towns," said they, "which lie on the road to the gold mines, and where they understand how to trade, are of very different manners: these people, though considering themselves as of most importance, have always been noted for their rude and obstinate behaviour" '.[91] The difference, Raffles later decided, was that in the gold-producing and gold-trading villages, '. . . the people seem to have some respect for authority, and it was evident that they had the advantage of more general intercourse with strangers'.[92]

The connection between the gold trade and the Minangkabau political system, particularly the royal families, will be discussed later. However, the place of mining and mineral-associated villages in the domestic economy of the plains requires elaboration. The major domestic mineral-based industry was iron. Villages could be connected with the Minangkabau iron industry in three different ways: they either owned land on which iron ore was mined, or were located near sources of wood which could be used as charcoal for smelting, or they possessed a blacksmithing industry for the making of iron implements. Those villages actually owning iron ore-bearing land were in fact the least significant of the three, at least by the 1820s.

The iron ore deposits of the Minangkabau uplands were in the Gunung Besi (iron mountain), a small mountain located on the western-most fringe of Tanah Datar near Lake Singkarak. It seems likely that the original centre of the iron industry in Minangkabau was located in a triangular area bounded by the mountain, the Umbilan river, and the very large village of Lima Kaum. Raffles mentioned a 'large town' just near Gunung Besi which had from 'time immemorial' worked the iron recovered from the mountain.[93] This was presumably Turawan, whose iron-working was, however, inconsiderable by the 1820s.[94] The reason was that by this period the iron mountain itself, and the villages nearby, lacked wood and even bamboo to provide charcoal for smelting.[95] It seems likely that the wood had become exhausted at some earlier time, and the major part of the iron industry had been transferred to a site further north, causing considerable dislocation in the south. By the 1820s the main iron-ore vein in the Gunung Besi belonged to one of the lineages of the adjacent village, and its head received payment for permission to work it, but the centre of the industry had moved far away. In 1838 the inhabitants of Padang Luar even claimed to know nothing of the methods used to extract the ore.[96]

Although iron-smelting gradually became an industry of the hills rather than the plains, its operation in the hills of northern Tanah Datar should be discussed in the present context because certain plains villages also participated in the iron production cycle. By the early 1820s iron-mining and iron-smelting was the province of one village, Salimpaung, lying on the slopes of Mount Merapi at a distance of one day's journey on foot from Gunung Besi.[97] The smelting industry had passed to this village from its previous location on the southern plains because Salimpaung possessed ample supplies of wood for charcoal growing on the mountain slopes behind the village.[98] Unfortunately we know little of the organization of the mining and carrying enterprises, but it seems that within Salimpaung itself labour was divided into specialized categories, the miners belonging to different lineages from those of the iron-smelters, although not even this is certain. The first stage of production required the Salimpaung miners to go to the Gunung Besi, which they did at irregular intervals for short periods. Their work was relatively easy, requiring no mine-works to be laid down. Only the layers of limestone covering the ore to a depth of several feet needed to be broken away, the ore then being worked loose with a hammer and other implements. Large, heavy stones were used by the miners to break the ore into pieces for transportation. No large expense was incurred; the *penghulu* whose lineage owned the land received only the equivalent of forty Dutch cents for each 'load' transported from the site.[99]

Once in Salimpaung, the ore came into the hands of the smelters. The smelters worked in teams; each team had its own furnace protected by a hut located right in the village, the wood and bamboo being brought down the mountain to the smelters.[100] The smelting process at Salimpaung was first described in 1833:

I saw this taking place at several locations, in a sort of brick smelting-furnace which was about 7 to 8 feet high and 8 to 10 inches across, with good vent holes at the bottom. In this furnace the iron-ore was placed in layers between charcoal made from bamboo, and subsequently liquefied; the liquefied iron gathered in the form of a cake at the bottom of the furnace, comprising naturally a brittle, hard iron which, however, after much forging acquires a considerable toughness and elasticity . . .[101]

Since each smelting team worked separately with different types of furnaces, the smelting process was carried out in very small-scale units, and the labour and effort required led to the finished product being very expensive. The process as it was described in 1833 produced barely enough iron to make half a gun barrel.[102] Even before the iron was put into the furnace, there was a preliminary process whereby the ore was roasted on an open fire made of piles of wood, and subsequently 'beaten into small dimensions the size of hazelnuts',[103] which were then stacked in the furnace. In 1838 it was claimed that it took a day and a night to smelt one lump of iron in a four-foot high cube-shaped stone furnace.[104] Once removed from the furnace the iron had to undergo further processing: it was treated by striking with a hammer to remove the charcoal adhering to it; then it was placed into an ordinary smith's fire and, when red, worked and drawn out on a square stone block. Next it was again returned to the fire and covered with charcoal, and finally it was forced into the square shape in which it was sold as a bar of iron.[105]

It is here that the connection of the iron industry with the plains becomes apparent, because at this point the villages which specialized in blacksmithing entered the production cycle. We know almost nothing of the way in which Salimpaung distributed its iron, but should note that, for reasons to be discussed in the next section, the majority of villages which specialized in smithing were also those on the hill slopes. However, there were one or two villages in the rice plains which contained certain lineages specializing in forging iron; the two main ones, Payakumbuh in Limapuluh Kota and Lima Kaum in Tanah Datar, were also noteworthy for their richness in *sawah,* presumably enabling some sort of arrangement for the support of the blacksmiths, or at least of the team leader, to be worked out. Payakumbuh specialized in sword-making, and Lima Kaum in farming and household implements, although neither did so to the exclusion of other branches of iron-working.[106] The smiths appear to have been organized in small teams, like the smelters, and, at least in Lima Kaum, one of the team would be deputed to travel to Salimpaung to buy the iron required. For cheapness iron could be acquired merely in a lump, as it came from the furnace; when sold by the prepared bar, the market price was much higher, although those smiths who were prepared to buy in bulk could often halve the price. In any case, by 1838 prices compared very unfavourably with those of imported Swedish iron, which was inevitable due to the small scale of production and the heavy costs of transport. We know little of the effects of foreign competition earlier, but certainly for some time before the 1820s the iron industry had been losing profitability, and yet no effort seems to have been made to amalgamate the small-scale units of production to combat this.[107]

The explanation for the tenacious retention of this small-scale method of production is unclear, but is certainly connected with the lack of working capital in Minangkabau society and the wealth-syphoning customs of village life mentioned earlier. The blacksmiths of the Tanah Datar plains village of Lima Kaum were investigated in 1838, and this investigation stressed features of production already mentioned by travellers who had visited smithies in the hills in the 1820s. The workshops of the smiths were located on the village market-place (*pasar*). There appear to have been twelve small teams, each with its own hut consisting merely of posts and a roof to cover the forge, and here the smiths made axes, hoes, rice-knives and such like. At least three men were required for the various operations, one to work the bellows, another to temper the product and a third to use the hammer. Capital equipment, however, was modest. It seems likely, from what we know of similar enterprises in Minangkabau, that a system of wage labour operated. It was the team captain, the *nakoda* who, while working with the others, actually owned the implements and financed the purchase of iron, paying the other workers from part of his profits.[108] The simplicity of the equipment is made clear: ' . . . the hearth is open to the ground; the bellows consist of two bamboos with pistons, the two or three foot long bamboo tubes of which shoot out in a somewhat oblique manner in a mould of clay. One man pumps the bellows by means of a lever; a piece of banana or coconut-tree trunk serves as a water cask; the anvil is a piece of trachyte; the hammer has a concentric level and its whole length or weight is on one side of the short handle'.[109] The market-places of Lima Kaum and Payakumbuh were among the largest in Minangkabau and the smiths' location obviated some of the costs of distribution but it is clear that by the 1820s the blacksmiths of Lima Kaum and Payakumbuh, like other participants in the iron industry, were suffering adversely from European competition.

By far the most important mining industry of the Minangkabau upland plains, gold, was suffering decline at the same time, though for quite different reasons. Of the four valleys, gold had existed for many centuries only in Tanah Datar, with a little being found also in a remote part of the Solok plain.[110] Just as the most important iron-working centres, Lima Kaum and Payakumbuh, with their large market-places and clear division of labour, were those which most nearly approximated a form of urban growth, so too the leading gold-mining centres in Tanah Datar were those which most closely approximated the development of courtly towns. From the fourteenth century a royal system connected with gold-mining and the gold trade had evolved in Tanah Datar, but, by the period dealt with here, the royal families of these gold-producing court centres – Pagarruyung and Suruaso, Buo and Sumpur Kudus – had lost their *raison d'être* due to the working out of the gold in the areas surrounding their courts. The Minangkabau royal system had survived due to its ability to supervise a chain of protected villages which allowed gold intended for export to pass freely to the coastal ports of both the east and west; as an aspect of Minangkabau external trade, gold and the royal families will be discussed in the next chapter. However, gold was also extremely important to the Minangkabau domestic economy, both in terms of distinguishing certain villages which possessed it and due to its having provided for centuries society's main means of exchange. Because of this, certain aspects of the acquisition and distribution of gold require inclusion in any account of the plains villages.

The effect of gold on the life of the villages in Tanah Datar possessing gold-bearing ground depended on the way it was mined. Gold could be acquired in two ways: where it appeared as small flakes or nuggets in 'placers', gravel deposited by running water, it could be recovered very easily by merely placing the gravel in a large pan with water and swirling the contents until the gold remained behind. Such gold of course originated in veins in solid rock, and where gold appeared in this form its recovery was altogether more difficult, requiring both exploration and the laying down of regular mineworks. The main areas for regular mining in Tanah Datar were in the south-west of the plain, in the low range of hills between Lake Singkarak and Suruaso, and in the extreme south-west in the area around Tanjung Ampalu on the river Umbilan.[111] The rivers Umbilan, Selo and Sinamar were the key to the location of villages which had grown up to exploit the gold. All cut through gold-bearing rock, and it was on their banks that the Tanah Datar court centres had evolved, with ready access both to gold and to *sawah* land.

By the 1820s and 1830s many of these mines were exhausted. Although the gold veins in the rocky region between Lake Singkarak and Suruaso were still being excavated, little profit was gained. Raffles, who passed nearby the main mines around Suruaso and Sulit Air, 'saw extensive excavations, where the miners had been at work; these, however, cannot be considered as regular mines, and they are not reckoned very valuable'.[112] Although previously near Suruaso 'gold had been procured in considerable quantities',[113] and although galleries of four to six foot square had been dug into the rock, the mines now produced comparatively little gold.[114] In the Sulit Air region the villages, which had little rice land, could only supply the miners with food at a very high cost, taking away what little profit there was.[115]

The other main gold-mining area, on the south-western fringes of Tanah Datar, lay on the plain of the river Umbilan around Tanjung Ampalu, where there were numerous villages which existed largely because of their gold mines. By the 1820s and 1830s a reasonable amount of gold was still being excavated here, but these mines too were coming to the end of their days. Most of the mines were already finished. 'Here, near Tandjong Ampalo, the whole surface area is full of mines which have now collapsed'.[116]

The other method of acquiring gold was to pan for it. As far as panning in the rivers Umbilan, Selo and Sinamar was concerned, the general evidence points to the fact that this too had markedly declined. The river Selo as it passed Suruaso was known as Sungai Emas, but little gold continued to be panned there.[117] The Umbilan, too, now carried only a little alluvial gold in its course from Lake Singkarak,[118] although the Sinamar still retained its reputation as a gold-bearing river; according to an 1838 report: 'In the Sinawang itself much gold is panned, and also in many of its more southerly tributaries . . .'[119]

Despite this general picture of depression in the gold-extracting industry of Minangkabau, the relationship of gold to the village economy is important. As with *sawah* and iron ore, the first question which arises relates to the ownership of gold-bearing land and rivers. In general, the rule followed was that pertaining to all other land in a village settlement, so that gold could occur randomly either on the land of an individual lineage or family, or on land regarded as the property of the village as a whole.[120] As far as panning for gold was concerned, this could of course only take place on communal property.

The next question to be addressed is whether, unlike iron ore, gold gave rise to large-scale production units and the organization of wage labour. In the case of panning, by its very nature it could be an individual enterprise leading to individual profits, and this it remained in Minangkabau.[121] Actual mining, however, was a very different matter and, as with iron, required the services of both a group of specialists and, even more than iron, a contingent of labourers. Interestingly enough, however, the organization of labour remained fluid and no class of miners appears to have arisen in particular villages, imparting to them a particular character. Before a mine could be worked, gold had to be discovered. For this there were specialist gold-seekers, who seem to have formed some sort of association and who were very much connected with the pre-Islamic religion of Minangkabau, using certain magical practices in the search for 'signs' of gold.[122] Once gold had been found, another specialist was required to organize the laying down of a mine and the actual mining for gold. Village life, however, remained unchanged. Very rarely did the individuals or villages on whose land the gold was found try to mine it themselves, and villages of specialist gold-seekers and gold miners never seem to have emerged. Instead, villages with gold-bearing land continued to devote their time to their *sawah,* which helped to feed the miners, and never developed their own specialist mining skills. They were content to call upon outside professional skills and outside mine labour and assure themselves of a percentage of the profits. Only occasionally as in the case of simple shallow mines on communal village land, such as those near Sulit Air, did a number of local individuals come together to organize joint exploitation of the gold. Even these had to call in a mining expert.[123]

This system of gold-mining specialists seems to have been a very ancient one in Minangkabau, and was certainly familiar to the Dutch in the late seventeenth century.[124] In general, the laying-down of a mine was organized by an entrepreneur (*kepala tambang* or *tua tambang, lit.* mine chief) who, like the *nakoda* in the blacksmithing team, would have the requisite knowledge and capital and who would be able to acquire the necessary workers to mine under his supervision. The *tua tambang* was an important member of society, although what his economic relations were with, say, the gold traders is impossible to say.[125] Certainly he required more capital than the iron-smithing *nakoda.* Mines were often very difficult to lay down and work, depending on the provenance of the gold. In Tanah Datar, gold occurred not only in veins running through the mountains, but also in detached rocks scattered around and mixed with earth.[126] The method of excavation used to acquire such gold in the plain around Tanjung Ampalu was described in 1838:

> Holes to the depth of about five men's height are dug through the red earth and the red marl and then through a loose grey sand called napar. A long bamboo, with notches for placing the feet, is placed in these holes or pits; the water is scooped out by hand or sometimes with a cask; they are not familiar with a paternosterwork. In a similar manner the stones are brought to the surface, and then sieved and washed out in small wooden dishes . . . . That gold which lies between the pits is sometimes brought out by making a wooden mine gallery, but naturally not all the stones can be obtained.[127]

In other areas there were different modes of operation, though the use of shafts and galleries was often essential. Mines were never cut very deep, due not to lack of skill but to fear of earthquakes.[128]

The first concern of the *tua tambang* was, of course, to acquire a labour force. Gold-mining was a much disliked operation, and no traditional class of miners ever evolved. Only the virtually destitute would work in the mines, so that recruitment was very difficult, other than in times of crop failure or other economic dislocation. The Dutch noted as early as 1688 that 'many thousands of poor people' could be recruited for a large mine in a time of hardship.[129] Two hundred years later it could still be recorded that: 'Among the natives there is proverbially no more wretched condition known than that of the gold miner (anak tambang)'.[130] Often the *tua tambang* had to organize his labour force over a considerable area, again requiring perseverance and initiative.

Next, tools and food had to be provided for this work force. This was generally done by the *tua tambang* making an agreement with the owners of the land, who would then undertake to provide the miners with food and the necessary iron tools such as crowbars, shovels, cleavers, hammers and handaxes; an alternative arrangement was for the *tua tambang* to supply all necessities, the owners' percentage of the profits being proportionately reduced.[131] The tools represented a considerable investment. The hammer used to pound gold-bearing lumps of rock had a head eighteen inches in length, was as thick as a man's leg, and had a handle in the middle.[132] Although the proportion of gold excavated paid to the owners of the land varied somewhat, sources make it clear that the traditional payment was one-sixteenth of every *tahil* excavated.[133] The remaining fifteen-sixteenths was distributed by the *tua tambang* as he saw fit. Since at the beginning of the work he generally gave the workers an advance in food and clothing, this was resumed on the completion of the season's mining. In general the miners were poorly paid, sixty Dutch cents per day being the maximum wage in 1838. Usually the wage was half this, and was extremely slight in relation to the amount of gold acquired.[134]

The advantages accruing to the *tua tambang* were described in 1838 in relation to a very small diluvial earth excavation in the vicinity of Rao in the northern *rantau* of Minangkabau, where the workers were in a far better position than that of wage labourers in a shaft mine.

> The exploitation of such a mine usually takes place in the following way. An entrepreneur employs four workers for the period of a year, or actually for a *moesim* (monsoon), omitting the sowing and harvesting months. One of them sees to the building of the hut at the mine site and the supply of food etc., while the

other three divide the mine work among themselves in this manner: one makes the water-course, one digs and collects the gold-bearing earth and the third washes out the gold. It costs the entrepreneur about f.80 to maintain each man for the length of a monsoon, costing thus f.320 for the four . . . At the end of the working year the entrepreneur weighs all the gold collected, subtracts his expenses, and divides the remainder into six equal shares: one for himself, one for each of the workers and one for the owner of the mine, who is usually the chief of the district. We were assured that whenever the outcome is reasonably successful, a share amounts to 10 tahil of gold, worth about f.600, so that the entrepreneur gets almost 200 per cent gain on his outlay of f.300 or f.320, and for that very small sum f.4,000 worth of gold is obtained in all.[135]

It can be seen from this description that, in general, gold-mining was never such a specialized activity that it could be cut off from the requirements of the agricultural cycle. Moreover, like iron production, the production units were small and independent. Individual *tua tambang* preferred to lay down small mines rather than to combine in larger-scale operations; the outcome of this *modus operandi* was that in 1811 there were reported to be 1,200 small gold mines in central Minangkabau alone.[136] However, despite the predominance of the rice village economy in Minangkabau plains society, gold-mining, unlike iron-mining, did have wider ramifications for at least the Tanah Datar political and social order. Various specialists grew up around gold and the gold trade, ultimately evolving into an elaborate system of royal courts and imported religious practices unlike anything else in Minangkabau. But before discussing this development of centuries, other variations of the Minangkabau village economy need to be added to the picture as it appeared in the early nineteenth century.

The hill village: manufactures and specialized crops

The four major rice plains of central Minangkabau are surrounded by volcanic mountains and ranges of hills which form part of the Bukit Barisan. On the slopes of these mountains – Singgalang, Merapi, Sago, Talang and the ranges between – the Minangkabau had also created village communities, indeed antedating those of the valley floors, which were originally too marshy for settlement and lacked the security which could be found in the hills. Also to the category of hill village may be added those villages which were properly on the valley floors but were so enclosed by hilly country as to have little rice land; this was the situation, for example, of villages to the east of Lake Singkarak. The different ecological conditions prevalent in the hills meant that the importance of the wet-rice cycle and of lineage lands was limited by the scarcity of land suited for *sawah*. Hence the lifestyle of the hills was determined by the need for village members to support themselves by methods other than those in use in the plains. This in turn led to differences in family and individual relationships in the typical hill village, differences which were becoming increasingly marked in the period under discussion.

Hill villages of course varied in height and in the amount of land available to them for cultivation as *sawah*. The higher up one went on mounts Singgalang, Merapi, Sago and Talang, the fewer were the opportunities for wet-rice cultivation.

Hill villages can therefore be divided into two categories, those which possessed some *sawah* land on the lower hill slopes, and those which had to depend entirely on dry-field cultivation in the form of permanent gardens on which short term crops or annuals such as dry rice, maize, potatoes, onions, cucumbers, cabbages and pulses could be cultivated.[137] Villages with *sawah* also engaged in dry-field agriculture, but the proportion of land used in this way became greater the higher one went up the mountains. In addition, both groups of villages also gave space to establishing gardens of perennials, such as sugar-cane, tobacco, indigo and bananas for internal trade, and cassia, gambir[138] and coffee for external trade.[139] Such variations in land use, based on the recognition that only certain lineages in a particular village could possess *sawah* land, created social relationships in the hill villages which, despite the persistence of matriliny, were often at variance with those of the plains. Individual effort was more necessary, more possible, and more apt to introduce strains into the village structure; particular methods had to be used to accommodate it.

The most common, which was just beginning to change in our period because of the external demand for certain of the hills' specialized crops, was for a considerable number of villagers to concentrate on artisan activities; as the homes of such specialized artisans, hill villages were often known to the inhabitants of the plains by the particular specialization with which they were associated. A concomitant of this artisan specialization was the institution of *merantau,* whereby large numbers of young men left the village annually, or even for a number of years, to sell the products of village labour and to trade in other articles as well. Because the introduction of new crops, such as maize in about the sixteenth century, had enabled the hill villages to maintain a high level of population, *merantau,* whereby a village lost up to two-thirds of its men in the periods between agricultural cycles, provided the safety-valve of out-migration which was provided by the circulation of lineage lands in the plains.[140]

Unfortunately we have no means of estimating the percentage of *sawah*-owning lineages in certain hill villages, nor the percentage of those engaged in artisan occupations, nor even whether the two categories, in the lower hills at least, were mutually exclusive. It does seem that, since villages were divided into different spatial sections, a large village having as many as eight hamlets, artisans of a particular craft lived in a particular locality of the village.[141] What we do know is that, whatever balance had been reached in these villages, the outside world's demands, from the mid-eighteenth century, for the three crops of cassia, gambir and coffee destabilized the social structure of all such villages. Before coming to this, however, and since nearly all hill villages were characterized by some form of artisan activity, the significance of the mode of production of these crafts for the village social structure should be dealt with.

Villages varied greatly in their specializations. In those which had relatively easy access to supplies of iron, smithing was the primary occupation. Sirukam, in the hills to the extreme east of the Solok plain, was a village of locksmiths, renowned for making locks for the big wooden chests in which household valuables were kept.[142] Sungai Puar and Bukit Betabuah, on the slopes of Mount Merapi in Agam, manufactured brass boxes and locks for guns.[143] Pandai Sikat, further south on the slopes of Mount Singgalang, specialized in making metal-tipped harrows for cultivating the fields.[144] Several villages in the hills bordering the Solok plain made heavy tools for use in both gold and iron mining.[145]

In Tanah Datar, the villages in the northern hills, stretching from the slopes of Mount Merapi to the slopes of Mount Sago, had strong artisan traditions connected with blacksmithing. This was due to their proximity to the iron-smelting centre of Salimpaung. Salimpaung itself possessed a gun-making industry, and swords and pikes were also made in the village.[146] Sipayang nearby made gun barrels,[147] while Tanjung Alam further north specialized in making the complete matchlocks.[148] Gun-making was a very important industry in Minangkabau, and dated from at least the sixteenth century.[149] In 1824 it was estimated that of every twelve men in Tanah Datar, one was armed, and of every six armed men, one was armed with a gun. An estimate of the same year gave 10,414 guns for the whole of the Tanah Datar population of 232,830; in 1822 the large village of Sungai Jambu, on the slopes of Mount Merapi, alone had 900 guns.[150] Candung, another large village on the Agam slopes of Mount Merapi, had 400 guns in 1824.[151]

Despite the widespread diffusion of the product of the gun-making industry, the industry itself was, like smelting, still pursued on a small scale, by individual entrepreneurs with simple equipment and one or two helpers. The small huts of the smiths contained an anvil which was in fact a large rock, a hammer made by attaching a smaller stone to two pieces of bamboo, tongs which were very small pieces of iron attached to bamboos and bellows made from large, hollow bamboos.[152] To make a gun barrel with these tools required great time and patience: 'After smelting the ore, they hammer the smolten metal into a long strip, twist it spirally round an iron pin, and thus fuse the coils of this strip together'.[153] Needless to say, such a gun barrel, which was about seven feet in length and heavy, was expensive; in 1833 a Salimpaung gun barrel cost 8 to 12 Dutch guilders.[154] The actual completion of the guns was yet another speciality, about which we know little. The guns were matchlocks, without flints but with a very simple fuse mechanism.[155] Lances, spears, swords and *keris* (daggers) were also the subject of careful manufacture in the hill villages of northern Tanah Datar.

Comparable to villages which specialized in blacksmithing were those which specialized in the working of gold and silver.[156] Certain Agam hill villages were particularly renowned for their goldsmiths, who specialized in filigree work in the form of flowers and foliage, and who often migrated to work in the coastal entrepôts where gold from all over Minangkabau was assembled for export.[157] Like blacksmiths, who were required to produce the humble spear in large quantities, goldsmiths were in considerable demand. Gold jewellery, after *sawah* and cattle, comprised the main wealth of a family; there were numerous types of such jewellery, and an authority in the late 1860s counted seventeen different varieties for men and twenty-two for women.[158] Gold armbands, ear-rings and chains, and gold *keris* were all objects of acquisition and wear, being a means of indicating a family's status. Silversmiths made small items of personal use, such as chains, tweezers, toothpicks and *sirih* boxes.[159] But here again, as in the blacksmithing industry, production took place by means of very small-scale units. Goldsmithing was always highly individualistic work; one and the same person worked the gold from its initial acquisition until it was sold as jewellery, and he would even make his own tools from iron he procured himself. This meant, in fact, that very few artisans were well-to-do, nor could they accumulate savings; often clients had to be prepared to finance the goldsmith's acquisition of his tools. Only by agreeing to work for a patron, by means of which they would secure some form of advance payment, could gold- and silversmiths live an existence that was not precarious.[160]

This small scale of production was apparent also in the other major hills craft, the dyeing and weaving industry. Here it should be noted again that not all villages pursuing artisan occupations were actually located on hill slopes; some were in very narrow valleys with only a small amount of rice land, and enclosed on all sides by hills. Such was often the case with many villages renowned for their role in the textile industry. An example is offered by the villages in the very narrow valley near Gunung Besi: Turawan, which was a large, prosperous village, its iron industry having decayed, specialized in dyeing cotton with *kasumba* and in weaving, whilst Padang Luar, even closer to Gunung Besi, supplemented rice farming in the same manner.[161] As far as the actual hill villages are concerned, those of Agam were particularly renowned for their dyeing and weaving of both silk and cotton cloths. Villages on the Agam slopes of Mount Merapi, where indigo was widely grown, had a ready source of livelihood in working as dyers for the cloth industry. An observer in 1824 claimed to have seen 'whole villages, which earned their livelihood by dyeing with indigo'.[162] Dark-blue dyed cloth was by far the most common Minangkabau wear.[163] Villages which specialized in dyeing required access to dyestuffs, either indigo, or the plant *kasumba,* or the roots of the *mangkudu* tree which produced red dye, or coats of the mangosteen fruit which were used to produce the black dye with which imported Indian blue cloth was dyed black for daily use. Dyeing was an art; dyeing yellow was particularly difficult in the absence of a suitable dyestuff.[164] In contrast to Agam, Limapuluh Kota had only a small dyeing and weaving industry and most of its cloth was brought in from outside.[165]

The organization of the weaving industry is not well documented, although in general it seems that there was little internal specialization, other than that on occasions between the dyeing and the weaving. Both were women's occupations. The best description we have of the operation of the industry comes from the late 1860s, and relates to the mountain weaving town of Silungkang south-east from Tanah Datar. Leaving aside the question of the origin of the cotton supply, in general once the cotton had been acquired by the women weavers, each family's women worked on their own, looms being placed under virtually every house. Little capital was required for such an enterprise, as each family could provide its own capital equipment.[166] A description of this undifferentiated labour dates from the 1860s, relating to silk weaving in Silungkang:

First the white silk . . . is given an initial preparation. It is wound onto a bamboo bobbin, and, as the threads are mostly too fine, two or three of them are twisted together by means of a wheel. After dyeing, either red with ambaloe pegou [sticklac] or blue with indigo, these fine strands are hung up, ketan [sticky rice] is rubbed in, and they are scoured with the raw shell of the coconut. In this way the threads which are not so good are removed; those remaining are wound on a wheel, then on bamboo bobbins, and finally from these onto the loeli, which is like our shuttle. Now the weaving can start. The loom, which is placed under the house, consists of 3 rows or lines of horizontal threads spun closely one above the other. The woman, who sits on a plank in front of it, throws the reels (small bamboo tubes which contain the loeli) backwards and forwards through the loom, and with every thread which is woven through in this way, she pulls the comb, which stands vertically on the loom, towards her, in order to intertwine the threads firmly![167]

Again, as with iron-working and goldsmithing, what is striking is the small scale of production.

Still other villages specialized in domestic necessities other than those made of metal or cloth. In the hilly area surrounding Lake Singkarak there was an 'extensive manufactory of coarse pottery',[168] and certain Tanah Datar villages also contained specialists in pottery-making.[169] The provision of materials and craftsmen for the construction of the large family houses was also an important branch of labour for people in the hill villages. Sulit Air was located in 'an unfertile terrain, where only a few grasses together with several clumps of Eurya grow',[170] but it was renowned as a village of woodcarvers, who specialized in decorating the large family houses of other villages by carving them and then dyeing the beautiful patterns red, white and black.[171] The hills derived advantage, too, from the natural forest which covered them. While poorer people had to be content to roof their houses with *alang-alang,* a type of savannah grass, the more prosperous preferred *ijuk,* a roofing material prepared from the leaves of the *anau*-palm, which grew on the hills at a height at which coconut would not grow.[172] This was of particular advantage to Agam, which was so high that coconut palms were rarely seen in any case. Bamboo too, which played a very important part in the Minangkabau economy, in housebuilding, irrigation, wall-construction and making implements, was also more prevalent in the hills, where it could be cut, fashioned and sold.[173]

Finally, in terms of domestic necessities which required some preparation, perhaps gunpowder can be included. Sulphur was available around all the volcanoes and merely had to be picked up by members of the nearby villages, some of which actually owned sulphur deposits.[174] Together with saltpetre it was used by the women of such villages to make gunpowder, which was kept in gourds and poured into small bamboo tubes which contained exactly one charge.[175]

Of the major industries of the Minangkabau hills – blacksmithing, gold- and silversmithing and weaving – the small scale of production is the leading characteristic. Unlike the Minangkabau of the rice plains with their *sawah* to maintain, family labour and family ownership of the means of production were not so important for the Minangkabau of the hills. Some of their crafts were highly individualistic pursuits, and others involved the elementary family only. Crafts involving metals were always individualistic; they had highly magical connotations, and craft secrets were handed down from father to son. Goldsmithing by its very nature was a private craft, but even trading ventures from the hills appear to have been personal and largely uncoordinated. Hence, the concept of property most suited to artisan families seems to have been that of *harta pencarian* or earned property.

However, too much emphasis must not be put on the individualistic nature of hills society. Tantalizing questions remain unanswered. Since artisans were generally not well-to-do, were not some in fact financed and supported by ownership of family land?[176] Industries such as smithing required the assistance of labour, which probably came from inside the lineage. Smiths also had to enter into commercial relations with others to acquire raw materials and to distribute their finished product. Weavers likewise entered into contractual relationships to acquire cotton and to sell the finished cloth. These satellite activities probably absorbed members of the lineages of the smiths and weavers to a similar extent to which those who cultivated *sawah* in the plains were absorbed into the agricultural cycle. This would explain why the *penghulu* and *mamak* system continued in the hill villages and, indeed, the way of life of the *sawah* villages of the plains seems to have remained the ideal to be aspired to in the hills. The story of Rancak diLabueh is set in a hill village in Bukit Kamang in Agam. The hero, however, due to lack of ricefields, has to make his way as a typical hill villager by drying the fibre of the leaves of the *anau*-palm and selling it for roofing material. He also establishes a garden with bananas, sugar-cane, maize, rice, cucumbers and other vegetables. His chief aim, however, is to acquire and increase his *sawah,* and only when he achieves this does his status in his home village become recognized.[177]

Agriculture was of course essential to the survival of the hill villages. Unfortunately their agricultural pattern is complicated, and lack of statistics make only a qualitative evaluation possible. It has already been noted that not all villages were very far up the slopes of the main mountains and some had access to land in the small valleys created by mountain spurs.[178] Such villages on the lower slopes of Mount Merapi in Tanah Datar, for example, were in a particularly favourable position, being able to combine both *sawah* and dry-field cultivation, mixing a little dry-field rice with vegetables and certain perennial 'trade crops'. The most favoured villages concentrated on the market gardening of vegetables. Simabur, for example, at about 2,000 ft., had ample water to irrigate its fields, and in addition to *sawah* the villager could also lay down gardens and cultivate maize and sweet potatoes for his own consumption, and onions and potatoes for sale: 'Within three months he has a bountiful crop of these which, as far as the maize and tubers are concerned, give him more profit than his rice'.[179] Sungai Jambu, further up Merapi, was in a similar position. On the Agam side of Mount Merapi Sungai Puar and Bukit Betabuah, at just above 3,000 ft., supplemented rice with potatoes.[180] Potatoes, onions and cabbages were also a feature of the villages lying on the slopes of Mounts Merapi and Singgalang in the area where the slopes of the two met to form a valley. Pandai Sikat, for example, produced such vegetables for sale, as did the hill villages on the Batipuh side of Mount Merapi, starting from about 2,300 ft. above sea-level.[181] Those lying on the hills around Lake Singkarak did likewise.[182] In the hilly region between Mount Merapi and Mount Sago, bounded by Salimpaung and Tanjung Alam at above 3,200 ft., a similar phenomenon was noted in 1833: 'many European garden vegetables such as cabbages, peas, beans and potatoes seem to grow extremely well here'.[183]

Villages higher up the mountains had to rely on dry-field rice, maize and potatoes to sustain their populations which, in the absence of *sawah,* were meagre. Such villages were small and poor, the large lineage houses being replaced by small, scattered bamboo dwellings.[184] With dry-field rice the land was quickly exhausted after two or three years, while at about 3,400 ft. above sea-level not even dry-field rice could be cultivated.[185] This was the area of true *ladang,* on which a variety of vegetables was grown. The highest village above Sungai Puar was at 4,700 ft.; rice fields were non-existent, 'but, on the other hand, extensive fields of onions take their place'.[186]

In addition to growing annual vegetable crops to provide a dietary supplement and an item for trade, the villages on the medium-level hill slopes were well suited for the establishment of gardens of perennial tree and other crops. The major crops grown, leaving aside those which by this period were important in external trade, were sugar, indigo and tobacco.[187] Unlike vegetables, which every village tried to grow, certain areas seem to have specialized in particular perennials, partly due to geographic conditions which did not always permit 'mixed gardens', although sugar cane and indigo are often mentioned together. Sugar was grown quite high up on slopes where the climate would normally be considered unsuitable. It grew particularly in Tanah Datar, on the hills around Lake Singkarak, around the Solok plain, on the slopes of the hills behind Pagarruyung, and on the slopes of the mountain ridge between Mount Merapi and Mount Sago around Tanjung Alam, Salimpaung and Sipayang.[188] It was also grown widely in the Agam hills: on the Merapi slopes around the Candung and Sungai Puar area, on the slopes of the northern hills enclosing Agam in the Bukit Kamang region, on the western slopes of Mount Singgalang around Melala, and on the slopes of the same mountain around Pandai Sikat.[189]

Raffles described sugar-growing and the industry associated with it as he observed it at Simawang, on Lake Singkarak:

> On the slopes of the hills which cannot conveniently be cut into terraces, or where streams of water cannot be carried, sugar-cane is the principal article. Of this the cultivation is considerable, and very neatly constructed mills for expressing the juice, which is afterwards manufacturered into a coarse sugar, are common. They consist of two perpendicular cylinders, the upper ends of which are formed into screws or grooves, which fit into each other so that the cylinders, which at the bottom are fixed into a stand, and are turned by an ox, revolve different ways. The expressed juice is received in a reservoir below.[190]

The juice was then boiled to make sugar. Sugar cane was also cultivated on hill slopes in Limapuluh Kota, particularly on Mount Sago, and exactly the same method of extracting the juice was in use.[191] None of this sugar was of export quality.

Indigo was widely grown on the slopes of Mount Merapi, both on the Tanah Datar and Agam sides, and on the hills surrounding the Solok plain, where of course it was vital to the continuance of the weaving industry.[192] To what extent weaving villages also possessed their own indigo gardens is not known; in any case, preparation was very simple, indicating that the dye was used on the spot: 'the ripe indigo is placed in water and boiled, after which the native adds quicklime and stirs it in, which causes the dyestuff to separate from the water; the latter is strained off and the dye is used in this liquid state'.[193]

Tobacco was also grown in Limapuluh Kota, Agam and northern Tanah Datar; although localities are not as readily definable as for sugar, its cultivation seems to have covered a similar geographic area, despite its not being cultivated to such a great height as was sugar. Around Tanjung Alam there were small tobacco gardens, the tobacco growing extremely luxuriantly. There were also tobacco gardens on the slopes of Mount Sago near Halaban.[194] Like sugar and indigo, it was cultivated for local use, and the cutting, cleaning, drying and sorting of tobacco leaves was not particularly well developed.[195]

While villages on the lower and middle slopes of the mountains seem to have actually opened up regular gardens for particular crops, higher-up villages possessed small *ladang* which tended to contain a mixture of crops which the individual establishing the *ladang* would dispose of as best he could; such a *ladang* would contain tobacco, maize, beans, coffee and several *anau*-palms. The latter was a useful complement, its sap being used to make sugar which was quite acceptable on the market, whilst parts of the trunk could be used to make an excellent cordage. The *anau*-palm also produced palm-wine or *tuak,* which was regarded more highly than that distilled from the coconut palm.[196]

To what extent did families in the major villages with both craft industries and crop gardens participate in both branches of the economy? It is impossible to answer this in the absence of any documentation, but the story of Rancak diLabueh indicates that *sawah* cultivation, garden cultivation and trading were combined to enable a family to maintain itself.[197] Artisans dealing with metals, however, seem likely to have come from distinct, separate lineages in such villages, and to have been engaged in full-time industry, but even they must have had access to land for their support.[198] Weaving was, of course, integrated into the agricultural cycle. Nevertheless, although agriculture was the *sine qua non* of the existence of a hill village, as it was for the plains, the demands of garden cultivation were certainly different from those of wet-rice cultivation, and the absorption of a large proportion of village land by gardens must certainly have affected the village social structure.

In the first place, availability of ample land within village boundaries was a prerequisite. In most areas the availability of land seems to have been no problem; even with the boom in commercial crops for international trade, it seems to have been possible for village entrepreneurs to use land higher and higher up the slopes, or to devise new, intensive methods for growing their crops. Travellers often mentioned large supplies of uncultivated land lying available, such as that in the hills behind Tanjung Alam and in the hills connecting Mount Merapi with Mount Sago,[199] although this was not universally the case in all commercial crop-growing areas, and may in any case have represented merely fallow land. However, in cases where there was not enough land in the immediate village surroundings, an enterprising villager would merely migrate up the slopes to lay down his own individual garden. Such a garden required little of the cooperative labour needed by *sawah,* and was less demanding as far as location was concerned. The higher gardens promoted highly individual settlement patterns, with only several simple buildings nearby belonging to the owners of the plots. More than one traveller observed the 'gardens with several huts and dry-rice fields' high up the western and northern slopes of Mount Singgalang.[200] Although such land belonged to the village as a whole, it was usually not difficult for an individual to gain permission to exploit it, and in a very real sense the produce of the garden was the property of the person who had established it.[201] To open up such a garden was a traditional means of escape from family and *penghulu* pressures; self-reliance and individual dynamism were the keynotes. The right to open up a garden did not, in the last resort, even depend on *penghulu* permission but on the fact of cultivation, and although the *penghulu* were there to protect the rights of other villagers – such as those to collect forest produce – from infringement, little tension seems to have been caused by the market gardening and trade crop system. The availability of land for market gardening helps to explain why the hill villages did not produce a large class of semi-proletariat in search of wage labour in the plains; instead, they produced peripatetic pedlars who would descend each season and travel even to the coast to earn a livelihood by trading.[202]

All these factors combined to make lineage and family claims on land less important than in the plains. Since land was never permanently alienated by gardening and producing tree crops in the way that *sawah* was, it was naturally of less interest to the lineage and was treated more like individual property. The stability of the garden of course varied with the crop produced. Vegetable crops and dry-field rice tended to rotate to provide periods of fallow, while gardens of perennials were longer lasting. But even these would require replanting with time, depending on the rate of deterioration, and so both tree and vegetable gardens tended to represent individual initiative and enterprise rather than the inherited wealth of a lineage. Since the garden plots themselves did not permit of any real improvement or expansion, they were of less interest to prospective heirs in the maternal line.[203]

If we can assume that up to the eighteenth century a variety of social mechanisms had evolved in the hill villages to control the disposition of private gardens, by the period we are dealing with these mechanisms had been rent asunder by the fact that certain tree crops which grew well as perennials in hill gardens had come to be in demand on the world market. This is not the place to discuss the historical development of the Minangkabau trade in cassia, gambir and *Arabica* coffee.[204] What must be noted here is merely the effect of the cultivation of these crops on the domestic economy at a particular point in time; since the effect of the production of these crops for the world market on village society is the theme of this book, only a beginning will be made here to look at the process, which had already disrupted the hill villages some time before the period we are dealing with here. The crops will be dealt with in the order in which world demand for them was experienced in Minangkabau.

An important point to notice is that the first of these crops – cassia – succeeded in the very areas, and even the very villages, which we have already mentioned as having access to *sawah* and as having also established successful market gardens. Cassia grew spontaneously in certain parts of Agam and, as demand grew for this wild cinnamon bark, gardens of the tree came to be planted. The chief ones were associated with Candung on the Agam slopes of Mount Merapi, where the soil was very suitable;[205] with the Bukit Kamang area in the northern hill boundary of Agam, where there were in 1832 'two very large cinnamon plantations';[206] and with villages such as Pandai Sikat on the slopes of Mount Singgalang and Kota Lawas on the slopes of Mount Merapi at the point where the two met to form a narrow valley. It seems possible that the latter was the original cassia area of Minangkabau; an investigator noted of the area in 1833:

'There were many cinnamon trees growing wild here, which produce a far superior product to the usual cassia . . .'[207] The Agam plateau was the highest area in central Minangkabau, and the cassia tree could be cultivated to a considerable height, enabling villages to use land higher up which had previously been part of their forest reserves. Since the tree could not be used until it was eight to ten years old, areas where cassia grew spontaneously had a great initial advantage. Preparatory to preparation of the cassia for the market, the tree itself had to be cut down close to the ground, as both the trunk and the branches were used in trade. Hence replacement of the trees was an ongoing process, once a market had been found for this product.[208]

While cassia was a speciality of Agam, gambir was confined to the northern and eastern hills, fanning out from Mount Bongso which bordered Limapuluh Kota and cut it off from the gently sloping coastal plains of the east coast of Sumatra. This area possessed ideal soil conditions for gambir, and those villages which were poor in *sawah* became almost dependent on the crop. The area also possessed adequate wood on the mountain slopes, wood being necessary for the preparation of the finished product.[209] Gambir was cultivated on the lower slopes of Mount Bongso by villages such as Sarilamak, and along the mountain range stretching north from Bongso by villages such as Mungkar which had previously had few sources of income.[210] It was noted in 1833: 'The low range of mountains is almost completely planted with gambir plantations; this product must spread a comparatively large amount of prosperity among the population here; very much gambir is transported from here to the East Coast for export'.[211] These villages were in fact located at the junction of the plains and the hill slopes. Mungkar and the villages further west were in an area very poor in ricefields, while Sarilamak and those to the east such as Taram and Halaban were well supplied with ample *sawah* and also grew their own fruit trees.[212]

Gambir cultivation required little work; very little, compared to cassia. The young gambir plant developed into a shrub which crept along the ground, because of its dense ground cover needing only once-yearly weeding until, at two or three years old, the leaves could be plucked ready for preparation for the market. A well-treated gambir shrub could be cut every six months and would usually reach ten or fifteen years of age before needing to be replaced; some shrubs were ready for plucking after one year, and continued bearing for another twenty years, or even longer. The most common cause of the abandonment of a gambir garden was the exhaustion of nearby wooded areas.[213]

It was neither cassia nor gambir, however, but another commercial tree crop which changed the fortunes of so many Minangkabau hill villages. From the 1790s there developed a world scramble for coffee. The result was a veritable boom in coffee cultivation in the Minangkabau hills. Like cassia, coffee was cultivated in virtually every area which had a tradition of successful market gardening and, moreover, it was adaptable enough for planters to be able to include it in gardens in both cassia and gambir areas. Coffee, unlike many agricultural crops, grows well in comparatively rugged terrain, on quite steep slopes, and particularly favours volcanic soils. Nevertheless, there were certain areas which were especially prolific in coffee, and since these were so much bound up with the Islamic movements which are our subject, they require to be carefully defined. Dating is also of the highest importance. The evidence indicates that it was in the eastern, south-western and northern hill areas of Agam that coffee cultivation was earliest and most assiduously fostered.[214] Villages on the slopes of Mounts Merapi and Singgalang were fortunate in being able to cultivate coffee to a considerable height up the mountains.[215] The earliest and most extensive cultivation in Minangkabau seems to have been on the Agam slopes of Mount Merapi stretching in both directions round the mountain from Candung. In 1824 this village was reported to have 'a large number of coffee trees',[216] while in 1833 the flourishing coffee gardens of Candung and surrounding hill villages were remarked upon again: 'Especially in *Tjandong* coffee grows very luxuriantly on the mountainside; at the same time the *Cassia* trees prevalent here thrive extremely well in suitable soil'.[217] Most important, the inhabitants of Candung, like those of other successful coffee villages, never had to rely wholly on the market for their coffee. They all had ample supplies of *sawah* to assure the population of rice at times when it was not profitable to put coffee on the market.

Following Mount Merapi round from Candung to the south, Bukit Betabuah and Sungai Puar at just above 3,000 ft., both known as villages of artisans and market gardens, were in the midst of an area 'extremely rich in coffee trees, which grow particularly well at this height'.[218] They too had a certain amount of *sawah* for their support. Further south again, where the slopes of Mount Merapi met those of Mount Singgalang to form a high, narrow valley, the bottom of which itself was about 3,400 ft. above sea level, the six main villages on the slopes of the two mountains had not only created considerable *sawah* to a fair height by irrigating with mountain streams, but were also known for their crafts and their market gardens and for the successful cultivation of cassia, and were now extensively engaged in coffee cultivation. Pandai Sikat and Kota Lawas, both with considerable *sawah,* were particularly remarkable for the extent of their coffee gardens.[219] To the north of Agam, where the valley was hemmed in by a limestone mountain chain, there was another area possessing the same characteristic as those previously mentioned. Here in the hills lay the seven large villages of Bukit Kamang, the main ones being Bansa and Sala which, 'seen from on high, gave the appearance of an enclosed garden with small hills, on which lie houses shaded by fruit trees and *areng*-palms and surrounded by bananas and sugar-cane . . . Its position on the slopes of the mountains with the river flowing through make this district a second Canaan, while the numerous coffee gardens yield considerable profits'.[220] The area had extensive *sawah,* and also grew cassia.[221]

In contrast to the widespread cultivation of coffee in Agam, Tanah Datar was not possessed of such ample opportunities for coffee-growing, other than on the slopes of the Merapi and in the hilly range linking the foot of the Merapi with Mount Sago. Coffee grew on the Merapi slopes above Batipuh and in the villages above Sungai Jambu, although it appears that these gardens were laid down after those of Agam.[222] The Tanah Datar Merapi coffee villages were only at a height of about 2,500 ft., not nearly as high as the equivalent coffee-growing area on the Agam side; the highest inhabited village on the Tanah Datar side was only at 3,200 ft., and coffee did not do very well on these lower slopes.[223] Coffee in the hilly areas to the south of Tanah Datar around Lake Singkarak was only a meagre affair as late as 1825, and in 1818 villagers from the hills around the Solok plain told Raffles that they had only recently begun to plant coffee.[224] It was in the villages of the northern hill areas of Tanah Datar that coffee was most prolific, beginning with Rao Rao at 2,400 ft. and stretching across the range between the Merapi and Mount Sago at a height of 2,800 to 3,100 ft.[225] At Tabatpatah in 1824 were found 'a great abundance of coffee trees',[226] and similar gardens were found around Salimpaung, Sipayang, Mandeling and, indeed, every other village in the area until the descent to Tanjung Alam on the Limapuluh Kota side. Again the area was one where coffee was never allowed to become a monoculture, and each coffee village had access to *sawah.*[227]

In Limapuluh Kota it was the areas in the extreme south and east which were best able to find land for coffee cultivation. The main villages here had the advantage of access to land for coffee both on the slopes of Mount Sago and the north-eastern mountain range, while on the well-watered plain below they could maintain their traditional *sawah.* One of the leading such villages was Taram, in the south-eastern corner of the plain, but also rising into the mountain foothills: 'This small district is extremely prosperous; the houses look very nice and are painted with flowers. There are considerable coffee gardens, an abundance of ricefields and well-stocked fishponds'.[228] A similarly situated village lay to the south of Taram, built partly against the slopes of Mount Sago and partly in the plain; this was Air Terbit. The part of the village built on the slopes was described in this way:

This latter area presents the appearance of a beautiful sloping ricefield that continues down into the plain, with which the valleys all join in their gradual descent. The mountain spurs between the valleys are planted with coffee trees and afford the planter, who often places his dwelling house in the middle of these coffee gardens, very considerable profits.[229]

Other villages higher up Mount Sago also planted coffee everywhere they could, and it was in fact grown at a considerable height.[230]

The other major coffee-growing villages of Limapuluh Kota were those in the north and north-west which also grew gambir. Coffee gardens were interspersed with those of gambir around Mount Bongso and along the northern mountain range at places such as Mungkar and Simalunggang. The latter village was particularly favoured because it had access to so much well-watered land in the plain for *sawah* cultivation. The villages in the extreme north-west, the main one of which was Suliki, were both able to water their fields by means of the river Sinamar which flowed through the area, and to produce coffee on the surrounding hills.[231]

Finally, it should be noted that coffee was by now bringing some of the remote hill areas surrounding the Minangkabau heartland into the Minangkabau economy in more than a marginal way. This was particularly true for the long narrow valley running south from Mount Sago, parallel to the main Tanah Datar valley but isolated by mountains of from 2,000 to 3,000 ft. on either side. On the southern and eastern slopes of Mount Sago, where the mountain formed spurs in its descent, lay a group of villages, the main one of which was Halaban. The spurs of the 5,000 ft. high mountain were inhabited up to about 2,000 ft., while coffee gardens had been laid down to over 3,000 ft.[232] Again, the villages also had access to *sawah.* 'These spurs are nearly all planted with coffee, while the valleys lying between them are filled with ricefields. On the highest point of these slopes lies the village *Alaban* . . .'[233] 'Coffee surrounds nearly every house and kampong here, is much more common than in the plain of the *50 kotta's* and, according to the natives, yields a very good product'.[234] Enclosing the valley on the eastern side was the 3,000 ft. high Mount Gabus, on the slopes of which lay the important village of Tebingtinggi where coffee was also grown.[235]

As the valley proceeded further south it became more and more enclosed by mountains, but the valley bottom was well watered by the river running through it and by mountain streams so that *sawah* cultivation had long been possible. This was the region of Lintau. Villages clung to the western mountain slopes at least as high as 2,400 ft. above sea level, with ricefields below and coffee above, all growing luxuriantly in the volcanic soil.

The position of this area means that it is amply provided with the necessary mountain streams for the irrigation of the numerous ricefields, which here constitute a gradually rising slope and which provide an abundant supply of food. Among these fields lie hamlets and villages in the midst of considerable coffee gardens which, to judge from the state in which we observed them, must provide considerable advantages to their owners in the form of not inconsiderable prosperity.[236]

The juxtaposition here of numerous ricefields and a considerable amount of coffee was noted by other travellers. Further south, however, in the Buo and Kumanis region, the valley became 'unusually hot and dry' and for the greater part, especially around Kumanis, was 'almost totally uncultivated'.[237]

The new prosperity of this area was paralleled by that of another region which had previously been on the fringes of Minangkabau classical culture. This was the hilly area to the west of Agam. In the west the Agam plateau broke up into a region of chasms and mountains, centred on the mountain lake, Lake Maninjau. On the western slopes of Mount Singgalang lay villages which had previously profited from *sawah* cultivation and market gardening but which now were actively participating in coffee production. This was a heavily-forested region and considerable enterprise had been required to plant the coffee trees. The chief village on the slopes was Melala at 2,400 ft.; 'it is located in a very fruitful area, almost completely planted with rice and coffee, and exhibits many signs of prosperity'.[238] Further west lay Lake Maninjau, ringed with mountains of 3,000 to 3,500 ft. high; to the east of the lake, however, the ideal combination of factors for coffee cultivation existed. Whilst the mountains to the west were especially steep, the east possessed a sloping, well-watered plain backed by hills 'on which, apart from rice, a considerable number of coffee trees and coconut palms appear'.[239] Further to the north-east of the lake lay broken ranges of hills in which lay villages which had made great strides in coffee cultivation.[240]

Having located the main areas of commercial crop cultivation, particularly coffee, it is possible to attempt to explain the significance of this cultivation for those villages which were engaged in it. Of course, the time-scale is important here, and about this it is difficult to be accurate. However, it seems that it was the villages on the Agam slopes of Mount Merapi and Mount Singgalang, and those in the northern mountain region between Tanah Datar and Limapuluh Kota around Mount Sago and Mount Gabus, which were the earliest cultivators of coffee for export. Some of the other main coffee-exporting villages presumably began their production later; a Dutch account of 1824 remarks that coffee cultivation was still expanding in the uplands, especially to marginal areas, and that it was also spreading to lowland areas wherever there was suitable land on the Barisan slopes.[241] The original coffee villages owed their early start to, firstly, location at a suitable height on the mountains, between approximately 2,500 and 3,000 ft.; secondly, their access to *sawah* land; thirdly, their tradition of market gardening; and, finally, the availability of land above them into which they could expand. This is not to say that all were equally favoured in respect to available land, and this land shortage of some villages seems to have been one of the causes of the tension imported into certain villages by the introduction of commercial crop cultivation. Villages on the slopes of Mount Merapi and Mount Singgalang such as Candung, Sungai Puar, Bukit Betabuah, Kota Lawas and Pandai Sikat, and around Tabatpatah on the other side, seem to have suffered most in this respect; moreover, they had a wide range of crops other than coffee growing, including commercial cassia gardens. Elsewhere, for example in the Merapi region between Candung and Tanjung Alam, there was still in 1833 much good, uncultivated land, covered with *alang-alang* interspersed with a little sugar cane and rice. This was true too of the northern slopes of Mount Sago between Tanjung Alam and Halaban.[242]

The question now arises, to what extent did the introduction of these commercial crops introduce tension into villages in which previously some sort of balance had been attained between *sawah*-owning lineages, market gardeners and artisan families? The existence of such tension is manifest in the violent disputes which broke out in these villages in the late eighteenth century and which intensified in the next century. However, the sources, which merely speak of 'parties' in such villages, make it difficult to identify the precise causes of dispute and crisis. That such disputes were fought out largely in religious terms does not obviate the necessity for seeking potential sources of tension in coffee-growing villages in particular. The first point to note is the manner in which coffee was grown. Coffee was first introduced into Minangkabau in the late seventeenth or early eighteenth century, and it seems to have been cultivated as a type of internal 'trade crop'. The trees generally began to bear within a maximum of five years from the initial seeding, and were producing well by the time they were eight years old. Yields were at their peak for the next fifteen to twenty years. Families with fruit trees around the family compound could also grow coffee in the same way, until it ultimately formed a dense hedge shaded by the other trees and known as *pagar kopi* (hedge coffee). Such bushes were not very productive, but since they required very little work and the product was in any case sold not as beans but in bundles of dried leaf-covered branches which the Minangkabau boiled to make a drink, such modest cultivation provided an additional means of livelihood.[243]

On the hill slopes, however, the situation was different. In the past villages had possessed wooded reserves which had now and again been disturbed for market gardening; now it was realized that coffee could profitably be planted on an extensive scale. Villages very high up the mountains were at a disadvantage because, having no access to *sawah,* they could not afford to risk too much to coffee cultivation exclusively; a sudden rise in the cost of daily necessities could be coupled with a downswing in the price of coffee, with disastrous results. The coffee planter in the medium-level villages with some *sawah* land was, however, to some extent cushioned, although what his relationship actually was to the rice-growers in his village is difficult to say. We do not know, for example, to what extent families were without *sawah,* nor to what extent *sawah*-owning lineages diversified into coffee. The basic change, however, was that now, with the profitability of coffee, there was considerable demand for the opening up of a village's wooded reserve. This was because coffee gardens could be established by reclaiming wooded land on which, in contrast to land around the villages which was often exhausted, excellent crops of coffee could be grown. The mountain ridges and spurs were particularly well-suited to coffee; little care of the crop was required, much of the natural growth being left standing to provide shade for the young trees and protect them from the strong winds. Two hundred and eighty-five fruit-bearing trees produced 1 *pikul* of coffee, and the tree planted in this way would continue to bear fruit for thirty to forty years.[244]

Uncultivated village land and village wooded reserves were, as has been noted, the property of the whole village and had very definite boundaries. In general, with market gardening we can presume that not large areas of village reserves were alienated. However with all the commercial crops, and coffee especially, there was increased demand from individuals within the villages for the opening up of village reserves on a fairly permanent basis. Whereas the ceding of land for gardening activities required little village involvement because permanent use was not really an issue, the opening up of a commercial garden meant consultation with the *penghulu* as representatives of the village so that the individual's rights to the land could be assured, by public marking and recognition of the boundaries. There could be considerable conflict of interest over to what extent to plant the new crops, given that such areas would then be removed from their traditional function as places where villagers could collect natural products, hunt, and cultivate on a small scale.[245]

It was this land hunger, especially of families which had in the past been without land, which seems to have caused extreme tension in those villages expanding into the new crops. The question of the rights to this individually owned *harta pencarian* and problems over who was to inherit the property of the owner of a commercial garden were not so acute, because family labour was necessary for the successful growing and processing of such crops for market, and therefore the family interest in the garden seems to have been recognized. But in addition to the land hunger of families there were other causes of tension; not all villages which wanted to diversify into the new crops had the necessary labour to help them exploit their reserves of land, and some villages at this time actually sought immigrants from elsewhere. Such migrants were known as *orang datang,* and required patrons in the host village. In some cases they never acquired full rights in the village or in the land they cultivated, and so their anomalous position produced an additional source of tension, particularly when they became vocal in demanding their rights in exchange for their contributions to the village's prosperity.[246]

A further source of friction caused by the expanding commercial crop production was experienced at inter- rather than intra-village level. It was induced by villages which did not have enough land for the ambitious plans of their inhabitants. Since village boundaries were known but not marked, it was possible for new gardens to be established in spots claimed by an adjacent village, thus causing disputes which could even lead to bloodshed. The expansion of commercial crops was marked by incessant boundary disputes, only absent in cases where villages had land to spare and an amicable agreement for the temporary cession of land could be made. Outright sale of land by one village to another was extremely rare, although one case is recorded for this period between two villages in the hills around Lake Maninjau.[247]

For the moment we will take the effects of commercial crop production in the hill villages of Minangkabau no further than to point out that many of these villages were in a condition of extreme volatility in this period, both because of land disputes and, of course, as a result of the new wealth flowing into them due to the external demand for their crops.

The west coast: villages of the foothills and the shore

It will be left to the final section to look at the commercial relationships between the various ecological zones of central Minangkabau. However, it is necessary to discuss two other zones, the economy of which was linked to that of the Minangkabau heartland. The first of these is the narrow coastal strip at the western foot of the high mountains of the Bukit Barisan. Two aspects of this coastal fringe of the Minangkabau world are important here: first, it provided those coastal ports which enabled the Minangkabau trader and his products to reach the outside world, and, second, it enabled the outside world, its products and ideas, to reach the Minangkabau in turn. In the period of the 1820s and 1830s only two ports on the coastal strip between Tiku in the north and Painan in the south had developed into genuine entrepôts where such an exchange of goods and ideas actually took place. One of these ports, Padang, had had a history of continuous contact with Europeans for over one hundred and fifty years, whilst the other, Pariaman, had a long history of contact with the Acehnese mercantile groups of north Sumatra. Both these entrepôts will be discussed later in relation to Minangkabau's external trade.

As far as the rest of the western coastal strip is concerned, its villages in general compared unfavourably in size, wealth and appearance with those of the highlands. Two different types can be distinguished, related to their mode of livelihood and the aspects of this which enabled them to integrate with the economy of the highlands.

Situated at the often-shifting mouths of the numerous swift-flowing rivers which catapulted down from the Bukit Barisan, and either stretching along the sea shore or removed somewhat back from it for security reasons, were small, drab-looking coastal villages which differed markedly from those of the uplands. They were small in terms both of size and population; even the leading ones, such as Ulakan, famous in Minangkabau history as one of the entry points of Islam into the Minangkabau world, presented 'a wretched appearance, matched by few villages on

Java . . .'[248] Behind these villages stretched sparsely peopled, marshy plains. In the mid-1830s it was estimated that the area stretching from the river Anai just north of Padang to the river Masang some miles north of Tiku and bounded inland by Lake Maninjau and the first peaks of the Bukit Barisan had a population of not more than 50,000.[249] Even where the plain was broadest, large tracts of marshy swamp and *alang-alang* grass separated one village from another.[250]

The inhabitants of the area adapted themselves to their unfavourable conditions as best they could. The typical village contained only a few houses. Ulakan had about twenty-five, and even a large fishing village such as Bungus, in the bay of the same name just south of Padang, had only three times that number. These houses, built of bamboo on piles six to eight feet off the ground and roofed with *alang-alang* grass, contained a household of not more than three or four people. They represented a marked break with uplands norms: the Minangkabau matrilineal house and family system were no longer applicable to the different conditions of the coast. Instead of the large rice barns of the uplands, symbolizing communal wealth, each house possessed a platform on which stood woven baskets filled with the family's meagre rice supply.[251] Bungus, described in 1834, was typical: 'It contains 80 to 100 bamboo houses, which stand in two parallel lines along the beach and has, in general, a poverty-stricken, old and decayed appearance'.[252]

Further back from the coast, not even nucleated settlements were in evidence; rather, isolated houses stood amidst patches of land which the owner was attempting to cultivate. All this is hardly surprising, considering that the coast suffered from very unfavourable climatic conditions. It was buffetted by the north-west monsoon from November to May and the heat and humidity had a debilitating effect, encouraging fevers and epidemics.[253]

In these unfavourable conditions, villages tended to specialize in what would most provide them with a profitable living, and imported rice where they could. Some concentrated almost exclusively on fishing and the fish trade; others on the carrying trade; others on the growing of cotton; others on cattle-raising, which could be carried out successfully in certain areas; others on weaving rattan or making lime or oil; and others still on salt-making.[254] Fishing, salt-making and cotton-growing were all occupations which had direct relevance to the life of the uplands, just as uplands rice helped to perpetuate the coastal economy. Being very often a rice-deficit area, the coast relied on rice brought down from the highlands to entrepôts such as Pariaman to be distributed to other ports, especially to Padang. The price of rice in the coastal ports fluctuated, but was often very high compared to prices in the uplands.[255] To buy their rice, coastal peasants concentrated on producing goods in which they were at an advantage and of which their uplands counterparts had need. Chief among such items was salt-water fish. Fishing took place all along the coast, although most villages engaged in a variety of other occupations. Those which cultivated only a little rice and lived almost entirely from the fish trade were in the area immediately north and south of Padang. Bungus, for example, was a village almost exclusively of fishermen, living on the shores of the bay of the same name, which teamed with fish. Fishing was highly organized, though, as with the blacksmiths of the highlands, the fishermen had never outgrown organization on a small scale. Few fishing teams consisted of more than seven men. Each team used a large trawling-net, made by its members from the fibres of the *anau*-palm, which needed seven pairs of hands to manage it. One man sat in the fishing-boat holding on to the net, whilst three men on each side gradually dragged it towards the shore. As with iron-working, because of the value of the capital equipment, one member of the team was in fact an entrepreneur who employed the others on a wage basis: the boat and the net together were estimated in the mid-1830s to be worth from f.100 to f.120. A village of several hundred people, with perhaps eighty adult males, would probably contain twelve such trawling-nets and boats. The twelve *nakoda* would take six or more men into service, paying them by dividing half the catch among them and keeping the other half for themselves. The fish so caught immediately entered into trade, either as fresh fish or, the greatest percentage, to be dried, salted and sold. Most of the fishing villages, especially those which held a market, had a certain number of full-time traders living among the population.[256]

Salt was another necessity for the uplands peasant, and salt-making was the speciality of a number of coastal villages. The villages centred on Narras north of Pariaman, on Ulakan between Pariaman and Padang, and on Jamba just north of Padang, were on stretches of the coast particularly suitable for this activity.[257] Salt-making was an important industry for these coast-dwellers, even though such salt could not compare in quality and taste with imported Javanese and Siamese salt; nevertheless, the small huts used by the salt-makers were conspicuous all along the beaches near these villages. Here the work was done, by lighting a fire and sprinkling it with sea water until ultimately the crystallized salt was retrieved from the fire's ashes boiled in a cauldron. Most of the process was carried out by women and children, the men completing the final stage of boiling the filtered sea water in the cauldron. In dry, warm weather one person could make a considerable amount of salt, although seasonal conditions such as the monsoon affected the work.[258]

Another commercial activity carried out along the whole coast between Padang and Tiku was the cultivation of cotton, an item of great interest to uplands weavers. Cotton was grown wherever there was suitable land, and attempts were made to improve the quality of the crop by using seeds found in Surat cotton-piece goods bales.[259] In addition to these readily marketable items, certain coastal villages had other specialities of their own. Tiku and the nearby villages were known for their excellent rattans and rushes from which the matting used by every Minangkabau household was made.[260] Though most villages had little *sawah* land, the ground being too sandy, there were higher, scrubby areas which formed good pasture land, and cattle-raising was a major occupation in villages such as Narras and Ulakan.[261] Other villages, especially those south of Padang, were able to burn lime from shell-fish found on the shore, and this lime was much preferred in *sirih*-chewing to that prepared in the interior from limestone.[262] Pariaman was well suited to the raising of cattle, it had good fishing grounds, it produced mats from rattan and it also supplied much of the rice consumed in less favoured coastal villages, including Padang.[263]

Extensive coconut groves were also an important economic asset along the coast. However, the oil so important in Minangkabau domestic use, especially for lighting, came largely from the coconut palms covering the small groups of islands off Tiku, Pariaman and Padang. The oil, which was widely traded, was extracted on the spot on these islands; they had been penetrated by entrepreneurs from the neighbouring coastal villages, who cared for and replanted the trees and used hired or bonded labour to prepare the oil all year round. The oil was vastly superior to that which could be obtained in the highlands.[264]

Behind the coastal villages and plain the land rose in a gradual slope towards the foothills of the Bukit Barisan. Closer to the foothills there was far greater possibility of *sawah* cultivation, but even here the uncertain climatic conditions kept the population small. The area between Padang and Limau Manis, for example, was one in which considerable *sawah* had been created, and cattle-raising was an important subsidiary activity; Raffles in 1818 remarked on the many herds of cattle and buffaloes in this area. Unlike the coastal villages, which were merely tiny hamlets strung out along the sea shore or the major rivers, the whole known by the name of the major village among them, in this area the villages became larger and, with their adjacent gardens and orchards, more prosperous.[265] This was not uniformly true, however; the ample *sawah* of Pau and Limau Manis contrasted favourably with the situation in the foothills behind Ulakan and Pariaman. Kayutanam and other foothills villages situated near the main trade routes to the uplands exhibited little signs of prosperity; Kayutanam itself, later to become so important because of its position, was described in 1824 as 'a miserable, small hamlet . . .'[266]

The social system of the coastal villages reflected their ecological singularity. In general, it may be said that the matrilineal system of the highlands had little relevance on the coast, despite the fact that many coastal villages owed a large part of their population to immigration from the highlands. In the coastal entrepôts in particular the *suku* system seems to have been irrelevant, although the title of *penghulu* was still retained for certain individuals. These entrepôts contained a mixture of migrants and foreigners such as the Acehnese, and their trade with the outside world had led to the rise of individuals of higher rank than the joint *penghulu,* bearing titles such as Raja, Tuanku and Panglima. Such individuals were able to represent the apex of local authority in dealing with foreign traders, and foreigners themselves had encouraged the evolution of such an institution. At Padang such a system was far evolved, the Tuanku Panglima and Tuanku Bendahara being important personages in comparison with the other eight *penghulu.* Often such individuals had precedence over a wide area; the Tuanku of Pariaman had a certain precedence in the whole area between Padang and Tiku.[267]

In the sixteenth and seventeenth centuries the coastal plains had flourished as a pepper-producing region. By the 1820s pepper growing on the plains had long fallen into decay, but at its heyday in the late sixteenth and early seventeenth centuries it too must have contributed to the rise of a hierarchy of landed lords and poor peasants. The small population on the coast made cultivation of land difficult in any case, and in 1825 it was estimated that the greater percentage of the population lived from trade.[268] What land there was under cultivation on the coast had become the hereditary property of a small group of landlords who had plots in small villages, satellites to the entrepôts in which they lived. Such land remained in the same family for generations, passing from father to children, and the only vestige remaining of the highlands matrilineal system was the fact that the *penghulu* titles remained and were sometimes passed down on matrilineal principles. This landed aristocracy cultivated its land with slave labour, slaves being an important item of trade from the island of Nias, and with debt bondsmen. The peasant, who had few rights to land, was also expected to provide a variety of goods and services, including work in the local lords' ricefields. In providing this labour, the peasant operated under a form of hiring agreement, which was the only way landlords could acquire labour. The peasant contracted himself for a stipulated sum, worked the fields and brought in the harvest, received a share of it, and then generally returned to his coastal village to occupy himself with fishing or salt-making until the next rice season came round, when he would again move inland with his wife and children. Even so, there was a severe shortage of labour, rice was expensive, and much land which could have been used for its cultivation lay waste.[269]

The east coast: riverine entrepôts and shifting cultivation

The east coast plain falling gently away from the Minangkabau mountain chain, and the rivers snaking through it, were important to the Minangkabau world in two ways: the rivers themselves formed major highways via which the Minangkabau could contact the commercial world of the Malacca Straits, while the river banks, especially in the area of their headwaters, provided limited opportunities for settlement by individuals who had made their way from the restrictions of the classic culture to a life of individual enterprise on the *ladang*. Some of these small river bank settlements were so situated as to be convenient assembly points for Minangkabau traders coming down over the Bukit Barisan on foot from the west to meet, bulk their cargo, and send it further downriver by *perahu* (boat, prow). At several points on the rivers *perahu* of deeper draught could be used to make the onward journey, and so at these points further bulking stations or riverine entrepôts arose, the major ones being not far from the river mouths, where cargoes of several *perahu* were bulked and transhipped across the straits to Penang, Malacca and, after 1819, to Singapore.

Of the character of the land adjoining the Minangkabau world to the east there is little that needs to be said. Minangkabau had settled from time immemorial around the headwaters and along the banks of the three main rivers, the Siak, the Kampar and the Inderagiri. Unfortunately we have no eye-witness descriptions of such settlements until the early 1880s, although it is difficult to believe that the areas had changed much since our period. The best description we have is of the region between the headwaters of the Siak and the Kampar Kanan. Here were a few small villages clinging to the river banks and populated by migrants from the heart of the Minangkabau world. The largest village in the area had only forty-four small houses, and ten or twenty was a more typical number. The villagers lived by fis̱hing and by cultivating rice, maize, sweet potatoes and sugar cane on widely scattered *ladang* hacked and burnt out of the forest. Trade was not a typical means of subsistence, although there was some commerce in rice, fishing nets and forest products on small riverside market-places, and *rameh* string and rattans were traded into the Minangkabau interior. But for young men, the only recourse from a life restricted to bare essentials was outmigration to the world of the straits, where fishing and small-scale trading could be combined. Such a form of existence could not support a very large population; the region between the headwaters of the Siak and the

Kampar Kanan contained in 1882 a population of about 1,057. Similar estimates were given for other areas; in 1858 the population of the whole Tapung Kiri-Tapung Kanan area of the upper Siak was estimated at only 1,000.[270]

This small Minangkabau population had, like the population of the west coast fringe, lost many of the classic Minangkabau characteristics. The typical Minangkabau family house was replaced by small, nuclear households of from five to six people and, although the Minangkabau in these areas regarded themselves as perpetuating Minangkabau *adat* (custom), in fact the *suku* system, although maintained in name, was irrelevant to these riparian villages. Instead each small village was headed by a *pucuk* or *datuk*, with the *datuk* of the original village in the area to be colonized exercising the greatest authority in a hierarchy of villages. Economically the family of a *datuk* differed little from that of other families in the village, being locked in the same cycle of *ladang* cultivation and fishing.[271]

The further down the great rivers these Minangkabau settlements went, the more the Minangkabau settlers became mixed with people of other origins, until they became incorporated into the state systems based on the major east coast entrepôts for straits trade, particularly the Siak state based on Siak Sri Inderapura, and the state of Kampar based on Palalawan. Here the Minangkabau *suku* system was merely a formality for identifying the areas of central Minangkabau from which the Minangkabau settlers along the river banks had originally come. The four *suku* recognized by the Siak state were Tanah Datar, Limapuluh, Pasisir and Kampar; they bore no relationship to the property-holding institutions of the classic culture, and indeed property was inherited in such riverine settlements by a man's wife and children. The nature of *ladang* cultivation of course made considerations such as governed the preservation of *sawah* quite irrelevant.[272]

Although these scattered settlements were important in providing another form of safety-value for people disadvantaged in the classical Minangkabau culture, of greater significance in our period were the riverine bulking stations which rose on the headwaters of the major rivers and which provided the first in a series of staging posts for the Minangkabau trader wishing to contact the international trading world of the straits. In their origins in the mountains of the Bukit Barisan the east coast rivers were fast-flowing, rocky and suited only for travel by rafts. During their progress towards the east, however, they became navigable by *perahu* of small capacity. At the point where this occurred there sprang up stapling-posts for Minangkabau trading goods coming over from the west and requiring to be taken down the rivers in successive stages. Such stapling-posts were known as *pangkalan*. Some of them, such as Patapahan on the Tapung Kiri branch of the upper Siak, and Durian Gedang on the upper Inderagiri, were very old; others, such as *pangkalan* Kota Baru on a branch of the upper Kampar Kanan, were only just becoming important in our period, as the outside world's demand for Minangkabau coffee and gambir increased. In this respect the headwaters of the river Kampar, being most accessible to the areas of coffee and gambir production, became particularly significant, and four very important *pangkalan* were flourishing there in this period.[273] Since the trade which took place at these stapling-posts, and the manner in which it was organized, is so intimately connected with Minangkabau external commercial networks and the changes they experienced from the late eighteenth century, a discussion of the *pangkalan*'s role in Minangkabau trade will be deferred until the next chapter.

Markets and traders

In the period we are dealing with here, the market system of Minangkabau had been experiencing extensive transformation, due to the requirements of selling Minangkabau commercial crops to international consumers. Coffee and cassia found their way to Pariaman and thence to Padang, or, via the east coast, to Singapore; gambir found that Penang was its chief market. Gold, the only other important Minangkabau export, came down to Padang. Here, an attempt will be made to discuss the Minangkabau internal market system without much reference to these commodities, but bearing in mind that their exchange and transport placed far more traders in the market-place than had existed a generation earlier.

Unfortunately we have little exact information on the spatial distribution of markets. However, some of the main ones seem definitely to have coincided with areas of transition between one ecological zone and another – markets lay on the borders between the world of the plains and of the hills, between the highlands and the west coast, between the shores of the Minangkabau world and the world outside, and between the headwaters of the main navigable east coast rivers and the Straits of Malacca. Not all of these market-places represented large villages. In addition to the important market villages of Tanah Datar such as Gurun, Sungai Tarab, Sumanik and Lima Kaum, all on the plains, it was calculated in 1825 that there were twenty-nine other market-places in Tanah Datar and its fringe areas; in the eastern part of Agam there were fifteen, and in Limapuluh Kota fourteen main ones, including the very large market-place of Payakumbuh, and many subsidiary ones.[274] Large, rich *sawah* villages naturally gave rise to large markets, but so too did small, poor villages strategically located. At the foothills of the Bukit Barisan some very important markets were held, which served to connect the uplands and the coast. Lubuk Asang, three miles from Mengoppo, provided a weekly market where traders from the Lake Maninjau area could meet those from Tiku and its surroundings. Going from Kayutanam through the Anai gorge and into the uplands, there was a market-place unconnected with any village just before entering the gorge.[275] Certainly it was the institution of the market-place which integrated the differing ecological zones of Minangkabau.

Pekan means both week and market in the Minangkabau language, the word for the actual place where the market is held being *pasar.* In general, such markets were grouped so that markets close together could rotate throughout the week, the market-place altering from day to day. Raffles, for example, states that seven main markets were held on the shores of Lake Singkarak in the most important villages such as Saningbakar, Simawang and Sumpur, the market taking place at a different village each day of the week.[276] There was a similar weekly rotating market system centred on Ulakan on the coast.[277] The daily alteration of venue meant that a full-time trader could cover a certain radius from his home base, this radius often being quite wide, though it is not possible to chart it in any meaningful way. We do have a description of the market system centred on the coastal port of Pariaman in 1831, giving some idea of its size and of the distances involved. About an hour inland on foot to the north-east of Pariaman there was a village market held every week. This market attracted between 3,000 and 4,000 people, who would come from as far away as the foothills of the Bukit Barisan. About two and a half hours from

Pariaman, further to the north-east, was yet another large weekly market at Pakandangan. To the north-west, at about the same distance from Pariaman as was Pakandangan, was yet another large market at Kota Ampalu, and there was another important one at Sungai Sarai.[278] It does seem that many of the confederations into which Minangkabau villages were united, confederations such as 13 Kota, 20 Kota, 6 Kota and so on, represented not only a system of mutual defence for the mother village and her daughter settlements, but also a locus of market activity and reciprocal market interaction. Such confederations were particularly prevalent on the fringes of the Minangkabau heartland.[279]

The actual location of the market-place is of some interest. It has been remarked that there were major markets on the borders of ecological zones, and also some large and famous markets right in the centre of important agricultural districts. Nevertheless, the actual *pasar* was generally located well outside the village or even, as was the case with some markets at the foothills of the Bukit Barisan, lay in a spot entirely unconnected with a nearby village. Such markets stood on the boundaries between different regions, and were of far greater importance than the village which gave the *pasar* its name. There was even a market held on top of Mount Merapi to permit trade to be carried on between the people of the western and eastern slopes, and the main market-place of the six major villages lying between the foothills of Mount Merapi and Mount Singgalang was outside the most obscure village of the six because it lay closest to the start of the route to the coast and the main route coming west from Tanah Datar.[280] Such markets were generally laid out on a large plain, surrounded with a stone parapet and shaded by banyan trees. The largest ones contained permanent constructions, such as booths for the sellers and even houses belonging to individuals who had some permanent interest in the market. This was particularly true in the coastal entrepôts, where the local merchants actually lived on the market-place, thus ensuring the safety of their goods, and even at the main foothills markets they built houses for themselves.[281] The desire for the market-place to be located well away from the village was because of the fights which often broke out on market day; these were occasioned not only by disputes over commercial transactions and by the attraction markets had for drifters in search of excitement, but particularly by the fact that the market-place was usually the scene of cockfighting, which caused considerable sums to change hands and aroused passions so that rioting by hundreds of participants was not uncommon. Most men on the *pasar* were armed. Markets were also the haunt of the opium-seller, waiting to prey on those who had made a successful transaction.[282]

Of course markets differed in relation to what was bought and sold; however, we do have descriptions of two of the main markets of the leading *sawah* areas of uplands Minangkabau, the market of Lima Kaum and a market near Payakumbuh. At these markets an extraordinarily wide variety of goods was offered for sale. The market was arranged according to the category of goods sold: in one section, staples such as dried fish, rice, fruit, vegetables, salt and other food items; in another, cloth, both cotton and silk; in another, items for leisure consumption such as snacks made from sticky rice and *anau* sugar, components of *sirih*-chewing such as betel leaves, tobacco, *pinang* (areca nuts), cakes of gambir and lime, and bundles of coffee tree branches to be used to boil the Minangkabau coffee drink; in another, items of household use such as pots, rattan mats, boxes, tubes of *damar* (resin) used for lighting etc.; in another, items of the blacksmith's trade such as hoes, spades, shovels and guns; gold dust was also sold, and a large market-place would also have a livestock market.[283]

The market-place of Lima Kaum was described in 1838, at a time when blacksmiths were still working there and selling the iron tools manufactured:

> Apart from a little iron, the bustling market place sold mainly fruit, salt, coffee, tobacco, cigar wrappers, a little brass, needles, thread etc.
>
> On one side sat the merchants with European cloth, Chinese silk, and Chinese gold thread; they also sold some of the splendid silk turbans bordered with gold thread which are made here, and also oval belt-plates [*pending*] made from a mixture of silver, tin and brass.
>
> On another side sat women who were selling the products of their own handicraft, native cotton cloth, blue and red sarongs with squares in the manner of the Buginese.[284]

A market near Payakumbuh in 1833 featured additional items, such as livestock:

> It was swarming with buyers and sellers, industry seemed to be very great here. One could especially observe a large amount of cotton piece goods, silk clothing, cotton yarn of particularly good quality, rice, coffee, a considerable amount of gambir, tobacco, salt, sugar . . . together with cows, buffaloes, goats, a lot of fresh-water fish etc., earthenware pots and pans, crucibles, copper, tin, smelted and unsmelted iron, guns, swords, pikes etc.[285]

It can be seen that the sellers in these markets were of a wide variety. First of all were the very small traders, usually women, who specialized in selling small quantities of domestically produced items; they of course financed themselves and operated on very small profit margins. An understanding of marketing was considered essential to a woman's upbringing; in Rancak diLabueh it is mentioned as one of the duties of parents to a daughter to teach her 'to judge the rise and fall in prices . . .'[286] Such women generally brought to market *beras* (hulled rice) in small bags, fruit, coffee tree branches, and also domestic cloth of their own manufacture; in addition they sold snacks to other market-goers. The amounts of rice dealt in were very small. Another important item which was sold as an adjunct to the domestic unit was livestock; livestock was of course part of the peasant's domestic capital, and a trader at the livestock market would be there to realize his assets. In the uplands, unlike the western coastal strip, there does not seem to have been much cattle- or horse-breeding for commercial purposes. Meat was also sold at markets, horse meat being the most highly regarded and most expensive.[287]

In addition to these small, face-to-face traders who traded with their domestic produce, the markets also attracted pedlars (*orang galas*; *menggalas,* to carry with a pole) who operated round a network of markets sometimes for weeks at a time until their loads were sold. Such pedlars generally financed themselves; they came mostly from the hill villages, from families with little or no *sawah,* and part of their load would consist of items produced in their home village; in the rest period after the end of the rice harvest, some villages would lose about two-thirds of their men in this way. The pedlars often travelled in pairs, one to trade and one to act as carrier or *kuli lama.*[288] The loads of these peripatetic traders did not only consist of items from their home villages. Often they would go far afield to acquire goods with which to supply the market, carrying on what can be called a relay trade across ecological zones. They were primarily responsible, for example, for the distribution of iron ware and guns to the lowlands, and they also participated in the dried fish trade. Dried, salted fish from the coast was the Minangkabau highlands' protein staple. Once the fish were caught on the coast, the catch was immediately sold to traders. Small coastal pedlars bought in small lots, but the vast bulk of the catch was sold to larger traders who, as middlemen, organized the drying process and then sold loads to the peripatetic pedlars who distributed the fish throughout the markets of the uplands. A similar form of relay trade seems to have operated in providing the highlands with the coconut products of the coast.[289]

Another type of trade was carried on mainly by pedlars from the eastern fringes of the Minangkabau world and comes under the category of group trading ventures. Pedlars banded together in a group would enter the highlands for three or four months of the year; for example, a group would come from the eastern borderlands of Minangkabau with the specialities of their area, such as rattan mats, wax and types of resin or, if from the south-east, with gold dust. This form of trade was more highly organized, with troops of up to twenty men headed by a *tua galas,* who was usually a professional trader. He carried gold dust in a little bag around his waist as his capital, and made some sort of arrangement to pay the others in cloths at the end of the journey. Such a group would sell cloths on their travels, but would also have a final destination in view, an important market centre where they would stay only a very short time and buy mainly cotton piece goods and guns.[290] A similar type of group trading venture was that operated by some uplands villages which required necessities from the west coast, particularly salt and cotton. Certain uplands villages laid claim to particular parts of the coast where they considered they had a right to make their own salt; 'the latter came down in troops now and then to prepare salt, and were a great burden to the coastal people . . .'[291] In the same way, a group of inhabitants of a weaving village would band together to go to the coast to buy cotton and return with it to their village.[292]

The final group of traders to be considered were those who traded in imported items such as cloth. In any market-place these were individuals of high status. However, for our purposes they can be dealt with in the following chapter, which discusses the changing external trading networks of Minangkabau. The imported cloth trade can be defined as being part of network trade rather than relay trade because the entry of cloth into the country was controlled by a very few individuals, mostly financed from sources outside Minangkabau. For this reason the export trade in coffee, gambir and cassia will also be dealt with as part of the export trading network. Nevertheless, it should be noted that, in addition to the high-status traders operating in the market due to the imported cloth trade, the export trade in commercial crops, which has been excluded from this account for purposes of analysis, had by the time with which we are dealing placed many more small traders on the market than ever before; these were the small-scale buyers of coffee beans, gambir cakes and cassia, who were either planters themselves or lived in some form of close connection with the planter, presumably in the same village. The members of these trading networks will be discussed in the next chapter.

It is not proposed to discuss the state of the roads or major trade routes here, since these were so greatly affected by the Islamic revivalist movements which are the subject of this book. The final point that needs to be made is the important role of gold in Minangkabau's domestic trade. Gold was not only a major item of export, but was also used as currency and actually sold on the market. In using gold dust as a means of exchange, the value of an article was expressed in terms of a gold weight. Gold traders therefore played a very important role in the domestic market; not only did they bring gold for sale, but they kept the scales and weights which were necessary to the operation of this means of exchange. Such weights were kept in attractive, carved boxes.[293]

At this point, now that we have observed the Minangkabau peasant in the field and the market-place in the 1820s and 1830s, what is required is to place his society in its historical context. For this we must look back at the great economic changes the Minangkabau lands had been experiencing over the previous fifty years, and place these in the context of even earlier changes. We will see a society rarely ever static, and participating quite markedly in the wider world of commerce, indeed the very antithesis of the static peasant community beloved of certain writers.

NOTES TO CHAPTER II

1 The European accounts used here were largely written by a team of Dutch scientific investigators sent into Minangkabau by the Netherlands Indies Government in 1833, and published right up to 1860. Prior to this we have an English account of 1818 and a Dutch account of 1824.
2 SFR vol. 47, f. 511, IOL.
3 ibid., f. 508.
4 ibid.
5 Treaty of Friendship and alliance between the Rajah of Menangcabau, and the Honble the English East India Company, 24 July 1818, SFR 47, f. 515-6.
6 See ch. III.
7 Treaty, SFR 47, f. 515.
8 Contract gesloten tusschen den Resident van *Padang, James Du Puy* . . . en de daar toe speciaal afgevaardigde Hoofden der Landen van het gewezen ryk van *Maninkabo* . . ., 10 Feb. 1821, Exh [ibitum] 24 Aug. 1826, no. 41, MK 513, ARA.
9 S. Raffles (ed.), *Memoir of the Life and Public Services of Sir Thomas Stamford Raffles* (London, 1835), i. 403.
10 ibid., pp. 425-6.
11 ibid., pp. 403, 412; H.G. Nahuijs, *Brieven over Bencoolen, Padang, het Rijk van Menangkabau, Rhiouw, Sincapoera en Poelo-Pinang* (Breda, 1826), p. 183.
12 Raffles to Dowdeswell, 12 Aug. 1818, SFR 47; Raffles, *Memoir,* i. 415.
13 Nahuijs, *Brieven,* pp. 133-4; Raffles, *Memoir,* i. 403.
14 J. van Swieten, 'Over het Grondbezit ter Sumatra's Westkust', *TNI* (1863), i. 300-1; Th. A.L. Kroesen, 'Het grondbezit ter Sumatra's Westkust', *TNI* (1874), ii. 3-4.
15 'Reizen Over Sumatra. Uittreksel uit het Dagboek van Wijlen L. Horner', *TBG,* x (1860), 350.
16 P.W. Korthals, 'Aanteekeningen over de Vijftig Kottas in de Padangsche Bovenlanden op Sumatra', *TNGP* (1835), ii. 18-19.
17 Elout to Riesz, 13 Aug. 1833, Bijlagen B and E, van den Bosch MSS. 394, ARA.
18 ibid., Bijl. B.
19 A.W.P. Verkerk Pistorius, *Studien over de Inlandsche Huishouding in de Padangsche Bovenlanden* (Zaltbommel, 1871), p. 43.
20 ibid., pp. 39-40.
21 Nahuijs, *Brieven,* pp. 162-3.
22 Raffles, *Memoir,* i. 416-7.
23 For a general discussion of this point see J.S. Migdal, *Peasants, Politics, and Revolution. Pressures toward Political and Social Change in the Third World* (Princeton, 1974), pp. 16-47, 68-9.
24 The very first observers make it clear that cultivated land was individual, not communal, property; de Stuers and Verploegh to van der Capellen, 30 Aug. 1825, L[a]E no. 2, Exh. 24 Aug. 1826, no. 41, MK 513.
25 'Reizen van L. Horner', p. 350; Nahuijs, *Brieven,* p. 178.
26 Raffles, *Memoir,* i. 412; P.Th. Couperus, 'Aanteekeningen omtrent de landbouwkundige nijverheid in de residentie Padangsche bovenlanden', *TBG,* v (1856), 286.
27 'Bijdrage tot de kennis van het grondbezit op Sumatra', *TNI,* xiv (1852), i. 111-2.
28 H. Burger, 'Aanmerkingen Gehouden op eene Reize door Eenige Districten der Padangsche Bovenlanden', *VBG,* xvi (1836), 208.
29 'Het grondbezit', p. 111.
30 Raffles, *Memoir,* i. 418; Couperus, 'Landbouwkundige nijverheid', p. 288.
31 Korthals, 'Aanteekeningen', p. 18; P.W. Korthals, *Topographische Schets van een Gedeelte van Sumatra* (Leiden, 1847), p. 37.

32 Raffles, *Memoir,* i. 407; Verkerk Pistorius, *Inlandsche Huishouding,* pp. 147-8.
33 Couperus, 'Landbouwkundige nijverheid', pp. 286, 288-9.
34 Korthals, 'Aanteekeningen', p. 20.
35 ibid.
36 Couperus, 'Landbouwkundige nijverheid', p. 296.
37 ibid., pp. 289-91.
38 Raffles, *Memoir,* i. 431.
39 Nahuijs, *Brieven,* pp. 140-1.
40 Burger, 'Aanmerkingen', p. 174.
41 ibid., p. 216.
42 ibid., p. 179.
43 Raffles, *Memoir,* i. 403.
44 Couperus, 'Landbouwkundige nijverheid', pp. 292, 296; Verkerk Pistorius, *Inlandsche Huishouding,* pp. 18, 50, 56-7.
45 Verkerk Pistorius, *Inlandsche Huishouding,* pp. 56-59.
46 'Het grondbezit', p. 109; Kroesen, 'Het grondbezit', p. 9.
47 Kroesen, 'Het grondbezit', p. 14; van Swieten, 'Over het Grondbezit', p. 301.
48 Kroesen, 'Het grondbezit', pp. 15-7; van Swieten, 'Over het Grondbezit', p. 301.
49 Verkerk Pistorius, *Inlandsche Huishouding,* pp. 48, 130.
50 Elout to Riesz, 13 Aug. 1833, Bijlagen A to H, van den Bosch MSS. 394.
51 Nahuijs, *Brieven,* p. 148; S. Müller, *Berigten over Sumatra* (Amsterdam, 1837), p. 16.
52 Raffles, *Memoir,* i. 405.
53 Elout to Riesz, 13 Aug. 1833, Bijlagen B and E, van den Bosch MSS. 394.
54 E.E. Graves, 'The Ever-Victorious Buffalo: How the Minangkabau of Indonesia solved their "Colonial Question" ' (University of Wisconsin Ph.D. thesis, 1971), pp. 40, 51-3.
55 A.H. Johns, *Rantjak diLabueh: A Minangkabau Kaba* (Ithaca, Cornell Southeast Asia Program Data Paper No. 32, 1958), pp. 142-4.
56 ibid., p. 2.
57 ibid.
58 ibid., pp. 28-30, 120.
59 Nahuijs, *Brieven,* p. 162.
60 ibid., p. 175.
61 J.C. Boelhouwer, *Herinneringen van Mijn Verblijf op Sumatra's Westkust, Gedurende de Jaren 1831-1834* (The Hague, 1841), pp. 56-7.
62 J.A.W. van Ophuijsen, 'Over het Grondbezit en de Onderscheiding der Gronden in de XIII Kota's (Sumatra's Westkust). Verzameld en uit het Maleisch Overgebragt', *TBG,* iii (1855), 480-1, 483.
63 Raffles, *Memoir,* i. 415.
64 Korthals, *Topographische Schets,* p. 15.
65 For the rich Payakumbuh region of Limapuluh Kota see ibid., p. 43.
66 Korthals, *Topographische Schets,* pp. 21, 37, 69-70.
67 ibid., p. 43.
68 Verkerk Pistorius, *Inlandsche Huishouding,* pp. 6, 31.
69 Korthals, *Topographische Schets,* pp. 27-8.
70 Burger, 'Aanmerkingen', pp. 204-5; Raffles, *Memoir,* i. 415.
71 Nahuijs, *Brieven,* p. 205.
72 Burger, 'Aanmerkingen', p. 190.
73 Nahuijs, *Brieven,* p. 205.
74 Verkerk Pistorius, *Inlandsche Huishouding,* pp. 45, 153-4.
75 Kroesen, 'Het grondbezit', pp. 17-8; van Swieten, 'Over het Grondbezit', p. 301.
76 Johns, *Rantjak diLabueh,* pp. 8-10; Kroesen, 'Het grondbezit', pp. 18-9; van Swieten, 'Over het Grondbezit', p. 301.
77 Modern *adat* experts' notions that land was rarely pawned is not borne out by historical evidence; see, for example, A.D. Batuah and A.D. Madjoindo, *Tambo Minangkabau dan Adatnja* (Jakarta, 1965), p. 92.
78 'Het grondbezit', pp. 110, 112.
79 Raffles, *Memoir,* i. 412.

80 Nahuijs, *Brieven,* p. 183.
81 Korthals, *Topographische Schets,* p. 21; Raffles, *Memoir,* i. 424.
82 Nahuijs, *Brieven,* p. 138.
83 'Reizen van L. Horner', p. 369; Korthals, *Topographische Schets,* pp. 29-30.
84 Nahuijs, *Brieven,* pp. 169, 172; Burger, 'Aanmerkingen', pp. 178-9; Korthals, *Topographische Schets,* pp. 69-70.
85 Burger, 'Aanmerkingen', pp. 177, 185; Korthals, *Topographische Schets,* pp. 68, 73-4.
86 Müller, *Berigten,* p. 20.
87 ibid.; Korthals, *Topographische Schets,* p. 42.
88 Korthals, *Topographische Schets,* p. 11.
89 Kroesen, 'Het grondbezit', p. 18.
90 See Ch. III.
91 Raffles, *Memoir,* i. 406.
92 ibid., p. 411.
93 Raffles to Dowdeswell, 12 Aug. 1818, SFR 47.
94 Korthals, *Topographische Schets,* pp. 24-5; W. Marsden, *The History of Sumatra* (3rd edn., London, 1811), p. 172.
95 'Reizen van L. Horner', p. 348; Burger, 'Aanmerkingen', p. 200.
96 'Reizen van L. Horner', pp. 343-6; Burger, 'Aanmerkingen', pp. 196-8.
97 Nahuijs, *Brieven,* p. 79.
98 'Reizen van L. Horner', pp. 343-5.
99 Burger, 'Aanmerkingen', pp. 196, 199-200; 'Reizen van L. Horner', pp. 343-6.
100 'Reizen van L. Horner', pp. 372-3.
101 Burger, 'Aanmerkingen', pp. 194-5.
102 ibid.
103 'Reizen van L. Horner', p. 372.
104 ibid.
105 ibid., pp. 372-3.
106 ibid., pp. 344, 373.
107 ibid., pp. 348-9.
108 For a modern parallel, see J. Kahn, 'Economic Scale and the Cycle of Petty Commodity Production in West Sumatra', in M. Bloch (ed.), *Marxist Analyses and Social Anthropology* (London, 1975), pp. 138-44.
109 'Reizen van L. Horner', p. 349.
110 Korthals, *Topographische Schets,* p. 14; Raffles, *Memoir,* i. 407.
111 'Reizen van L. Horner', p. 358; Korthals, *Topographische Schets,* p. 14; Raffles, *Memoir,* i. 407, 420.
112 Raffles, *Memoir,* i. 420.
113 ibid., p. 427.
114 Korthals, *Topographische Schets,* pp. 14-5, 23-4.
115 ibid., p. 14.
116 'Reizen van L. Horner', p. 358.
117 Raffles, *Memoir,* i. 427.
118 Korthals, *Topographische Schets,* p. 55.
119 'Reizen van L. Horner', p. 358.
120 P.Th. Couperus, 'Eenige Aanteekeningen Betreffende de Goudproduktie in de Padangsche Bovenlanden', *TBG,* v (1856), 128.
121 ibid., p. 125; Verkerk Pistorius, *Inlandsche Huishouding,* p. 154.
122 Couperus, 'Goudproduktie', pp. 129-30.
123 ibid., pp. 124, 129; Verkerk Pistorius, *Inlandsche Huishouding,* pp. 154-5.
124 Van Outhoorn, 30 Nov. 1697, *GM* 5 (The Hague, *RGP* 150, 1975), p. 844.
125 Couperus, 'Goudproduktie', pp. 124, 128.
126 Burger, 'Aanmerkingen', p. 172.
127 'Reizen van L. Horner', p. 359.
128 Marsden, *Sumatra,* pp. 166-7; Couperus, 'Goudproduktie', pp. 125-6.
129 Camphuys, 27 Dec. 1688, *GM* 5, p. 229.
130 Verkerk Pistorius, *Inlandsche Huishouding,* p. 155.

131 ibid., p. 154; Couperus, 'Goudproduktie', p. 128.
132 Marsden, *Sumatra,* p. 166.
133 Verkerk Pistorius, *Inlandsche Huishouding,* p. 155; Camphuys, 27 Dec. 1688, *GM* 5, p. 229. One *tahil* equals 1 1/3 oz. avoirdupois.
134 'Riezen van L. Horner', pp. 359-60; Verkerk Pistorius, *Inlandsche Huishouding,* p. 155.
135 Müller, *Reizen,* p. 153. The sign f. equals one Netherlands guilder.
136 Marsden, *Sumatra,* p. 168.
137 This was equivalent to Javanese *tegalan,* the permanent cultivation of annuals in dry fields, not to *ladang* or shifting cultivation on dry fields.
138 *Cassia lignea vera* or *cinnamomum aromaticum,* a form of cinnamon originating not in Ceylon but in South China, coarser and darker than that of Ceylon; *gambir,* a scrambling plant used as one of the ingredients in *sirih*-chewing and in tanning leather.
139 Korthals, *Topographische Schets,* pp. 26, 66-8; Müller *Berigten,* p. 9; Burger, 'Aanmerkingen', pp. 172-3; Raffles, *Memoir,* i. 403.
140 Verkerk Pistorius, *Inlandsche Huishouding,* p. 65.
141 Ophuijsen, 'Over het Grondbezit', p. 478; for 1972 figures of holdings of rice land in the hill village of Sungai Puar see J.S. Kahn, 'Imperialism and the Reproduction of Capitalism: Towards a definition of the Indonesian Social Formation', *Critique of Anthropology,* ii (1974), 4-5, 7. In 1972, 58% of Sungai Puar residents had access to lineage land.
142 Verkerk Pistorius, *Inlandsche Huishouding,* p. 30.
143 Korthals, *Topographische Schets,* p. 71.
144 H.A. Steijn Parvé, 'De Secte der Padaries (Padries) in de Bovenlanden van Sumatra', *TBG,* iii (1855), 253.
145 Raffles to Dowdeswell, 12 Aug. 1818, SFR 47.
146 Burger, 'Aanmerkingen', pp. 194-5; 'Reizen van L. Horner', pp. 372-3.
147 Nahuijs, *Brieven,* p. 79.
148 'Reizen van L. Horner', p. 344.
149 Marsden, *Sumatra,* p. 347.
150 Nahuijs, *Brieven,* pp. 140-1; E.B. Kielstra, 'Sumatra's Westkust van 1819-1825', *BKI,* xxxvi (1887), 43-4.
151 Nahuijs, *Brieven,* p. 171.
152 ibid., p. 166.
153 Korthals, *Topographische Schets,* p. 31.
154 Burger, 'Aanmerkingen', p. 195.
155 Boelhoewer, *Herinneringen,* p. 174.
156 Minangkabau gold contained a considerable amount of silver.
157 Müller, *Reizen,* p. 28; Marsden, *Sumatra,* pp. 178-9.
158 Verkerk Pistorius, *Inlandsche Huishouding,* p. 30.
159 Nahuijs, *Brieven,* p. 143.
160 Marsden, *Sumatra,* p. 179; Verkerk Pistorius, *Inlandsche Huishouding,* pp. 150, 155-6.
161 Nahuijs, *Brieven,* p. 180; 'Reizen van L. Horner', pp. 343, 347; *kasumba* is the orange-red flower of the *carthamus tinctorius,* which produces a saffron dye.
162 Nahuijs, *Brieven,* p. 70.
163 Korthals, 'Aanteekeningen', p. 10.
164 Marsden, *Sumatra,* pp. 94-5.
165 Korthals, *Topographische Schets,* p. 20.
166 Verkerk Pistorius, *Inlandsche Huishouding,* pp. 36-7, 151.
167 ibid., p. 37.
168 Raffles, *Memoir,* i. 432.
169 Verkerk Pistorius, *Inlandsche Huishouding,* p. 20.
170 Korthals, *Topographische Schets,* p. 14.
171 Raffles, *Memoir,* i. 408; Verkerk Pistorius, *Inlandsche Huishouding,* p. 28.
172 Korthals, *Topographische Schets,* pp. 67, 73.
173 Müller, *Berigten,* p. 9; 'Reizen van L. Horner', p. 373.
174 Nahuijs, *Brieven,* p. 79; Burger, 'Aanmerkingen', p. 180.
175 Boelhouwer, *Herinneringen,* p. 175.

176 See Kahn, 'Imperialism and the Reproduction of Capitalism', pp. 25-6, where Sungai Puar statistics show that individual cash crop producers as well as owners of small enterprises tend, on average, to own more rice land than do others in the village. They require this to enable them to enter the market.
177 Johns, *Rantjak diLabueh,* pp. 16, 18, 22, 28.
178 Korthals, *Topographische Schets,* p. 27.
179 ibid., p. 26.
180 ibid., p. 71.
181 ibid., pp. 6-7, 9.
182 Raffles, *Memoir,* i. 435.
183 Burger, 'Aanmerkingen', p. 188.
184 Korthals, *Topographische Schets,* p. 44; Korthals, 'Aanteekeningen', p. 18.
185 Müller, *Berigten,* p. 9.
186 'Reizen van L. Horner', p. 330.
187 Tobacco is strictly an annual, but exhibits perennial tendencies.
188 Raffles, *Memoir,* i. 403, 419, 425; Burger, 'Aanmerkingen', pp. 186, 190.
189 Burger, 'Aanmerkingen', pp. 169, 172-3, 178-9; Korthals, *Topographische Schets,* pp. 66-8; Steijn Parvé, 'De Secte', p. 253.
190 Raffles, *Memoir,* i. 419.
191 Korthals, 'Aanteekeningen', p. 19; Burger, 'Aanmerkingen', p. 218.
192 Burger, 'Aanmerkingen', pp. 178-9; Raffles, *Memoir,* i. 403.
193 Nahuijs, *Brieven,* p. 70.
194 Burger, 'Aanmerkingen', pp. 189, 218.
195 Nahuijs, *Brieven,* pp. 68-9.
196 Korthals, 'Aanteekeningen', p. 18; Marsden, *Sumatra,* p. 88.
197 Johns, *Rantjak diLabueh,* p. 22.
198 See J.S. Kahn, ' "Tradition", Matriliny and Change Among the Minangkabau of Indonesia', *BKI* cxxxii (1976), 76.
199 Burger, 'Aanmerkingen', pp. 189, 218.
200 Müller, *Reizen,* p. 62.
201 Ophuijsen, 'Over het Grondbezit', pp. 479-80.
202 Kroesen, 'Het grondbezit', p. 6; van Swieten, 'Over het grondbezit', p. 302.
203 Kroesen, 'Het grondbezit', pp. 13-14; van Swieten, 'Over het grondbezit', p. 301.
204 See Ch. III.
205 Korthals, *Topographische Schets,* p. 70.
206 Dagboek . . . 30 Jul. 1832, Vermeulen Krieger MSS. 3, ARA.
207 Burger, 'Aanmerkingen', p. 180.
208 Couperus, 'Landbouwkundige nijverheid', p. 310.
209 'Schets van de Bereiding der Gambier te Paija Komba (Padangsche Bovenlanden)', *TNNI,* iii (1852), 21.
210 Korthals, *Topographische Schets,* p. 39; idem, 'Aanteekeningen', pp. 11, 12-3, 19.
211 Burger, 'Aanmerkingen', p. 212.
212 Korthals, *Topographische Schets,* pp. 39-40.
213 'Schets', pp. 22-3.
214 Nahuijs, *Brieven,* p. 171; Burger, 'Aanmerkingen', pp. 78-9.
215 Korthals, *Topographische Schets,* pp. 64-5.
216 Nahuijs, *Brieven,* p. 171.
217 Korthals, *Topographische Schets,* p. 70.
218 ibid., p. 71.
219 ibid., pp. 6-7; Burger, 'Aanmerkingen', p. 181.
220 Korthals, *Topographische Schets,* pp. 66-8.
221 Dagboek . . . 30 Jul. 1832, Vermeulen Krieger 3.
222 Müller, *Berigten,* p. 9; Nahuijs, *Brieven,* p. 171; Korthals, *Topographische Schets,* pp. 10, 27.
223 Burger, 'Aanmerkingen', pp. 189-90; Korthals, *Topographische Schets,* pp. 18-9.
224 Letter of Friendship . . . from the Chiefs of Tigablas . . ., 20 Jul. 1818, SFR 47, f. 508.

225 Korthals, *Topographische Schets,* p. 28.
226 Nahuijs, *Brieven,* p. 160.
227 Korthals, *Topographische Schets,* pp. 28, 30-1; Burger, 'Aanmerkingen', pp. 189-90.
228 Korthals, 'Aanteekeningen', p. 14.
229 Korthals, *Topographische Schets,* p. 42.
230 Korthals, 'Aanteekeningen', pp. 15, 19-20.
231 ibid., p. 11; Korthals, *Topographische Schets,* p. 39.
232 Müller, *Berigten,* p. 21; Korthals, 'Aanteekeningen', p. 16.
233 Korthals, *Topographische Schets,* pp. 45-6.
234 Burger, 'Aanmerkingen', p. 218.
235 Korthals, 'Aanteekeningen', p. 17.
236 Korthals, *Topographische Schets,* p. 50.
237 'Reizen van L. Horner', pp. 364-5.
238 Burger, 'Aanmerkingen', p. 169.
239 Korthals, *Topographische Schets,* p. 77.
240 Cochius to de Eerens, 29 Apr. 1837, no. 34/99, Exh. 23 Oct. 1837, no. 250 Geh [eim], MK 4247.
241 Nahuijs, *Brieven,* pp. 63-4.
242 Burger, 'Aanmerkingen', pp. 186, 218.
243 Nahuijs, *Brieven,* p. 65; Raffles, *Memoir,* i. 394; Korthals, *Topographische Schets,* p. 37.
244 Couperus, 'Landbouwkundige nijverheid', pp. 297-9, 303-5; one *pikul* equals 133 lbs.
245 Kroesen, 'Het grondbezit', pp. 11-3; 'Het grondbezit', p. 113; Ophuijsen, 'Over het Grondbezit', p. 479.
246 Kroesen, 'Het grondbezit', pp. 20-2, 24-6; 'Het grondbezit', pp. 111-2; Ophuijsen, 'Over het Grondbezit', p. 478.
247 Kroesen, 'Het grondbezit', pp. 4, 23-4; Verkerk Pistorius, *Inlandsche Huishouding,* pp. 132-3.
248 Nahuijs, *Brieven,* p. 128.
249 Müller, *Reizen,* p. 61.
250 ibid., p. 4; Boelhouwer, *Herinneringen,* p. 99.
251 Müller, *Reizen,* pp. 60-1; Nahuijs, *Brieven,* pp. 129-30.
252 Müller, *Berigten,* p. 2.
253 Nahuijs, *Brieven,* p. 129; Müller, *Reizen,* p. 25; Korthals, *Topographische Schets,* p. 1.
254 Een nota en statistique bijzonderheden over Padang, c. 1825, Bijlage A, van Zuylen van Nijevelt MSS. 102, ARA.
255 ibid.; de Stuers and Verploegh to van der Capellen, 30 Aug. 1825, L[a]E no. 20, Exh. 24 Aug. 1826, no. 41, MK 513.
256 Müller, *Reizen,* pp. 42, 47; idem, *Berigten,* pp. 2-3.
257 Müller, *Reizen,* p. 59; Burger, 'Aanmerkingen', p. 161.
258 Nahuijs, *Brieven,* p. 89; Müller, *Reizen,* pp. 50-1.
259 Een nota, Bijlage A, van Zuylen van Nijevelt 102; Consideratie, Nopens den Handel . . . in de Besittingen der Nederlandse Oost Indische Compagnie op Sumatras West Cust, 22 Dec. 1789, par. 219-21, Koloniaal Archief 3800, ARA.
260 E.B. Kielstra, 'Onze kennis van Sumatra's westkust omstreeks de helft der achttiende eeuw', *BKI,* xxxvi (1887), 518.
261 ibid., pp. 519-20; Burger, 'Aanmerkingen', pp. 162-3.
262 Müller, *Reizen,* pp. 38, 43.
263 Kielstra, 'Onze kennis', pp. 520-1.
264 Kielstra, 'Sumatra's Westkust van 1819-1825', p. 18; Müller, *Reizen,* pp. 19, 59; Korthals, 'Aanteekeningen', p. 18.
265 Raffles, *Memoir,* i. 391, 393; Müller, *Reizen,* p. 30.
266 Nahuijs, *Brieven,* p. 130; see also Raffles, *Memoir,* i. 393-40, 430.
267 J. van der Linden, 'Het Inlandsche Bestuur in het Gouvernement van Sumatra's Westkust', *TBG,* iv (1855), 261; Een nota, Bijlage A, van Zuylen van Nijevelt 102.
268 De Stuers and Verploegh to van der Capellen, 30 Aug. 1825, L[a]E no. 20, Exh. 24 Aug. 1826, no. 41, MK 513.
269 Een nota, Bijlage A, van Zuylen van Nijevelt 102; Elout to Riesz, 13 Aug. 1833, Bijlagen B and F, van den Bosch 394.

270 E.Th. van Delden, 'Dagverhaal van eene Reis naar Gloegoer VI Kota', *TBG,* xxvii (1882), 128, 131, 134-6, 141-3, 161; idem, 'Verslag over den Toestand van het Landschap Gloegoer VI Kota', *TBG,* xxvii (1882), 170-1; F.N. Nieuwenhuijzen, 'Het rijk Siak Sri Indrapoera', *TBG,* vii (1858), 393, 414-6.
271 Van Delden, 'Dagverhaal', pp. 148, 161; idem, 'Verslag', p. 169.
272 Nieuwenhuijzen, 'Siak Sri Indrapoera', pp. 397, 403, 411, 414-5.
273 Van Delden, 'Verslag', p. 171; Müller, *Berigten,* p. 26; Korthals, *Topographische Schets,* p. 21.
274 Korthals, 'Aanteekeningen', p. 11; Kielstra, 'Sumatra's Westkust van 1819-1825', p. 124.
275 Boelhouwer, *Herinneringen,* p. 127; 'Reizen van L. Horner', pp. 322-3.
276 Raffles to Dowdeswell, 12 Aug. 1818, SFR 47; Raffles, *Memoir,* i. 415.
277 Boelhouwer, *Herinneringen,* p. 61.
278 ibid., pp. 27-8, 30, 35, 38, 42; Nahuijs, *Brieven,* p. 130.
279 Raffles, *Memoir,* i. 411-2; Korthals, 'Aanteekeningen', p. 6.
280 Korthals, *Topographische Schets,* pp. 7, 48; Boelhouwer, *Herinneringen,* pp. 61, 80; Müller, *Berigten,* p. 14.
281 Boelhouwer, *Herinneringen,* pp. 35, 38, 56; Nahuijs, *Brieven,* p. 41; Raffles, *Memoir,* i. 390.
282 Boelhouwer, *Herinneringen,* pp. 41, 144.
283 Verkerk Pistorius, *Inlandsche Huishouding,* pp. 16, *et seq.*
284 'Reizen van L. Horner', p. 349.
285 Burger, 'Aanmerkingen', pp. 215-6.
286 Johns, *Rantjak diLabueh,* p. 140.
287 Verkerk Pistorius, *Inlandsche Huishouding,* pp. 16, 18, 20; Raffles, *Memoir,* i. 404; Nahuijs, *Brieven,* p. 174.
288 Verkerk Pistorius, *Inlandsche Huishouding,* pp. 14-15, 36-7, 65, 125, 168.
289 Marsden, *Sumatra,* p. 347; Nahuijs, *Brieven,* p. 164; Müller, *Berigten,* pp. 3-4; Korthals, *Topographische Schets,* p. 78.
290 Verkerk Pistorius, *Inlandsche Huishouding,* pp. 238-9.
291 Müller, *Reizen,* p. 59.
292 Verkerk Pistorius, *Inlandsche Huishouding,* pp. 36-7.
293 ibid., p. 35; Marsden, *Sumatra,* p. 171.

CHAPTER III

DEVELOPMENT AND CHANGE IN EXTERNAL COMMERCIAL NETWORKS, 1347-1829

The significance of the Minangkabau gold trade, 1347-1795

Although great changes occurred in Minangkabau as a result of its involvement in the export of agricultural products to the growing world market of the late eighteenth century, it would be wrong to assume that Minangkabau had been previously isolated from the wider world of economic exchange. A particular area of central Minangkabau for centuries played an important role in the economy of the Indian Ocean, an economy more dynamic in many ways than that of Europe in the same period. The Tanah Datar region of Minangkabau was one of the chief sources of an important commercial lubricant for the Indian Ocean economy, gold. It was upon gold that the Minangkabau state and commercial system was built, and its presence in the hills and rocks of Tanah Datar profoundly influenced that area's political, religious and cultural life.

For most of the history of the Minangkabau gold trade our sources are mainly archaeological or represent oral tradition written down at a much later date. Little can be stated about the gold trade in terms of quantifiable statistics, relating either to exports, to imports or to the level of demand for outside goods in Minangkabau society; nor can an adequate profile of the Minangkabau gold merchant be constructed. Nevertheless, much can be said of the gold trade in terms of its political impact on Minangkabau, and the decline of this trade in the late eighteenth century loosened political ties, aggravated the imbalance between regions and assisted the penetration of the country by forces seeking to benefit from the new export agriculture.

It has already been shown how the major gold-producing areas of central Minangkabau were confined to two adjacent regions, the valley and hills of the river Selo and the valley and hills of the rivers Sinamar and Sumpur, both located in the area known as Tanah Datar. To export the gold so located required either a short but arduous trip on foot down the steep slopes of the Bukit Barisan to the west, or a calmer but much longer journey by boat down either the rivers Inderagiri or Kampar, after a short overland march to the nearest point to which boats could ascend. In either case, because of the worth of the item carried, security was required to protect the gold traders from the bandits who infested rugged areas. In addition, an organized transport system was necessary, not for carrying a low-bulk commodity such as gold to the coast, but for returning with the high-bulk cotton cloths which formed the staple of the trade.

Very little is known about the organization of the trade throughout this whole period. We do know, however, that it attracted both foreign merchants and foreign adventurers into the Minangkabau interior, all of whom were, in a sense, trying to tap the trade at its source. These merchants and adventurers entered by the major trade routes, which have to be deduced from later evidence. To the west coast the main ones were the so-called Jalan Jawi, leading out of Tanah Datar by way of Batipuh and the southern slopes of Mount Merapi and then to Tambangan and over the Ambacang mountain, and the Jalan Bukit Tujuh which went through the Anai gorge; both emerged in the Barisan foothills at Kayutanam, from whence the coast and the chief gold-exporting port of Pariaman could be reached. There was a subsidiary, more difficult route by way of Lake Singkarak, which involved going from Suruaso to Simawang on the shores of the lake, crossing the lake by boat to Saningbakar and the Solok plain, and thence over the mountains and down to the coast at Kota Tengah or Padang.[1] To reach the east coast from the areas in the valley of the Sinamar around Buo and the Sumpur around Sumpur Kudus, the main route was either by water or land to assembly points on the headwaters of the Inderagiri river such as Siluka or Durian Gedang, or overland to *pangkalan* Sarai on the headwaters of a tributary of the Kampar Kiri.[2]

It was by these routes that the gold trade was carried on for centuries, and it was through them that foreign influence entered Minangkabau. The preference given to routes coming from the west or the east varied, of course, with the safety of the Straits of Malacca. At the time when Minangkabau or, speaking more correctly, Tanah Datar, first enters historical focus, it seems that the west coast route was that most favoured by Indian traders due to the decline of Srivijaya and the unfavourable situation in the straits.[3] Archaeological evidence and oral tradition indicate that some time in the twelfth or thirteenth centuries South Indian traders, referred to as *chettis,* actually entered Tanah Datar and established themselves at or near Pariangan, on the southern slopes of Mount Merapi, from whence they had an excellent opportunity to survey the main trade route out of Tanah Datar.[4] At that time the focus of Minangkabau life seems to have been around Lima Kaum, which probably had both practical and magical significance as an iron-working centre, the role of smiths in pre-Indianized Minangkabau having undoubtedly been as important as in other parts of the archipelago. The South Indians apparently established their own separate commercial-cum-political centre at Pariangan. They had a political leader entitled Maharajadiraja, and we know from an inscription of the mid-fourteenth century that South Indians were still living as a separate community in Minangkabau at that date.[5] Meanwhile they had influenced considerable areas of Minangkabau life, and many Dravidian and Sanskrit words passed into common usage for the most basic Minangkabau family, village and legal institutions. *Nagari* (Indon. *negeri*) and *kota* are only the best known among many, and it seems possible that Malabar traders, in which area matriliny had only recently been adopted, either introduced or reinforced matrilineal institutions in the Minangkabau rice-growing areas.[6]

Gradually the centre of Indian influence seems to have moved further west into Tanah Datar and a system of 'rajas' developed near the main gold-bearing areas.[7] This developing polity was disrupted by the appearance in Tanah Datar in 1347 of members of the court of the Javanese Kingdom of Majapahit. From this time dates our knowledge of the first readily verifiable figure in Minangkabau history, King Adityawarman, a man of mixed Sumatran-Javanese parentage brought up in the royal *kraton* of Majapahit. Adityawarman came to Sumatra in the 1340s to take control of the Dharmasraya gold-exporting region of the upper Batang Hari river, which had been tributary to Majapahit's predecessor on Java from the 1270s. Inscriptions dating from 1347 indicate that Adityawarman threw off his allegiance to Majapahit and moved into central Tanah Datar by way of the Inderagiri river and the Buo region, where, in the area surrounding Bukit Gombak and Suruaso, he formed a kingdom known to us through his many stone inscriptions. Here he claimed for himself the titles Maharajadiraja and Kaṇakamedinīndra, 'sovereign of the gold-bearing ground',[8] and he seems to have been particularly associated with gold-rich Suruaso. His long reign lasted until at least 1375, and inscriptions indicate that his kingdom was never merely a Javanized polity; the Minangkabau element in the kingdom remained extremely important, and it was under the rule of Adityawarman that Minangkabau began to develop its own higher culture, with its own art, language and script in which Javanese and Malay elements were synthesized.[9]

It appears, however, that after Adityawarman's death the royal family was unable to provide a ruler of his ability, and its members were pushed into the background by more powerful figures. The inscriptions indicate that Adityawarman had a *patih* or chief minister who was of great importance in the Javanese penetration of Tanah Datar. According to a 1347 inscription, this *patih* 'acquired riches and gold'; the inscription prays that he may 'enjoy the treasure which he has amassed for himself by his conduct on the warrior's path of the Kṣatriyas . . .'[10] Adityawarman's inscriptions also mention other high functionaries, including a *tumanggung* and an army commandant, *mahasenapati pamanan.*[11]

From this point, however, we enter the realm of Minangkabau oral tradition. This tradition consistently refers to two Minangkabau lawgivers, Datuk Perpatih nan Sabatang and Datuk Ketamanggungan who, according to legend, quarrelled and established two different legal systems for Minangkabau, each village being obliged to adhere to one or the other. What seems to have happened is that the chief officers of state did quarrel after Adityawarman's death, and there was in fact a civil war between the followers of the *patih* and the *tumanggung,* Perpatih nan Sabatang being identified with the *patih* and Ketamanggungan with the *tumanggung.* The followers of the *tumanggung* identified themselves with the royal family, with hierarchy in village government, and with the gold trade and the need to regulate both production and the routes to the coast. The followers of the *patih* identified themselves more with pre-Javanized Minangkabau, with matriliny and with the Indianized elements in the population, who presumably had suffered in the period 1347-1375.[12] The result was that, after the conflict was settled, two major centres remained in Tanah Datar, each espousing a different legal tradition, called *laras*: Lima Kaum was the focal point for all villages following the legal tradition laid down by the followers of the *patih,* the tradition known as Bodi Caniago. Sungai Tarab became the focal point of the rival tradition, known as Koto Piliang. From the very beginning the main gold villages and the villages on the gold-exporting route adhered to this latter system, and Koto Piliang was known as the legal tradition of the area 'Where the merchandise goes out and in, Where the traders sell and buy.'[13]

An hierarchical system of office-bearing grew up around the *laras* Koto Piliang, in which resonant titles were granted to office-bearers who controlled the gold routes. The most famous of these was the Tuan Gedang of Batipuh, whose territory was strategically located across the main route from Tanah Datar down to Pariaman, and the villages on the banks of Lake Singkarak were drawn into the same system and were also given Koto Piliang titles.[14] In all of this the royal family seems to have been pushed more and more into the background, as the *tumanggung* metamorphosed himself into a Bendahara and established himself at Sungai Tarab, one of the oldest villages in Minangkabau and possibly then an iron-working centre. The pre-eminence of the Bendahara was noted by the first Europeans to write about Minangkabau, and in the 1820s he was still regarded as the leading personage of the realm after the royal house. The *patih* remained at Lima Kaum as the Bendahara yang kuning, in contrast to the Bendahara yang putih at Sungai Tarab, and this Bodi Caniago area was regarded by the first European writers as rivalling Sungai Tarab.[15] In fact, the history of Tanah Datar for several centuries after Adityawarman's death seems to have represented a continual contest for supremacy between Sungai Tarab and Lima Kaum. Both were apparently connected with iron-smelting, an important means of assuring a supply of weapons, and with gold-mining. Lima Kaum had some sort of traditional access to the gold mines of Bukit Gombak and Suruaso, whilst Sungai Tarab seems to have specialized in keeping the trade routes open.[16]

With time and movement of population, of course, some villages came to contain both *adat* traditions, though generally speaking pure Koto Piliang villages predominated in Tanah Datar and Bodi Caniago ones in Agam, while Limapuluh Kota exhibited a mixed arrangement.[17] In any case, the differences between villages of the Bodi Caniago and Koto Piliang *laras* were scrupulously observed, and even as late as 1825 were said to be maintained with 'an indescribable jealousy.'[18] These differences, and the arrogated superiority and influence of the Koto Piliang villages, have been discussed here so extensively because the Koto Piliang system was an important target for reform by the later Islamic revivalists.

With the rise of Sungai Tarab and Lima Kaum to pre-eminence in central Tanah Datar, it appears that the royal family was pushed into the background and lost much of its *raison d'être.* A change in its fortunes, however, came with a change in Minangkabau's trade routes. The rise of the Malacca sultanate during the fifteenth century led to security in the straits, and Minangkabau gold became one of the mainstays of Malacca's trade, a situation which continued throughout the sixteenth and early seventeenth century after Malacca had passed into the hands of the Portuguese.[19] The Buo and Sumpur Kudus area at the headwaters of the Inderagiri route down to the straits was an important gold-bearing region, and the area north of Buo on the banks of the Sinamar right up to Tanjung across the Marapalam is mentioned in the *Nagara-Kertagama* (1365 A.D.) as containing two 'states' tributary to Majapahit. Possibly this area was in some way linked to Adityawarman's new state, and doubtless he and his followers passed through it on their way to central Tanah Datar and the banks of the Selo.[20] With the civil war following Adityawarman's death, it seems that the royal family moved back to this area and gradually established its position as a trading partner of Malacca. Members settled at various points in the valleys of the Sinamar and Sumpur, including Buo on the Sinamar and Sumpur Kudus on the Sumpur, and at the place then called Pagarruyung, near Kumanis, where the Sinamar was navigable for trading *perahu* coming up the Inderagiri. It was while living here that the royal family came into contact with Muslim traders and Islamic ideas, and in the late sixteenth century it was gradually Islamicized. At some stage the royal functions were divided among three members of the family, three being a number of great significance in Minangkabau thought, with the Raja Ibadat or King of Religion closest to the trading world of the straits at Sumpur Kudus, the Raja Adat or King of Tradition at Buo and the Raja Alam or King of the World at Pagarruyung nearby.[21] Sumpur Kudus was probably Islamicized early, having access to both the Kampar and the Inderagiri rivers for trade; during the heyday of the Malacca sultanate Kampar and Inderagiri had evolved around the mouths of their respective rivers as important tributary states of the sultanate, bound by marriage ties to the sultan of Malacca and living off the transit trade in gold and Indian cloth. Tomé Pires referred to Inderagiri as 'an important kingdom. It has a fair number of trading people, and people go there from many places to trade. It is the chief port of Menangkabau.'[22]

While the eastern Minangkabau gold trade with the world of the Malacca Straits continued after the Portuguese capture of Malacca, the Selo region of Tanah Datar was also able to pursue the gold trade via the west coast, under the control of the Bendahara of Sungai Tarab. Even before the fall of the Malacca sultanate, the newly rising commercial interests of Gujarat had replaced the South Indians on the west coast route, trading with Java by way of the Sunda Strait. Tomé Pires wrote in the early sixteenth century of the importance of Gujarati ships for the trade of Minangkabau, coming as they did to the main Tanah Datar port of Pariaman: 'One, two or three ships come every year; they sell all their clothing, and take in a great deal of gold . . .'[23]

With the rise of the Portuguese at Malacca and the Islamicization of Gujarat, many Gujarati merchants made the Islamic sultanate of Aceh on the northern tip of Sumatra their stapling place, leading to an increase in Gujarati trade with Minangkabau by way of the west coast. The result was that the blossoming Acehnese sultanate sought to engross the Minangkabau gold trade for itself, so that the Acehnese sultans could act as intermediaries in the valuable bilateral gold and cloth trade. The gold port of Pariaman was the first harbour on Minangkabau's west coast to be incorporated in the developing Acehnese monopoly system, and about 1575 one of the sultan's sons was installed there as *panglima* (governor), with supervision also over the port of Kota Tengah. Under sultan Iskandar Muda (1607-1636) all foreigners were barred from the coast and the sultan claimed fifteen per cent of all gold exported as tribute, in addition to stipulating prices for the remainder.[24]

With the decline of the Acehnese the Minangkabau acquired new partners in the gold trade, particularly as far as the west coast was concerned, and once again these partners profoundly affected the Minangkabau, or rather Tanah Datar, political system. The Dutch traders of the United East India Company (VOC), who had originally been attracted to the coasts of Sumatra in the search for pepper, gradually became aware of the role Minangkabau gold played in Indian Ocean trade, and of their need to have access to it in order to participate in that trade. Short of specie to pay for the pepper and spices they desired throughout the archipelago, the Dutch company soon learnt that, if it could transport Minangkabau gold to the Coromandel coast, it would be able to mint its own gold coins and thus pay for the cotton cloths from both Western and Southern India which had to be the stock-in-trade of anyone wanting to engage in commerce in the archipelago, and at the same time eliminate the Indian merchants based on Aceh.[25] So began the Dutch company's attempt to make itself the sole trading partner of the gold-producing Minangkabau interior. Gold was first acquired officially on behalf of the VOC at Pariaman in 1651, but Acehnese insistence on continuing to monopolize that port pushed the Dutch further south to Padang, near Kota Tengah, where the Lake Singkarak gold route to the coast terminated, and in 1663 a Dutch factory was established at that port. In the same year the company was given the right by certain southerly ports to monopolize their trade in gold, and from then on the Dutch attempted to channel all Tanah Datar gold exports to the ports of Padang and Kota Tengah, robbing the northern port of Pariaman of its ancient function. They also insisted, from 1668, that gold would not be taken other than in exchange for cloth, the sales of which brought the company seventy-five per cent clear profit.[26]

The Dutch gold trade on the coast was based on some sort of bilateral arrangement with the Bendahara of Sungai Tarab, to whom the first Dutch emissaries – in fact, Minangkabau merchants – seem to have addressed themselves, reporting back that Sungai Tarab and Lima Kaum were still the two most powerful centres in Tanah Datar and that from here alone could it be decided when gold was to be sent to the coast. The Bendahara of Sungai Tarab was the leading figure in the interior and the Raja Alam's 'absolute *wakil*'; the royal family was completely in the background, the Raja Alam being regarded more as a sacral figure with certain magical powers.[27] The Bendahara seems to have hoped that his connection with the Dutch might help him to make himself Raja Alam. On his own initiative in 1667 he appointed the company's representative at Padang the Raja Alam's *wakil mutlak* (absolute representative; Dutch *stadthouder*) for the whole coast from Barus to Inderapura, an appointment apparently made without the Raja Alam's knowledge, and in the hope of strengthening the Bendahara's ties with the Dutch, whose commercial treaties on the west coast he recognized.[28]

One of the reasons for the pre-eminence of the Bendahara at this period was that the royal family seems to have been still in the Buo-Sumpur Kudus area in the 1660s and 1670s. The coming of the Dutch on the scene, however, tipped the scales once more in favour of central Tanah Datar as the commercial centre of the Minangkabau world. This was only a gradual process. The Dutch were aware of the importance of the Inderagiri gold route, and in fact the establishment of a company 'residency' at the river's mouth took place only one year after the Dutch establishment at Padang, 'in the hope that by this means it will in future be able to acquire control of the gold available there.'[29] However, unlike Padang, the Inderagiri route could never be monopolized by the Dutch; the revival of the sultanate of Johor and its ports in the latter part of the seventeenth century, particularly Riau after 1673, led to large numbers of Indian Muslim merchants being attracted to the rivers of the east coast and proving strong competition for the Dutch in the bilateral gold and cloth trade, particularly on the Inderagiri. The Minangkabau interior seems to have been well supplied with cloth by this route, at prices which the Dutch could hardly match.[30]

Despite the fact that the gold trade in the Buo-Sumpur Kudus region continued to flourish, it was at this period that the royal family returned to the old Bukit Gombak-Suruaso core of Adityawarman's realm. Why they did this is a question that can never be satisfactorily answered. It appears that the royal family's position had gradually strengthened as a result of its commercial ties with the east, and that in 1674, when the Raja Alam died and there were two claimants for the succession, the family tried to come to some sort of arrangement whereby it could take advantage of both the eastern and the western commercial links. A compromise was gradually worked out whereby one claimant would take control of the Tanah Datar heartland, thus superseding the Bendahara of Sungai Tarab and taking over the links he had forged with the Dutch, and the other would control the old eastern areas.[31] The name of the old eastern capital, Pagarruyung near Kumanis, was brought over into Tanah Datar to an area near Suruaso known traditionally as Tiga Balai, and sometime in the 1680s certain members of the royal family gradually moved west, leaving behind in the east one member as the so-called Raja di Buo. Gradually the eastern family lost its trade partners, with the decline of the Johor sultanate about 1700, and the troubles in the straits caused by claimants to Johor's former power. In the Pagarruyung-Suruaso area the old triumvirate of the three *raja* was re-established, based on intermarriage between the royal houses of Pagarruyung and Suruaso; the title Raja Ibadat was reserved for Raja Suruaso and that of Raja Alam for Raja Pagarruyung, while the wives of the two *raja* obtained alternately the title Raja Adat. With this reorganization of the Minangkabau royal system, which lasted until the fall of the dynasty at the hands of the Islamic revivalists about 1815, Suruaso in addition to Sungai Tarab came into direct contact with the Dutch and maintained links by regularly sending emissaries with letters, considering it was in their mutual interest to do so. The letters from this court were numerous, all calling for the establishment of safe conditions for trading.[32]

The fifty years after the move back to central Tanah Datar must have been the heyday of the Minangkabau royal family. This is the only period for which we have any adequate statistics at all for the volume of the gold trade, though even these are open to question because they represent only the volume of gold which came into Dutch hands and, although the Dutch were able to establish a monopoly at Padang, some gold must certainly have escaped them by way of ports further north on the west coast, and certainly on the east coast the Dutch were never the sole or even the chief buyers. Nevertheless, Dutch figures indicate a steady supply of gold from Tanah Datar throughout the seventeenth century and well into the middle of the next century.[33]

Gradually, however, economic catastrophe struck the royal family. From the late eighteenth century supplies of gold in Tanah Datar were beginning to be worked out; the figures and prices for gold exports tell the story, and the first Europeans to investigate Tanah Datar's natural resources after 1818 confirmed the reason, noting the evidence of exhausted mines around Suruaso and other places. In 1834 only enough gold was being mined and panned in Tanah Datar to satisfy local exchange needs, and the considerable quantities which were still coming onto the Padang market came largely from the far south, around Sungai Abu.[34]

There is no doubt that the Minangkabau royal family's economic position was gravely weakened by the failure of gold mines in the late eighteenth century. But what in fact was the relationship of the royal family to the gold mines? Here again the situation is obscure. Gold-mining in Minangkabau was always a small-scale operation; the veins were small and scattered, and it has already been noted that no large-scale entrepreneur ever seems to have been able to take control of even a few of the estimated 1,200 gold mines, not to mention the gold-panning operations. However, where organization on a larger scale was needed was to cope with the transportation of that portion of the gold which was to be exported to the coast. It was here that the Minangkabau royal family and its ministers entered the commercial network. The first concrete evidence we have is that given by Tomé Pires at the beginning of the sixteenth century, when political authority in the Minangkabau world was divided between the Bendaharas of Sungai Tarab and Lima Kaum and the royal family at Buo, whom Pires calls the three kings of Minangkabau. Pires indicates that part of the gold from lineage and village lands was passed on to the apex of the political system:

They say that all the three above-mentioned kings can collect from one mine and the other, which is the law of the land, and that no Moor may go to the mines. Only the heathen lords [*penghulu*] have the mines and they have the gold and from there it is distributed to the kings of Menangkabau, and from the three kings it is distributed to others, and [as for] the amount of gold which is obtained from the said mines every year, they say that they get two bahars of gold, and more according to the Moors.[35]

What percentage the political authorities actually got is impossible to say, and of course it must have varied over this very long period. But their existence was vital to the regulation of the gold route and, in the west in particular, Sungai Tarab and Lima Kaum must have owed their importance to their ability to provide weapons and guards for the caravans of gold-traders who, once out of the 'protected villages' of the heartland, had to pass through bandit-infested mountains and woods down to the coast. The development of firearms in the early sixteenth century in particular must have given Sungai Tarab and Lima Kaum, with access to these important items, great importance as protectors of the gold trade.Neither was as close to the sources of gold as was Suruaso, but instead derived their position from the protection they could give the gold caravans.[36]

Dependent as they were on this political protection, no really independent merchant class ever developed in Minangkabau. The Minangkabau gold merchant was often a leading mining entrepreneur, who relied on the Tanah Datar political system to protect him as he led his caravan of one hundred or more men on foot down the rugged slopes of the Barisan mountains. The majority in such a caravan consisted of carriers with provisions for the journey lashed to frames on their heads or backs, their numbers swollen by those needed for the return journey to carry the bulky imports of iron or cloth required by the interior. Each carrier could cope with loads of fifty to sixty pounds on such a lashed frame.[37] Once on the coast, the merchant found the leading seaports of his country in the hands of others, and himself a mere link in a trading network which originated in other parts of the Indian Ocean. This was as true for the east coast, where water-borne carriage made the journey somewhat easier, as for the west. The Minangkabau political authorities, in exchange for trying to keep the roads in reasonable repair and encouraging the establishment of shelters and overnight resting-places for the gold caravans, were able to establish toll-posts at the main entry points into Tanah Datar, at fixed spots on mountain passes or at the headwaters of rivers, and to raise duties on trade, those on gold, iron and cloth being the highest. These duties formed the economic basis of the royal family's existence. With the decline of the gold trade, this whole apparatus declined too, and the royal family was left with the meagre revenue of three toll-posts, never having acquired any *pusaka* lands. By the late eighteenth century their fortunes had reached a nadir.[38]

Can more be said about the courts of the Minangkabau political authorities and the position of the gold merchants within the village system? Gold merchants do seem to have had specific characteristics and to have been over-represented in certain villages clustering near the court centres or on the main gold routes.[39] Of the court centres of the royal family we know very little. A Portuguese emissary of the Dutch, Thomas Dias, did visit Pagarruyung when it was still near Kumanis in 1684, and reported it to have a large population of 8,000, not including the 'suburbs'. Sumpur Kudus was equally populous. The *raja* lived in considerable state, with numerous armed retainers – Dias claims to have been accompanied on one stage of his journey by 4,000 royal retainers – and court ceremonial was very much modelled after that of the old Malacca court, with niceties such as yellow banners and umbrellas, golden dishes for letters and silver dishes for gifts. Guns and armed retainers were obviously very important for the maintenance of the ruler's position and for the protection of trading convoys; the outer gate of the royal palace was guarded by one hundred soldiers, all armed with guns, and Dias speaks of 3,000 armed soldiers accompanying him on his departure from Pagarruyung for Siluka, 'who continually fired their guns into the air.'[40] There also appear to have been royal slaves, about whom we know little, but can presume that they were people repudiated by their families due to crime.

Of Suruaso and Pagarruyung in central Tanah Datar we know even less because both, together with their palaces, had been deliberately destroyed in the Islamic revivalist movement of the early nineteenth century before any European could describe them. It does seem, however, that Malacca ceremonial and conscious refinement were aimed at. A 1730 Dutch manuscript describes the inhabitants of Pagarruyung and Suruaso as 'certainly somewhat more civilized and courteous than the majority of Malays . . .'[41] Raffles speaks of Suruaso in 1818 representing 'the wreck of what had once been great and populous' and mentions 'the distant boundaries of this once extensive city'; he also speaks of 'many an extensive building now no more.'[42] A late seventeenth century figure placed the population of Suruaso at 4,000 and of Pagarruyung at 1,000.[43] Pagarruyung, two miles north of Suruaso, lay like it between the river Selo and the hills, and also showed signs of having accommodated a large court town; the entrance, from which led a highway to the former palace and *balai* (council hall), was three-quarters of a mile from the palace. Later evidence also indicates that Pagarruyung was unusually large by Minangkabau standards; it took three-quarters of an hour to ride from its furthest boundary to the royal palace.[44] In fact it consisted of three separate sections, each of which was allotted to one member of the royal triumvirate, and there also seem to have been slave hamlets, the slaves and criminals who had sought refuge in Pagarruyung being used by the royal family in all kinds of work. There also appear to have been royal soldiers, well-armed, who were prepared to use force on the surrounding population.[45]

Of the gold merchants our knowledge is equally limited. However, the key point is that, because of the small scale on which all operated, no really large gold merchants are known to have developed, the mercantile system being directly linked to the small-scale mining operations. Like the *tua tambang,* the gold trader was a specialized component of the mining team, who had to be able to organize a party of carriers and defend them:

> Of those who dig for it, the most intelligent, distinguished by the name of *Sudagar* or merchants, are intrusted by the rest with their collections, who carry the gold to the places of trade on the great eastern rivers, or to the settlements on the west coast, where they barter it for iron (of which large quantities are consumed in tools for working the mines), opium and the fine piece-goods of Madras and Bengal, with which they return, heavily loaded, to their country . . . . they carry on their backs a weight of about eighty pounds, through woods, over streams, and across mountains; in parties generally of one hundred or more, who have frequent occasion to defend their property against the spirit of plunder and extortion which prevails among the poorer nations, through whose districts they are obliged to pass.[46]

These large parties consisted of course chiefly of carriers, known as *orang bangsat,* for whose sustenance provision had to be made, food generally being provided by the leader of the expedition and carried with it. Often it ran out on the coast, causing considerable disruption in coastal villages.[47]

Of course there were some gradations between merchants; in 1761 a Dutch account made a distinction between richer and poorer operators in the gold trade, according to their buying strategy once they reached the coast: 'if they are well-to-do traders they go direct to our warehouses, otherwise they go to the native merchants who buy goods in lots from our warehouses and sell them in even smaller lots to the single trader.'[48] Generally speaking, we can describe the Minangkabau gold trade as not being highly centralized and as being in the hands of a large number of people in relation to the bulk of the item dealt in. With the gradual limiting of the supplies of gold in the later eighteenth century, there were fewer gold traders operating. By the end of the company period, the main traders were only coming down from the interior once a year, bringing with them their carriers to bear the amount of cloth with which the leader of the trading venture wished to return. In any case, by this time the Dutch were only sending one ship a year to Padang from Batavia, which was supposed to arrive in late June or early July to bring goods needed for the *puasa* (fasting month) and the new year which followed, so that the Minangkabau traders could supply the interior with the necessary clothing for the post-fasting celebrations.[49]

As far as their relations with the interior villages are concerned, the gold merchants tended to be restricted to a limited number of villages, which they called home, villages located either near the mines or on the gold routes. Batipuh, for example, and its two nearby villages of Sumpur and Bunga Tanjung on the main trade route out of Tanah Datar, were said in 1730 to be 'largely inhabited by merchants, whose number is very great. The number of inhabitants is estimated to be about 4,000.'[50] A similar situation existed in the east near the Buo-Sumpur Kudus gold regions, where villages with a large mercantile component developed. While some villages concentrated on extracting gold from lumps of earth and rock, feeding themselves by agriculture at the same time, others such as Menganti and Ungan had two hundred to three hundred traders living in villages whose population was under one thousand. Entrepôt villages developed on the banks of the main navigable rivers near this region; Siluka and Durian Gedang, for example, on the Inderagiri, and *pangkalan* Sarai on a branch of the Kampar Kiri, a village which had two hundred traders in a population of one thousand. A whole network of villages dominated by traders developed down the Kampar Kiri as far as Lipat Kain, from whence there was an overland route to Air Tiris on the Kampar Kanan, and further facilities for overland and waterborne trade as far as the Siak. In the eleven main villages down the Kampar Kiri from *pangkalan* Sarai to Lipat Kain there was a population of 9,300 of whom 2,200 were traders, the villages being prosperous and well-fortified.[51]

While little can be said of the volume of gold exported from central Minangkabau in the period of the flourishing of the gold trade, equally little reliable information can be given concerning demand for outside products within Minangkabau. In general the main item exchanged for Minangkabau gold was cloth, and at ports where the Dutch were in command, in particular Padang after 1665, gold was only accepted in exchange for cloth, with the aim of fostering the company's cloth trade by two complementary means. It is impossible to estimate the demand for cloth because Dutch statistics have always to be complemented by the imports originating with Indian Muslim traders on the east coast and those made by the Acehnese and later the English north of Pariaman, a trade which the Dutch found impossible to stop. An interesting point, however, is that this trade was not a luxury trade and that large quantities of Indian cloths were demanded by gold traders on the coast; quality was not an important consideration, and the items in most demand were coarse Coromandel cloths, either unbleached or blue, originally intended for the West African trade, which could be transported to the uplands and dyed dark blue and black by the Minangkabau dyers themselves. The demand for this type of cloth was constant right throughout the company period. However Dutch losses in Coromandel after 1784, together with the burdening of company cloths with all the costs of transport and packing and the demand for a fixed amount of profit above that, led to gradual Minangkabau buyer resistance for the finer types of cloth, especially when so many were now unavailable. The five hundred to six hundred bales which had been disposed of annually in the early years of the century declined by 1788 to less than 275 bales, and by 1792 to about one hundred. This does not, of course, mean a decline in Minangkabau cloth consumption, but only that alternative sources of supply were available.[52]

European, chiefly Swedish, iron was also in demand, as it was highly regarded for use in tools, particularly gold-mining tools. So was Javanese salt.[53] The other item in steady demand was Dutch copper coinage, which the Dutch agreed to sell for gold at Padang from 1732 and which, since Minangkabau had none of its own copper, was highly prized for use in jewellery. The custom developed of upland traders taking for their gold only two-thirds of the full value in cotton cloths, and the remaining in copper coins, which were sold by weight in *pikul*. This proportion gradually increased in favour of copper towards the end of the century, until by 1789 nearly all gold was being exchanged for copper coinage.[54]

West coast entrepôts and coastal brokers, 1529-1795

We have spoken of network trade in connection with Minangkabau products exported to the outside world, in contrast to relay trade or the exchange system on which internal trade was based. In the Minangkabau network trade the key link between the sellers of the interior and the foreign suppliers of imports was the coastal brokerage system, which had developed on the coast at points where trade routes from the highlands converged on a good, safe anchorage. In the early centuries of the gold trade the chief coastal entrepôt was without doubt Pariaman, and Pariaman retained this position right down until the mid-seventeenth century, the whole coast being known in fact as 'the Pariaman coast.'[55] There were other, smaller coastal settlements at points where trade routes from the interior met the sea, such as Tiku, Ulakan, Kota Tengah and Padang, but of these only Tiku had any real importance because it lay at the confluence of two routes, one of which came from the Rao area of northern Minangkabau, an important gold-producing region.[56] How the commercial system operated at these ports we do not know until the seventeenth century, but the ports themselves seem to have been founded and developed by people from a particular village or group of villages in the highlands, in order to further their own commercial interests. Kota Tengah, for example, was founded by emigrants from Saningbakar on the shores of Lake Singkarak, a village on one of the gold routes, and Padang was founded by emigrants from the Solok plain. Pariaman owed its origin to villages in the Batipuh area, and was in fact regarded as a royal foundation.[57]

The leading men of these coastal entrepôts acted as brokers between foreign merchants and uplands traders. They were the typical *orang kaya* (lit. rich man) known throughout the Malay maritime world, men seeking to rise in the world by their own efforts in a way which agrarian life did not always make possible. In addition to acting as brokers for the main items of import and export, they tried to provide stable conditions at their entrepôts so that a wide variety of items would be stapled there, brought often from a considerable distance by small coastal *perahu* of which they were the principal owners. As well as the *orang kaya* each port had its own *raja*, nominally linked to the Minangkabau royal court, each of whom administered his port and the surrounding area as a territorial entity. Although the Minangkabau genealogical system was inapplicable in coastal conditions, the *orang kaya* retained the old uplands title of *penghulu*, and recognized their *raja* as *primus inter pares*.[58]

Under such a regime Pariaman, in addition to providing facilities for the gold and cloth trades, stapled camphor, benjamin, wax and honey coming from the area north of Air Bangis, horses from the Batak country, which were an important item of export to West Java, and coconut oil from the islands off the west coast.

Pariaman was also fortunate in that, unlike some other ports, it had good land for rice-growing in its hinterland, although it seems that to make good the labour shortage for cultivating this, slaves had to be imported from the islands, and a flourishing slave trade developed, particularly with the island of Nias. Rice shortages were also made good from this source.[59]

Some time in the early or mid-sixteenth century a great change came over these coastal entrepôts, although we still do not understand its full ramifications for the coastal brokerage system, and the economic history of the west coast, using the ample Dutch documentation available, still waits to be written. The change came about due to the commencement of the cultivation along the west coast of Sumatra – from Air Bangis in the north to Benkulen in the south – of a commercial crop of great value in international trade. For the first time, part of the Minangkabau world undertook a new role, and began to pursue the precarious existence of commercial producer of an agricultural commodity for foreign markets. The agricultural commodity in demand was pepper. Discussion of the establishment of pepper-growing on the coast has significance for us not only because of the changes it caused in the nature of the coastal brokerage system, but also because the experience of the pepper planters was in so many ways similar to that of the Minangkabau coffee planters in the early nineteenth century, and a comparison of the two cases is conducive to understanding that the problems of peasants involved in commercial agricultural production for foreign markets were no mere nineteenth century development.

In the sixteenth century the major demand for west coast pepper came from the Chinese market, although Gujarati traders were also eager to supplement Indian supplies of pepper which were exported to Europe. Demand in Europe was extremely high; pepper was the first great European consumer product from the tropics, long predating sugar, coffee and tea. Once the demand became established, Minangkabau peasants from the highlands began to come down to both the west coast and the east coast in far greater numbers than ever before, stimulated by the profits to be made from pepper cultivation. What these profits were we do not know, but the incentives to cultivate pepper must have been considerable, given the difficult work required to establish and maintain a pepper garden, the deferment of benefits until the vines began to produce in their third year, and the relatively quick decline of the garden after it had reached its optimum production between its eighth and twelfth years.[60]

Not all areas of the coast were suited to pepper-growing. The gardens did best on level ground on the banks of a river, somewhat inland so as not to be flooded, but with ready access to water transport. On the Minangkabau west coast only a few areas met these conditions, and in fact the existing gold entrepôts of Pariaman, Kota Tengah and Padang did not have a hinterland suitable for pepper. Although we have few records for the sixteenth century, it seems that from the early decades of that century the most favoured areas for pepper-growing were the broad coastal stretch north of Tiku, centred on the river Masang and Pasaman, and certain parts of the coast south of Padang, in particular around Bayang and Inderapura.[61] As migrants came down to the coast and established numerous new villages, so did the older entrepôts seek to maintain their privileged stapling position by establishing contacts with the pepper villages and encouraging them to use their port facilities. Kota Tengah, for example, developed itself as the stapling point for Bayang pepper, Padang for that of the Sepuluh Buah Bandar, and Pariaman for that of Inderapura, where the harbour facilities were poor. Tiku developed to such an extent that by the early seventeenth century it was the leading pepper port on the central part of the coast.[62]

The transformation of the traditional entrepôts into pepper ports must have led to a considerable development in the trade undertaken by the port brokers. The pepper districts were usually a considerable distance inland and pepper required an extensive transport network, small *perahu* being sent upriver to collection points; the pepper was then assembled in warehouses at the stapling port, and an increasing number of port officials was required to carry on the trade with visiting Chinese and Indian traders. A labour supply was also needed for loading and unloading. All important for the coastal brokers was the maintenance of good relations with the pepper villages of the interior, but this relationship was often very volatile. Disputes over prices and weights must often have arisen, with the increasingly numerous planters in the interior wishing to assert their interests at the expense of the coastal brokers, who controlled the transport and exporting network. It was just such disputes in the hinterland of Tiku which led to foreign intervention in the port, and there are reports of attacks on the Bayang pepper region by armed parties from Padang and Kota Tengah. The entrepôts themselves also contended with one another for economic supremacy and the right to establish prices. In some areas, such as Inderapura, pepper proved the basis for independent political development.[63]

The question which most demands an answer is, to what extent were these coastal brokers independent and well-to-do merchants who could have formed a nascent commercial class? The question is an important one because the position of the coastal mercantile class becomes an issue with the massive exports of commercial crops from Minangkabau in the early nineteenth century, when the absence of large Minangkabau merchants in this trade is very marked. Did pepper-exporting ever produce a well-to-do commercial class in the west coast ports? The evidence on which to base an answer is very slender. Certainly in 1529, when Tiku was only just beginning to expand as a pepper-stapling entrepôt, French visitors found it a poor place, despite the extent of its trade: '. . . the town of Ticou is not big, and has only two or three streets: it is enclosed at both ends by wooden posts driven into the ground, and there are also gates; for fencing there are transverse pieces of wood slotted through holes in the larger posts; the houses are not made of timber and are all alike, except that some are larger than others.'[64] The inhabitants led a simple existence: they slept on the floor on rattan mats in houses with only one storey, roofed with palm leaves, and had few domestic utensils. This austerity was reflected in their food. Chicken was reserved for special occasions; on all other occasions 'their meals consist of a little rice boiled in water without salt, and sometimes accompanied by a little sun-dried fish as small as one's finger.'[65] There certainly were *orang kaya* who were remarkable for their gold armbands and gold-handled *keris,* but though these men were the leading traders, nothing is said about their commercial operations.

How the coastal brokerage class might have developed had these west coast entrepôts been left alone is impossible to say. With the rise of the Acehnese sultanate in the late sixteenth century, however, the port of Pariaman was incorporated into the Acehnese trading system about 1575. It was not primarily the gold of Pariaman which concerned Aceh, but the fact that by this time Pariaman, although without a pepper-producing hinterland, had become an important stapling-place for southern pepper.[66] Pepper was becoming increasingly vital to Aceh's economy, and the sultanate wished to become the leading stapling-place for pepper in the archipelago, in order to be able to supply both the Gujaratis who conducted the Red Sea pepper trade and the China trade which was so vital to its existence. With the exhaustion of the north-east Sumatra pepper districts, Aceh cast its net towards the west coast of Sumatra to ensure itself of supplies. For a time control of Pariaman ensured Aceh's position in Indian Ocean trade. But with the coming of the northern Europeans to the waters of Sumatra, competition for pepper supplies made it impossible for Aceh any longer to regulate even partially the Sumatran end of the trade. In addition to those Chinese and Gujarati traders who went direct to the pepper ports, the English and Dutch, who had founded commercial companies with the very aim of supplying Europe with pepper, were seen to be trying to buy up pepper along the coast. Such competition led to greatly rising prices, an incentive to which upland peasants seem to have responded by migrating in greater numbers to the pepper villages and increasing production.[67]

For Aceh it now appeared that the only way to hold down prices to a reasonable level and to ensure that the sultanate engrossed the major share of the trade was to occupy the main pepper ports and, establishing political control there, take over part of the functions of the Minangkabau coastal brokers and reduce them to agents of the Acehnese officials sent to the ports, who then became mercantile bureaucrats specializing in the initial and final import-export stage. This process was completed by the Acehnese sultanate in the reign of Iskandar Muda (1607-1636) but had begun much earlier; from Tiku in the north to Inderapura in the south, all the leading entrepôts on the coast were gradually placed under the control of Acehnese *panglima*. Iskandar Muda's policy was one of attempting to conduct all pepper sales through the Acehnese capital Kotaraja, to prevent any more 'pepper ports' coming into existence on the west coast by a rigorous policy of stapling at the three major ports of Tiku, Pariaman and Inderapura, and to bar all foreign traders, including Gujaratis and Europeans, from the coast.[68] Thus for the first time, as a result of the international nature of the pepper trade and of her role in the international economy, Minangkabau found her ports in foreign hands and a system of monopoly enforced over her sole cash crop.

How the Acehnese system actually operated in relation to the indigenous coastal brokers is not clear, but it seems that they were indispensable to the Acehnese as later to the Dutch. Since the Acehnese *panglima* were only appointed for three years at a time and received no fixed salary, it was in their interests, while themselves acting as the chief merchant importer/exporter and regulator of duties and taxes, to encourage the coastal brokers to keep open the pepper supply lines. However the position of the coastal brokers was not what it had been. From this period, and continuing for over three centuries, the initial and final control of imports and exports passed into foreign hands, first Acehnese and then European, and the coastal brokerage system was metamorphosed into a form of agency system. The relationship of Acehnese officialdom with the coastal brokers contained certain elements which were later to become familiar in the Dutch system. Many of the brokers' former functions were removed: the *panglima* was able to fix all anchorage dues and customs duties at his port; he was obliged to remit all pepper to Aceh and to fix prices in accordance with the sultan's wishes; he could force the local brokers, and ultimately the pepper planters, to accept imports of Spanish dollars or of Gujarati cloth sold on the sultan's behalf; he took fifteen per cent of all pepper delivered without paying for it and sent it as tribute to Iskandar Muda.[69] Even so the Minangkabau brokers or *orang kaya* continued to play a significant role in commercial transactions. The pepper trade could not have operated without the transport facilities provided by the brokers; numerous small boats were vital to all stages of the trade, including the final loading onto foreign ships, and the payments made by foreign traders to the brokers indicate that it was only through them that the pepper producers could be reached.[70]

Nevertheless, it was now the Acehnese *panglima* who actually enjoyed the lion's share of the profits of commerce. While the brokers' capital was tied up in the transport network and advances to planters and there are no records of rich brokers, it is reported that the *panglima* of Pariaman on his death in 1662 left at least 4,000 Spanish dollars, in addition to gold ornaments and jewellery.[71] Furthermore, the Minangkabau brokers experienced competition from Acehnese settlers who entered their profession independently. At the leading port of the coast, Pariaman, these settlers were very much in evidence, having come there in considerable numbers and intermarried with the population. In 1664 there were between 500 and 700 Acehnese in Pariaman, in addition to their offspring, and at Tiku too there was much intermarriage with the Acehnese. Considerable Acehnese effort seems to have gone into organizing Pariaman's commerce, since the entrepôt had a dual role as a pepper-stapling port and as the main terminal point of the gold export route. While the Minangkabau brokers' boats brought in the pepper from considerable distances down the coast, a system of horse relays was organized for transporting the gold from the Anai gorge to Pariaman, and slaves were also used for this purpose.[72]

If the coastal brokers had lost to the Acehnese their main function as importers and exporters, what was their relationship with the Minangkabau peasant who grew pepper and on whom their prosperity depended? Even here other, outside, traders placed obstacles in the way of their monopoly of contact with the planter, and the coastal brokers were engaged in competition with outside traders to maintain face-to-face relationships with the planters. Foreign traders, particularly the Chinese, were willing to leave the established entrepôts and go inland up distant rivers to contact the pepper planters themselves, and even European traders attempted this. In this way the planters could avoid the transport costs charged by the coastal brokers and receive a higher price for their product. Some planters became well-to-do by skimming the profits of the brokers; the pepper planters of Bayang, for example, were reported in the 1660s to be so well off that they could afford to hold back their crop if prices did not suit them.[73]

The introduction of Iskandar Muda's system, however, affected the peasants' desire to plant pepper, to the further disadvantage of the coastal brokers. Pepper planting was discouraged by Acehnese demands for free deliveries of pepper in the form of tribute, and by the *panglimas'* fixing of prices, which now no longer fluctuated according to demand and supply. The coastal brokers were even more disadvantaged when the Acehnese began to try to contact the pepper planters directly; in the pepper villages behind Tiku, and in the south, a tax per pepper-planting household was introduced, obviously to be paid in pepper, and though this caused considerable dislike of the Acehnese, it did not help the brokers.[74]

With the decline of the Acehnese sultanate in the 1640s another period of fierce international competition for west coast pepper developed. It seems likely that the coastal brokers were beginning to re-establish themselves, there being so many foreign traders – including Indian Muslims who never went inland – coming directly to the coast to acquire pepper, and new plantings were made almost daily. It was at this time that representatives of the Dutch East India Company on the coast, acting on instructions from the main Dutch settlement in the Indonesian archipelago at Batavia in West Java, began to make a concerted bid to enter the pepper trade on their own terms. Pepper was at that time the most important item in the company's commerce, and on Acehnese terms the Dutch were at a severe disadvantage. Even when they could get Acehnese permission to trade at the pepper ports, they were competing with the sultan's own imports, which always had to be sold first, and then those of Gujarati merchants, whose long experience on the coast enabled them to assess local taste and demand. They also had to face arbitrary price-fixing by the Acehnese *panglima,* and in addition they were handicapped in the cloth trade by not having adequate sources of supply in India, whilst the demand for Spanish dollars at the ports was a severe strain on them.[75]

The declining Acehnese, therefore, were not immediately replaced by the Dutch. Throughout the 1640s and 1650s Indian Muslim traders conducted by far the greatest volume of commerce on the coast and were the main suppliers of Pariaman and Tiku.[76] The Dutch now decided to use a new strategy. Instead of working through the Acehnese *panglima* system, as did the Indian Muslims, or contacting local suppliers, as did the Chinese, the Dutch decided to eliminate the Acehnese *panglima* importer/exporter and his Indian collaborators and form a direct alliance with the Minangkabau coastal brokers, whose loyalty to the Acehnese system could not be regarded as indubitable. Dutch strategy was twofold. First, pressure was put on the troubled Acehnese court to fix by treaty prices on Dutch terms at west coast ports, and to exclude all foreign traders other than the Dutch from these ports. By contemporary advances in India the Dutch were able to acquire cloth supplies which enabled price equivalents to be fixed for pepper and allowed the Dutch to enter the intra-Asian barter trade and so relieve the burden of the need for specie. Secondly, the Dutch at the same time were looking for allies among the old Minangkabau coastal brokerage class who would be prepared to overthrow the Acehnese system completely and to admit the Dutch company to their ports, replacing the Acehnese as the leading merchant importer/exporter.[77]

The success of this policy is well known and its development has been well documented. Representatives of the coastal brokerage class up and down the coast, beginning in 1657 with the Sepuluh Buah Bandar area in the south, and later including leading coastal brokers in Tiku and its hinterland, Padang and Inderapura approached the Dutch with offers to sell pepper and gold exclusively to the company, in exchange for the removal of the Acehnese *panglima* and continuing Dutch protection. The result was the signing in 1663 of the Treaty of Painan, on which all subsequent Dutch claims to the coast rested.[78]

The irony is, however, that just at the period when this treaty was signed, Dutch commercial interests on the coast were changing. Now it was the acquisition of gold, rather than pepper, which was becoming the company's chief concern. Pepper consumption had reached saturation point in Europe by the 1680s, but there was a booming demand for Indian cottons on the European market after 1670, and cottons soon overtook pepper as the most valuable part of the company's homeward cargoes, although interest continued in pepper as a commodity in intra-Asian trade. To acquire cottons, vast amounts of bullion and specie were shipped to India, giving Minangkabau gold considerable importance.[79] In the 1660s the company therefore established its chief settlement at Padang, a coastal entrepôt which, with nearby Kota Tengah, received little pepper but was at the terminus of a minor gold route from Tanah Datar and did not have the disadvantage of a large number of Acehnese settlers.[80] It is at this point that the European presence on the coast, which had previously been restricted to trading within the existing system, began to affect the relative positions of the coastal ports and their inhabitants in a manner which has continued until today.

Before looking at the coastal brokers of Padang and their relationship with brokers in other major coastal entrepôts, it is not out of place to summarize the fate of the coastal pepper villages after 1663, subject as they were both to fluctuations in the price of pepper on the European market and to the overall priorities of the Dutch trading system. With the stagnation of the European pepper market in the late seventeenth century and the reduction of orders from the Netherlands, coupled with the injunction to ensure low buying prices, the coastal pepper planters in areas where the Dutch were able to prevent outside buyers from approaching the coast were placed completely at the mercy of Dutch commercial policy, which fluctuated throughout the eighteenth century according to the state of the European market and the possibility of acquiring cheaper pepper in other parts of the archipelago.[81] One of the first acts of the Dutch, once in control of the west coast entrepôts, was to lower the buying price of pepper; in addition, white rather than black pepper was demanded from the planter, requiring the removal of the black shell of the pepper corn, which caused much extra trouble. Further, the planter's transport costs became higher, the company having other uses for what transport there was on the coast, obliging the planters to find their own boats to bring their pepper to the few and distant stapling places. Moreover, the Dutch would pay for pepper only in cloth and not specie, thus disrupting the pepper planters' own trading network and hampering the coastal rice trade, on which the pepper villages largely depended for their subsistence. Rice was shipped from the few rice surplus areas along the coast to the pepper areas where insufficient rice for consumption was grown, but this rice had to be paid for in specie.[82]

Under these circumstances many pepper villages showed their flexibility and sought salvation in an alternative crop. Now used to commercial agriculture, they did not immediately return to rice-growing; instead many once flourishing pepper areas turned to a crop which had been the coastal commercial staple before the pepper boom. Prior to the mid-sixteenth century, cotton had been cultivated on the coast to supply the upland weavers.[83] Cotton was an attractive competitor for pepper, doing well in exactly the same warm climate and alluvial soils of the river floodplains as did pepper; moreover, it was an annual, requiring a growing season of only 180 to 200 days, and the labour involved was certainly no greater than for pepper. While former pepper areas such as Bayang and Inderapura turned to rice, the areas in between – the coastal strip at the foot of the Sungai Pagu highlands, comprising the hinterlands of Painan, Salida and the so-called Sepuluh Buah Bandar – moved into cotton cultivation as early as the period 1656-1665, the cotton being shipped out to Padang, Kota Tengah and elsewhere and thence transported to the uplands to be manufactured by the increasing number of weavers in the hill villages. In this way the former pepper districts transformed themselves into direct competitors of the company's cloth trade.[84]

The coastal planters of pepper and cotton never ceased to experience Dutch interference and pressure, in different ways. In the latter decades of the seventeenth century and the early ones of the eighteenth, Dutch policy towards pepper fluctuated, but every period of discouragement made it harder to revitalize pepper cultivation at a later date. Typical was an attempt to reduce the buying price of west coast pepper from f.17½ to f.12½ per *pikul* in 1698, due to low prices on the European market. When in 1710 the price was raised, in anticipation of a fall in the company's stocks of pepper, planters who had gone out of production after 1698 simply could not be won back to the labour of pepper cultivation. When in subsequent decades of the eighteenth century Batavia began to realize the usefulness of pepper for the China tea trade and tried to make new efforts to promote its cultivation, in most areas on the Minangkabau west coast it was already too late.[85]

As part of this renewed interest in Minangkabau pepper for the China trade, the Minangkabau coastal brokers were further transformed into agents of the Dutch, this time of Dutch agricultural interests. They were given a function which had never been theirs previously, that of encouraging and supervising pepper cultivation in the satellite settlements of their own villages. In recognition that their authority did not stretch much further afield, efforts were particularly centred on the brokers of the two main entrepôts, Pariaman and Padang where, of course, pepper cultivation had never flourished before and in the environs of which cotton-planting was beginning to be pursued with success. As well as being transformed into Dutch agents for the promotion of pepper, the coastal brokers were urged to use all their influence to stamp out cotton cultivation and to recognize that their best interests were bound up with peasant cultivation of pepper.[86] In 1690 the Dutch-appointed *panglima raja* of Padang, after steady urging, finally promised to forbid cotton cultivation and 'to set all hands to work to plant the fields of Padang with pepper . . .'[87] In 1747 the buying price of pepper was raised even higher, to f.20 per *pikul,* and the coastal brokers were again urged to promote pepper-planting and extirpate cotton.[88] In 1755 a series of treaties was made with the coastal ports which were quite new in their implications for the west coast. By these treaties the coastal brokers both north and south of Padang committed themselves to preventing the planting of cotton. In addition they promised to take no part in the cotton trade, to declare any cotton arriving at their ports contraband, and to store cotton being sent to the mountains. They further agreed to cultivate pepper themselves, and to persuade the inhabitants of their areas to do likewise; each treaty contained the clause: 'Each of the panghoeloes must bring his pepper gardens into a good state of cultivation, and also must persuade the rest of the community to plant pepper vines.'[89] Rice, too, had to be cultivated annually to prevent shortages on the coast.

Little success attended the signing of these treaties. Cotton was too profitable to be extirpated, while by the 1780s the regular cultivation of pepper on that part of the Minangkabau coast within the Dutch orbit had virtually ceased. Pressure on the Padang brokers continued with little result, and Dutch attempts to encourage pepper in non-traditional pepper areas in the vicinity of Padang, Pau and Kota Tengah had only a brief success when, in the period between 1785 and 1792, the product was paid for in silver instead of the traditional cloth.[90] In areas more accustomed to pepper the crop never returned, so ending Minangkabau's first experiment with a commercial crop for the world market. Large sections of the coastal plain, their soil exhausted and their inhabitants gone, returned to scrub such as had existed there before the pepper boom.[91]

The Dutch and the growth of the Padang brokerage system, 1665-1795

It now remains to trace the history of the coastal brokerage system from the period when the Dutch company replaced the Acehnese and hoped to use the port brokers to foster its own trade, until the period when the exigencies of Dutch agricultural interests led to attempts to turn them more and more into agricultural supervisors and finally, to replace them by another, alien, group, the Chinese. The first point to notice is that not all coastal brokers were convinced of the wisdom of replacing the Acehnese by the Dutch. The coastal entrepôts themselves were in no way homogeneous: the families of the earliest settlers were often at odds with those of later settlers; wealth could be made and unmade rapidly; different families were linked with different and often competing economic activities – some with the coastal trade, others with island trade, others with trade with the interior; some families benefited a great deal from the Acehnese presence and, related to leading Acehnese traders by marriage, were not always eager to snap the links of the alliance.

Because of this, different entrepôts took up different attitudes to the Dutch connection, or rather, what was seen as beneficial by certain groups in a particular entrepôt was not seen as such by others. The leading brokers of Tiku, for example, considered that the removal of the Acehnese would allow them to regain control of the area's pepper trade and regulate prices. In Pariaman only the richest brokers wanted to get rid of the Acehnese, whilst the remainder, the vast majority, wished to continue in partnership with them. At both ports, the Acehnese had to be driven off by force by Dutch expeditionary troops.[92] In these circumstances, the Dutch came more and more to rely on the southerly port of Padang, an insignificant spot compared to its two northern neighbours, and, initially, on nearby Kota Tengah and the southern pepper port of Salida. Kota Tengah was cultivated because it provided an alternative terminus to Pariaman for the Anai gorge gold route, and the Dutch aim was to destroy Pariaman's trade completely.[93]

Padang owed its rise to the leading position it has retained on the west coast until today entirely to the astuteness of the majority of its leading merchants in recognizing the advantages which might accrue to them by replacing the Acehnese, to whom Padang was an out-station, with the Dutch. Originally a poor village of fishermen and salt-makers trading on a limited scale with the surrounding areas, Padang was settled in two main waves, first by people from other parts of the coast as far north as Pasaman and as far south as Inderapura, and secondly by people from the Singkarak-Solok region of the highlands. There was considerable tension between the two groups, heightened by the fact that the former traced their origin back to Pariangan on Mount Merapi and regarded themselves as belonging to the Koto Piliang or 'royal' *laras,* while the newcomers were Bodi Caniago. Eventually an administrative system for the port was worked out, recognizing four main lineages in each of the two groups. This gave Padang eight *penghulu* acting as brokers in the coastal trade, until the port was taken over by the Acehnese in the early seventeenth century.[94]

The use of the term *penghulu* for the heads of these port lineages helped to maintain the continuity of institutions with the Minangkabau homeland, but in fact such a *penghulu* represented something very different from the controller of lineage *sawah* in the uplands. As at the other entrepôts he was above all a commercial broker, enabling the commerce of the port to be carried on between the local traders, who came to Padang by land and sea with small amounts of gold, cotton, pepper, coconut oil, fish, salt, straw mats, cloth and slaves, and the foreign merchants. Although lineage titles were often handed down in the female line, this was not invariably the case, and by the seventeenth century at least property, in the form of commercial assets rather than land, generally passed from father to children.[95]

The brokers of Padang felt there would be great advantages to their neglected port in a commercial alliance with the Dutch, although two – Padang's richest and most important traders, descended from the Solok plain settlers – dissented from this view, wishing to keep up the Acehnese connection through which they had prospered. They were subsequently exiled, with their families, by the Dutch. There was also reason to think that many of the ordinary inhabitants of the port were opposed to allowing the Dutch to establish an actual factory at Padang.[96] However, forging an alliance with the European company did lead to considerable advantages for other Padang broker families; this was true in particular of the family of the so-called Orang Kaya Kecil, who was the client of an important Padang broker and who was the leading spirit in conducting negotiations with the Europeans. When Dutch forces drove out the Acehnese *panglima* in 1664 and removed pro-Acehnese elements – often more recent settlers – in the population, Orang Kaya Kecil and his family were rewarded for their collaboration. The Dutch preserved the *panglima*-ship and gave the position to Orang Kaya Kecil in 1667, his title being *panglima raja.* The *panglima raja* was also later given a supervisory role in places which were Padang's commercial rivals, such as Tiku, in an attempt to establish a coastal 'capital'. The *penghulu* system was also subject to Dutch interference:

twelve *penghulu* were appointed from families loyal to the Dutch, whilst Orang Kaya Kecil's brother was rewarded with the position of Bendahara, the leading *penghulu* of the twelve.

Of course, the Minangkabau *panglima raja*'s position was substantially different from that of the Acehnese *panglima*; the Dutch company's representative on the coast now functioned in the old Acehnese role of governor, and the *panglima raja* and the twelve *penghulu* merely continued as brokers to the Dutch merchant importer/exporter, the controlling point in the commercial network. Although descent was taken into account in appointing *penghulu*, the *penghulu* were subject to Dutch decisions concerning the fitness of an occupant for the title, and *panglima raja* too had to be seen to be loyal to Dutch interests if they wished to retain their position.[97]

The importance of fitness or merit as a criterion for the position of *penghulu* was linked to the use to which the Dutch wished to put these coastal brokers. It was soon discovered that the newly-collaborating class was not a class of independently rich traders. What capital the coastal brokers possessed seems to have been sunk in shipping, which was required to go as far north as Nias for rice and slaves and as far south as Inderapura for pepper. In fact, it was this coastal trade in essential supplies which had always formed the basis of the brokers' livelihood. Rice had constantly to be taken by boat from rice surplus to rice deficit areas; salt had to be brought in from outside, expecially Java, and salt vessels were often owned by the brokerage class. All this trade was carried on with small profit margins, transport costs absorbing much of the profit on goods which were destined to be sold in the interior.[98] To carry on their own trade in pepper, the Dutch had to advance cloth and specie to these brokers, who then operated through itinerant traders and boat managers until the pepper could be assembled. A similar system enabled the gold trade to function, the Dutch advancing the brokers large sums, in which cloth more and more predominated because of Dutch difficulties in acquiring specie. In such a system, the honesty and reliability of the broker was a prime consideration. The entire commercial system operated on credit, and risks were high. The commercial network consisted of, firstly, foreign merchant importer/exporter; secondly, Minangkabau brokers or intermediaries, who broke into lots imported bulk cargoes and dealt with the producers; thirdly, itinerant traders, who were often agents of the brokers; and fourthly, small pedlars.[99]

In this system by far the greatest margin of profit was made by the foreign importer/exporter; the coastal brokers in the key pepper and gold trades remained a sort of administrative or agency class, operating on small profit margins due to the large number of intermediaries functioning within the trading network between the coast and the interior. Their 'wealth' consisted in the amount of credit of which they were regarded as worthy, rather than in their own capital assets. There is little evidence of combination by brokers to increase capital assets, form guilds and trade on their own account, and indeed the tenacity of the lineage system and of factional struggle for prestige even on the coast seems to have prevented this. Some of the leading brokers do form exceptions to this picture, though estimates of their wealth are impossible to arrive at. Those who had a considerable number of vessels to engage in the coastal stapling trade were often married into families at comparable ports and joint commercial ventures on this basis were then more readily undertaken, though many of the products transported, such as *atap* and rattan matting, gave low profits. Combination was particularly necessary for trading ventures to the north; there is a report in 1667 of a ten-year old partnership trading regularly with Barus in which the boat was owned jointly by a broker from Padang, one from nearby Kota Tengah, and a *nakoda* from Sungai Tarab in the uplands.[100]

The credit system was the key to the gold trade in the earliest days of Dutch settlement at Padang, the acquisition of gold being Padang's chief *raison d'être* from the Dutch point of view. The first company representative at Padang found that the Acehnese had also had to operate on credit and, in imitation of their system, he advanced to particular brokers the considerable sum of cloths worth up to 400 *tahil* of gold. This system of advancing credit was not confined only to the leading brokers. While the pepper trade still continued, because of the need to use smaller traders to actually travel considerable distances and collect the pepper in order to have supplies ready for shipment, company officials extended credit even to these small men. Unfortunately, it soon became apparent that, although leading brokers could be made answerable for their debts, small traders could not, and such men, failing in business, would simply return home to their uplands village, whence they could not be pursued.[101]

Gradually, therefore, the company moved over to another system. No credit at all was now given to small traders, who were eliminated as brokers in the import/export trade, their function in any case having become less important with the decline of the pepper trade. Only established *penghulu* were to be recognized as brokers, and in 1667 advances to them were also stopped, and instead they became more and more paid agents of the company. Payment was directly related to the volume of trade passing through those entrepôts where the Dutch had a factory, of which Padang of course was the main one. Toll-houses and fixed tariffs were established at the ports, and the resultant duties collected by the company's officials on all imported and exported goods were divided among each port's *penghulu*. At Padang the *panglima* received one-third of such duties and the other *penghulu* together two-thirds. In addition, the Pariaman and Padang *penghulu* were paid a certain sum for each *tahil* of gold and each *bahar* of pepper they delivered to the company's warehouses, in the hope that this would give them a greater interest in encouraging the flow of trade. Whatever advances the *penghulu* required as trading capital could now only be negotiated as charges on their regular payments from the customs duties, which could then be withheld if the credit was not repaid.[102]

In the early years of the new system the coastal brokerage class acquired considerable trading capital. As trade flourished, so too did customs duties. In 1667 the *penghulu* of Salida alone got f.4,500, and Padang and Kota Tengah did well too.[103] However, gradually the Dutch position on the coast, which had looked so hopeful, began to deteriorate, and with it the fortunes of those who had allied themselves with the company. The decline of the pepper trade, and therefore of port customs duties, has already been noted. But far worse was the fact that the gold trade, which was to have been Padang's staple, became increasingly erratic because the Dutch were unable to retain the collaboration of villages near Padang through which the gold traders had to pass. The rise to influence and prosperity of Padang excited bitter resentment elsewhere on the coast, and various villages whose cooperation was vital to keeping the gold routes open displayed marked hostility to the Padang merchants, which was exhibited by entering into alliances with those Acehnese traders and adventurers who were still on the coast. Kota Tengah and Pau to the north-east of Padang are only two examples of villages which united at various times to attack Padang and disrupt its trade. Dutch response was to rely more and more on Padang and its brokers, and to treat every other port on the coast with suspicion. Every effort was made to restrict the trade of Pariaman and Tiku, in particular to break the Acehnese supply lines of these ports and to ensure that they never regained their old commercial pre-eminence. It was stipulated that those coastal traders, including the Chinese from Java, to whom Dutch passes were granted for trade on the west coast, ignore Tiku and Pariaman and go no further north than Padang and Kota Tengah. Pariaman was of interest only in relation to its agricultural hinterland, which it was intended would be the 'larder' of Padang, and its trade gradually declined to such an extent that the company removed its factory.[104] By 1730 it was reported that Tiku's trade had declined almost to nothing due to Dutch restrictions; even the Tiku coconut oil trade with the islands off Air Bangis was deflected to Padang.[105]

Gradually, with the decline of southern pepper and the southern ports, Padang became the focus of all the company's activity. However, in attempting to destroy the trade of other ports along the coast, the company also greatly harmed that of Padang, since Padang had a long tradition of involvement in the coastal trade. For this the gold trade could never be an adequate substitute but, having entrusted so much of its commercial fortune to this trade, Padang was particularly hard hit by its decline from the mid-eighteenth century. The twists and turns of Dutch commercial policy along the coast cannot be entered into here; the key point, however, is that, by its alliance with the Dutch, the Padang brokerage class lost all opportunity of participating in a flourishing foreign and coastal trade, and so declined in both wealth and consequence, after its brief hour of glory in the 1660s and 1670s.

In particular, Dutch policy towards free navigation and private trade on the coast underwent innumerable changes which could not fail to damage the Padang brokers. In 1686 salt imports and sales were declared a company monopoly, and private trade, especially from Java, was seen as a threat to both this and to the company's cloth trade. On the other hand, whenever the Javanese trade was banned, Padang and other ports which depended on Padang as a stapling place went short of basic necessities; near famine in the areas surrounding Padang is reported more than once.[106] Although the Java traders, who were mostly Chinese, could provide Padang with numerous domestic items in which the company did not trade, quite apart from the essential salt and rice, the company found that these traders introduced so much salt onto the coast that the profits the company gained on its own salt trade markedly declined. This was a problem the Dutch never solved in relation to Padang right up to 1795, when they were removed from the port by the English. Not only was Padang often short of necessities such as salt and rice as a result of the changeable policy on private trade, but the brokers' links with this trade were gradually broken.[107]

The company also attempted to break some of Padang's commercial links with the uplands. Cotton from the south coast shipped to Padang and other nearby ports for transportation to the upland weavers of Agam was ordered confiscated, as were the finished products coming down to Padang to be retailed along the coast by Padang traders. The trade in coastal salt with the uplands, which was based on coastal villages renting out salt pans to certain upland villages, which sent salt-makers down at certain times of the year, as well as on direct trade, was also disrupted in favour of the company salt monpoly. Coastal salt pans were first destroyed in 1687 and, until this was forbidden by Batavia in 1718, regular destruction of the pans took place.[108]

Equally bad for Padang was the company's own supply problem with Indian cloths, which began in the first decades of the eighteenth century and gradually became worse as the century progressed due to European struggles in Coromandel. The upland Minangkabau, for whom most of the imported cloth was destined, had very definite preferences, and the shortage of the desired type, or of any type, on the coast was a constant complaint of the company's officials at Padang. The company gradually lost many of its customers and, whereas at the height of Dutch success at Padang in the 1660s and 1670s 1,500 bales of textiles had been disposed of on the coast every year, by the 1750s demand was down to 550 bales p.a.[109]

The sufferers in all this were the Padang brokers, whose fortunes went from bad to worse with the decline of the entrepôt's trade. There was intense internal factionalism, which increased the more Padang came to depend for its existence on the gold trade, a trade which gave the advantage to those *penghulu* with family connections in the villages on the gold route. The closed nature of the *penghulu* system itself, with the immutable number of twelve, also affected commercial relations between the brokers; individuals who did succeed in trade in their own right were excluded from the benefits of the existing system and often aroused the jealousy of the existing brokers. But the gravest problem was financial. The collapse of the pepper trade struck the first blow; in 1704 it was reported that a year's total in customs duties 'is now very small in comparison with earlier times, when this coast exported large quantities of pepper, and recently it amounted to no more than 402 rijksdaalders for the period of a whole year, which the panglima wanted for himself alone . . .'[110] By 1749 the situation was so bad for both the Dutch and their collaborators that Padang officials asked Batavia to allow them to grant the leading brokers of Padang credit, without which trade could not continue because the brokers were so poor that they 'had to hawk around in small quantities the goods sold to them to even poorer individuals in the community, before they could pay the stipulated amount of gold.'[111] The rising price of gold from the 1770s also made it difficult for the brokers to make any trading profit on their own; they could not sell any cloth because of the very high price of gold, which first had to be acquired before they could go to the company warehouse for cloth supplies.[112]

By tying Padang's fortunes so firmly to the gold trade and destroying all subsidiary trades, the Dutch had reduced Padang by the end of the eighteenth century to the condition in which they had found it in the days when it had been thought thousands of *tahil* of gold would flow through the port. It was a small coastal village, lying on the banks of the Padang river, with houses and market-place well inland from the shore to afford protection. The main settlement was on the right bank of the river, separated from the shore by thick groves of coconut and *nipah* palms. Small, scattered Minangkabau houses and gardens then began, until, where the island in the Padang river lies, a quarter of a mile from the shore, a portion of land was reached which the company had been able to acquire from the *panglima raja* in 1685, and where it had built its 'town' and fort. The town in 1781 was described as 'consisting of 22 houses along the river, mostly built of wood with atap roofs, and with a few small gardens. Next to these was the fort.'[113] In that year the 'town' contained 56 European servants of the company and their families, and 31 soldiers from India and Sulawesi. In addition, there were the 'Christian burghers', of whom by 1790 there were 77 adults and 102 children; these 51 families were the generally impoverished descendants of earlier company servants who had retired on the coast, each with their own small house and plot of land.[114]

On the opposite bank were most of the company's official buildings, including pepper warehouses and a hospital. Further upriver from the fort lay the main *pasar* of Padang, where the leading brokers and other local merchants lived. In addition to the twelve *saudagar* (merchants) or *penghulu* through whom the company disposed of its cloth and salt, and whom the gold traders coming down from the mountains would first approach for their necessities, there were also smaller traders living on the *pasar*; they can be classified as itinerant traders, who were the third link in the network joining foreign merchants to the uplands consumer. They often set themselves up as 'agents' for uplands villages. Most came from the Solok region, or from leading Tanah Datar villages, from Lake Singkarak and Batipuh, and were valuable for their skills as gold 'buyers', sorting, selecting, cleaning and valuing the gold as it was brought to market in the lumps and sand with which it had been excavated. They were an integral part of the gold trade. Their aim was to stay in Padang only as long as it took them to make a small competence, after which they would return home with sufficient wealth either to mount a challenge for a *penghulu*-ship in their own village or, if debtors, to repay their debt. There were also gold- and silversmiths living around the *pasar,* mostly from Agam. North of the *pasar* began the main village settlement of Padang, with its nine satellite hamlets; here lived the overwhelming majority of Padang's inhabitants, who were peasants concentrating on provisioning the traders and carriers who came to their village. They were often hard pressed to supply the upland carriers with food if the Dutch ship was late and the latter's food supply ran out.[115]

It was in this depressed condition that Padang and its brokers existed when the first exports of coffee from the uplands began to trickle down to the port. Its sorry state was augmented in 1797, when a severe earthquake destroyed virtually every house and public building.[116] However, one final point needs to be made about the fortunes of Padang and its brokerage class, in order to be able to account for the nationality of the chief brokers at Padang in the early ninteenth century, at the beginning of the coffee trade. Before the Dutch and the English came to Sumatra for pepper, Chinese pepper traders had been visiting west Sumatra from their commercial base at Banten. They frequented both Tiku and Pariaman, bringing with them the highly desired Java salt and specie, and also took part in the coastal stapling trade as far north as Barus. In the 1630s their vessels were reported to be swarming to the coast in search of pepper, and it seems likely that there were Chinese settled at Pariaman to act as agents for their compatriots;

certainly they were reported to be established there in 1663.[117] Very few of these Chinese traded with their own capital, and they had meagre capital resources; they were generally agents for Banten Chinese, who in turn operated a *commenda* trade using money and goods supplied by merchants in China and, later on, by Europeans in Banten.[118]

With the establishment of the Dutch position at Padang, those Chinese with commercial links with the Minangkabau coast experienced the same advantages as did their compatriots on Java, where Dutch policy from the time of the settlement of Batavia was to use the Chinese to extend their trading network. The company had no desire to see the Chinese buy up and trade in those archipelago products over which it wished to exert a monopoly, products such as Minangkabau gold and pepper, but it was keen to encourage Chinese coastal trade and retail trade as a counterpart to its own monopoly wholesaling. Chinese were therefore encouraged in the Minangkabau coastal trade at a time when the Dutch were discouraging Minangkabau participation in this trade in order to break the coast's links with the Acehnese ports further north. It was rare for any other than Chinese traders to get passes to trade to the north, where they specialized in the Nias provision and slave trade, and also in the coconut oil trade. As a result of their usefulness to the Dutch in Batavia, Batavian Chinese were also given passes to keep up the coastal supply trade from Java, although they could not always get permission to bring salt, at a time when Minangkabau coastal traders were finding it difficult to get passes.[119] Right until the end of the company period the vessels of Batavian Chinese were used in provisioning Padang and importing everyday items such as domestic utensils, although their fortunes oscillated with the continuously changing Padang regulations concerning the salt trade and private trade.[120]

Almost immediately after the establishment of the Dutch factory at Padang some Chinese must have settled there as agents for Batavian Chinese, possibly moving south from Pariaman. In 1673 there are reports of a Chinese 'Nakoda Banten' living at Padang in his own house, and other Chinese were also settled there performing services for company officials as they did at Batavia. In that year several Chinese bought land from the *panglima raja* to establish a brickworks, and by 1682 there were so many Chinese at the entrepôt that a Lieutenant Chinese had to be appointed to regulate matters concerning them.[121] One hundred years later there were sufficient Chinese to warrant a Captain Chinese, who lived in the most substantial house in Padang after that of the company's representative, and members of the community operated their own vessels in the Java trade.[122]

Like the Java Chinese, their relationship to the company had gradually become one of closer collaboration, which gave them commercial advantages quite apart from those acquired by their own commercial acumen. The company operated a monopoly lease system, a system of farming out different company monopolies and rights to private individuals, and for these leases the Chinese were nearly always the most successful competitors. The oldest company lease was the right to levy import and export duties on the incoming and outgoing cargo of vessels according to a fixed tariff, a lease introduced at Batavia in 1622 and farmed out to the highest bidder. In the late eighteenth century, with the running down of the company's personnel at Padang, this system was introduced there too. In 1785 the farm for collecting import and export duties at Padang was sold to the Captain Chinese,

Lau Ch'uan-ko. With the decline of the gold trade, it was agreed by the Batavia government in 1790 to accept specie for a certain percentage of the company's cloth sales at Padang, so that the cloth trade would not be totally paralysed by the absence of gold. This too benefited the Padang Chinese, who were the only group at the port with access to specie, and enabled them now to act as brokers in the company's cloth trade, bypassing the Minangkabau brokerage system which relied on exchanging gold for cloth. In the last years of the company much of the cloth trade fell into Chinese hands, foreshadowing the day when the Chinese would accede to importance at the expense of the traditional Minangkabau brokerage class.[123]

The English and the first commercial revival, 1760-1795

There can be little doubt that the decline of the gold trade and of the Tanah Datar-Padang trading network in the latter part of the eighteenth century affected the prosperity of the leading villages of Tanah Datar, of the royal family and of the Padang brokers. But as this old system declined, new opportunities were opening for other parts of the Minangkabau world. It was not only the gold villages of Tanah Datar which had had an ancient relationship with Pariaman. The villages of Agam, particularly those lying on the slopes of Mounts Singgalang and Merapi, had equally strong links to the coast around Pariaman and Ulakan. It was through these ports that the Agam weavers received the raw cotton grown on the Minangkabau coast further south. Agam traders from the weaving villages would themselves hire vessels from these ports to transport the cotton in their own trading ventures.[124] In addition, certain Agam villages specialized in salt-making on the coast at times of the year when agricultural work was light, renting saltpans in the vicinity of Pariaman and Ulakan and often causing distress to the coastal villagers in times of food shortage.[125]

Although the Dutch East India Company largely succeeded in its aim of deflecting the main international trade of Pariaman to Padang, the Pariaman brokers were flexible enough to grasp at whatever new opportunity presented itself to them. The key factor here was that the English East India Company had not completely lost interest in the west coast of Sumatra after being outmanoeuvred by the Dutch, and after its exclusion from the Banten pepper market by superior Dutch strategy in 1682 its interest once again returned to the Minangkabau coast. A group of Pariaman brokers sought to take advantage of this interest, and in 1684 offered a pepper monopoly to the English company in exchange for protection against the Dutch, even travelling as far as Madras to sign a treaty with the English. Unfortunately for them their manoeuvre failed, the English company in the following year choosing to contract with Benkulen for pepper supplies, because of its closeness to a pepper-producing region.[126]

However, a new opportunity now came Pariaman's way. This was the gradual development of the so-called 'private trade' in India, trade carried on mostly by Europeans based in Bengal and Madras, who took advantage of the growth of British dominion in India to undertake trading ventures in pursuit of personal profit. Often the private traders were in the employment of East India Company agents in India and had access to considerable capital to expand their commercial activities. From the 1680s and 1690s the ships of these private traders began coming to the Minangkabau coast in the area of Pariaman and the ports to her north, often not even landing but selling goods to local boats offshore.[127] They were encouraged in their ventures by both the veniality of the Dutch company's servants at Pariaman, who were prepared to trade with the English in their own interest and, after this was put a stop to, by the growing Dutch difficulty in the early eighteenth century in providing adequate naval surveillance of the coast. Gradually the English traders at Pariaman built up contacts with the uplands, particularly Agam, from whence traders began to come down to Pariaman, attracted by the possibilities of obtaining supplies burdened with far lower transport costs than those which had to be brought all the way from Padang. The Acehnese were also able to take part in this trade, and re-establish to some extent their contacts with both Pariaman and Tiku.[128] Matters had gone so far that in 1707 the English East India Company requested permission to build a factory at Pariaman.[129]

Supplying the coast was no problem for these English traders; they had increasing access to the cloth weavers of Coromandel and Bengal. In 1710 they were alleged by the Dutch to have 'filled every place with their cotton goods.'[130] But for the Minangkabau who wished to trade with them, there were problems in finding return cargoes desirable to the English traders. The coast itself still offered small quantities of pepper, mostly coming from the more northerly Pasaman area, but other, more profitable products were also in demand. Pariaman could supply the highly profitable benjamin, a resin derived from a tree which grew in the Batak highlands to the north of the port, but this had to be collected and brought from a considerable distance.[131]

What was found to be close at hand, however, growing spontaneously in the Agam hill districts, was a tree the bark of which when dried, produced a coarse variety of cinnamon known as cassia (*cinnamomum aromaticum*). Real cinnamon (*cinnamomum Zeylanicum*) was in particular a product of Ceylon, which the Dutch had conquered in 1658, later establishing a monopoly over the cultivation of and trade in cinnamon in 1707. This trade brought considerable profits to the Dutch company on the European market, so that the English, both private traders and the company, were always seeking alternative sources of supply.[132] The realization that cassia grew in Agam and could be advantageously acquired at Pariaman as a return cargo led to English encouragement of Agam traders to bring down supplies of cassia to the port. With the acquisition of this profitable cargo English private trade at Pariaman and at ports to the north expanded rapidly in the 1740s, as did Agam's trade with Pariaman, based on cassia exports.[133]

Unfortunately, due to the lack of documentation of the activities of English country traders we have no reliable details of the trade, how it was managed at Pariaman, or to what extent it fluctuated. We do know, however, that not only did English private traders from Bengal and Madras trade at Pariaman, but Chinese and Malay agents of the English East India Company's settlement at Benkulen also did so. At one stage in the 1760s there was a boom in the demand for Minangkabau cassia, officials of the English East India Company becoming aware of its potential for the London market, and in 1763 it was declared a company monopoly, supplies being sought as far south as Kerinci and as far north as Tapanuli. However the London side of the trade never prospered, the quality of the cassia not being good enough to compete with Dutch cinnamon, but the trade itself continued, gradually in the 1770s and 1780s slipping back into the hands of private traders, who could profitably export cassia to both Canton and India.[134]

By the mid-eighteenth century Dutch trade at Pariaman was at a standstill. One of the main reasons for this, already noted in the case of Padang, was the increasing inability of the Dutch to supply Minangkabau with cloth. Moreover, when the Dutch did receive supplies, they were never able to sell them as cheaply as did the English, who by 1750 were even attracting Tanah Datar gold to Pariaman for cheap cloth supplies. More and more private traders swarmed onto the coast; according to the Dutch Resident at Air Bangis in 1766, there were at least 200 English vessels from Madras, Bengal and Bombay on the coast annually, with a greater share of the local trade than the Dutch.[135] The crucial period for English influence on the Minangkabau coast was between 1781 and 1784 when, as a result of war in Europe, officials of the English East India Company took over Padang from the Dutch. As a result the English were able to attract a wider spectrum of Minangkabau traders into their marketing orbit, selling as they did Coromandel cotton cloths far more cheaply than the Dutch and also operating more freely with credit. Once the Dutch returned to Padang when the war in Europe ended, these new customers were not lost to the English, but turned from Padang to the Pariaman area where they were supplied by the regular Pariaman traders, most of whom were from Agam.[136] This of course contributed further to the commercial development of Agam, at the expense of Tanah Datar.

One unfortunate aspect of Agam's burgeoning trade was that it came to be connected with the importation into the Minangkabau world of opium. Opium-smoking had been known in the Malay world from at least the fifteenth century, being prevalent among Malay seamen, and the habit had to some extent spread to the higher levels of society, particularly in the seaport towns. It soon became apparent to the English private traders from Bengal that opium was an ideal outward trading cargo, bringing huge profits and requiring little space, and it soon stood side by side with cloth as the leading item imported by the English onto the Minangkabau coast. Opium was first brought to the Pariaman area by the English in 1701 and progressively increasing amounts were imported during the eighteenth century, leading to the tragedy of addiction in both the coastal ports and, probably for the first time, in the interior. The importation of opium of course promoted trade in Agam: opium-smokers mixed the drug with tobacco, which encouraged tobacco-growing in the uplands. It was often consumed on the *pasar* where it was sold, leading to some *pasar* gaining a bad reputation.[137]

By the late eighteenth century it was estimated that about 150 chests of opium were consumed annually on Sumatra's west coast, though what percentage of this went to the central Minangkabau coast is impossible to estimate. Each chest contained 140 lbs. of opium, prepared in cakes weighing 5 to 6 lbs. each and capable of storage and sale for two years. Opium traders made a considerable profit. The purchase price of a chest at port of entry was 300 Spanish dollars, but once the opium was broken down into smaller lots for sale the wholesale buyer could resell for 500 to 600 Spanish dollars; in times of scarcity far higher prices were reached. The trading network itself was complemented by individuals who specialized in preparing the raw opium for sale, boiling and straining it, then mixing it with shredded tobacco and finally making it up into the small pills about the size of a pea in which form the prepared opium (*madat*) was sold. Given the retail costs, transport costs and preparation costs, not surprisingly opium was extremely expensive and was largely used by the well-to-do; addiction could of course lead to a rapid change in family fortunes if the addict happened to be a lineage head. It seems that lineage heads, too, were the only individuals able to organize the buying of raw opium, the preparation of *madat* and its sale, and the *madat* trade in the uplands became associated with certain *penghulu*.[138]

In the latter part of the eighteenth century Agam's internal trade was further stimulated by Dutch problems in supplying the coast. In the heyday of the Dutch-Tanah Datar alliance Agam must have received much of its imported cloth by way of Tanah Datar gold merchants, who also brought Dutch-imported Javanese salt. Dutch attempts in the earlier part of the eighteenth century to persuade coastal ports and their brokers to prevent uplanders making salt near their villages and importing raw cotton from the south seem to have been fairly successful; although there were difficulties with continual cruising to entrap the English, lightning raids could be made on coastal salt pans or on cotton warehouses to prevent losses on Dutch imports to the interior. With the gradual breakdown of the Dutch supply system, however, more and more coastal villages saw their interests as lying in direct, bilateral trade with the uplands rather than being used as middlemen in the Dutch system. From the 1760s coastal villages in the Pariaman vicinity turned increasingly to the planting of cotton, which they could then sell to Agam weaving villages, allowing, as a Dutch report put it, 'the native weavers to be able to supply a considerable quantity of cloths at moderate prices.'[139] The dearness of Dutch-imported salt also gave a new impetus to salt-making by coastal villages or entrepreneurs from the uplands, the product being transported to the interior and sold. This trend was intensified after the Dutch return to the coast in 1784, when the company was unable to restore its warehouse at Pariaman, leaving that part of the coast totally dependent for supplies of cloth and salt on passing English or Acehnese traders; under such circumstances, cotton-planting and salt-making increased.[140]

Coastal cotton-planting and the Agam weaving industry developed hand in hand, and in fact some of the planters were emigrants from Agam to the coast. The burgeoning of the weaving industry by the late 1780s can be estimated from the Dutch assertion that 32 *pikul* of Surat cotton could be sold to weavers each year were it available. The coastal planters were able to get f.48 per *pikul* for their cotton from Agam and Tanah Datar weavers.[141] The cloths manufactured by Agam weavers were poor in quality, but because they were so cheap there was a considerable demand for them. The stimulation of the weaving industry also stimulated those villages which specialized in dyeing.[142]

Doubtless the rice-growing villages of the Agam plain also benefited from this bilateral trade; cotton-planting must have caused more than the usual rice shortages on the coast, and with the coming of fewer and fewer vessels from Batavia it is likely that Agam fed at least that part of the coast to which it was indebted for cotton. Upland gunsmiths seem also to have been supplying the coast with an increasing number of guns, for which there was a new demand.[143] The salt trade was also brisk by the late 1780s, and was competing with that of Padang. In 1789 the Dutch were not able to sell even 100 *koyan* of salt at Padang, although in earlier and better years 400 to 500 *koyan* had been disposed of; such figures indicate the extent of the coastal salt trade with the uplands.[144]

By the next decade the Dutch counted for little in the Minangkabau coastal commercial world. In 1792 they had shut down their northernmost posts on the Minangkabau coast at Air Bangis and Tiku; small military posts remained at Pariaman, and in the south at Pulau Cingkuk and Air Aji, where little trade was done. The Batavia government decided to retain Padang only to protect Java itself from enemy machinations arising in western Sumatra, and in 1792, to relieve its desperate situation, Padang was opened to free navigation and trade, all foreigners were welcomed provided they paid import and export duties, and the company withdrew from all trade other than that in pepper. The aim was to make Padang pay its way so that it could be maintained for strategic reasons.[145] European events, however, once again affected the Minangkabau world, and in 1795 the port once again fell to representatives of the English company, beginning over twenty years of direct English influence on the Minangkabau.

The English, Penang and the second commercial revival, 1786-1819

The impact of the expansion of English influence from India was felt not only on the western Minangkabau coast, but also in the commercial world of the straits, to which world Minangkabau had long been linked commercially. In 1786 the English East India Company established a port at Penang off the Malay peninsula which, in addition to its naval role, it was hoped would attract some of the trade of the straits and so pay its own way. The location of this port, and the ample supply of Indian and archipelago produce which soon became available here, meant that it became a natural focus for the trading aspirations of the traders of Limapuluh Kota, the easternmost of the four Minangkabau valleys.

Limapuluh Kota seems to have long traded with the east coast by way of routes leading to the headwaters of the Kampar Kanan, and also via the adjacent Siak river. In the late seventeenth century, with the discovery of tin in the area between the upper Kampar Kanan and the Siak, the Minangkabau entrepôt of Patapahan on the Siak, and other entrepôts on the Kampar Kanan, experienced a period of feverish commercial activity, heightened by competition between the Dutch and officials of the Johor state for access to the tin.[146] What the part of the Limapuluh Kota traders was in this trade we do not know; the valley was famous for its rush matting and for forest produce such as *damar* (resin used for lighting), and some Payakumbuh traders seem to have hoped they could obtain sufficient supplies of Tanah Datar gold to enter the new trading network. The chief *pangkalan* of Limapuluh Kota, *pangkalan* Kota Baru, certainly experienced a period of expansion as a result of association with the tin villages.[147] However, trade was presumably on a relatively small scale and, with the decline of both the Dutch and Johor in the straits in the eighteenth century, Limapuluh Kota's trade, lacking commercial partners, must have been meagre. The appearance of the English in the straits as a result of English development of the China trade altered the situation and, even before the founding of Penang, Limapuluh Kota traders were renewing their contacts with the east coast in an effort to gain the supplies of salt and cloth of which they had been deprived by Dutch problems at Padang. Trade was particularly active in the months of January and February, when the English ships passed through the straits.[148]

With the founding of Penang those Minangkabau traders who wished to trade with the English and others in the straits now had a permanent entrepôt available to them where, in particular, the much desired Coromandel cloth could be acquired. The English at Penang sold cloth for as little as five per cent profit in order to attract trade, whilst the Dutch commercial system at Padang required a profit of at least fifty-nine per cent on quite ordinary cloths.[149] The traders of Limapuluh Kota also found that they had the wherewithal to trade with Penang, for they produced a crop for which there was demand in eastern trade similar to that for the cassia of Agam. This was gambir, for the cultivation of which the soil of the hilly parts of Limapuluh Kota was exceptionally well suited. Gambir was desired in archipelago trade because it was in such universal use as a component of *sirih*-chewing, for cleansing and cleaning the mouth, and in addition it was used in the tanning of leather, the gambir of Limapuluh Kota being far more highly regarded than that of its only other competitor, Riau, because of its high tannin content.[150]

The cultivation and preparation of gambir for the export trade had different social results in Limapuluh Kota to that produced by cassia in Agam. Cassia was a product of the hills only and, at the beginning of the trade at least, required little labour; the trees grew wild and only required to be felled, the bark pared off and dried in the sun for several days before entering into trade.[151] Cultivation and replanting was not an issue in Agam hill villages for some time. With gambir, however, much more work was required to maintain regular cultivation, whilst the preparation of gambir for export demanded some capital equipment and some degree of organization. For this reason, despite the fact that the plant was only grown in certain hilly areas, several plains centres became associated with the preparation of gambir for export, and the hill peasants who grew it were often dependent on members of the richest lineages in leading villages such as Payakumbuh for the necessary equipment to make the gambir marketable. Because of this a wide range of villages and groups in the valley came to have an interest in the trade, including the plains *penghulu.* By 1835 it was reported that the buying up of gambir for export had become a monopoly of the leading *penghulu* of Payakumbuh.[152]

Gambir preparation required both the organization of manpower and the provision of equipment. After cutting off the branches of the gambir plant, the leaves were removed and hacked very fine, boiled in water, evaporated and then poured into thin tubes of bamboo which were left to cool. Once cooled, the tubes were split and the hardened gambir cut into small slices and then dried, the finished product looking like biscuits or large coins. It was estimated that three men could make 3,000 to 4,000 of these slices in three days, gambir being sold not by weight but by the number of slices;[153] in 1824, 10,000 pieces were selling for five Spanish dollars at Padang.[154] Such a process required, in addition to the workers, a shed made of bamboo and covered with *alang-alang* grass, an extremely large iron pot for boiling about 50 lbs. of leaves, and the requisite supply of bamboo tubes. With time, particularly in large centres such as Payakumbuh, equipment became more efficient though also more expensive, but the work never became less labour-intensive, and the basic 'team' for preparing gambir remained fixed at three workers. New features were the introduction of a wooden press to remove water from the boiled leaves more efficiently – a large piece of equipment operating by means of beams and a wooden hammer – and of a more complicated drying-rack procedure to dry out the gambir before and after it was shaped in the bamboo tubes.[155]

We know virtually nothing of the respective capital contribution and distribution of profits between the gambir growers, the workers in the preparation teams, the lineage heads in the main villages, and the gambir traders. Transport costs must certainly have been heavy, but not heavy enough to discourage the grower. The Limapuluh Kota merchant himself seems unlikely to have gone beyond the riverine entrepôts of Kota Baru and Patapahan, the latter in particular developing into the leading transit point for goods coming into various parts of Minangkabau from Penang. However, because gambir was a low-value, high-bulk commodity when compared with gold, and because such large amounts of cloth and salt were being transhipped to Patapahan, considerable numbers of individuals in Limapuluh Kota must have been earning their livelihood merely by operating on this particular sector of the trade route, as Dutch evidence concerning the opening up and improvement of paths in the area between Sarilamak and *pangkalan* Kota Baru testifies.[156] Traders on each stage of the network must have operated on very small profit margins, because Coromandel cloths from Penang could still be sold throughout central Minangkabau cheaper than those bought from the Dutch at Padang, only a few days' journey away.[157] In 1789, with the appearance of these Coromandel cloths for sale on the shores of Lake Singkarak, long within Padang's orbit, the Dutch *opperhoofd* of Padang noted in desperation: 'One can truthfully say that half of this island, from the tip of Atchien right down to Palembang, and as far inland as the centre, has been drawn to trade in Pulo Pinang, and that it supplies all nearby small trading places on this coast such as Jambij, Patapahan, Indragoerij, Siak, Benkalis, so that people are not only drawn away from here but also they return and import goods even on to the west coast.'[158]

After Patapahan the trade passed out of the hands of Minangkabau from the central valleys and into those of what can quite properly be called the Minangkabau trading diaspora. Minangkabau had for centuries been migrating down the Siak river, and were settled at intermediary points along the river, and also along the east coast as far north as Batu Bara and Asahan, where they earned their livelihood by engaging in the intermediate trade. They connected the straits entrepôt of Penang with the internal supply and consumption markets of Minangkabau, river markets having arisen due to the need to break up bulk cargoes at various stages of the voyage up and downstream. After Patapahan, the next main bulk-breaking centre on the Siak was Pakan Baru and, after this, the capital of the Siak sultanate, Siak Sri Inderapura, about eighty miles from the mouth of the river. Pakan Baru in particular had by 1823 developed into 'the principal mart of the country'[159] because vessels of considerable burden could ascend to this point. Ships loaded at Pakan Baru could carry 30 to 50 *koyan,* so that the cargoes of small *perahu* were assembled here for the outward journey and, conversely, on the return journey here they were broken down into smaller lots for the upriver trip in the smallest *perahu.*

The journeys varied in time, because the outward journey was always much faster than the return journey.[160]

By the time Siak Sri Inderapura was reached, much of the trade on the river between Pakan Baru and the coast was in the hands of traders of a variety of origins, including the sultan and the ruling class of the Siak sultanate, and various Arab traders and their descendants who had settled at the capital. By 1823 the Arabs had become particularly successful in the cross-straits trade: 'The Arabs own many large tops; and there is a small brig or two owned by some of them.'[161] One such vessel could hold a cargo worth anything up to 20,000 Spanish dollars, and the huge variety of goods imported up the Siak has been recorded.[162] Four hundred *perahu* belonged at home in Siak Sri Inderapura alone; they were encouraged by the sultan, who not only built his own vessels but also raised duties on imports and exports passing along the river, and on the basis of this transit trade the sultan and nobility of Siak had by 1823 acquired considerable wealth.[163]

For negotiating the straits and carrying the exports to Penang yet another group of intermediate traders entered the trading network. These were the Minangkabau coastal settlers of Batu Bara, to the north of Siak, the descendants of Minangkabau who some centuries earlier had migrated to the coast and lived by engaging in cross-straits trade. They were highly regarded in Penang, and by 1823 there were no less than 600 Batu Bara *perahu* engaged in cross-straits commerce, some being owned by wealthy individuals with several *perahu* at their disposal.[164] Of course, not all these *perahu* were engaged in the Minangkabau gambir trade via the Siak; but the earliest port statistics from Penang show that not only did the Batu Bara *perahu* initially take the lead in coming to Penang from the east coast, but that those which came from Siak brought with them gambir as their main cargo.[165] The first *perahu* from Siak is recorded on 7 July 1787, with a cargo of gambir,[166] and these gambir *perahu* from Siak continue to be reported into the 1790s, as long as full port statistics continued to be compiled.[167] In addition, the first *perahu* recorded as having come from Padang, on 10 September 1789, also carried gambir as their chief cargo.[168] A further effect of the gambir trade was to induce numerous ships from other parts of the archipelago, attracted to the straits by the Penang trade, to come themselves to the mouth of the Siak. In the 1790s and early 1800s thirty to forty large Bugis *perahu* visited the Siak every year, importing salt, raw silk, cloth and other items in an immense boost to trade; ships from Java, Borneo and Coromandel also came.[169]

We know very little about the mechanics of this Malay trade, and next to nothing about its financing. What is of most concern to us here, in any case, is the impact of the gambir trade on Limapuluh Kota. It does seem that the differences between prices at Penang and in the Minangkabau interior were sufficient to ensure small profit margins for each of the groups of intermediate traders through whose hands the goods passed, whilst not causing these items to be too exorbitantly priced for the consumer, and all accounts bear witness to a strong consumer demand in Limapuluh Kota; the good quality of the general population's clothing there is often remarked on by the earliest travellers, as is the prosperity and good order of Payakumbuh, where all roads in Limapuluh Kota seemed to meet and trade was as much a way of life as agriculture.[170] Nevertheless, as at Padang, most of this trading network was financed by the strongest thread in the net, the European exporter/importer of Penang, most of whom were private traders from India. The majority of the Batu Bara *perahu* owners, particularly the well-to-do ones, seem to have operated on credit from these European merchants, or their Chinese agents, who were authorized to advance them cargoes or Spanish dollars for the return journey across the straits.[171] It is remarkable that we have no examples of large-scale Minangkabau merchants. No Minangkabau trader seems to have been prepared to expose himself to large losses; all preferred to act on a small scale in a small commercial venture, and rested content with the concomitant small profits.

The gambir trade to Penang appears to have continued until the founding of Singapore, although there is little information for the early years of the nineteenth century apart from a recorded decline in the period between 1808 and 1817, due partly to internal troubles in Siak.[172] Thereafter the trade revived, though much of it was channelled towards Singapore; in 1833 it was estimated that 15,000 *pikul* of gambir was exported to that port annually from Limapuluh Kota via the east coast rivers.[173]

The Americans and the rise of the Minangkabau coffee trade, 1790-1829

The apogée of the Minangkabau commercial revival was reached with foreign demand for another crop which, like cassia, simply grew spontaneously in Minangkabau. This was *Arabica* coffee, which had been introduced into the highlands either by Mecca pilgrims or by Dutchmen interested in the Java coffee experiments, presumably in the seventeenth century. In 1789 coffee was already recorded as available on the market at Padang, probably as an item of internal trade.[174] Although we do not know from what areas the first coffee exports came, some coffee was cultivated by villagers in the coastal foothills, and it was probably they who initiated the trade; however, it was in the hill villages of the highlands that coffee did best, and there is no doubt that these villages very soon entered the trade, making use of the old route from Agam down to Pariaman, the coffee then being sent further south to Padang by sea.[175]

Coffee, together with tea, gradually became an important item of world trade during the course of the eighteenth century due to rising European demand, and the Dutch on Java were quick to adapt to this trade, until Java coffee became one of the most profitable commodities in the Dutch company's commerce. The Dutch, whose policy was one of monopoly, limited supplies and high prices, were not without rivals. By the 1780s two-thirds of the world's supply of coffee was produced in the Caribbean colony of St. Domingue; the 1791 slave uprising in this colony led to a virtual cessation of production, giving far greater importance to Java as a producer.[176] Other contemporary international developments now conspired to give prominence to Minangkabau coffee, and to produce for the Minangkabau a new trading partner. By 1783 the independence of the American colonies had become a reality and Americans who had become rich from speculation and profiteering during the revolutionary wars saw the desirability and possibility of financing voyages to the east to get from their countries of origin items which had previously been imported into America by way of Britain. The first ship flying the

United States flag called at Aceh Head in Sumatra on a voyage to India in 1784, and as early as 1788 it was reported that merchants of Salem, Massachussetts, were looking for coffee supplies in the east. The outbreak of the French revolutionary and Napoleonic wars in Europe gave great impetus to American trade, particularly as the Netherlands' links with her colonies were cut for a time, and high prices were paid on the European market for coffee brought by neutral shipping.[177]

In 1788 the first American ship arrived at Padang and acquired a cargo of cassia; thereafter the Americans joined the English private traders in carrying this item right up to the 1820s.[178] Even after coffee had overtaken it, cassia remained the second main agricultural export of the western part of Minangkabau throughout the 1820s and certainly brought advantages to those relatively limited areas which produced it.[179] The Americans were also interested in Minangkabau indigo, and cargoes of this too were taken from Padang.[180] However, interest in these items was very soon surpassed by that in coffee, and in 1790 the first American cargo of coffee was shipped from Padang. Hereafter eight to ten American ships called at Padang every year, although in the period of English control of the port, between 1795 and 1819, they generally came rather to the Pariaman-Ulakan area so as not to break regulations concerning American trade with British Indian ports.[181]

Unfortunately we have no way of estimating coffee exports or prices for this period, Padang port statistics for the duration of English rule being non-existent. However, they were doubtless considerable. Using the records of Salem vessels alone it can be seen that individual ships often acquired large cargoes; one vessel in 1803 returned with 10,460 lbs. of coffee, and another in the same year with the huge cargo of 425,000 lbs.[182] In addition English private traders, who included East India Company servants at Padang, began to compete for coffee deliveries, and between 1798 and 1801 the English company's resident at Padang made the first recorded English export of coffee from the hills north-east of Padang; in 1800 alone he exported 4,000 *pikul* on his own account.[183]

Although there is some scant information about prices paid at the point of export and about quantities exported, we know very little of the amounts actually paid to the planter and the profits acquired by the large number of middlemen who were called into being to cope with this new, high bulk trade. Before trying to look at this question, however, the general statistics concerning the coffee trade should be reviewed, using both Padang prices and Padang export figures but remembering that much coffee was exported from ports north of Pariaman and via the east coast rivers. About 1800 the buying price for a *pikul* of coffee at Padang was f.7, and in the early 1800s the price was stable at between f.6 and f.7 per *pikul*; thereafter it rose to f.10 and subsequently to f.20 per *pikul,* until by 1820-22 the price was as high as f.30 and f.40.[184] The high prices in the second decade of the nineteenth century were the result of a European and American descent on the archipelago at the end of the Napoleonic wars in a 'coffee mania' which pushed prices to unprecedented heights. An American ship's captain writing from Batavia in 1818 referred to his fellow countrymen as 'coffee mad; no price is too great for them.'[185]

By the time the Dutch returned to Padang in 1819 as part of the postwar settlement, coffee stood at f.40 per *pikul.* A Dutch merchant sent from Batavia to investigate the trade reported that Americans at Padang were paying enormous prices for cargoes, transporting as much as 3,000 *pikul* on one single ship. The amount exported annually was now 20,000 *pikul,* compared with 5,000 *pikul* a few years previously.[186] In response to the demand, Minangkabau in both the highlands and the foothills were turning over more and more areas to coffee wherever conditions were suitable and, in the race to export, were plucking beans before they were ripe, aware that the American buyers were prepared to buy even wet beans.[187] Dutch representatives at Padang were now, and for some years, encouraged by Batavia to keep the port open to foreign traders, and coffee exports remained buoyant, rising from 16,000 *pikul* in 1821 to 33,000 *pikul* in 1825 and 49,000 *pikul* in 1826.[188] American ships came regularly to take the coffee to Antwerp, and English ships from India also continued to come. By 1827, however, the peak had been reached. Fewer English ships began coming from about 1825, and by 1828 fewer Americans than usual were visiting Padang.[189] In July 1829 it was reported that, since the start of 1828, not a single *pikul* of coffee had been exported by Americans, although several had visited Padang for the purpose.[190] By 1830 only three American ships visited Padang in the entire year.[191] There were at least two reasons for the decline in the Padang coffee trade. One was the low price of coffee on the European market from 1827, which persisted for a number of years. The other was the gradual Dutch retreat from a fairly open system at Padang to one of discriminatory duties on foreign shipping, which bore hardest on American and English ships.[192]

It must of course be noted that the decline of the Minangkabau coffee trade via Padang does not necessarily mean an absolute decline in the coffee trade itself, and here it is very difficult to draw conclusions. Certainly the coffee growers and traders of Agam and Limapuluh Kota were able to find outlets for their coffee outside the network of Dutch regulations and duties, Agam using ports north of Pariaman and Limapuluh Kota the east coast rivers linking that area, after 1819, with the new entrepôt of Singapore.[193] Dutch investigations in 1830 led to the conclusion that coffee production was still expanding and that large stocks were on the market, destined for outlets where there was no Dutch supervision of trade.[194] The previous year a Singapore source claimed that about 1,000 *pikul* of Limapuluh Kota coffee came to that port every month by way of the Kampar river.[195]

Three aspects of the coffee trade now deserve to be looked at more closely. The first is the role the two main west coast exporting points, Padang and Pariaman, played in the trade, and here an attempt should be made to elucidate why a class of important Minangkabau brokers did not develop to service this trade. The second is the part played by the east coast riverine bulking stations in the trade, and the role of Minangkabau merchants in this sector. The third is the impact of coffee-growing on the Minangkabau highlands themselves, and, in particular, on the balance of forces inside the villages which were able to move into coffee production.

The development of Padang, so important to the future of Minangkabau, requires the greatest amount of comment. Practically destroyed by an earthquake at the end of the eighteenth century, there was little in the next few decades to distinguish it from any other village along the coast, apart from the European and Chinese element in its population. Even as late as the mid-1830s its appearance was ramshackle. By then it had developed into a settlement of about 2,000 houses, of which barely one hundred – belonging to the Netherlands Indies government or to English and Chinese merchants – were brick. About four hundred were of wood, and the remainder of bamboo; standing high off the ground, on pillars of coconut palm trunks, with their long, overhanging roofs of palm leaves or *alang-alang* grass, they presented a wretched appearance.[196] The port served virtually no function for the surrounding area, but operated merely as an outlet for the highlands and to supply them with imports.[197] Population figures are unreliable; an estimate of 1825 put the population at 13,441, and one of 1835 at between 11,000 and 12,000.[198] The 1825 estimate indicates to what extent foreigners had been attracted to the port by the prospects offered by the coffee trade. Padang contained 10,816 'Malays', among whom were included both Minangkabau and the descendants of those brought from west coast islands such as Nias to work as slaves; in addition, 770 individuals were still recorded as slaves. There were 419 Europeans, very few of whom were Dutch official or military personnel, representing rather settled families with 154 women and 116 children in the total. Many Chinese, too, were established settlers; they were 1,422 in number, including 436 women and 548 children.[199]

The structure of trade at Padang had changed in terms of personnel from the days of the VOC, but not in terms of the basic links in the network. In the period of Padang's occupation by the English from 1795 to 1819, the Dutch company as merchant importer/exporter had been replaced by the English private trader, who now took advantage of the Benkulen administration's lack of interest in Padang to settle there and expand his trading opportunities, either in the coastal supply trade between Natal, Padang and Benkulen and in the north Java salt trade, or by functioning as west coast agent for firms in British India.[200] These private traders were disparaged by the first Dutch resident of Padang in 1819: '. . . all these individuals call themselves merchants, though they largely consist of former masters or mates of merchant vessels who, to avoid their creditors in India, remain here, out of reach of English law.'[201]

In fact the individuals who set up English agency houses at Padang were largely men who had been in the employ of the East India Company at Benkulen, and their activities at Padang were a direct outgrowth of the flourishing private trade carried on by company servants in the north from the 1760s, which was partly financed by the establishment of the Benkulen Bank in 1760 with an initial capital of 40,000 Spanish dollars. This expansion was in turn a result of the 1767 prohibition of company servants' participation in the inland trade of Bengal, which led to a great increase in the so-called country trade and the development of the system of agency houses, financed almost wholly by the capital of the company's servants and run by ex-servants of the company enjoying their successors' confidence and drawing on their savings.[202] In the period of the English interregnum at Padang it is impossible to be sure of the relative position of company servants and private traders in the commerce of the port, although it seems that for some time the port was run as a private concern by the resident Giles Holloway, who between 1798 and 1801 moved into coffee-exporting after a long career in private trade.[203]

In 1829 a survey was made of the English agency houses at Padang. By this time there were three, and in addition there was operating one private Dutch agency house, that of A.F. van den Berg and Co., founded by a man who had come to Padang as a government official after 1819 and had been discharged. All these houses, including A.F. van den Berg, were agents for commercial firms established in Bengal and they worked with Bengal capital, although they conducted business with other parts of India, especially Coromandel and Bombay, and even with Europe. The English agency houses were Townsend and Ingram, W. Purvis and Charles Hay, and all had expanded to Padang after successful commercial ventures at Moko Moko, an important Benkulen out-settlement which flourished as a centre for private trade in the late eighteenth century. Both Townsend and Ingram and A.F. van den Berg had one brig each, which they used in trade with the Coromandel coast, but the only really 'well-to-do' operator of an agency house at Padang was Purvis of W. Purvis. Purvis began with an establishment in the south, at Inderapura, and was then harbour-master of Padang under the English administration; he had a brig engaged in the Coromandel trade, several small vessels occupied in the coastal trade, and seven *perahu* with which he was able to monopolize the loading and unloading of ships in the Padang river and which he rented to Dutch officials.[204]

These firms specialized in the Coromandel trade, particularly in importing Coromandel cotton piece-goods, continuing the old trade of the coast from Acehnese and VOC days, coarse, unbleached Coromandel cloths still being in great demand among the Minangkabau. They also imported opium, a now well-established article of commerce of the English private trader.[205] Bombay cotton piece-goods gradually also became significant, and demand for them increased due to the prosperity of the interior. In addition, attesting the continued strength of the highlands weaving industry, raw cotton was imported from Bombay; the demand was placed at 1,700 *pikul* p.a. in the period 1820-27, although in 1828 4,400 *pikul* was imported.[206] However, because of the way the commercial system had developed at Padang since the American involvement in the coffee trade, the agency houses had difficulty in getting return cargoes which would be profitable in India, and largely took instead silver dollars, imported by the Americans to pay for the coffee, gold when they could get it, and cassia.[207]

The agency houses also continued the old VOC commercial system by operating through the Padang brokerage class. The institution of a *panglima* and twelve *penghulu* was retained by the English and reconfirmed by the Dutch when they returned to Padang, although now of course there was virtually no Dutch trade at the port and, as far as the Dutch government was concerned, the brokers were rather paid local officials settling local disputes and maintaining law and order, however unsuccessfully. In fact, it was discovered soon after the Dutch return that they had organized a system of taxing trade, independent of the Netherlands Indies government's own import and export duties; they collected taxes on items sold at the *pasar,* from Minangkabau vessels bringing goods up the river, on local ricefields and on business transacted with the *panglima.*[208] In terms of operating as brokers they seem to have been replaced by other Minangkabau traders who had acquired a reputation for reliability at the port and who represented specific uplands villages with trading interests at Padang; they were described in reports simply as Padang's *saudagar* (merchants). Both groups lived on the main *pasar* together with small, transitory traders.[209]

As far as their own trading capital was concerned, both classes of Minangkabau brokers remained poor, living in 1824 in 'a collection of decrepit, cheek-by-jowl houses, most of them raised on rocks, with very tiny window frames, or rather air-holes, which would be more suited for jail-houses than for the dwellings of free men.'[210] Ten years later these conditions had not altered, and the 'two rows of dark, dirty-looking houses'[211] of the leading Minangkabau merchants on the Padang *pasar*, where they both lived and operated their business, were still thought worthy of notice. They traded on capital advanced to them by the Padang agency houses at a twelve per cent rate of compound interest, and some individuals were entrusted with up to f.100,000 worth of credit.[212] Their part in commercial operations was described more fully in 1829:

The [European] merchants are never in immediate contact with the main body of consumers, who live in the interior. All sales take place by way of the second hand, or at least using intermediaries, especially by means of the Soedagers, who call themselves the bridge over which all goods pass. The inhabitants of the interior come to them with their products, which they buy or at least see that they are sold; in return the Soedager provides the bringer of the products with what he needs, either from his own supply or by acquiring the necessities from others . . . The profits which the Soedagers take are so moderate that they cannot put much aside. The majority have only a small amount of wealth or none at all, and none of them can be called rich. The only security the European agents have from them is good faith. They pay according as they sell. This can sometimes be a very slow process if it is a question of goods for which they can find no customers, as they do not feel responsible for the advance until they have resold the goods, but with not too much exertion the debts are easily recovered. This cannot be said of the other native traders. It is dangerous to give them credit.[213]

Whatever had been the case under the English administration, in the 1820s this agency house-broker operated trading network was very fragile. In the early 1820s we hear of one agency house, that of John Kemp, agent for Guyon Mackintosh of Madras, breaking up, and by 1829 it was reported that Townsend and Ingram and W. Purvis were on the point of winding up their affairs, whilst A.F. van den Berg and Co., which appeared to be doing good business with Coromandel, Bengal and Europe, was not making the profits desired and van den Berg was planning to move into the commercial cultivation of sugar and indigo near Padang. There were, of course, some replacements; in 1833 one of the chief European merchants of Padang, Boyle, was an Englishman, but in general, despite the increasing trade of the port of Padang in the early 1820s, the English agency houses did not share in it, having no markets for coffee and being gradually disadvantaged by Dutch commercial policy in relation to the items in which they had built up their trade.[214] This was particularly true with regard to the importation of Java salt, in which English agency houses at Padang had had a flourishing trade from about 1811, and the importation of Bengal opium. The reintroduction of the salt monopoly on behalf of the Netherlands Indies government damaged the salt trade, at least as far as Padang was concerned, although Dutch salt prices were so high that private traders continued to run in Siamese salt at other ports. Imports of opium declined from about 1823 because the Dutch abolished the bonded warehouse system which had been established at Padang under the English administration. This had enabled goods to be stapled there for a certain period without paying full import duty and had thus encouraged the stapling of opium at Padang, which attracted a variety of traders, including the Bugis, to the port.[215]

The other trading network which had been established at Padang from the late eighteenth century was that involving the Minangkabau coffee grower, the Padang Chinese broker and the American buyer. How the Chinese came to specialize as brokers in the coffee trade is not known due to the absence of records for the English interregnum; certainly they seem only to have gained their position in the trade gradually. It has already been noted that Padang Chinese were operating the Dutch monopoly lease system in the 1790s. Under the English a system of farming or licensing the sale of a particular item to a private individual was the norm; opium was the leading such item, and the privilege of its sale was farmed to certain Chinese on payment of a fixed sum. The Dutch continued this system from 1820; the exclusive sale of opium was by far the most profitable farm, and this was leased to Padang Chinese, as were the farms for the sale of *arak,* the collection of the duty on imported tobacco and the collection of a cattle-slaughtering tax. In 1824 the exclusive sale of opium was farmed for a monthly amount of f.14,824, whilst the lessee of the *arak* farm had the right to sell *arak* for f.1 per bottle, producing f.6,600 p.a. for the Dutch in 1823.[216]

All this indicates that the Padang Chinese, unlike the Minangkabau brokers, were men of some capital; they were described in 1824 as 'reasonably well-to-do people',[217] living in houses far superior to those of the rest of the population in the Chinese quarter on the site of the old Dutch fort, and specializing in branches of trade in which they had an advantage. They imported Chinese goods such as cloth and porcelain for domestic use from Batavia, Penang and later Singapore and, in particular, raw silk, for which there was an increasing demand in the interior; with growing prosperity the uplands weaving industry seems to have burgeoned rapidly, and in the early 1820s sometimes sixty chests of silk were sold each year.[218] Their exports included wax and birds' nests, much desired in China. Members of the community were also involved in producing lime from coral and shells in the bays near Padang.[219]

With their increasingly flourishing trade, their contacts with Chinese merchants in the newly burgeoning Chinese ports of Penang and Singapore as well as Batavia, and their old connections with the European commercial establishment, members of the Padang Chinese community not surprisingly emerged as the port's leading brokers. With the arrival of the American coffee buyers they quickly perceived the role they could play as intermediate traders, buying up the crop for which the American ship's captains had come and delivering it to them in the condition they desired. Since the Americans had little to offer for the coffee apart from the famous Spanish milled or silver dollar, in the Chinese they were able to find customers willing to accept this coin, which was then used to lubricate Chinese trade elsewhere, particularly with Penang. Silver dollars in such huge amounts were not acceptable in the Minangkabau uplands, where copper coins were still preferred. The greater part of the dollars returned to European trade, being taken by the English agency houses in payment for their Bombay and Coromandel cloth, which the Chinese also bought to re-sell to uplands traders.[220] Between 1826 and 1829 only 2,176 *pikul* of coffee was sent by these houses to India, while f.472,165 worth of silver was exported, almost the full sum of the f.476,318 imported by Americans in the same period.[221]

The four leading Chinese brokers in Padang in 1829, just as the American coffee boom was passing, were Li Heng, Li Ma-ch'iao, Li Sing and Hu A-chiao. Unlike the Minangkabau brokers they were

> well-to-do individuals. Until now they have specialized in the buying up of coffee for cash and selling it again to the Americans, by which they have earned a lot of money. For this purpose they used to place buyers on roads which the inhabitants of the coffee districts had to use to get to the coast. On arriving at these points they would sell their coffee for silver money, and what slipped from their grasp by this method was acquired by their buyers at the passer [i.e. of Padang] itself.[222]

Most of the coffee came down to Padang not by way of the Lake Singkarak route, but from Agam via the Anai gorge and thence to Pariaman. Pariaman therefore also became important to the Padang Chinese brokers. With their commercial expansion they were able to resume their old role of coastal traders, travelling north in their own *perahu* to collect coffee, which in any case was delivered to the Americans outside Padang in the English period.[223] By 1825 Pariaman had a population of twenty-five Chinese, and these specialized in buying up that two-thirds of Padang's coffee exports which actually originated in Agam, and transhipping the cargoes. By 1833 their number had grown to sixty, and they had also moved into another important branch of the coffee trade, that of drying and preparing the beans for sale, the upland planter finding such processing not always worth the trouble.[224]

With the disappearance of the Americans from the Padang coffee trade about 1829 the Chinese suffered severely, and the lack of silver affected the trade of the port in general. However, they were resilient enough to turn to another branch of commerce, and entered into competition with the Minangkabau brokers to buy up Indian cloth and cotton imports from the European agency houses. For this purpose they also entered the gold trade, which was now of course open to private traders, and bought up gold both to finance their cloth trade and to send it to Penang and Singapore, where gold prices were high.[225] By 1829 it was noted that, although they had started with the initial disadvantage of having no direct contacts among Minangkabau highland traders, and were therefore unable to sell direct to them, European agency houses were willing to accept lower Chinese prices because they were far more punctilious about payment than were the Minangkabau brokers and, operating as they did under a system of joint liability, offered more security for bad debts.[226]

It was at this point that the Nederlandsche Handel-Maatschappij entered the scene as the official Dutch government-sponsored trading corporation, and gave new life to the commercial activities of the Padang Chinese. An 1829 survey of the NHM's Padang activities noted that it was vital that Chinese cooperation be sought, and the old Dutch system of selling to Minangkabau brokers with no capital and no security be abandoned.[227] It is, of course, unlikely that the Chinese brokers themselves had substantial amounts of working capital, but the services they performed were such that it was felt credit could be safely advanced to them and they would perform reliably the service of buying up, often in small quantities, whatever crops were needed by the European exporter, whose business interests did not make it worth his while to come into direct contact with the producer.

Padang remained the centre of foreign trade on the coast, although Pariaman regained a little of the position it had held in the seventeenth century. Its participation in the cassia trade with English private traders in the late eighteenth century doubtless had some impact on it as an entrepôt, and though it was described in 1824 as 'a town or leading negorij of little importance'[228] its reflorescence had undoubtedly begun, because by 1831 a Dutch officer, with considerable familiarity with the place, noted it was 'an important Kampong, due to its trade and its considerable extent . . .'[229] Its 1825 population of 1,662 Minangkabau, 25 Chinese, 6 European military personnel and 72 slaves[230] had also considerably increased by 1831. The reason was the role of Pariaman in the coffee trade, coffee coming down particularly from the area between Mounts Singgalang and Merapi by way of Pakandangan, the subsequent sea journey from the port to Padang taking five hours. The *pasar* of Pariaman gradually expanded and was brought into the centre of the settlement, with fifty permanent booths for traders being set up. Large coffee warehouses were erected and the Chinese population grew rapidly, diversifying from coffee into growing sugar and distilling *arak.* There were also Minangkabau traders in Pariaman, some quite prosperous, and all apparently either *penghulu* or connected with *penghulu* lineages. By the mid-1830s there were also Arab traders at the port, living in the type of wooden houses favoured by the Chinese and distinguished from the bamboo houses on piles of the rest of the population. Itinerant Arab traders had long been a feature of the Padang commercial scene; one, Syekh Ahmad, was settled at Padang for a number of years prior to 1822 and had commercial relations with the uplands.[231]

The other major Minangkabau coastal entrepôt, Tiku, did not share in the commercial expansion of Padang and Pariaman. In 1825 its population was a mere 126; midway between the reviving Pariaman and those more northerly Minangkabau ports which were flourishing outside the Dutch orbit, it became depopulated. Its weekly market fell into decline, and was only re-established in 1833 by a Dutch official from Pariaman, who found that even so only a few hundred people were attracted to this location.[232]

The role of the riverine ports of the east coast in the Minangkabau coffee trade is somewhat analogous to that of the west coast entrepôts, although these ports had more the character of bulking stations for the handling of staples than of entrepôts, and the traders operating through them had more the character of intermediate traders than of brokers. The true brokerage class in the east coast coffee trade was found in Singapore and was entirely Chinese. *Pangkalan,* it has already been noticed, flourished on the headwaters of the main navigable east coast rivers wherever there was a demand in the outside world for Minangkabau products; the rise of *pangkalan* Kota Baru on the upper Kampar Kanan in connection with the Limapuluh Kota gambir trade has been discussed. With the rapid expansion of coffee-growing in the early decades of the nineteenth century and the founding of Singapore in 1819, the Kampar Kanan in particular became the river by which most of Limapuluh Kota's coffee was shipped to the new entrepôt, and flourishing settlements expanded on its banks to act as bulking stations.[233] Three other *pangkalan* of importance flourished on the upper tributaries of rivers which ultimately flowed together to form the Kampar Kiri: *pangkalan* Kapas, *pangkalan* Sarai and *pangkalan* Indarung. All represented bulking stations which had been in use at least as early as the seventeenth century, at the time when Johor was encouraging trade on the Kampar, and probably long before.[234]

The Kampar Kanan and Kampar Kiri flow together to form the river Kampar, emerging into the straits and, despite a difficult bore, ideally situated for trade with Singapore. Trade along the Kampar, like that along the Siak, remained in the hands of Minangkabau intermediate traders down to the final bulking station nearest the Kampar mouth, Palalawan, where it then passed into the hands of cross-straits traders, a mixed group of 'coast Malays'. The headwaters *pangkalan* developed to serve different parts of the Minangkabau interior and represented independent Minangkabau riverine settlements established there centuries earlier by emigrants from the Minangkabau world. All were approached on foot through a broad band of nearly trackless jungle, *pangkalan* Kota Baru being at the junction of two separate paths from Mungkar and Sarilamak in Limapuluh Kota; *pangkalan* Kapas was the nearest bulking station on the route from Taram, servicing the eastern part of the valley of Limapuluh Kota, whilst *pangkalan* Sarai was reached by three different paths from Halaban, and *pangkalan* Indarung by a path from Menganti in the Sumpur valley. The river Inderagiri also retained some of its old position as an exit route for Minangkabau products, Menganti still being connected by path to Siluka on the upper Inderagiri. Of the five bulking stations *pangkalan* Kota Baru, servicing the northern Limapuluh Kota, and *pangkalan* Sarai, servicing Halaban and the adjacent Lintau area and also the upper Sumpur valley, all extensive coffee-producing regions, were the most important, although neither was particularly large in terms of its own population; Kota Baru in 1834 had only fifty houses.[235]

The commercial system operating on these rivers was similar to that described for the Siak; since distances were long and the time involved in carrying goods there and back to Singapore commensurate, the intermediate traders working these routes must have operated on very small profit margins in order to import goods into Minangkabau at prices cheaper than those imported via Padang where, of course, imports were burdened with duties. Using the *pangkalan* Kota Baru trading network as an example, the trader and his carriers had first to go overland from Sarilamak to the *pangkalan,* a journey taking two days for a man carrying a burden. Such trading parties generally consisted of bands of eight to ten men, two of whom carried about half a *pikul* of coffee each, the rest carrying provisions for the journey. At the *pangkalan* river transport began, with successive unloading and reloading at the various bulking stations along the Kampar due to the possibility of changing to larger *perahu* as the mouth of the river was approached. At *pangkalan* Kota Baru the river was navigable for *perahu* carrying somewhat in excess of 100 *pikul* and manned by three to six men. Further down river at Taratakbuluh, goods could be loaded onto larger *perahu* and taken down to Palalawan, the main bulking station on the Kampar, or, if destined for Penang, taken overland to Pakan Baru on the Siak, a six- to eight-hour journey on foot.[236]

Palalawan had experienced phenomenal growth with the founding of Singapore, and was the place where unloading and reshipping of all goods coming down both branches of the Kampar from the three other *pangkalan* took place. From here trade was carried on in large, three-masted vessels manned by twenty to thirty men, who took the bulked cargoes across to Singapore. Much time was required. From Kota Baru to the confluence of the Kampar Kanan and Kampar Kiri took ten to twelve days, and from there to Palalawan three to four days; the crossing from Palalawan to Singapore took six more days. The downward journey to Palalawan could be carried out by rowing, but on the return journey long bamboo poles had to be used, and the return journey from Palalawan to Kota Baru took about one month. The other routes operated in the same manner, and with similar time-schedules; the bulking station between *pangkalan* Kapas and Palalawan on the Kampar Kiri was Kuntu, and there were also many overland paths through the jungle between villages on the Kampar Kanan and the Kampar Kiri, paths already well used in the seventeenth century.[237]

Minangkabau intermediate traders operated only as far down as Palalawan, after which the products were handed over to Malay ship's captains. Unfortunately we have no reliable data on transport costs and price differentials. In 1834 it was estimated that coffee was bought on the *pasar* at Halaban, Taram or Mungkar for f.8 for half a *pikul* and was burdened with f.1.60 transport costs to the nearest *pangkalan*, bringing the buying price for coffee at this point to f.9.60 per half *pikul*. This left f.8.30 for transport costs and local duties for the remainder of the journey to Singapore, if a *pikul* of coffee at Singapore was not to exceed the buying price of a *pikul* at Padang, taking into account the transport costs and duties of the Padang route. Dutch investigators thought it likely that coffee was in fact fetching much higher prices than this at the markets of origin, intermediate traders being content to make their profits on the large variety of goods they could import into Minangkabau from Singapore extremely cheaply:[238]

The markets of the fifty *Kotta's, Alaban,* and other districts lying further to the South always exhibit a quantity of white and coloured cotton piece goods, silk materials, salt and many other articles which appear to bear the mark of foreign origin and which, according to the testimony of the merchants themselves, are imported from the other side of the island.[239]

Large numbers of traders must have operated via this eastern route, judging by the quantity of coffee which went down to Singapore and by the rapid rise of Palalawan. It was a typical east coast riverine settlement built on rafts and piles in the midst of thick, uninhabited scrub, with a mixed population of Minangkabau, Johorese and coast Malays, some of whom turned to market gardening to service the growing number of traders based on the port. At Palalawan the trading community lived and carried on business quite separately from the Siak *orang kaya* who established control of the region.[240] The actual mode of financing and organizing the cross-straits *perahu* is, however, like so much concerning Malay trade, obscure. Many of the vessels were in the hands of the Batu Bara *perahu*-owners who had already established themselves in the Penang trade and the east coast trade in general, though there is some evidence that Palalawan *orang kaya*, like those of Siak, also became owners of large vessels for hire. The *perahu* generally crossed to Singapore in fleets of ten or twelve for mutual protection; each boat carried up to 200 *pikul* and was manned by 15 to 30 men, each of whom had some share in the cargo in addition to the captain's own major share. They were well armed with guns against pirates.[241]

The coffee trade with Singapore grew only gradually, gambir and cassia being Minangkabau's initial exports to the new port, but Singapore's rapid burgeoning as an entrepôt for the whole of Southeast Asia meant that ultimately there was an active trade in coffee. In 1825, 1,088 *pikul* of coffee from Minangkabau came to Singapore via the Kampar and in 1826, 4,452 *pikul,* whilst by 1829 it was estimated that between 9,600 and 12,000 *pikul* were being imported every year.[242]

There is no need to go into the organization of the Minangkabau coffee trade at Singapore, other than to say that, as at Padang, Minangkabau coffee became the preserve of Chinese brokers, working with credit advanced by the European agency houses which quickly established themselves in Singapore. These houses were agents for merchants in Europe rather than India; by 1827 there were fourteen of them in Singapore, their concern being principally to dispose of the surplus cotton cloth produced by the now booming cotton mills of Britain. It was in the form of cloth that credit was advanced to the Singapore Chinese brokers. The cheapness of British piece goods provided strong competition for Coromandel cloths in the straits, and explains why Minangkabau intermediate traders could operate profitably over such a long distance and were able to bring goods onto the market at reasonable prices despite high transport costs.[243] Heavy Dutch duties on certain items coming via Padang also helped to lessen the western route's initial cost advantages. By 1829 brokers were sending across the straits vessels carrying cargoes worth up to 2,000 Spanish dollars, when a Singapore writer noted of the Minangkabau side of the trade:

> . . . if we suppose that 100 of these prows bringing 100 piculs of coffee each, come here annually, and that it produces 6½ dollars per picul, it will give us the respectable sum of 65,000 dollars as the annual amount of our trade with the Menangcabao country by this means only.[244]

In return, Limapuluh Kota traders at Palalawan were accepting British manufactured cloth, raw silk and cotton, Coromandel cloth, Bugis cloth, lead, iron, steel, gold thread, salt and Javanese tobacco, and then beginning the long journey home, disposing of small lots at various points to petty traders, who peddled them slowly around Limapuluh Kota and elsewhere. It took two to three months to dispose of a whole cargo and to collect and bulk coffee again in Limapuluh Kota, preparatory to a new commercial venture.[245]

Enough has been said already to indicate the effects of foreign demand for coffee on the Minangkabau village, and so discussion of the third point mentioned above will be brief. If has been remarked that only certain villages could seize the commercial opportunity offered by the demand for coffee; these were the villages on the hill slopes surrounding the plains of Agam, Limapuluh Kota, Tanah Datar and Solok-Singkarak. Within these villages, which were traditionally short of land, only certain lineages had access to *sawah* for cultivation; the possibility of cultivating coffee in the hills and on the ridges behind the village opened up new sources of wealth and opportunity to members of other lineages in the village, thus creating considerable social tensions and internal feuding. Between villages, too, coffee cultivation caused friction when ill-marked boundaries were ignored in the efforts of individuals in a particular village to expand their holdings of coffee. All this created a situation of extreme volatility in the hill villages.

It also disturbed their traditional relationship with the plains villages, which had previously supplied them with rice in what were basically face-to-face encounters; now, although in some hill villages the old service industries remained strong, others entered into a new commercial network which gave them direct relations with the east and west coasts, a network which had in the past been the exclusive concern of a relatively few traders and mining villages in Tanah Datar. Of course much still depended on the continuing prosperity of the plains rice villages and their ability to supply rice at a reasonable price; but meanwhile, coffee-growing expanded with relatively little effort. Preparation and processing of the coffee for the market was undertaken only to a minimal degree. The beans were extracted from the cherries by throwing them into water-filled pits where they lay for several days until the outer husk rotted away; then they were hulled, which was generally done by crushing them in *keranjang* (containers) made of oxen or buffalo skin, pressed into the ground in funnel-shaped holes. Usually no further trouble was taken and the beans came down to the coast uncleansed of impurities, generally wet, and ungraded, with black, white and broken beans mixed up together. Cleansing, drying and grading were all done by Pariaman Chinese, whose willingness to undertake the task meant that coffee was a crop which was very little trouble to the planter.[246]

The second important effect of coffee-planting in the interior was the entry into trade of large numbers of individuals whose role it was to see that the coffee reached the European exporter. Just as numerous households could enter coffee-planting with little capital, few tools and using family labour, there were also few barriers to entry into the circle of coffee traders. This distinguished the rising group of traders from the old gold traders, who were part of a small, elite fraternity operating in connection with an ancient, almost mystical calling. Minangkabau society, particularly in Agam and Limapuluh Kota, had to adjust rapidly to the physical task of transporting large quantities of low-value, bulky commodities quite different from the high-value, low-bulk gold brought down to the coasts in the past. There was called into being a very large group of 'intermediate traders', about whose organization and profits we know, unfortunately, next to nothing. They were, of course, middlemen, buying up the coffee of a particular village in small lots, assembling it at a convenient, large *pasar,* and then making arrangements for its transportation in stages to either the west or east coast.[247] These peasant traders or micro-traders should be seen as distinct from the coffee growers themselves, although it is likely that members of coffee growers' families took part in at least the first stage of the trade, from the coffee garden to the nearest *pasar.*

Obviously differentials between the price the planter got for his crop, either in the village or at the nearest main *pasar,* and the buying price on the coast, were large, and of course the planter was further affected by changing world prices for coffee over which he had absolutely no control. However, it does not seem that any household or village ever specialized in coffee to such an extent that it was impossible to withhold the crop when prices fell on the coasts, and there were often examples of coffee being withheld until prices rose.[248] The profit margins of the Minangkabau peasant traders are impossible to estimate, because we do not know through how many hands the coffee passed before it reached the coast, nor what was the economic relationship between the trader or buyer and the carrier. In 1833, when coffee was selling at Padang for f.12 to f.16 per *pikul,* a planter who could get his crop to the nearest market could expect to get f.6 to f.8 per *pikul,* the remaining half thus being absorbed by the intermediate trade.[249] A similar situation was revealed in an 1844 investigation, although by this time the price of coffee had declined considerably: the planter was estimated to be getting f.3½ to f.4 per *pikul* for his crop, the intermediate trade absorbing f.6 to f.6½ and the coffee being sold at Pariaman for f.9 to f.10.[250]

The extent of division of labour between traders and carriers is unknown. An 1844 survey estimated there were at least 12,000 men involved as carriers in the coffee trade to Pariaman alone, who earned f.6 per *pikul* for one downward journey from Agam, the same for a return journey, and absorbed c.f.200,000 in a year, assuming that they undertook one journey per month. Each journey was estimated to take five days either way, leaving the remaining twenty days a month for 'recuperation'.[251] Not all of these carriers were working for traders, and in general such a category of people can be regarded, in the words of Peter Worsley, as 'very commonly occupationally indeterminate, "floating" between self-employment, employment of others and sale of their own labour-power. They do not constitute a distinctive and consolidated social class'.[252]

The important point to note is that, in the coffee trade and, to a lesser extent, in the cassia and gambir trades, new opportunities had arisen for large numbers of Minangkabau, particularly from hill villages, to earn their livelihood on the basis of participating in an impersonal commercial network, where village norms and village relationships no longer applied. The disruption caused by these changes leads us back once again to the Minangkabau political and social structure and, for the first time, to the role of religion and ideology in Minangkabau society, for it was these elements in the Minangkabau world which first sought to cope with the changing commercial environment.

NOTES TO CHAPTER III

1 Korthals, *Topographische Schets,* p. 9; Nahuijs, *Brieven,* pp. 127-8, 130, 184; Raffles, *Memoir,* i. 388 *et seq.*
2 F. de Haan, 'Naar Midden Sumatra in 1684', *TBG,* xxxix (1897), *passim.*
3 W.J. van der Meulen, 'Suvarṇadvīpa and the Chrysê Chersonêsos', *Indonesia,* xviii (1974), 12-3.
4 N.J. Krom, *Hindoe-Javaansche Geschiedenis* (2nd edn., The Hague, 1931), pp. 83, 303; idem, *Inleiding tot de Hindoe-Javaansche Kunst* (2nd edn., The Hague, 1923), ii. 422-3; L.C. Westenenk, 'Opstellen over Minangkabau. II', *TBG,* lvii (1916), 241-2.
5 Krom, *Geschiedenis,* pp. 414-5; idem, *Inleiding,* ii. 427; J. Minattur, 'Some Notes on Indian Influence on Malay Customary Law', in D.C. Buxbaum (ed.), *Family Law and Customary Law in Asia: A Contemporary Legal Perspective* (The Hague, 1968), pp. 55-6; D.S. Sjafiroeddin, 'Pre-Islamic Minangkabau', *Sumatra Research Bulletin,* iv (1974), 43-4.
6 *Nagara* is Sanskrit for 'city', *kota* a Dravidian word for 'fort'; Minattur, 'Indian Influence', pp. 50-1, 56-8; E.P.N.K. Pillai, *Studies in Kerala History* (Kottayam, 1970), pp. 292-323. I am indebted to Robin Jeffrey for this reference.
7 L.C. Westenenk, 'Opstellen over Minangkabau. I', *TBG,* lv (1913), 248; Sjafiroeddin, 'Pre-Islamic Minangkabau', p. 35.
8 H. Kern, 'Het Sanskrit-inschrift op den grafsteen van Vorst Ādityawarman te Kubur Raja (Menangkabau; ± 1300 Çāka)', in Kern, *Verspreide Geschriften,* vii (The Hague, 1917), 219. Adityawarman's major inscriptions have been translated in Kern, *Verspreide Geschriften,* vi (The Hague, 1917), 251-62, 267-3, and in ibid., vii, 169-72.
9 Krom, *Geschiedenis,* pp. 413-4; idem, *Inleiding,* ii. 427; Westenenk, 'Opstellen. I', pp. 248-9.
10 H. Kern, 'De wij-inscriptie op het Amoghapāça-beeld van Padang Candi (Midden-Sumatra); 1269 Çāka', in Kern, *Verspreide Geschriften,* vii. 169, 173, 174.
11 Krom, *Geschiedenis,* p. 415.
12 F.W. Stapel, 'Een verhandeling over het ontstaan van het Menangkabausche rijk en zijn Adat', *BKI,* xcii (1935), 463-4; W.J. Leyds, 'Larassen in Minangkabau', *Koloniale Studiën,* x (1926), 390-1, 395; Westenenk, 'Opstellen.II', p. 246; Minattur, 'Indian Influence', pp. 50-1; Sjafiroeddin, 'Pre-Islamic Minangkabau', pp. 44, 51.
13 Minattur, 'Indian Influence', p. 53; for the major villages in each *laras* in 1715, see Stapel, 'Een verhandeling', p. 464.
14 Leyds, 'Larassen', pp. 392-4; A.D. Batuah and A.D. Madjoindo, *Tambo Minangkabau dan Adatnja* (Jakarta, 1965), pp. 34-5.
15 Subsequently three other 'ministers' evolved to join the Bendahara: the Indomo of Suruaso, the Kadi of Padang Ganting and the Makhudum of Sumanik; Leyds, 'Larassen', pp. 394-5; Batuah and Madjoindo, *Tambo,* pp. 34, 151; H. Kroeskamp, *De Westkust en Minangkabau (1665-1668)* (Utrecht, 1931), p. 46.
16 Leyds, 'Larassen', p. 395; Kroeskamp, *De Westkust,* p. 46.
17 Stapel, 'Een verhandeling', pp. 463-4; Burger, 'Aanmerkingen', pp. 191-2; Leyds, 'Larassen', pp. 395-6.
18 De Stuers and Verploegh to van der Capellen, 30 Aug. 1825, L^{a}E no. 20, Exh. 24 Aug. 1826, no. 41, MK513.
19 M. Dion, 'Sumatra Through Portuguese Eyes: Excerpts from João de Barros' *Decadas da Asia', Indonesia,* ix (1970), 141; A. Cortesão (ed.), *The Suma Oriental of Tomé Pires* (London, 1944: The Hakluyt Society, Series II, vols. lxxxix and xc), ii. 276.
20 Krom, *Geschiedenis,* p. 416; Westenenk, 'Opstellen.I', pp. 234-5; idem, 'Opstellen.II', pp. 261-2.
21 De Haan, 'Naar Midden Sumatra', p. 361; Westenenk, 'Opstellen.I', pp. 234-5, 236-40.
22 *Pires,* i. 153.
23 ibid., p. 161.

24 Kroeskamp, *De Westkust,* pp. 11-13; W.J.A. De Leeuw, *Het Painansch Contract* (Amsterdam, 1926), p. 19; D. Lombard, *Le Sultanat d'Atjèh au Temps d'Iskandar Muda 1607-1636* (Paris, 1967), pp. 64-5, 98; J. Kathirithamby-Wells, 'Acehnese Control over West Sumatra up to the Treaty of Painan of 1663', *JSAH,* x (1969), 460.
25 Kroeskamp, *De Westkust,* p. 45; De Leeuw, *Painansch Contract,* p. 3; Brouwer, 27 Dec. 1634, *GM* 1 (The Hague, 1960, *RGP* 104), p. 454; Maetsuyker, 16 Dec. 1660, *GM* 3 (The Hague, 1968, *RGP* 125), p. 323.
26 Reniers, 19 Dec. 1651, *GM* 2 (The Hague, 1964, *RGP* 112), p. 521; Kroeskamp, *De Westkust,* pp. 92, 145; De Leeuw, *Painansch Contract,* pp. 30-1, 44.
27 Maetsuyker, 2 Sept. 1671, *GM* 3, p. 742; Maetsuyker, 31 Jan. 1675, *GM* 4 (The Hague, 1971, *RGP* 134), p. 7; Kroeskamp, *De Westkust,* p. 47; Camphuys, 30 Dec, 1689, *GM* 5, p. 327.
28 Maetsuyker, 31 Jan. 1675, *GM* 4, p. 7; Kroeskamp, *De Westkust,* pp. 96, 98-100.
29 Maetsuyker, 30 Jan. 1665, *GM* 3, p. 476.
30 Maetsuyker, 16 Dec. 1660, *GM* 3, pp. 322-3; Maetsuyker, 30 Jan. 1666, *GM* 3, p. 524; L.Y. Andaya, *The Kingdom of Johor 1641-1728* (Kuala Lumpur, 1975), pp. 69-73, 75-6.
31 Maetsuyker, 31 Jan. 1675, *GM* 4, p. 7; Maetsuyker, 28 Nov. 1676, *GM* 4, p. 143.
32 Westenenk, 'Opstellen.I', pp. 244-5; Camphuys, 27 Dec. 1688, *GM* 5, pp. 227-8; Andaya, *Johor,* pp. 251, 321-2, 330-1.
33 C. Dobbin, 'Economic Change in Minangkabau as a Factor in the Rise of the Padri Movement, 1784-1830', *Indonesia,* xxiii (1977), 2-7, 16-7.
34 Marsden, *Sumatra,* pp. 27, 166, 168; Raffles, *Memoir,* i. 407, 420, 427; Nahuijs, *Brieven,* p. 76; Korthals, *Topographische Schets,* p. 24.
35 *Pires,* i. 164-5; see also Maetsuyker, 31 Jan. 1672, *GM* 3, p. 786; Kroeskamp, *De Westkust,* p. 44.
36 Maetsuyker, 23 Nov. 1675, *GM* 4, pp. 65-6; Kroeskamp, *De Westkust,* pp. 44, 46, 158; Marsden, *Sumatra,* p. 335.
37 Raffles, *Memoir,* i. 394, 430; Nahuijs, *Brieven,* pp. 163-4; Kroeskamp, *De Westkust,* p. 44.
38 De Stuers and Verploegh to van der Capellen, 30 Aug. 1825, L^aE no. 20, Exh. 24 Aug. 1826, no. 41, MK 513; Raffles, *Memoir,* i. 393-4, 396, 400-1, 428; Kielstra, 'Onze Kennis', p. 501.
39 Raffles, *Memoir,* i. 407.
40 De Haan, 'Naar Midden Sumatra', p. 353; also pp. 341-5, 355.
41 Kielstra, 'Onze Kennis', p. 502.
42 Raffles, *Memoir,* i. 421, 423.
43 Kielstra, 'Onze Kennis', p. 502; Andaya, *Johor,* p. 111.
44 Raffles, *Memoir,* i. 424; 'Reizen van L. Horner', pp. 340, 351.
45 De Stuers and Verploegh to van der Capellen, 30 Aug. 1825, L^aE no. 20, Exh. 24 Aug. 1826, no. 41, MK 503; Elout to Riesz, 13 Aug. 1833, Bijlage B, van den Bosch 394; Marsden, *Sumatra,* pp. 336-7; Westenenk, 'Opstellen.I', p. 250.
46 Marsden, *Sumatra,* pp. 168-9.
47 E. Netscher, *Padang in het laatst der XVIIIe eeuw* (Batavia/The Hague, *VBG* xli, 1881), pp. 14-5.
48 De Radicaale Beschrijving van Sumatra's West Cust, 1761. KI MSS. H. 167, ch. 3, par. 16, p. 216.
49 Netscher, *Padang,* pp. 12, 14-5.
50 Kielstra, 'Onze Kennis', p. 501.
51 De Haan, 'Naar Midden Sumatra', pp. 339-41, 353-6.
52 De Radicaale Beschrijving, ch. 3, par. 16, p. 217; Netscher, *Padang,* pp. 26, 36, 52, 54; Kroeskamp, *De Westkust,* pp. 49, 145.
53 Netscher, *Padang,* pp. 54-5; Kroeskamp, *De Westkust,* p. 49.
54 De Radicaale Beschrijving, ch. 2, par. 90, p. 156; Consideratie, 22 Dec. 1789, par. 104-19, 133, KA 3800.
55 Camphuys, 28 Feb. 1687, *GM* 5, p. 86.
56 *Pires,* i. 161.
57 Een nota, van Zuylen van Nijevelt 102; Kielstra, 'Onze Kennis', p. 505.

58 Ch. Schefer (ed.), *Le Discours de la Navigation de Jean et Raoul Parmentier de Dieppe* (Paris, 1883), pp. 64-5.
59 *Pires,* i. 160, 167; 'Beschrijuingh van de Westcust van Sumatra [in ±1630]', *BKI,* iii (1855), 114-5; Maetsuyker, 17 Dec. 1657, *GM* 3, pp. 155-6; Maetsuyker, 17 Nov. 1669, *GM* 3, p. 688.
60 Marsden, *Sumatra,* pp. 136-7; De Carpentier, 3 Jan. 1624, *GM* 1, p. 146; Brouwer, 4 Jan. 1636, *GM* 1, p. 541.
61 W. Foster (ed.), *The Voyages of Sir James Lancaster to Brazil and the East Indies 1591-1603* (London, 1940: The Hakluyt Society, Series II, vol. lxxxv), p. 113; W. Foster (ed.), *The Voyage of Sir Thomas Best to the East Indies 1612-14* (London, 1934: The Hakluyt Society, Series II, vol. 1xxv), pp. 65-6, 270; De Carpentier, 3 Feb. 1626, *GM* 1, p. 193; De Leeuw, *Painansch Contract,* pp. 18-9, 37-42.
62 Sepuluh Buah Bandar refers to ten small ports south of Painan; De Leeuw, *Painansch Contract,* pp. 16, 37-42, 53; Kroeskamp, *De Westkust,* pp. 20-1; J. Kathirithamby-Wells, 'The Inderapura Sultanate: The Foundations of its Rise and Decline, From the Sixteenth to the Eighteenth Centuries', *Indonesia,* xxi (1976), 65.
63 De Leeuw, *Painansch Contract,* pp. 17-8, 24-5, 27, 37-42, 69; Kathirithamby-Wells, 'Inderapura', *passim*; N. MacLeod, 'De Oost-Indische Compagnie op Sumatra in de 17e eeuw. IV', *IG,* xxvi(ii) (1904), 1269.
64 Schefer, *Le Discours,* p. 72.
65 ibid., pp. 72-5.
66 *Lancaster,* p. 167.
67 ibid., p. 100; *Best,* p. xxxv; De Leeuw, *Painansch Contract,* p. 3; Kroeskamp, *De Westkust,* p. 11; A. Reid, 'Sixteenth Century Turkish Influence in Western Indonesia', *JSAH,* x(1969), 400-4.
68 De Carpentier, 3 Feb. 1626, *GM* 1, p. 193; Brouwer, 15 Aug. 1633, *GM* 1, p. 385; Kroeskamp, *De Westkust,* p. 14; De Leeuw, *Painansch Contract,* p. 20; *Best,* p. xxxvi.
69 De Carpentier, 3 Feb. 1626, *GM* 1, p. 192; Brouwer, 15 Dec. 1633, *GM* 1, p. 413; Kathirithamby-Wells, 'Achehnese Control', pp. 460-4; *Best,* p. xxxviii; De Leeuw, *Painansch Contract,* p. 20; Kroeskamp, *De Westkust,* pp. 12-3; the silver Spanish dollar had a contemporary value of between 4s6d and 5s.
70 *Best,* pp. 67-9; De Leeuw, *Painansch Contract,* p. 20.
71 De Leeuw, *Painansch Contract,* p. 35.
72 ibid., pp. 18, 49, 77; Kroeskamp, *De Westkust,* pp. 36, 88, 101; Lombard, *Sultanat d'Atjéh,* p. 65; MacLeod, 'Oost-Indische Compagnie. IV', pp. 1267, 1270.
73 Brouwer, 4 Jan. 1636, *GM* 1, p. 541; *Best,* pp. 65-7; Kroeskamp, *De Westkust,* p. 57.
74 Brouwer, 4 Jan. 1636, *GM* 1, p. 543; Reniers, 20 Jan. 1651, *GM* 2, p. 464; Kroeskamp, *De Westkust,* pp. 29-30.
75 K. Glamann, *Dutch-Asiatic Trade 1620-1740* (Copenhagen/The Hague, 1958), p. 73; van Diemen, 18 Dec. 1639, *GM* 2, p. 55; Kathirithamby-Wells, 'Achehnese Control', pp. 463-4.
76 Van Diemen, 9 Jan. 1644, *GM* 2, p. 230; De Leeuw, *Painansch Contract,* p. 5.
77 De Carpentier, 3 Jan. 1624, *GM* 1, p. 145; Reniers, 19 Dec. 1651, *GM* 2, p. 520; De Leeuw, *Painansch Contract,* pp. 6-10, 18-4; *Best,* p. 206; Kathirithamby-Wells, 'Achehnese Control', pp. 467, 469-70.
78 Maetsuyker, 17 Dec. 1657, *GM* 3, p. 155; De Leeuw, *Painansch Contract,* pp. 32, 43, 58, 85, 87.
79 Glamann, *Dutch-Asiatic Trade,* pp. 73-9, 142-7; Kroeskamp, *De Westkust,* p. 43.
80 The company's first permanent lodge at Padang was built in 1665; De Leeuw, *Painansch Contract,* pp. 14-5, 17-8; Kroeskamp, *De Westkust,* p. 49.
81 Glamann, *Dutch-Asiatic Trade,* pp. 76-7, 81, 83, 86-8.
82 Maetsuyker, 19 Dec. 1668, *GM* 3, p. 657; Kroeskamp, *De Westkust,* pp. 48, 64, 146.
83 Schefer, *Le Discours,* p. 74; *Pires,* i. 160-1.
84 Marsden, *Sumatra,* p. 157; De Leeuw, *Painansch Contract,* p. 17; Kroeskamp, *De Westkust,* pp. 48-9; MacLeod, 'Oost-Indische Compagnie.IV', p. 1269.
85 Van Outhoorn, 4 Feb. 1695, *GM* 5, p. 725; van Outhoorn, 6 Dec. 1698, *GM* 6 (The Hague, *RGP* 159, 1976), p. 28; Kielstra, 'Onze Kennis', pp. 551, 555; Glamann, *Dutch-Asiatic Trade,* p. 90.

86 Camphuys, 27 Dec. 1688, *GM* 5, p. 227; Camphuys, 26 Mar. 1691, *GM* 5, p. 413; De Radicaale Beschrijving, ch. 2, par. 38, p. 92; Kroeskamp, *De Westkust,* pp. 104-5.
87 Camphuys, 14 Mar. 1690, *GM* 5, p. 363.
88 De Radicaale Beschrijving, ch. 2, par. 96, p. 166; ch. 3, par. 21, p. 126.
89 F.W. Stapel (ed.), *Corpus Diplomaticum Neerlando-Indicum* (The Hague, 1955) vi. 51; see also pp. 35, 38, 50-1, 54, 64-6.
90 Ter Hoeff to Alting, 13 Feb. 1793, par. 79-83, KA 3876; van Riebeeck, 12 Feb. 1712, *GM* 6 p. 840; Netscher, *Padang,* pp. 13, 26-7, 55.
91 Von Erath and van der Stengh to Alting, 30 Jan. 1788, par. 38, KA 3752.
92 De Leeuw, *Painansch Contract,* pp. 69-79; Camphuys, 28 Feb. 1687, *GM* 5, pp. 85-6.
93 Kroeskamp, *De Westkust,* p. 83.
94 Stapel, 'Een verhandeling', pp. 461-6.
95 ibid., p. 469; Kielstra, 'Onze Kennis', p. 531; Kroeskamp, *De Westkust,* p. 73; De Leeuw, *Painansch Contract,* pp. 14-5, 17.
96 Stapel, 'Een verhandeling', p. 466; De Leeuw, *Painansch Contract,* pp. 16, 48, 74.
97 Stapel, 'Een verhandeling', pp. 467-9; De Leeuw, *Painansch Contract,* pp. 24, 26, 46; Kroeskamp, *De Westkust,* pp. 73, 102, 115-6.
98 Maetsuyker, 31 Jan. 1673, *GM* 3, p. 851; Maetsuyker, 31 Jan. 1674, *GM* 3, p. 904; Maetsuyker, 28 Feb. 1675, *GM* 4, p. 23.
99 Brouwer, 4 Jan. 1636, *GM* 1, p. 542; De Leeuw, *Painansch Contract,* pp. 14-5, 33, 35-6; Kroeskamp, *De Westkust,* p. 34.
100 De Leeuw, *Painansch Contract,* pp. 14-5, 33, 35-6, 60, 75; Kroeskamp, *De Westkust,* pp. 34, 138.
101 Kroeskamp, *De Westkust,* pp. 51-2, 57, 74, 109, 133.
102 ibid., pp. 54, 107-9, 115-6; De Radicaale Beschrijving, ch. 2, par. 28, p. 38.
103 Kroeskamp, *De Westkust,* p. 130.
104 ibid., pp. 40, 42, 56-7, 68, 78-9, 87, 94-5; Camphuys, 31 May 1684, *GM* 4, p. 693; Camphuys, 13 Mar. 1688, *GM* 5, p. 179; van Outhoorn, 26 Feb. 1704, *GM* 6, p. 282; van Riebeeck, 29 Nov. 1710, *GM* 6, p. 684.
105 Beschrijving van Sumatras West-Custe. 1730. KI MSS. H. 166, pp. 35-6, 51-2.
106 For changing regulations on free navigation and private trade from Batavia, see i.a.: Maetsuyker, 7 Feb. 1676, *GM* 4, p. 91; van Goens, 21 Dec. 1678, *GM* 4, p. 253; Camphuys, 31 May 1684, *GM* 4, pp. 693-4; Camphuys, 27 Dec. 1688, *GM* 5, pp. 226-7; van Outhoorn, 30 Nov. 1702, *GM* 6, p. 202; van Hoorn, 30 Nov. 1704, *GM* 6, p. 305; De Radicaale Beschrijving, ch. 2, par. 52, p. 109; par. 54, p. 113; par. 76, p. 138; par. 97, pp. 168-9.
107 Maetsuyker, 13 Feb. 1677, *GM* 4, p. 161; van Goens, 21 Dec. 1678, *GM* 4, p. 253; van Goens, 13 Feb. 1679, *GM* 4, p. 285.
108 Maetsuyker, 19 Dec. 1671, *GM* 3, p. 763; van Riebeeck, 30 Nov. 1711, *GM* 6, p. 770; De Radicaale Beschrijving, ch. 2, par. 54, pp. 113-4; par. 79, p. 144; par. 83, p. 148; par. 84, p. 149; par. 91, p. 158.
109 Van Outhoorn, 31 Jan. 1692, *GM* 5, p. 473; van Outhoorn, 6 Dec. 1698, *GM* 6, p. 28; van Hoorn, 30 Nov. 1705, *GM* 6, p. 362; De Radicaale Beschrijving, ch. 3, par. 6-8, pp. 193-201.
110 Van Hoorn, 30 Nov. 1704, *GM* 6, p. 306. One rijksdaalder equalled f.2.50. For factionalism among the brokers, see van Outhoorn, 30 Nov. 1702, *GM* 6, p. 201; van Hoorn, 30 Nov. 1705, *GM* 6, pp. 359-61; von Erath and van der Stengh to Alting, 30 Jan. 1788, par. 93-131, KA 3752.
111 De Radicaale Beschrijving, ch. 2, par. 96, p. 165.
112 Consideratie, 22 Dec. 1789, par. 104-19, 133-5, KA 3800.
113 Netscher, *Padang,* pp. 6-7; see also Beschrijving van Sumatras West-Custe, pp. 76-9.
114 Netscher, *Padang,* pp. 7, 22, 29, 38, 42.
115 ibid., pp. iii-iv, 12, 14-5; Nahuijs, *Brieven,* pp. 77-8; Consideratie, 22 Dec. 1789, par. 49, KA 3800.
116 Netscher, *Padang,* pp. 93-4.
117 *Lancaster,* p. xxx; *Best,* pp. 65, 206; van Diemen, 9 Dec. 1637, *GM* 1, p. 634; De Leeuw, *Painansch Contract,* p. 35.

118 M.A.P. Meilink-Roelofsz, *Asian Trade and European Influence in the Indonesian Archipelago between 1500 and about 1630* (The Hague, 1962), p. 254.
119 Maetsuyker, 31 Jan. 1673, *GM* 3, p. 851; Maetsuyker, 31 Jan. 1675, *GM* 4, p. 113; De Radicaale Beschrijving, ch. 2, par. 54, p. 113.
120 Camphuys, 14 Mar. 1690, *GM* 5, p. 372; De Radicaale Beschrijving, ch. 2, par. 38, p. 92; Netscher, *Padang,* p. 2.
121 Beschrijving van Sumatras West-Custe, p. 79; De Radicaale Beschrijving, ch. 2, par. 49, p. 104.
122 Netscher, *Padang,* pp. 17, 24.
123 ibid., pp. 27, 56, 66, 79; Consideratie, 22 Dec. 1789, par. 110-20, KA 3800.
124 Camphuys, 27 Dec. 1688, *GM* 5, p. 22.
125 Camphuys, 23 Dec. 1687, *GM* 5, p. 134; van Riebeeck, 12 Feb. 1712, *GM* 6, p. 840; De Radicaale Beschrijving, ch. 2, par. 84, p. 149.
126 J. Bastin, *The British in West Sumatra (1685-1825)* (Kuala Lumpur, 1965), p. xii.
127 Camphuys, 11 Dec. 1685, *GM* 4, p. 811; Camphuys, 13 Dec. 1686, *GM* 5, p. 50; van Outhoorn, 8 Feb. 1696, *GM* 5, p. 756; van Hoorn, 30 Nov. 1704, *GM* 6, p. 305; van Hoorn, 15 Jan. 1711, *GM* 6, pp. 717-8; R.J. Young, 'The English East India Company and Trade on the West Coast of Sumatra, 1730-1760' (University of Pennsylvania Ph.D. thesis, 1970), pp. 14-5.
128 Van Outhoorn, 26 Feb. 1704, *GM* 6, p. 282; van Hoorn, 25 Jan. 1706, *GM* 6, p. 394; van Hoorn, 25 Nov, 1708, *GM* 6, p. 546; van Hoorn, 18 Feb. 1709, *GM* 6, p. 592.
129 De Radicaale Beschrijving, ch. 2, par. 74, pp. 136-7.
130 ibid., ch. 2, par. 76, p. 139.
131 Young, 'English East India Company', pp. 69-71.
132 De Radicaale Beschrijving, ch. 1, par. 12, pp. 23, 25.
133 Beschrijving van Sumatras West-Custe, p. 45; Young, 'English East India Company', pp. 70, 96, 107; J. Kathirithamby-Wells, *The British West Sumatran Presidency (1760-85): Problems of Early Colonial Enterprise* (Kuala Lumpur, 1977), p. 138.
134 Young, 'English East India Company', p. 117; Bastin, *British in West Sumatra,* pp. xxxi-ii, 53, 70; Kathirithamby-Wells, *West Sumatran Presidency,* pp. 114-6, 144, 164-6.
135 Kathirithamby-Wells, *West Sumatran Presidency,* pp. 147, 161; Young, 'English East India Company', pp. 54, 62-4, 69; De Radicaale Beschrijving, ch. 2, par. 98, pp. 170-2.
136 Netscher, *Padang,* pp. 26, 49; Kathirithamby-Wells, *West Sumatran Presidency,* p. 171; von Erath and van der Stengh to Alting, 15 Jan. 1789, par. 16-7, 167-8, KA 3800; Consideratie, 22 Dec. 1789, par. 243-6, KA 3800.
137 De Radicaale Beschrijving, ch. 1, par. 10, p. 19; ch. 2, par. 68, p. 131; Young, 'English East India Company', pp. 96, 124; Bastin, *British in West Sumatra,* pp. 47-8.
138 Marsden, *Sumatra,* p. 277; Nahuijs, *Brieven,* pp. 94-5.
139 De Radicaale Beschrijving, ch. 3, par. 5, p. 190-1.
140 ibid., ch. 3, par. 10, pp. 205-9; von Erath and van der Stengh to Alting, 15 Jan. 1789, par. 166-71, KA 3800.
141 Consideratie, 22 Dec. 1789, par. 219-21, 226-34, KA 3800.
142 Von Erath and van der Stengh to Alting, 30 Jan. 1791, KA 3853; Netscher, *Padang,* p. 36; Nahuijs, *Brieven,* p. 70.
143 Van Outhoorn, 26 Nov. 1701, *GM* 6, p. 156; De Radicaale Beschrijving, ch. 3, par. 1, p. 183; Kroeskamp, *De Westkust,* p. 108.
144 Consideratie, 22 Dec. 1789, par. 215-7, KA 3800. One *koyan* equals between 27 and 40 *pikul.*
145 Netscher, *Padang,* pp. 34-5, 40-2, 79.
146 Camphuys, 27 Dec. 1688, *GM* 5, p. 225; Andaya, *Johor,* pp. 105-6, 133.
147 Camphuys, 13 Dec. 1686, *GM* 5, p. 50; Camphuys, 27 Dec. 1688, *GM* 5, p. 227.
148 Von Erath and van der Stengh to Alting, 15 Jan. 1789, par. 21-2, KA 3800; Consideratie, 22 Dec. 1789, par. 194, KA 3800.
149 Light to Cornwallis, 5 Mar. 1789, SSFR 3, IOL; Consideratie, 22 Dec. 1789, par. 153, 201, KA 3800.
150 Marsden, *Sumatra,* p. 160.
151 Couperus, 'Landbouwkundige nijverheid', p. 310.

152 Plate to Nederlandsche Handel-Maatschappij, Batavia, 23 Apr. 1835, Baud MSS. 429, ARA.
153 Korthals, 'Aanteekeningen', p. 19; Nahuijs, *Brieven,* p. 74; 'Schets van de Bereiding der Gambier', pp. 26-7.
154 Nahuijs, *Brieven,* pp. 74-5.
155 'Schets van de Bereiding der Gambier', pp. 24-6.
156 Consideratie, 22 Dec. 1789, par. 105-6, 196-205, KA 3800; Marsden, *Sumatra,* p. 357.
157 Von Erath to Alting, 30 Jan. 1788, par. 48, KA 3752; von Erath and van der Stengh to Alting, 15 Jan. 1789, par. 23, 32, KA 3800.
158 Consideratie, 22 Dec. 1789, par 192, KA 3800.
159 J. Anderson, *Mission to the East Coast of Sumatra, in MDCCCXXIII* (Edinburgh/London, 1826), p. 350.
160 ibid.; Müller, *Berigten,* p. 30.
161 Anderson, *Mission,* p. 352.
162 ibid., pp. 168, 253.
163 ibid., pp. 172-4, 352.
164 ibid., pp. 115-7, 310-2; L. De Scheemaker, 'Nota Betreffende het Landschap Batoebarah', *TBG,* xvii (1869), 461, 474.
165 A List of the Prows which have arrived at this Port, since the 22[d] December Last, Con [sultations] 11 Apr. 1787, SSFR 2.
166 Account of Prows arrived at Prince of Wales Island between 1st April and 9th July 1787, Con. 17 Sept. 1787, SSFR 2.
167 Import by Prows at Pinang . . . 1789-1792, Con. 5 Apr. 1793, Enclosure No. 9, SSFR 5.
168 An Account of Goods etc. Imported into Prince of Wales's Island 1789, Con. 14 Jan. 1790, SSFR 4.
169 Anderson, *Mission,* pp. 346-7.
170 Korthals, *Topographische Schets,* pp. 40, 44; Burger, 'Aanmerkingen', p. 216.
171 Anderson, *Mission,* pp. 117, 122; idem, *Acheen, and the Ports on the North and East Coasts of Sumatra* (London, 1840), p. 194; Wong Lin Ken, 'The Trade of Singapore, 1819-69', *JMBRAS,* xxxiii (1960), 55.
172 Anderson, *Mission,* p. 352; idem, *Acheen,* pp. 184-5.
173 Van den Bosch to de Stuers, 20 Dec. 1833, no. 467, Baud 480.
174 Consideratie, 22 Dec. 1789, par. 278, KA 3800.
175 Du Puy to van der Capellen, 12 June 1819, no. 21, in P.H. van der Kemp, 'Eene Bijdrage tot E.B. Kielstra's Opstellen over Sumatra's Westkust', *BKI,* xviv (1894), 283-4.
176 S. Ahmat, 'Some Problems of the Rhode Island Traders in Java, 1799-1836', *JSAH,* vi (1965), 94-5; M. de Young, *Man and Land in the Haitian Economy* (Gainesville, 1958), pp. 16-7.
177 Ahmat, 'Rhode Island Traders', pp. 94-5; G. Bhagat, *Americans in India 1784-1860* (New York, 1970), pp. 4, 25; J.W. Gould, *Americans in Sumatra* (The Hague, 1961), p. 2.
178 G.G. Putnam, *Salem Vessels and Their Voyages. A History of the Pepper Trade with the Island of Sumatra,* Series I (Salem, 1924), p. vii.
179 ibid., pp. 21-2, 34, 45, 49; Nahuijs, *Brieven,* p. 73; de Stuers to Elout, 17 May 1826, no. 4, Exh. 23 Oct. 1826, no. 48, MK 523.
180 Putnam, *Salem Vessels,* p. 22.
181 De Stuers to Elout, 15 Feb. 1828, no. 3, Exh. 11 Jul. 1828, no. 52, MK 625; Putnam, *Salem Vessels,* pp. 21-2, 25, 34, 40, 45, 49, 51; Gould, *Americans,* p. 14.
182 Putnam, *Salem Vessels,* pp. 15-7.
183 De Stuers to Elout, 15 Feb. 1828, no. 3, Exh. 11 Jul. 1828, no. 52, MK 625; de Stuers to van den Bosch, n.d. Mar. 1838, Exh. 12 Mar. 1838, Kab[inet] L[a]X, MK 4417.
184 De Stuers to Elout, 15 Feb. 1828, no. 3, Exh. 11 Jul. 1828, no. 52, MK 625.
185 Ahmat, 'Rhode Island Traders', p. 100.
186 Rapport omtrent den handel in Koffie ter Padang door A. Bezemer, MK 3070.
187 ibid.
188 See Dobbin, 'Economic Change', p. 23 for full export figures and prices between 1820 and 1830, and the relevant sources.
189 De Stuers to Elout, 17 May 1826, no. 4, Exh. 23 Oct. 1826, no. 48, MK 523; de Stuers to Elout, 17 May 1828, no. 8, Exh. 31 Dec. 1828, no. 47, MK 652.
190 De Stuers to Elout, 10 Jul. 1828, no. 10, Exh. 29 Dec. 1829, no. 53, MK 721.

191 Elout to Clifford, 6 May 1831, no. 1/109, Exh. 26 Sept. 1831, no. 28, MK 810.
192 De Stuers to Elout, 16 Mar. 1828, no. 5, Exh. 16 June 1829, no. 130, MK 683; de Stuers to Elout, 10 Jul. 1828, no. 10, Exh. 29 Dec. 1829, no. 53, MK 721.
193 MacGillavry to Elout, 6 Aug. 1829, no. 38, Exh. 26 Nov. 1829, no. 59, MK 717.
194 Rapport omtrent den staat van den handel, 21 Apr. 1830, no. 315, Exh. 15 Sept. 1830, no. 6/A, MK 767.
195 *Singapore Chronicle,* Sept. 1829, in J.H. Moor, *Notices of the Indian Archipelago, and Adjacent Countries* (Singapore, 1837), p. 102.
196 Nahuijs, *Brieven,* pp. 37-8; Müller, *Reizen,* p. 27.
197 Travel Report no. 13, F.H. Spengler, Sept. 1829, Archief Nederlandsche Handel-Maatschappij, ARAH.
198 Een nota, Bijlage A, van Zuylen van Nijevelt 102; Müller, *Reizen,* p. 27.
199 Een nota, Bijlage A, van Zuylen van Nijevelt 102.
200 Spengler 1829, ANHM; Nahuijs, *Brieven,* pp. 23, 89.
201 Du Puy to van der Capellen, 13 June 1819, no. 22, in Kemp, 'Eene Bijdrage', p. 262.
202 Kathirithamby-Wells, *West Sumatran Presidency,* pp. 148-9; Wong, 'Trade of Singapore', pp. 12-3.
203 De Stuers to van den Bosch, n.d. Mar. 1838, Exh. 12 Mar. 1838, Kab. L[a] X, MK 4417; Kathirithamby-Wells, *West Sumatran Presidency,* p. 148.
204 Spengler, 1829, ANHM.
205 ibid.; Nahuijs, *Brieven,* p. 80; de Stuers to Elout, 14 May 1826, no. 3, Exh. 30 Sept. 1826, no. 79, MK 519.
206 De Stuers to Elout, 10 Jul. 1829, no. 1, Exh. 29 Dec. 1829, no. 53, MK 721; Nahuijs, *Brieven,* p. 80.
207 Spengler, 1829, ANHM; de Stuers to Elout, 17 May 1826, no. 4, Exh. 23 Oct. 1826, no. 48, MK 523.
208 Nahuijs, *Brieven,* pp. 35, 54-5; du Puy to van der Capellen, 15 June 1819, no. 28, in Kemp, 'Eene Bijdrage', p. 266.
209 Spengler, 1829, ANHM; Nahuijs, *Brieven,* p. 57; Een nota, van Zuylen van Nijevelt 102.
210 Nahuijs, *Brieven,* p. 41.
211 Müller, *Reizen,* p. 28.
212 Nahuijs, *Brieven,* p. 41; Rapport omtrent den staat van den handel, 21 Apr. 1830, no. 315, Exh. 15 Sept. 1830, no. 6/A, MK 767.
213 Spengler, 1829, ANHM.
214 ibid.; Boelhouwer, *Herinneringen,* pp. 116-7; Kemp, 'Eene Bijdrage', p. 316.
215 Nahuijs, *Brieven,* pp. 82-4, 87.
216 ibid., pp. 93-4, 96.
217 ibid., p. 93.
218 ibid., pp. 40, 93; Spengler, 1829, ANHM.
219 Nahuijs, *Brieven,* pp. 73, 75; Müller, *Reizen,* pp. 6, 38, 43.
220 De Stuers to Elout, 17 May 1826, no. 4, Exh. 23 Oct. 1826, no. 48, MK 523; de Stuers to Elout, 10 Jul. 1829, no. 1, Exh. 29 Dec. 1829, no. 53, MK 721.
221 Rapport omtrent den staat van den handel, 21 Apr. 1830, no. 315, Exh. 15 Sept. 1830, no. 6/A, MK 767.
222 Spengler, 1829, ANHM.
223 ibid.
224 Een nota, van Zuylen van Nijevelt 102; Boelhouwer, *Herinneringen,* pp. 131, 172.
225 De Stuers to Elout, 10 Jul. 1829, no. 1, Exh. 29 Dec. 1829, no. 53, MK 721; Spengler, 1829, ANHM; Nahuijs, *Brieven,* p. 75.
226 Spengler, 1829, ANHM.
227 ibid.
228 Nahuijs, *Brieven,* p. 216.
229 Boelhouwer, *Herinneringen,* p. 25.
230 Een nota, Bijlage A, van Zuylen van Nijevelt 102.
231 Boelhouwer, *Herinneringen,* pp. 133-6, 149-50; Nahuijs, *Brieven,* pp. 216-7; Müller, *Reizen,* p. 61; Burger, 'Aanmerkingen', p. 163; Kielstra, 'Sumatra's Westkust van 1819-1825', pp. 41-2, 51.
232 Een nota, Bijlage A, van Zuylen van Nijevelt 102; Boelhouwer, *Herinneringen,* p. 148.

233 *Singapore Chronicle,* Sept. 1829 in Moor, *Notices,* p. 101.
234 Müller, *Berigten,* p. 26; de Haan, 'Naar Midden Sumatra', pp. 356, 365; Andaya, *Johor,* pp. 146-7, 173-4.
235 Müller, *Berigten,* pp. 28, 31-3.
236 ibid., pp. 28-9; Korthals, *Topographische Schets,* p. 21; *Singapore Chronicle,* Sept. 1829, in Moor, *Notices,* p. 102.
237 Müller, *Berigten,* pp. 29, 31-2; de Haan, 'Naar Midden Sumatra', p. 356.
238 Müller, *Berigten,* p. 29; Korthals, *Topographische Schets,* pp. 57-8.
239 Müller, *Berigten,* p. 34.
240 J. Faes, 'Het Rijk Pelalawan', *TBG,* xxvii (1882), 490-1, 496-7, 503.
241 *Singapore Chronicle,* Sept. 1829, in Moor, *Notices,* p. 101; Wong, 'Trade of Singapore', p. 55.
242 *Singapore Chronicle,* Sept. 1829, in Moor, *Notices,* p. 102; C.D. Cowan, 'Early Penang and the Rise of Singapore 1805-1832', *JMBRAS,* xxiii (1950), 102, 112, 114, 119, 178-9; Anderson, *Acheen,* pp. 171-2.
243 Wong, 'Trade of Singapore', pp. 18-9, 84, 163, 167; Anderson, *Mission,* pp. 212-3.
244 *Singapore Chronicle,* Sept. 1829, in Moor, *Notices,* p. 102.
245 ibid., p. 101.
246 Spengler, 1829, ANHM; Travel Report no. 38, C.A. Granpré Molière, 1844, ANHM, p. 38.
247 Memorie van toelichting, 11 Oct. 1833, no. 311, Exh. 9 Apr. 1834, no. 74K Geh[eim], MK 4233.
248 Nahuijs, *Brieven,* pp. 64-5.
249 Memorie van toelichting, 11 Oct. 1833, no. 311, Exh. 9 Apr. 1834, no. 74K Geh., MK 4233.
250 Granpré Molière, 1844, ANHM, p. 43.
251 ibid., pp. 43-4.
252 P. Worsley, 'Social class in emergent countries: bourgeoisie and petty bourgeoisie', in A. Béteille (ed.), *Social Inequality* (Harmondsworth, 1969), p. 218.

CHAPTER IV

ISLAMIC REVIVALISM, 1784-1832

Islam in Minangkabau society

The historical study of peasant religion is notoriously difficult. In Minangkabau, as in other parts of the Indonesian archipelago, peasant culture rested on a substratum of animistic beliefs which were still flourishing in the nineteenth century. Other strata of society may have adopted the forms and beliefs of outside cults, but even these social groups – such as the royal family or artisan families – remained powerfully influenced by the prevailing animism of the society in which they lived.

The key figure in the religion of the Minangkabau peasant was the shaman, for whom the Minangkabau term *pawang* was generally used. The peasant household might be visited in the course of the year by serious illness, death, danger to the harvest, and numerous other terrors. Its only recourse was to the *pawang,* who could conjure with invisible forces and bring comfort to the stricken family. The theoretical justification for the work of the *pawang* was peasant belief in the dualism of the soul. Each individual was thought to have a real soul, and a soul which could disappear; it was the latter, called *semangat,* which represented life's vital power. In this way illness could be explained as the capturing of the *semangat* by an evil spirit, and it was the role of the *pawang* to call on his or her familiar spirits to track down the lost *semangat* and return it to the sufferer. The *pawang* would sometimes merely consult with spirits, but at other times he or she would become possessed, after going into a trance often accompanied by music and singing.[1] It was not only humans who possessed *semangat*; so did animals and plants. The *semangat* of rice was carefully preserved by a variety of ceremonies at planting and harvesting, as was that of other crops.[2]

Implicit belief in spirits was an essential component of this explanation of the world and its ills. Everything was considered to harbour spirits, so that even a track in the jungle or a tree possessed its own spirit. To placate evil spirits sacrificial offerings were made. Spirits of mountains were particularly frightening, and a Minangkabau journeying to the top of Mount Merapi would first slaughter a buffalo to placate the spirits of the mountain, at the same time taking great care not to utter certain words which might be offensive to the spirits.[3] Belief in spirits led to attachment to fetishes. Spirits were thought to reside in certain objects, so that individuals could protect themselves with amulets made of special stones or animal bones, whilst the community at large recognized objects with supernatural power or *sakti* which could perform good for the whole village.[4]

In every village the shaman was a person of considerable influence, and each shaman passed on his art to an heir, who got possession of a familiar spirit by inheritance.[5] In addition to village shamans, it has already been noted that Minangkabau peasant culture regarded those who worked with metals as having supernatural powers. *Sakti* was especially present in metals such as iron, and so blacksmiths were regarded as magically dangerous, magically 'charged' personalities, needing magic power in order to be able to cope with their tasks. Secret rites of initiation attended the instruction of an apprentice in the techniques of forging.[6] Seekers for gold and exploiters of mines were also regarded as having particular powers. The spirits which inhabited the gold mines had to be handled with the greatest care, and gold-seekers formed a fraternity, members of which alone knew the secret signs of gold and could perform the magical feats necessary for the successful prosecution of a mining venture.[7]

Overlaying the religion of the Minangkabau peasant were certain cults which had been introduced into Minangkabau from outside. Unlike peasant animism, these cults had altered markedly over the centuries with each fresh wave of foreign influence, though it should be remarked that much that had gone before was incorporated in the new. The first evidence we have of Minangkabau 'higher religion' centres on the appearance of megaliths (large stones), erected about the beginning of our era in the course of rites designed to protect the soul from the dangers of the underworld or to ensure eternal life; some were carved to represent human beings and female fertility symbols. With the eruption into the Minangkabau world of Indian traders and the Hindu-Javanese court of Adityawarman, a new form of higher religion was introduced. Where possible, however, this new religion was associated with the former megalithic cult. Adityawarman used the stone pillars for his inscriptions, or carved additional markings on their summits, and sacred centres such as the three stone seats near Lima Kaum were used by the king in his own court ceremonial.[8] But he also introduced the religion of which he was a devotee, a Tantric form of demonic Buddhism with Shivaite elements. The most notorious aspects of this cult, which flourished at the Javanese court of Majapahit, do not appear to have survived long in Minangkabau: they included rites of human sacrifice, the drinking of blood and the rattling of human bones in ecstatic dances which took place at night in graveyards, all as part of ceremonies designed to produce mystic union with the godhead.[9] What did survive, however, was the concept of the divinity of the ruler, who was transformed by the miracle of his accession into a divine being and became the sustainer of the cosmic order. The ruler could never afford to neglect magical ceremonies to sustain his power, and in Minangkabau this sacral character of the ruler remained very marked through the centuries.[10]

Islam is the outside religion introduced into the Minangkabau world which most concerns us here. It had to contend with several factors which hardly guaranteed its successful adaptation to the society. First of all, it was a religion very much associated with the city, in its original environment and in its earliest years in the Indonesian archipelago. Indeed, it has been pointed out that Islam requires the city in order to realize its social and religious ideals. Its cornerstone, communal prayer, requires a fixed and permanent mosque, and its other religious obligations, too, are more suited to the rhythm of life of the town-dweller than that of the peasant. The tradition of Islam is in fact filled with a spirit hostile to the peasantry.[11] Furthermore, the well-developed religious system of the Minangkabau peasantry, with its own religious specialists, proved an obstacle to a religion which could never be satisfied with individual converts but stressed continually the *ummat*, the Islamic community. In addition, the Minangkabau royal family possessed its own sacral system and beliefs, which Islam would have in some way to adapt to if the ruling group was not to be alienated from the new religion.[12]

It is hardly surprising that Islam achieved its first and most lasting successes in the Minangkabau west coast entrepôts, which most resembled in function the Islamic city of the Middle East, revolving as they did around a central market-place. Tiku, the leading port for the west coast trade of Indian Muslims from Gujarat, was Islamicized by the second decade of the sixteenth century. The main administrative and port officials all had Muslim titles, and Islamic teachers well versed in the Koran were in evidence in the port.[13] The conversion of Pariaman and Ulakan seems to have followed,particularly after the establishment of Acehnese control over the coast. The outer forms of Islam are easily learnt and adopted, and commercial relations with the Indian traders who poured onto the coast in the hey-day of the pepper trade were greatly simplified when the local brokers adopted the religion of their trading partners. Their traditional roles were left undisturbed and no radical change in behaviour was called for.[14] As late as 1761 Islam was largely confined to the leading broker families of the ports; Islamic law, particularly that connected with inheritance, proved suited to their needs, providing them with an alternative to the matrilineal system of inheritance of the uplands. The coastal peasants, however, remained attached to their animistic beliefs and to their own religious specialists.[15]

As far as the Minangkabau interior was concerned, conversion proceeded both by way of the west coast and via the east coast rivers. The move of the royal family to the Buo-Sumpur Kudus area, and its involvement in the straits gold trade, led to relations with the Malacca royal court which had been Islamicized in the fifteenth century.[16] Sultan Mansur Syah of Malacca, who died in 1475, was the suzerain of the states of Kampar and Inderagiri. This led to the adoption of Islam by the rulers of these states, and it became more and more important for anyone dealing with these Islamicized courts at least to transact business by using Muslim merchants and scribes. Such scribes were able to acquire considerable influence over their royal masters; they indicated what was good form in other courts of the Muslim world, showed the ruler how his own power and prestige could be increased by acceptance of Islam, engaged in correspondence with foreign powers and kept court records.[17] Yet there can be no doubt that this conversion to Islam by members of the Minangkabau royal family – and by other officials of the realm – did not cause them to abandon many of their earlier beliefs and practices. Items in the Minangkabau royal regalia retained their magical significance, and merely acquired an Islamic veneer; further items were sought for well after the conversion.[18] The Raja Alam also strove to retain his reputation for supernatural powers right down to the nineteenth century. He kept out of the public eye, and in 1825 told a Dutch inquirer that he had the power to punish refractory *raja* in the *rantau* by causing failure of the rice crop or an epidemic among people or cattle.[19]

By the mid-seventeenth century all the centres of the gold trade, and the villages with a high proportion of gold merchants among their inhabitants, had been converted to Islam. Sumpur Kudus became known as the 'Mecca of the *darat*',[20] and other gold centres such as Talawi and Padang Ganting became Muslim, as well as the earlier Hindu-Buddhist centres around Suruaso and Pagarruyung which were possibly converted when the royal family moved back there.[21] But it should not be forgotten that Islam was merely added to what had gone before, and it exhibited itself in Minangkabau in a highly syncretic form. For the royal family it was an additional means of increasing their inner strength or *sakti,* whilst in the gold-producing villages the magical practices of the gold-seekers still continued undiluted.

As far as the numerous agricultural villages of Minangkabau were concerned, villages with no connection with the gold trade, their relationship to Islam took two forms. The first was the affiliation the new religion was able to evolve with the family and lineage system, and the second was the relationship of Islam to the village community as a whole. It was the second connection which was the more difficult to establish. Agricultural life persisted in its rhythm of planting and harvesting, its round of placation of spirits and consultation with the shaman. Islam seemed to have little to offer here, and it is not surprising that, even in the early nineteenth century, there were whole villages with no connection at all with the Muslim faith.[22] Where Islam made its initial impact, therefore, was not at the level of the community, but rather within the lineage. Village shamans received their calling quite apart from the lineage system. However, lineages which were prosperous and flourishing also desired to have their own religious functionary, which gave them added prestige in the eyes of fellow villagers. In pre-Islamic days this functionary appears to have been somewhat similar to the Brahman priest attached to prosperous Indian households, and was in fact called a *pandita.* Now this functionary gradually took on an Islamic veneer and adopted the title of *malim.* Like the lineage *penghulu* his position was hereditary and, like the *penghulu,* his installation was marked by expense and ostentation, as befitted his prestige-giving role. He had no place whatever in the *penghulu* council, and his religious role inside the lineage was more involved with matters of custom (*adat*) than with enforcing the injunctions of Islam. He was present at births, deaths and family ceremonies such as the first bathing of a newborn child, house-moving, the start of a journey and so on.[23] Right down to the early nineteenth century the *malim* had few opportunities to exercise a wider village role, even though he might be the *imam* (leader of prayers) of the village mosque. Most mosques were still excluded from the village; they were small, unpretentious buildings located away from the main population centres and even from roads.[24] For the rest, the *malim* was indistinguishable from other villagers in his participation in the agricultural round, and even the leading *malim* of the Minangkabau state, the Kadi of Padang Ganting, was remembered as having worked his *sawah* with his own hands in the early nineteenth century.[25]

There was, however, another means by which Islam could penetrate the Minangkabau highlands, in a manner suited both to its own genius and that of the Minangkabau. In this way, too, whole villages were involved in an Islamic institution, although the village itself might not form a Muslim community. An important facet of life in any Minangkabau village was the *surau,* the house where young men lived after puberty away from the lineage house, which was the dwelling-place of women and children. The position of men in Minangkabau society was always problematic, as they could never be more than guests in the home of their marriage-partners. Although we know little of the Hindu-Buddhist period in Minangkabau, it is established that in 1356 Adityawarman established a Buddhist monastery in the vicinity of Bukit Gombak, and it seems that such a gathering together of young men to learn sacred lore provided an ideal solution for a very definite social problem. In certain villages, therefore, Islam constructed a whole edifice of learning on the basis of the pre-Islamic *surau*.[26]

This was made possible by the fact that, in the early Islamic centuries, Muslim brotherhoods (*tarekat*) had sprung up in response to a popular need for more intimate communion with God than that provided by the dry legalism of the official doctors of Islam. Devotees of these brotherhoods, called Sufis, concentrated on following a *ṭarīḳa* (Arabic: path, way) laid down by a teacher or *syekh*, in whose school they gathered, often for many years. These *tarekat* and their schools could fit into the existing *surau* system of Minangkabau without the least disruption, and so become an acceptable addition to village life in certain villages. The brotherhoods were adept at taking on a local colouring, and their stress on the inward condition of a man's heart rather than his acts and on the spiritual progress of the individual rather than the ethical demands of the *ummat* posed few problems for the host village, which need in no way function as an Islamic community.[27] Moreover, certain of the religious exercises carried out in the *surau* in the hope of receiving visions – the repetition of the names of God, singing, swaying to music etc. – had much in common with the way a village shaman attained a trance, and so continuity with village life was again preserved.[28]

It has been pointed out that the term Sufi brotherhood is not a useful sociological classification, because the brotherhoods or orders came to be very much affected by the social setting in which they operated.[29] By the eighteenth century there were three Sufi orders functioning in Minangkabau, the Naksyabandiyah, the Syattariyah and the Kadiriyah. Before looking at their penetration of Minangkabau and their geographical distribution in the highland valleys, we should note what they possessed in common. Their chief characteristic was the utter devotion of the students (*murid*) in the *surau* to their *syekh*, who taught them the Islamic faith with reference to the particular precepts of his own *tarekat*, after having himself passed through a discipline prescribed by a spiritual director whose credentials could ultimately be traced back to the *tarekat*'s founder.[30] In addition to teaching the reading of the Koran and of the commentaries, the *syekh* and the various *guru* who gave instruction in a large *surau* would teach the particular rules, methods and religious practices which constituted the 'path' laid down by their own order for the seeker after God. The *syekh* would also teach his own secret *ilmu* (esoteric knowledge) concerning methods of self-defence, means of making oneself invulnerable in the face of weapons, and ways of consulting numerological treatises to decide upon auspicious days, such learning, with its pre-Islamic overtones and magical colouring, having been readily assimilated by Minangkabau Islam.[31] In the evenings the *murid* would gather together to perform the *dikir*, a recitation of short religious phrases, sitting in a semi-circle around the leader until their shoulders touched, swaying from left to right, and repeating formulae such as the names of God.[32]

Another feature common to the different *tarekat* was the actual organization of the *surau*. The big *surau* which developed in connection with certain teachers in the highlands attracted hundreds of students; a typical one would have at least twenty buildings, which were divided among students coming from different geographical areas, who preferred to live together in a separate dwelling, each under the care of a *guru.*[33] To cope with this large concentration of students the *surau* had to be organized on an economic basis. A visitor to one of the largest *surau* of the highlands in 1886 noted this economic aspect immediately, and there can have been little change from the previous century: 'The small soeraus were all built on high piles, and looked exactly like lapaus [small inns or shops]. In the beginning I was not able to think of them as soeraus, especially when I saw hanging from the windows bunches of bananas and other fruit, obviously for sale'.[34] Students had to help their *guru* in his garden or *sawah,* and instruction often ceased during busy agricultural periods. To provide food and clothing for themselves they also engaged in trade in small articles, particularly in fruits growing around the *surau* such as bananas, or in items needed by local people, such as banana leaves. Older students, and those who felt they had many years to devote to their studies, engaged in a craft such as carpentry, by means of which they provided for their wants. The largest and most famous *surau* would be established in villages with important market-places, and the students depended for their livelihood on what they could sell at the weekly market. Smaller *surau* were even more dependent on their agricultural activities, and pupils would be instructed only in the early morning and for a few hours in the evening, the day being devoted to agricultural tasks and taking care of the cattle.[35]

Yet another characteristic common to all the *tarekat* was the nature of their teaching. Though there were disputes among the brotherhoods, these seem to have been based largely on personal jealousies and inter-village rivalry. Some village teachers even established village *tarekat,* usually temporary institutions dying out with the death of the teacher, but which could arouse much zeal in their students over questions of religious ritual.[36] But generally speaking the teaching of the *tarekat* were very similar. All the *tarekat* represented in Minangkabau were orthodox in their thought; the heterodox Sufism which had caused pantheistic speculations to flourish in Aceh in the seventeenth century was not represented in Minangkabau. This is not to say that the *tarekat* neglected one of their chief aims, the individual search for truth and knowledge of God, but this was clearly to be achieved within an orthodox framework, and no individual was ever exalted above the ritual and the law. In this Minangkabau followed the trend towards orthodoxy throughout the Malay world in the late eighteenth century, manifest in the numerous Malay translations of orthodox Sufi texts from the Arabic made at that time.[37]

The individual's submission before the gamut of Islamic learning was hardly surprising because the young student had much of a practical nature to grasp before he could advance very far. The beginning of all learning for every properly educated Muslim is the recitation of the Koran, with less stress placed on understanding and more on the correct intonation of the Arabic sounds. No progress can be made in Islamic studies without a sound knowledge of Arabic, so that all *murid* who wished to do more than merely intone the portions of holy writ needed for daily prayers had to study Arabic by means of a series of grammatical texts. Many students never got past this early obstacle. Those *guru* who had never been to Arabia were barely proficient in Arabic themselves, and so their students could not advance beyond the simplest texts. Those who did surmount the difficulties of learning Arabic then moved on to the study of Islamic law, the *syariat.* This branch of study, called *fikh,* was regarded as the most profound for any Muslim, and it also happened to be the easiest as *fikh* books were written in simple Arabic.[38]

In teaching *fikh* the *tarekat* schools were all alike. Most *syekh* had a clear understanding of the spiritual capacities of the majority of their students, and the mysteries of the 'way' were reserved for only the few; the majority was taught first the basic duties of Islam and then guided in right behaviour, through a study of the *syariat.*[39] Throughout Minangkabau the outstanding handbook for the study of the law was the same; it was *Minhāj aṭ-ṭālibīn (A Guide of Believing Students),* which the Minangkabau called simply 'the fikh book' (*Kitab Fikh*).[40] All the leading *fikh* books of Islam are very similar. They deal first with the five pillars of Islam – the confession of faith, prayer, fasting, the pilgrimage and almsgiving – which can be subsumed under the heading *ibadat* or the laws governing man's conduct towards God. Those who advance further can study in addition those aspects of Islamic law which govern human relationships, such as the law of inheritance, marriage law, and so on. All the leading *surau* of Minangkabau tried to gain a reputation in the study of the law, which was thought to be the greatest form of learning here below.[41] Its study was never merely an empirical exercise, but was regarded rather as the practical aspect of the religious and social doctrine preached by Muhammad, deriving naturally from the Koran where God appears as commanding and forbidding, rewarding and punishing.

After reviewing all that the Sufi brotherhoods in their institutionalized form in Minangkabau had in common, some attempt must be made to see them in their diversity. Of the Kadiriyah very little is known, though it seems to have been represented on the coast and in Agam.[42] Of the other two *tarekat,* the Naksyabandiyah seems to have been introduced into Minangkabau somewhat earlier than the Syattariyah, and to have predominated in Limapuluh Kota and Tanah Datar. It was possibly brought in the first half of the seventeenth century by a scholar from Pasai in north-east Sumatra, who entered Minangkabau by way of Pariaman and then stayed for some time in both Agam and Limapuluh Kota. In the typical manner of *tarekat* teachers he did not disdain to do agricultural work to earn his livelihood, although he was at the same time the author of a Malay *fikh* book based on Arabic sources and introducing Naksyabandiyah prayers and recitations to the Malay public.[43] It is impossible to construct a religious geography for the *tarekat,* other than to say that the Naksyabandiyah, like the other *tarekat,* established *surau* near large, prosperous agricultural villages, rich mining villages, or villages located at the junction of trade routes. The largest Naksyabandiyah *surau* in the late eighteenth century seem to have been located in two *sawah*-rich villages, Taram in Limapuluh Kota and Cangking in Agam, and in the gold-mining centre of Talawi in Tanah Datar.[44] In general, they were a phenomenon of the plains rather than the hills, although some famous hills *surau* did exist.

Much more is known about the Syattariyah *tarekat,* because in the late eighteenth century its members became involved in religious controversies. Like the Naksyabandiyah an order which was particularly dynamic in India, the Syattariyah was introduced into Sumatra by the famous Abdurrauf of Singkil (c.1615-c.1693).[45] A Minangkabau pupil of Abdurrauf's, Burhanuddin, brought the *tarekat* from Aceh to Ulakan sometime in the latter part of the seventeenth century, and from thence it moved up the trade routes to the villages of Kapas Kapas and Mensiangan, close by modern Padang Panjang, to Kota Lawas, and to the rich *sawah* country of southern Agam, in particularly to Kota Tua near Naksyabandiyah-oriented Cangking.[46] In the villages west of Kota Tua the *tarekat*'s *surau* became so prolific that it was described by one of its members as 'the leader in this world and the hereafter of all beings in this part of the region'.[47] The region became known as Empat Angkat (the four exalted ones) after the fame of four leading Syattariyah teachers who lived at Kota Tua and nearby.

The students who came to study at Syattariyah *surau* were exposed to the full gamut of Islamic learning. Abdurrauf's writings show his considerable respect for the *syariat*;[48] he had even requested one of his teachers in Medina to write a book for Indonesian pupils largely devoted to expounding the significance of the law in the life of the mystic, to counteract the idea that mystic enlightenment brings exemption from the provisions of the law.[49] Different Syattariyah *surau* specialized in different branches of learning, which were added to and reinforced by the increase in the number of pilgrims leaving Minangkabau for the holy land in the latter part of the eighteenth century. Kamang specialized in *ilmu alat,* the study of the Arabic language; Kota Gedang in *ilmu mantik maana,* the logical exposition of the meaning of the Koran, appealing to reason rather than to feelings; at Kota Tua resided a scholar from Aceh who had come to teach *ilmu tafsir* or commentary on the Koran.[50] A typical Syattariyah *kitab* (book) completed by a teacher at Ulakan in 1757 indicates that a variety of instructional matter was available to Syattariyah pupils: there are notes on Arabic grammar; a commentary by an Arab author on a well-known Arabic grammar; notes on verses from the Koran; Malay notes on medicine and on numbers, to help in the choosing of auspicious days; and notes on Arabic syntax.[51]

Nothing so far mentioned differentiates the Syattariyah from other orders. However, the brotherhood did also have its own way of looking at the world of God and man, and it was characterized by its own peculiar teaching of the *martabat tujuh,* the doctrine of the seven phases of emanation of the Absolute.[52] This teaching was outlined in the early seventeenth century work of a Gujarati teacher, *al-Tuḥfa al-mursala ilā rūḥ al-nabī (The Gift addressed to the spirit of the Prophet),* which postulated that God is Being, and that this Being proceeds to the visible world through six further stages of emanation, but is involved in no change thereby. Abdurrauf made use of this system of seven grades of Being in his writings, and its promulgation became a mark of the Syattariyah order in Indonesia.[53] Devotees of the Naksyabandiyah order found much to dislike in the *martabat,* and there is a Minangkabau account of disputes between Syattariyah centres and Naksyabandiyah-oriented Taram and Talawi, where scholars lived who 'opposed the martabat'.[54] These disputes became so serious as to lead to open fighting, but it seems likely that much of this disputation was related more to matters of precedence and prestige than to actual doctrinal disagreement.[55]

By the late eighteenth century the study of the law was important in all *surau*; students were able to move readily between one order and another with little intellectual dislocation. As far as the Syattariyah was concerned, both the *Tuḥfa* and the works of Abdurrauf were eager to present to their readers the basic minimum of Islamic practice. Syattariyah writings made clear the need to follow the path of obligation – the law – as a guide to right living here on earth,[56] and about this none of the *tarekat* introduced into the fabric of Minangkabau life disagreed.

The first Islamic revivalist movement, 1784-1803

In the late eighteenth century the area surrounding the Syattariyah centre of Kota Tua in Agam was experiencing commercial stimulation and a new influx of wealth, occasioned by the cassia trade of the neighbouring hill villages. Individuals who had done well in trade were able to afford to make the pilgrimage, and more and more people from this small region went to Mecca, exposing their villages on their return to fresh currents from the Muslim world outside.[57] From 1790 the profits of the coffee trade were added to those of the cassia trade, earned by numerous individuals who now had the opportunity to enter the market as 'micro-traders', buyers and sellers of products required in foreign commerce. Although we do not know from exactly which villages the bulk of the traders came, there is no doubt that many men from the plains villages in this region must either have travelled up to their hill counterparts offering to buy and transport their products, or have bought up small lots of coffee or cassia as they were brought down from the hills by their growers, assembling them for transhipment to the point where descent to the coast began and another group of traders took over.

About 1784 a renowned *syekh* presided over the Syattariyah *surau* in Kota Tua. This was Tuanku Nan Tua, an outstanding teacher who had attracted literally thousands of pupils to Kota Tua and to other Syattariyah *surau* in nearby villages. These *surau* had in the past blended peacefully into the agrarian landscape; they issued no challenge to the wider society, and prior to the commercial revival much of their teaching had been concerned with *ilmu hakikat,* the mystic knowledge required by the seeker after God. Tuanku Nan Tua himself was profoundly occupied with pursuing this path to God: 'Completely immersed in his speculations, he could maintain the same position unaltered for hours on end, losing himself in the religious question with which his spirit was occupied, and this abstraction seemed to release him from the turmoil of the world to such an extent that on these occasions his soul was reputed to go on a pilgrimage to Mecca'.[58] This concentration on the other-wordly aspects of Syattariyah teaching was ended by the rapid growth of commercial agriculture in the area. There was no objection to any of the students of the *surau,* or the teachers, becoming involved in trade, and in fact Tuanku Nan Tua became personally well-to-do as a result of his participation in commerce.[59] But such involvement led to a renewed interest among *surau* teachers in Islamic regulations for the successful prosecution of commercial ventures.

Conditions in southern Agam were hardly conducive to the well-regulated progress of commercial contacts with the outside world. Despite booming demand on the part of foreign customers, the society exhibited an inability to organize a secure trading network. Making for particular difficulty was the existence of widespread banditry, and even of whole villages of bandits who pursued their calling as an hereditary occupation. Bandits from these villages waylaid traders and robbed them of their goods or even, in the worst cases, abducted them and sold them to east coast traders. Apart from this social cancer, individuals' personal morality often frustrated the needs of commerce. The larger village markets, which had the potential for becoming bulking points for cassia and coffee, were only too often the scene of cockfighting and its concomitant, gambling, when a successful trader might lose all the profits of his recent venture; they were frequently places of ill-repute, to be avoided where possible, and the haunt of the seller of *tuak* and of opium.[60]

Even when confronting one another in the market-place, traders were in a difficult situation. According to Minangkabau custom they were supposed to settle disputes among themselves, coming as they did from various villages and being withdrawn from the jurisdiction of the *penghulu* council of the village in which they might trade.[61] In any case, with all the new commercial activity and the far greater numbers of traders in the market, the *penghulu* councils' methods of settling disputes were inadequate. Even in serious cases such as murder and theft bribery would postpone a council's decision, resting as it did on mutual consultation and agreement. Lack of justice for the traders of one village in another might lead to a flare-up between villages, and ultimately to blows. Villages were heavily fortified, and inter-village battles on specially-designated land outside the boundaries, in which even guns were used, were not uncommon.[62] These disputes were not only or necessarily the result of corruption on the part of members of the council; laws were not written, and *adat* sayings were open to a variey of interpretations, necessitating long drawn out discussions in the council hall.[63]

It was at this point that the *surau* was able to stand forth in society, offering an alternative to the existing mode of regulating society's affairs, especially its commercial affairs. The texts of Islam show a particular interest in the activities of traders; Muhammad himself was of course a merchant, and both the Koran and the *sunnah* (the custom of the Islamic community, handed down in the form of short narratives, the *hadis*) look with favour on commercial activity. The *sunnah* approves of economic activity, the search for profit, commerce and production for the market, and trade is even regarded as a superior way of earning one's livelihood.[64] The *syariat* as it was codified came to contain numerous provisions concerning commercial activities. It was within this framework that, from about 1784 – whatever may have been the case earlier – Islamic law became an important field of study in the *surau* of the Empat Angkat area. Movements dominated by the cry 'back to the *syariat*' have been common throughout the historical development of the Sufi brotherhoods, and displacement of hope from this world to the next never entirely dominated any of the orders, so that social and political action was always part of a brotherhood's potential. Even more than the Syattariyah, the Naksyabandiyah *tarekat* was marked by its disciples' study of jurisprudence and by its succession of teachers emphasizing the role of the *syariat* in the believer's life. In India this culminated in Shaikh Ahmad Sirhindi's 'back to the *syariat*' movement in the late sixteenth and early seventeenth centuries, a movement which undoubtedly influenced Indonesian *tarekat* teachers.[65] Now for the first time in Central Sumatra conditions became ripe for a similar movement; for Minangkabau's Muslim schools to challenge further accommodation with society, and to couch this challenge in terms of elevating Islamic law to a position of pre-eminence.

As the Syattariyah *surau* in the environs of Kota Tua began to concentrate on the teaching of Islamic jurisprudence, Tuanku Nan Tua took upon himself the special mission of trying to induce neighbouring villages to accept Muslim law in relation to trade and dealings with traders. As part of this enterprise he was prepared to attempt conversion of individuals in these villages, trying to persuade them to adopt the five pillars of Islam and lead the life of good Muslims. For this purpose he sent out groups of his students under a leader, and he particularly sought to operate inside bandit villages, which he felt were most in need of reform. This campaign was not always carried on without violence, just as in the past religious disputes between villages with Naksyabandiyah and Syattariyah *surau* had led to bloodshed; indeed, one of the functions of *surau* was to teach pupils the Malay martial arts, and a *guru* generally had on hand a body of fit young men who could be armed and made ready for a clash.

> First Tuanku Nan Tua worked out the places where the people who were robbed and sold as slaves were held captive, and also the regions where all those rules and regulations [i.e. of Islam] were violated, and in addition how many traders were robbed and captured in the course of time. He ordered that they should be recovered and brought back and the robbers punished. Their villages were attacked and captured, and therefore the robbers became very afraid of robbing and selling their captives.[66]

It seems that these tactics had some success, and towards the mid-1790s the Empat Angkat area was experiencing a great improvement in the regulation of commercial matters. Tuanku Nan Tua became known as 'the patron of traders'.[67]

The best of Tuanku Nan Tua's pupils determined to carry on his work in other villages outside Empat Angkat where the new commerce needed regulating. One of the most famous, Jalaluddin, established a *surau* in Kota Lawas, a market-gardening village on the slopes of Mount Merapi, already home to a famous Syattariyah *surau*. Kota Lawas was another newly prospering village, growing and selling both cassia and coffee. Jalaluddin's aim was to establish a genuine 'Muslim community', so that a revolution would be brought about in the village's way of life on the basis of following what he calls in his account of this period 'the rules of an Islamic religious adherent':[68] the saying of the five daily prayers (*sembahyang*) and carrying out the other four pillars of Islam. He also taught other aspects of Islamic law, including commercial law.[69]

None of the evidence from this period tells us exactly what sections of the village listened to his call, and on this point we must proceed by deduction. Kota Lawas was a village where families and individuals were gaining a considerable supplementary income by laying down cassia and coffee gardens and by entering the market as small traders either in their own or others' products. There can be little doubt that the puritanical, hard-working life, bounded by readily comprehensible regulations, preached by Jalaluddin attracted such people. Moreover the *syariat*, as well as providing guidance in matters of trade, provided a whole legal framework which offered an attractive code for a village in which many people did not own *sawah* land and whose previous codes of conduct had been modelled on those of the *sawah*-rich villages of the plains. Changing conditions made the need for such a code all the more apparent. The recently established gardens of tree crops led to a considerable increase in *harta pencarian* or self-earned property in the hill villages, and whilst the multiplication of such a form of property could readily be dealt with by the Muslim law of inheritance, *adat* was not designed to cope with such an alteration in the common pattern of land ownership. The Koran itself lays down the fixed fractional shares of the estate to which various relatives are entitled, and so here again the call 'back to the *syariat*' was appropriate to existing conditions in the hill villages.[70] Jalaluddin made considerable progress with conversion in Kota Lawas, although he also met opposition, presumably from the *sawah*-owning lineages in the village, and there were armed attacks on his *surau* from time to time.[71]

The Padri movement, 1803-1819

This domestic revivalist movement common to the life of Sufi brotherhoods in the Islamic world was rudely interrupted somewhere about 1803 by currents which swept into Minangkabau from the heartland of Islam. We have already noted that the new wealth to be gained from trade enabled more and more individuals to undertake the *haj*, and so to become sensitive to developments in the holy city. Those who were in Mecca in 1803 lived through a stirring episode; the city was conquered by an army of desert warriors whose cry was not simply 'back to the *syariat*', but rather expressed itself in a demand for a return to the most fundamental tenets of the Prophet and his Companions. These were the Wahhabis from eastern Arabia, and it was Wahhabi teaching which so impressed certain Minangkabau pilgrims that they determined to launch a full-scale revival when they returned home. They became known as Padris, men of Pedir (Pidië), after the port in Aceh from which most Minangkabau pilgrims sailed for Arabia.

In times of crisis in the history of Islamic communities great religious revivalist movements have exploded, usually with a strong military and political dimension and based on the firm distinction made in the Koran between believer and unbeliever, between the Muslim *ummat* and the communities of the *dār al-ḥarb* (abode of war). In delineating the characteristics of the true believer, the definitive source for such movements has always been the teachings of the Koran pure and simple and the tradition of the Prophet, so that these movements tend to idealize the earliest Islamic centuries and to deprecate all later developments. In the mid-eighteenth century just such a revivalist movement arose in Nejd, in eastern Arabia, preached by Muḥammad Ibn 'Abd al-Wahhāb (1703-1792) who was shocked at the lawlessness and irreligion prevalent in his home region. His views were very similar to those of an earlier revivalist preacher, Aḥmad Ibn Taimīyah (1263-1328), who had urged a return to the Koran and to the example of Muhammad, in opposition to the interpretations of later philosophers and the Sufis and who encouraged *ijtihad* or individual interpretation of the Koran. He, like 'Abd al-Wahhāb, was an adherent of the Ḥanbali school of law, the most conservative of the four schools of Islamic law, which is characterized by uncompromising adherence to the letter of both the Koran and the *hadis,* which transmits the *sunnah,* the tradition or practice of the Prophet.[72]

Unlike Ibn Taimīyah, 'Abd al-Wahhāb was able to give his movement a political dimension by enlisting the aid of one of the leading families of Nejd, the Sa'ūd family. In 1741 he formed an alliance with Muḥammad Ibn Sa'ūd, aimed at restoring true religion and purging Arabia of heresy, and the two declared a *jihad* or holy war which lasted over sixty years. Everywhere they went they made clear what they were fighting for. Their central theological dogma was the absolute incomparability of God and His unity and oneness. They had great objection to *tasauf,* the mystic's attempt to get nearer to God, and they condemned both students and *syekh* of the Sufi orders because they aimed at just such a special relationship with God. For this reason they opposed worship at the tombs of holy men and the practice of using others to intercede with God, and in their conquests they commonly destroyed elaborate tombs, including the tombs of Mecca and the dome covering Muhammad's tomb at Medina. In their attitude towards the Muslim community on earth the Wahhabis stressed that, as in early Islam, the main purpose of the community is to apply the law of God, the original law stripped of the innovation of intervening centuries. Strict observance of the prescribed religious duties was felt to be of the utmost importance, and the lawfulness and unlawfulness or prohibited nature of certain actions they considered must be scrupulously observed. In all this, it was not the books of codified law but the practice of the earliest Muslims which was to be followed, to be judged independently on the basis of accounts in the Koran and the *hadis;* whatever had been introduced after the third generation from Muhammad was regarded as *bid'ah* (innovation, i.e. heresy) and therefore sinful.[73]

A Wahhabi pamphlet distributed in Mecca in 1803, giving account of the conquerors' view to a questioning Meccan, states:

So we informed him of our belief which is as follows: We believe, our sect holds the real true religion, is the sect of the Ahl-us-Sunnat and al-Jamá'at, and that our way to salvation is that of the pious ancient departed, most easy and excellent, and opposed to the doctrines of those who hold that the modern way is the best. We construe the Qorán and Hadíṣes according to the meaning apparent on the face of them, and leave the interpretation of them to God, for He is the Ruler.[74]

Elsewhere the pamphlet made clear that the Wahhabis 'obeyed those proofs which were clear and open without caring whether they were opposed to what our ancestors had or had not done.'[75] However, this is not to say that they merely interpreted the words of the Koran without making use of certain explanatory material; in fact they consulted the usual orthodox commentaries as aids to understanding both the Koran and the *hadis*: 'As to those liars and concealers of the truth who say, that we explain the Qorán according to our own views and only hold those traditions which agree with our opinions, without having recourse to the well known commentaries on the one or taking into consideration the narrators of the other; . . . All this is simple nonsense.'[76]

The Wahhabi army entered Mecca in early 1803, although Wahhabi groups had previously attended the *haj* on occasions and many of their doctrines had already been discussed in Mecca before 1803, owing to their disputes with that city's scholars.[77] Now, however, the content of Wahhabi teaching must have been immediately clarified for those Minangkabau pilgrims who were in the city. First and foremost it was apparent that violence was an integral part of the Wahhabi *jihad.* Not only did they plunder towns for booty as a right, they also massacred the inhabitants of several settlements on their way to Mecca. In Mecca itself they strictly enforced regular attendance at prayers, banned tobacco smoking, prohibited the wearing of silk clothing and the use of the rosary. When the hour of prayer arrived, the Wahhabi soldiers patrolled the streets armed with large sticks and drove the inhabitants by force into the mosques. By 1804 the Wahhabis were in complete control of the Hejaz, and by 1811 their empire extended from Aleppo in the north to the Indian Ocean, and from the Persian Gulf in the east to the Red Sea. In every town they simplified the administration by appointing one supreme official, a *kadi,* who was to deal with all disputes by relying less on the opinions of legal scholars and more on his own judgements based on consultation of the Koran and the *hadis.* Having intruded into Ottoman territory, however, they were ultimately confronted with an Ottoman army under Egyptian command. By 1812 they were driven out of Medina and in 1813 out of Mecca, leaving the Hejaz securely garrisoned by the Turks for another century, while the Wahhabis themselves remained shut up in their desert fastness of Nejd for the same period.[78]

Some time in 1803 three Minangkabau pilgrims who had witnessed the Wahhabi occupation of Mecca returned home.[79] The best known among them is Haji Miskin, who had been involved in Tuanku Nan Tua's local revivalist movement before leaving for Mecca and had himself preached conversion for four years in the Agam plains village of Batutebal, near Kota Tua, which was his home. On his return to Minangkabau he spent some time at Batutebal, but ultimately he felt called to go and live in the hill village of Pandai Sikat, which was now actively producing both cassia and coffee for the market. He became the client of one of the Pandai Sikat *penghulu,* Datuk Batuah, who on his own initiative was trying to promote reforms in the community so that the newly burgeoning commerce of Pandai Sikat could be subject to suitable regulation. The example of Datuk Batuah's patronage of Haji Miskin is only one instance of many in the Padri movement of *penghulu* and religious teachers working together to introduce a new regime; the notion of the movement solely as an uncompromising attack on the *penghulu* system is quite misleading, although this interpretation still holds sway in even the most recent literature.[80] In Pandai Sikat Haji Miskin 'with all his strength preached religion and improved the state of the district.'[81] The centre of Haji Miskin's and Datuk Batuah's campaign was the market-place, which continued to be a scene of disorder; it was here that money flowed into the community and was immediately squandered in the cockfighting ring near the *pasar,* and on the drinking of *tuak* and the smoking of opium, all of which led to inflamed passions and volatility at the end of market-day, passions which could ultimately erupt into fighting, robbery and even murder. Despite all Haji Miskin's preaching, however, Pandai Sikat was in too volatile a state to pay much attention to his call. Finally, to demonstrate his earnestness in his cause, the *haji* burnt down the new *balai* of Pandai Sikat, the pride and glory of the village, and fled to Kota Lawas.[82]

At this stage Haji Miskin seems to have thought that his failure in Pandai Sikat was due to the absence among his adherents of prominent religious teachers,who could give weight to his cause. Kota Lawas, unlike Pandai Sikat, was an old centre of Syattariyah endeavour. Not only had Jalaluddin paved the way here by preaching the 'back to the *syariat*' cry, but Kota Lawas was also the home of one of the most revered Syattariyah *syekh* in Agam, Tuanku Mensiangan, whose grandfather had been that very Syattariyah teacher who had introduced the *tarekat* to Kapas Kapas and Mensiangan from the coast.[83] Tuanku Mensiangan, assailed first by the views of Jalaluddin and then by the zeal of Haji Miskin, became won over to the Wahhabi principle that, if all else failed, force must be used to convert the country to Islam, so that each village could become a genuine Islamic community. He extended his patronage to Haji Miskin, who gradually acquired a following in the village presumably comprising the same families which had extended a welcome to Jalaluddin's message. Like Jalaluddin, however, he also encountered opposition, so that ultimately the village was ranged into two camps and fighting ensued. In a particularly fierce battle which took place on the village *pasar* Haji Miskin and his supporters were defeated. The *haji* was forced to flee to another protector, in the more northerly hills of Bukit Kamang, but Tuanku Mensiangan's prestige in the village was so great that he was left undisturbed by the victors on condition that he restricted himself merely to teaching in his *surau* as before.[84]

Haji Miskin's new patron in the hill area of Bukit Kamang was another religious teacher, a former student of Tuanku Nan Tua's called Tuanku Nan Rinceh. This man had been an early convert to the 'back to the *syariat*' movement and had followed Jalaluddin to Kota Lawas to see the effect of the latter's teachings. His home area of Bukit Kamang was deeply involved in the cultivation of cassia and coffee, and on his return he determined to put the ideas of his teachers into practice. Like Tuanku Nan Tua he devoted his first efforts to trying to see that the numerous small traders now on the market had recourse to an adequate legal code; in particular he established a special council in his home village of Bansa, to which traders who had been robbed of their merchandise could apply for redress. Also in imitation of the tactics of his *syekh* he drew up a list of bandit villages and began a series of open attacks on them, receiving help both in men and firearms, dispatched by his old teacher from the Kota Tua area.[85] With the appearance of Haji Miskin in Bansa, about 1805, Tuanku Nan Rinceh's cause took on a more militant aspect.

Tuanku Nan Rinceh soon came to be regarded as the archetypal Padri. According to a Dutch account based on the testimony of various Minangkabau in the 1830s, he was thin, small of stature, could be reduced to frenzy by the violence of his emotions, and possessed eyes which 'glistened with unusual fire'.[86] Because he had been a favourite pupil of Tuanku Nan Tua's, and because the aims of his movement were initially inchoate and seemed to be still part of Tuanku Nan Tua's 'back to the *syariat*', the old *tuanku* at first lent Tuanku Nan Rinceh his support, the more so because he himself was under threat of attack and Jalaluddin's *surau* at both Batutebal and Kota Lawas had been burnt down. The new allies now resolved that force should be used not only against bandit villages, but also against certain villages which were in every way outwardly respectable. The villages chosen to feel the wrath of the intensified movement were those where the village market-place was disfigured with large, prominent cockfighting rings. The hill village of Bukit Betabuah, as a result of its commercial agriculture, had acquired enough money to build a new, splendid cockfighting ring (*gelanggang*). As a preliminary manoeuvre, Tuanku Nan Tua visited the village with a group of his students, seeking to get the ring closed by negotiations. On his arrival, however, he was surrounded by a mob armed with stones and rifles, negotiations quickly broke down, and ultimately a fierce battle ensued from which neither side emerged the victor. Tuanku Nan Tua and his following were able to escape, and they kept up sorties against the village until the ring was finally destroyed four months later.[87] After this ring had been smashed, another ring was established in the nearby hill village of Banuhampu and a similar situation arose, the local religious teacher appealing to Tuanku Nan Tua for help: 'So the cock-fighting ring was banned by the orders of Tuanku di Padang Luar. He asked Tuanku Nan Tua to assist him, and the latter agreed to come with his men. Battle ensued, and many were killed and wounded on both sides. But the battle was short, only ten days, because Tuanku di Padang Luar was an able protector of his village.'[88]

This piecemeal action now became annoying to Tuanku Nan Rinceh, and he decided that each village must be turned into an Islamic community as rapidly as possible, using the simplicity of the Wahhabi system as a model along the lines of which such new communities were to be organized. He decided to use the typical instrument of Islamic revivalism, the *jihad,* and to move immediately to the final stage of the *jihad,* the combating of unbelievers by the sword, considering that the other two stages of holy war – *jihad* of the heart, directed against the flesh, and *jihad* of the tongue and hands, directed towards prohibiting unlawful actions – had already failed in Minangkabau.[89] His argument was that the time had come to move on to the violent stage of the *jihad* because the non-violent warnings of himself and his fellow revivalists had been ignored. Tuanku Nan Rinceh began his *jihad* spectacularly in his own village by killing his mother's sister for using tobacco, and went on to announce to Bansa the regime of extreme puritanism which must henceforth be followed: the outward signs of a revivalist village were to be the abandonment of cockfighting, gambling, and the use of tobacco, opium, *sirih* and strong drink; white clothes symbolizing purity were to be worn, with women covering their faces and men allowing their beards to grow; no part of the body was to be decorated with gold jewellery, and silk clothing was to be eschewed. Needless to say, prayer five times a day was made obligatory. A system of fines was instituted for infringement of these rules.[90] Regimes of such puritanism are, of course, a feature of revivalist movements, and had even accompanied Islamicization in other parts of the archipelago. In Banten in the late seventeenth century many religious authorities had discarded Javanese dress for Arab garb, and had prohibited opium and tobacco smoking, whilst the Budiah movement in mid-nineteenth century north Java exhibited similar tendencies.[91]

Was there more to Tuanku Nan Rinceh's system than just a general Wahhabi puritanism? Unfortunately we understand little of how Islamic law was forced upon the village. The introduction of this legal system was certainly the *tuanku*'s aim, and village administration was to be remodelled along the lines of the Wahhabis' reforms in Arabia. In Minangkabau, however, the lineage system seems to have remained too strong for this innovation to be ever more than partially successful, and the *penghulu* council continued to play a leading role in all village affairs.

Nevertheless, each village conquered by the Padris, or converted to their system, was obliged to appoint a *kadi* who functioned side by side with the village council; his judgements had to exclude many areas of village life, but in matters relating to Islam – its rites and duties – he was the supreme judge, and since trade was so often excluded from the council's purview, it too fell within the sphere of the Padri *kadi.* As far as the content of his judgements went, he was obliged to consult only the Koran, a more extreme position than even the Wahhabis had taken up. The village was also required to appoint an *imam,* to be occupied with expounding the scriptures and carrying out religious ceremonies. Overseers of the new regulations were also appointed, to be on the look out for individuals who missed the prayer hour, or simply left their knees uncovered.[92]

Apart from the institutionalization of its teachings, the most characteristic mark of the Padri movement was its organized violence against villages which would not submit to the Padri notion of an Islamic community. Tuanku Nan Rinceh saw the futility of Tuanku Nan Tua's practice of going into battle simply with an armed crowd of his own students and followers. Instead, his strategy was to set one entire village against another, no very difficult task given existing inter-village rivalries and the possibility of booty and *adat*-prescribed tribute from the defeated village. Tuanku Nan Rinceh's first successes with this strategy were achieved in his home area. Three hill villages of Bukit Kamang, Sala, Magek and Kota Baru, were converted to the new system, presumably because they saw the wisdom of austerity and social regulation if they were to conserve the new wealth brought to them through coffee and cassia and also because, in the past, they had been despised for their poverty and isolation and called *kerbau yang tiga kandang* (waterbuffaloes of the three stables) by their more prosperous plains counterparts. Now, as good Muslims, their inhabitants felt they were morally and socially superior to their neighbours, and they were persuaded by Tuanku Nan Rinceh to take revenge on the chief among their past tormenters, the inhabitants of the rich plains village of Tilatang. They fell on this village, settling old scores by killing some members of the population and driving many others away with loss of their property. Next Tuanku Nan Rinceh set his Bukit Kamang villages to attack Kurai, between Bukit Tinggi and Kota Tua, which was reduced to ashes, and then the more easterly Padang Tarab, which suffered the same fate.[93] The populations of all defeated villages had to pay a fine in gold or goods, the tribute sometimes amounting to up to fifty per cent of the village's gross product. In all these attacks it was easy to set a new, less respected village against an ancient, prestigious one, and also to set Bodi Caniago villages against villages of the Koto Piliang *laras,* which traditionally considered that in Minangkabau 'they had the most exalted position.'[94] Most of the original Padri villages did in fact belong to the Bodi Caniago tradition.

A similar strategy was found to work successfully within villages. Particularly in the plains, many villages exhibited far greater extremes of wealth and status than was common in the hills. In these villages members of lineages with no claim on a *penghulu* title and without much *sawah,* called by one Dutch observer 'vagabonds and dregs of the population',[95] could be convinced of the virtues of the new system and it was they who prepared the way for a Padri onslaught; they then had the satisfaction of seeing some of the leading *penghulu* families flee, and could appropriate their property. Many villages in any case held a sizable nucleus of people ready for reforms, particularly in the hills, where the most genuinely Padri villages came to be located. Once converted, a village could be persuaded of its moral duty to attack a plains neighbour and enforce the new system.[96]

Gradually Tuanku Nan Tua became more and more averse to the inter-village violence which was becoming the hallmark of the Padri movement, and refused any longer to lend his prestige to Tuanku Nan Rinceh's campaign. With most of the hill villages of north-eastern and southern Agam now solidly Padri, Tuanku Nan Rinceh therefore entered into an alliance with their leading *malim* for mutual support. Seven *malim* from the hill villages of Candung, Sungai Puar and Banuhampu joined with Tuanku Nan Rinceh in a league which, due to its ferocity, earned its members the epithet *harimau yang delapan* or eight tigers. But, despite their position as war leaders, all had been pupils of Tuanku Nan Tua and their original bond of submission to their master could not be regarded as broken; they were still *anak murid* or *anak saksian* (pupils). Hence they decided, in the interests of carrying their campaign forward, to try to win over Tuanku Nan Tua once more and to get his blessing on their enterprise. Negotiations were started and a feast was arranged at Kota Tua, where it was hoped to persuade Tuanku Nan Tua to remain in his *surau* as a teacher, whilst the Padri leaders would gain his sanction for spreading their principles in a somewhat different manner.[97]

During the negotiations Tuanku Nan Rinceh argued from the very words of the Koran and from Nawawi's *fikh* handbook that all customs not sanctioned in the Koran must be abolished, and that death was a fitting punishment for those who disagreed. Tuanku Nan Tua, a man of far wider learning, turned to the several Koranic commentaries sanctioned by the Syattariyah brotherhood, and argued that the Prophet had never intended such a meaning to be attached to his words: many passages in the Koran bore witness to the peace-loving, conciliatory spirit of the Prophet, who had made it clear that the only person who deserved death was he who had consciously renounced Islam, and that no village containing a single *mu'min* (believer) should be attacked.[98]

The outcome of the debate was that the Padri leaders were unable to get Tuanku Nan Tua's blessing, and instead they were induced to swear an oath to their teacher. When they had had time to reflect after the meeting, however, they decided that they wished to pursue their cause, and that the only way to legitimize it now was to find a new *syekh* in Agam whose prestige was equal to that of Tuanku Nan Tua and who would support their endeavours. The obvious candidate was Tuanku Mensiangan, descended as he was from the earliest teacher of the Syattariyah in the highlands, a man renowned for his learning and with considerable influence in the Kota Lawas region. Since he had already shown interest in Haji Miskin's movement, it was not difficult to win him over. The prospect of wider fame now opened before him and he was given the title Imam Besar, whilst Tuanku Nan Tua was labelled by the Padri leaders Rahib Tua (old Christian monk) and Jalaluddin execrated as Raja Kafir (King of Infidels) and Raja Yazid.[99]

The Wahhabis of Arabia, although themselves Ḥanbalis, recognized all the four Islamic law schools, and so the Padris had no motivation to try to replace Shafi'i teachings with those of the Ḥanbali school in Minangkabau. Nor were the Wahhabis opposed to forms of Sufism which did not deflect the individual from the path of the law.[100] The eight *tuanku,* however, now conceived the notion that opposition to their movement was being stirred up by those who remained loyal to the Syattariyah order. To show their contempt for the order, and with Tuanku Mensiangan's agreement, they burnt down Paninjauan, a village next to Kapas Kapas and one of the earliest Syattariyah centres in the highlands, with a large population of religious students.[101] Next they turned their attention to the Empat Angkat area, and a war was waged against Kota Tua and surrounding villages for six years. At times it took on a savage fury: 'They looted and robbed the wealth of the people and insulted the orang kaya. They killed the ulama and all the orang yang cerdik [pandits]. They captured married women, wedded them to other men, and made their women captives their concubines. Still they called all their actions, "actions to perfect religion".'[102] At one stage a truce was called and an attempt was made to confound Tuanku Nan Tua by inducing him to test his scholarship against that of a leading Naksyabandiyah scholar from Talawi, but this strategem foundered when the visiting scholar declared himself to be in agreement with Tuanku Nan Tua on all important matters. The war therefore continued, with numerous small villages near Kota Tua being razed to the ground and Tuanku Nan Tua losing his sons in battle. Nevertheless Kota Tua and nearby villages such as Cangking were able to hold out, until in 1821 the Dutch arrived on the scene; by this time all the Agam hill regions were solidly Padri, including the Kota Lawas-Pandai Sikat area on the slopes of Mounts Merapi and Singgalang, and the Bukit Pau region in the northernmost corner of the valley of Agam.[103]

The movement had also spread throughout the Lake Maninjau and Matur area to the west of Agam, where the hilly nature of the country made coffee-growing a flourishing activity. Dynamic individuals here were able to carve out a role for themselves both as agricultural entrepreneurs and as Padri leaders, witness the career of Tuanku Nan Tinggi in the area just north of Matur: 'Toewankoe nan Tinggi is a clever native who raised himself by his own ability from hoeloebalang of the former Toewankoe to ruler of this land; starting in the early days of the Padries he has been able to maintain the administration in his own hands, ensuring prosperity to his people because he leads and commands them in cultivating the land to their own advantage; he has especially encouraged coffee cultivation, rightly seeing the profits which can be made from this.'[104]

Much less is known about the Padri movement in the other valleys of Minangkabau, but each seems to have pursued its own particular route to conversion. Limapuluh Kota is interesting because its villages appear to have embraced Padri teaching wholeheartedly, and little in the nature of internal warfare is recorded. It has already been noted to what an extent all the villages of Limapuluh Kota were involved in the new commercial opportunities, exporting both gambir and coffee. A regime promising law, order and justice was attractive to villages whose trading proclivities were well developed. A Dutch commercial observer in 1844 remarked of Limapuluh Kota: '. . . as is well known, more wealth, more prosperity, more commercial spirit reigns than in any other district: apart from the 10,000 to 12,000 pikuls of coffee produced by this region every year, the cultivation of rice is carried on here with an industriousness unusual among the Malay, so that the district has been able to feed not only its own population, which is estimated at 600,000 to 700,000 people, but exports rice practically every year to Agam and other districts.'[105]

About 1811 Haji Miskin, after having made his mark in Bukit Kamang and seen Tuanku Nan Rinceh's successes, left for Limapuluh Kota to propagate his message. He settled in the coffee-rich village of Air Terbit on the slopes of Mount Sago, and began to win a name both for his teachings and for the holiness and purity of his life, passed very simply and with great personal austerities. In the village he gained the support of a wide variety of people of influence, both *penghulu* and *adat* religious authorities, and although there was some initial resistance from a section of the village, finally the village council agreed unanimously to follow the prescripts of the Koran more closely.[106] Other villages throughout Limapuluh Kota quickly declared their intention to do the same, both out of conviction and from fear of raiding parties from Agam if they did not show themselves to be followers of the new system. When the Dutch first entered the valley they found the adherents of Padri tenets had zealously set about promoting many works designed to improve their commercial prospects; roads and bridges were well maintained, houses large and attractive, and the market-places models of their kind. A Dutch visitor to a market-place near Payakumbuh in 1833 remarked: 'The good order which reigned here and everywhere in the Padri lands was remarkable: no disputes could be heard among all these people at the passer; each enquired the price and paid, if it satisfied him, without any bargaining.'[107]

A similar spirit seems to have marked the conversion of the Solok plain, where the earliest foreign visitor saw no signs of destruction,[108] and every mark of outward conformity to Padri usage:

On entering the country, we were struck by the costume of the people, which is now anything but Malay, the whole being clad according to the custom of the *Orang Putis,* or Padris, that is to say, in white or blue, with turbans, and allowing their beards to grow, in conformity with the ordinances of Tuanku Pasaman, the religious reformer. Unaccustomed to wear turbans, and by nature deficient in beard, those poor people make but a sorry appearance in their new costume. The women, who are also clad in white or blue cloth, do not appear to the best advantage in this new costume; many of them conceal their heads under a kind of hood, through which an opening is made sufficient to expose their eyes and nose alone . . .[109]

Quite different was the introduction of Padri principles into Tanah Datar, where the whole movement was once again marked by violence. The conversion of Tanah Datar is most closely associated with the name of Tuanku Lintau, a native of Lintau in the valley of the Sinamar running south from Mount Sago and parallel to the main Tanah Datar plain. This was an area which had experienced sudden riches from coffee exporting, and Tuanku Lintau was one of those who had become sufficiently well-to-do to go and pursue Islamic studies on the coast, first at Natal and then at Pasaman.[110] He became impressed with stories he had heard of Tuanku Nan Rinceh's movement in Agam, and about 1813 he returned home convinced that, as an inhabitant of Tanah Datar, it was his mission to reform manners and morals in the valley and, in particular, to make the royal family aware of its own unIslamic way of life. It appears that the Raja Alam of Minangkabau, Raja Muning Syah, was not averse to the introduction of some of Tuanku Nan Rinceh's teachings, and under his patronage the need for moral improvement was proclaimed in several villages. However, although the villages of Lintau itself were easily converted, the *penghulu* of the Tanah Datar *sawah* villages, wedded as they were to the existing royal system with its practice of non-interference in village life, were almost universally hostile, the more so as the proclamations excited some of the ordinary villagers against *penghulu* families and led to outbreaks of conflict within certain villages.[111]

As disorder spread in the villages of eastern Tanah Datar, Tuanku Lintau decided that the Raja Alam had neither the strength nor the desire to carry the reforms through, and that in some way he must try to impose a uniform system of administration throughout Tanah Datar, putting an end to the old village autonomy. It seemed to him that a prerequisite for the success of this plan was the removal of the royal family from the scene, and he began the second stage of his campaign by attacking those villages which were most intimately associated with royalty, such as Tanjung Berulak east of Suruaso. The Raja Alam, who was an old man of about seventy, stepped in to recover the village by arms, but after several contests Tuanku Lintau and his followers were victorious. The *tuanku* now became convinced that the royal system was a barrier to all he hoped to achieve. Some time in 1815 he persuaded the Raja Alam and other members of the royal family, as well as certain important state functionaries, to attend a meeting for negotiations at Kota Tengah between Suruaso and Tanjung Berulak. Suddenly, after the meeting had begun, he turned on the Raja Alam and all the assembled officers of state, accused them of corruption and irreligion, and ordered his followers to attack them. Many were killed, including the Raja Alam's two sons, though the Raja Alam and his grandson were able to escape, and ultimately made their way to Lubuk Jambi on the Inderagiri.[112]

Tuanku Lintau now turned to the task of legitimizing his position in the eyes of the inhabitants of the court centres. He married a daughter of the last Raja Ibadat, who died in 1817, changed the name of the latter's traditional seat, Sumpur Kudus, to Lintau, and assumed in his own person the consolidated offices of Raja Adat and Raja Ibadat.[113] Nevertheless, there was fierce resistance to Tuanku Lintau in the old royal centres; when Raffles visited Pagarruyung in 1818 he found it had been burnt three times and all buildings associated with the royal house destroyed. Suruaso suffered the same fate.[114] The Lintau Padris made successful raids into Tanah Datar as far west as Gurun, which they burnt numerous times, and as far south as Padang Luar at the food of Gunung Besi. The slopes of Mount Merapi in the west were their stopping-point; although they raided Batipuh, they were extended too far from their base to do much damage, and Batipuh remained throughout the Padri wars a gathering place for all those driven from their homes through opposition to the Padri system.[115]

One of the reasons the Lintau Padris organized persistent raids into the Tanah Datar plain was that, the more they turned their narrow valley over to coffee and devoted their labour to coffee cultivation, the greater was their need to acquire rice from outside. The granary of the Tanah Datar valley became essential to the operation of the Padri system further east. Also essential to the operation of the system was the market in slaves. The Agam Padris also made slaves of some of the inhabitants of the villages they captured, though how slavery was organized in Agam we do not know. Tuanku Lintau took considerable numbers of captives from Tanah Datar into service with his army, where as slaves they were essential for transporting equipment and the food needed for expeditions. Other captives he sold as slaves in the markets of Tanah Datar, and still others he had transported to areas in the east where there was need of labour and sold them there. It is unlikely that the Padris could have survived so long on a war-footing in their narrow valleys had they not had slave auxiliaries for their armies and slaves to cultivate the fields at home while they were away. Of some villages in the eastern valleys it was reported in the 1860s that the descendants of slaves captured in the Padri wars made up one-third of the entire population. At Silungkang, a village located in a sparsely populated region in the extreme east, while the inhabitants worked their *sawah,* they settled their newly acquired slaves outside the village boundaries and set them to work cultivating *ladang* or excavating small mountain gold mines nearby.[116]

Tuanku Lintau was able to extend his system administratively by means of some of his *hulubalang* or war chiefs, who took certain areas as fiefdoms and imposed Padri discipline. In the eastern hills, unlike central Tanah Datar, this was largely acceptable to the population of the villages, and so the entire Buo and Kumanis region became Padri under two separate *tuanku.*[117] Talawi, further south, exhibited an unusual arrangement; the main village of the area, also called Talawi, split into two parts, one half becoming Padri and the other remaining unconverted. This large village was divided by a stout wall, and there was no communication between the two halves.[118] To the north of the valley of Lintau, on the slopes of Mount Sago, the rich coffee-growing district of Halaban submitted to a *hulubalang* of Tuanku Lintau who became known as Tuanku Halaban; his region became zealously Padri.[119] In general all these new *tuanku* were renowned less for their learning and more for their fighting skills; they were war leaders first and religious teachers second. All seem to have been markedly concerned for agricultural improvement.

In addition to the attention he paid to the rice villages of Tanah Datar, Tuanku Lintau determined to try to gain control of part of the commercial network on the Inderagiri river. Lintau and Buo carried on an extensive coffee trade along this river, exchanging coffee at Lubuk Jambi, the main stapling point on its higher reaches, for cotton goods and salt. As a result of this trade the markets of Lintau and Buo were reported to be well-stocked. In 1823 the Lintau Padris mustered all their forces and besieged Lubuk Jambi for several days with about 1,200 men. They burnt most of it down, but were never able to install their own administration, and the place soon recovered as an independent river port.[120]

In the remainder of Tanah Datar, the pattern of conversion to Padri principles was similar to that observable elsewhere. While the plain remained resolutely unconverted, the other main hill regions became Padri independently of the activities of Tuanku Lintau. All the coffee villages of the northern hills were Padri by the second decade of the nineteenth century, beginning with Rao Rao on Mount Merapi, which was regarded as the 'forward line' of the Padris against the plains.[121] In the limestone range joining Mounts Merapi and Sago, coffee and artisan villages such as Tabatpatah, Salimpaung, Mandeling and Tanjung Alam were all strongly Padri.[122] To the south, the ten villages on the hilly plateau above Lake Singkarak, of which the woodcarvers' village of Sulit Air was the most important, also became zealous converts.[123]

Although the Padri movement failed to create a unified administration for all the Minangkabau highlands, Padri villages did have certain common characteristics. In addition to those already mentioned, it is interesting that most made use of some of their new income to build large, splendid mosques, replacing the small, obscure buildings of the pre-Padri period. One of the typical features of a strongly Padri village was a newly-constructed, large, wooden mosque, surrounded by ponds well stocked with fish.[124] Some were spectacular, such as the mosque at Sala in Bukit Kamang which had three conical roofs, one poised above another. Tuanku Halaban erected one of the largest mosques in the highlands at Tebingtinggi, with five roofs. The main village of Lintau, Tapi Selo, boasted a similar one; the pond surrounding it was so extensive that small boats could be used to go from one part of the mosque to another. Much labour was expended on these buildings. To construct the mosque at Tebingtinggi men were recruited from Limapuluh Kota as well as Halaban; work gangs were divided into five troops, each troop representing the manpower of ten villages. Specialists were also brought in; woodcarvers, for example, executed beautiful carvings on the doors and window posts.[125]

The other important characteristic of Padri villages, as indeed of all villages in Minangkabau in the Padri period, was that they were heavily fortified and their male population was kept almost constantly on a war-footing. The general practice was for a village to surround itself with a thick, impenetrable hedge of thorny bamboo (*aur-aur*), then a deep trench or moat which could be flooded, and finally a parapet of stones. Generally the fortifications simply followed the line of the village, so that it was always possible to enclose some ricefields within them. Outside the final parapet the ground would be impregnated with thousands of *ranjau,* sharp, pointed pieces of bamboo which could do severe damage to the feet of approaching soldiers, whilst at strategic points covered pits containing sharpened sticks were there to trap the unwary. There was little fighting in the open field, the hilly terrain in any case being unsuited to this form of warfare. For defence against besiegers, large numbers of hollow bamboo tubes would be inserted into the outer parapet; in one of these the defender's gun could be placed and against the other he would place his eye. Usually the outer stone parapet was also covered with a hedge, so that the guns were invisible and anyone who approached exposed himself to danger. The defenders' batteries were usually behind this parapet too. Although there was little open field combat, not all the defenders would remain within the fortifications; some generally came out, armed with guns and pikes, to try to outflank the attackers.[126]

Not only individual villages were fortified. Where adjacent villages of a naturally defensible region were of the same persuasion, they threw up joint fortifications as the first line of defence of an entire area. The Bukit Kamang Padris had a line of defence against Empat Angkat which stretched one and a half miles from near Bukit Tinggi to Baso near Candung, ending against a spur of Mount Merapi. The line consisted of trenches and walls planted with thorny bamboo, on which at intervals were erected small, square forts. Kota Lawas, Pandai Sikat and their allies were surrounded by defensive works, being completely ringed by large trenches which had been dug as high as 4,000 feet on Mount Merapi. The trenches were protected by stone ramparts, grown with thorny bamboo hedges, and the only break in the fortifications was to make provision for well-guarded entry paths. One reason for these elaborate constructions was that it was only in this way that fields could be protected and agriculture carried on while a state of war persisted. The northern hill region of Tanah Datar, commencing at Rao Rao, was surrounded by double defensive works; in addition each tiny valley between the mountain spurs, which might be open to surprise attack, was surrounded by strong walls grown with impenetrable hedges, inside which fields and coffee gardens could continue to be cultivated. The valley of Lintau was fortified in the same way, trenches being dug high up on the western mountains.[127]

Good use was made of mountainous terrain for defence. If a district could only be approached through mountainous country, the mountain passes and heights would be occupied and fortified. In the case of the Marapalam approach to Lintau, the mountain was covered with circular entrenchments which it was impossible to outflank. The defenders were able to use the descending ground to place heavy stones and beams attached to ropes in front of the trenches, which were then let loose on any attackers on the mountain. Water was also conducted to certain spots in such a way as to flood the steep ground and make it slippery.[128]

In areas where the terrain was flatter, watchhouses were erected as part of the defensive ramparts. They were generally mounted on four pillars eighteen to twenty feet high, and occupied by one or two defenders during the day and by six or eight at night. The watchhouse sentries would place bamboo ladders over the trenches so that the defenders could rapidly reach the ramparts after being called by shrill cries, and the village women would play their part by manning the trenches and drawing in the ladders. Outside the general fortifications there were also constructed small advance forts or *benteng,* made either of lumps of turf or of the trunks of coconut palms. Where these *benteng* were placed high up on a mountain, women, children and old men would be sent into them when a village was under attack.[129]

Despite the lack of open field combat, it was customary for the village *hulubalang,* those young men who had inherited the position of defender of their lineage, to mount the ramparts armed with lances and jump over on to open ground to challenge an approaching enemy. Since their lineage position was one of service to a *penghulu,* they could always be seen clustered around a *penghulu* if the latter appeared in the open field and, of course, the various Padri *tuanku* acquired large bodyguards of such men; three hundred was not an uncommon number. They were easily distinguishable by their red clothing, and generally they did not carry guns but were armed with one or more pikes, a sword and a shield, which they wielded dexterously to avoid bullets. Their function was to show courage rather than profound judgement in battle; they would advance several paces in front of their lines with fierce cries, much dancing and flashing of teeth, their long hair flying across their faces, and urge the enemy *hulubalang* to join battle.[130]

Final judgement in battle was left to the village's war leader who, as the Padri system evolved, was generally the village *imam.* During sorties into other territories, if the war leader was wounded the whole force would immediately retreat. War leaders were generally given the epithet *bertuah* (endowed with magic powers) and thought to be invulnerable, so that a wound was regarded as a sign of God's unfavourable judgement on the enterprise. This was linked with the widespread use of astrology to choose an auspicious day for an attack; when failure seemed imminent, it was felt that the day had not been properly chosen and retreat was viewed as the wisest course.[131]

It has already been noted that various villages specialized in making guns, and that a considerable percentage of the male population of many villages had guns. The guns used were long matchlocks, though, having no ramrods, they could only be loaded clumsily. Villages also had their own small iron cannon of Minangkabau manufacture, and large, rounded stones were used as cannon balls. Tapi Selo, the main village of Lintau, was found to contain forty-two large and small cannon when it was taken in 1832.[132]

European penetration of the Minangkabau highlands, 1818-1832

While the Padri villages of the interior were concentrating on expanding agriculture and carrying on a vigorous trade with all comers, Europeans in the Minangkabau world remained bottled up in the west coast port of Padang. From 1795 the port had been in the hands of the English, who had removed the Dutch as a consequence of conflict in Europe. The English policy was one of complete political passivity, and there was no other English factory on the coast north of Padang until Air Bangis and the fringes of the Minangkabau world were reached.[133] The Padri trading network was a successful rival to that of Padang, with Pariaman blossoming once again as the port to which the cassia and coffee trade of Agam was directed. The English by the second decade of the nineteenth century laboured under the fear that the Lintau Padris, who had penetrated as far as Saningbakar on the main route to Padang, might lay claim to the port and entirely cut off its trade to force submission. By early 1818 the Lintau Padris were showing every sign of wishing to attack Padang; they sent raiding parties quite close to the port, and sealed the roads to prevent traders from going there. The English Resident was daily expecting an attack.[134] No European challenge was thrown down to the Padris, however, until the arrival at Padang in July 1818 of the English Lieutenant-Governor of Benkulen, Sir Thomas Stamford Raffles.

Raffles viewed the Minangkabau highlands in the context of Britain's position in Southeast Asia. After the British surrender of Java to the Dutch at the end of the Napoleonic wars, Raffles was of the opinion that Britain must have a foothold somewhere in the Indonesian archipelago to forestall Dutch control of all the trade of the region. He felt it was only just that Sumatra should be brought within the British sphere of influence, as compensation for the loss of Java.[135]

The prevailing political situation in Minangkabau gave Raffles considerable ammunition with which to support his case. Arriving at Padang he encountered two relatives of the last Raja Alam of Minangkabau, who had escaped the Kota Tengah massacre and were living in the port under the designation 'The Tuankus of Suruaso'. Accompanied by a party of Minangkabau in which these two were included, he made his famous journey to Suruaso and Pagarruyung, and was convinced by his reception from the last remaining female representative of the royal house that Britain would acquire a good claim to Sumatra if she acted to support the 'legitimate authority' of the Minangkabau royal family.[136] A treaty was signed promising this support in return for the cession of the western coastal strip to Britain, and so was inaugurated a period of direct European interference in Minangkabau's affairs in alliance with the royal family. Raffles was clear that this alliance represented the most prudent course: 'By upholding their authority, a central government may easily be established, and the numerous petty states, now disunited and barbarous, may be again connected under one general system of government. The rivers which fall into the Eastern Archipelago may again become the high roads to and from the central capital; and Sumatra, under British influence, again rise into great political importance'.[137]

On his departure from Tanah Datar Raffles left a detachment of Bengali soldiers at Simawang, with the aim of protecting the villagers from the Lintau Padris and keeping open the mountain passes between Lake Singkarak and the coast.[138] However, all of Raffles' acts were annulled by the Directors of the East India Company, and the Minangkabau coast was duly handed back to representatives of the Netherlands Indies government, who arrived at Padang in May 1819.[139] Padang once again became the centre of Dutch activities on the coast, all ports between Tiku in the north and Inderapura in the south being deemed to be now under Dutch control. It was not long before the Dutch Resident at Padang, James du Puy, came to espouse the same views that Raffles himself had held. The British garrison at Simawang had been withdrawn when the British left Padang, but Raffles' two protegees, the Tuankus of Suruaso, remained in the port to keep the new Resident informed of the vices of the Padris of Lintau and their alleged destruction of the Tanah Datar trading system. From June 1819 du Puy began to urge the Batavia government to again garrison Simawang so that the Padris could not completely strangle the trade of Padang or, worse still, descend from the mountains and attack the port.[140]

It was a very old fear of the Dutch, dating from their first settlement in Padang, that opposition to their position would arise in the interior, leading to the possibility of a combination of their internal and external enemies which they could never withstand.[141] Batavia therefore, while refusing at this moment to remove badly needed troops from Padang, agreed that connections should be maintained with the Tuankus of Suruaso. Raffles had granted the two a monthly pension and had recognized them as representatives of the Minangkabau court; Batavia assented to this, and, in a remark which indicated that only financial stringencies were preserving the government's caution, conceded that the two might be useful 'in the eventual occupation' of the highlands.[142]

Du Puy continued to press for the reoccupation of Simawang, arguing still that the disruptions in Tanah Datar had markedly affected Padang's trade, had isolated it from its previous trading partners, and had exposed it to the danger of an attack. In a letter written in August 1820 he requested, again following Raffles' model, permission to make a treaty with the 'chiefs of the interior', based on the cession of their lands to the Netherlands Indies government. He then went to Batavia to press his case, and was rewarded with a government decision that, for the sake of the protection of Padang, there could be 'an unconditional cession' of the lands in question to the Netherlands Indies government; the lands were to be occupied, and a military garrison of one hundred men was to be placed at Simawang or some other strategic spot.[143] The result was the signing of a treaty in Padang on 10 February 1821 between du Puy and the nephew of the last Raja Alam of Minangkabau, Sultan Alam Bagagar Syah of Pagarruyung, the two Tuankus of Suruaso, and designated *penghulu* from the main villages on the gold route from

Suruaso to Padang. Cession was made of the core of Adityawarman's old realm – Pagarruyung, Suruaso, Sungai Tarab and 'the remaining lands of the State of *Maninkabo*' – in return for a Dutch military detachment at Simawang. In the same month a Dutch force of one hundred men occupied Simawang, and conflict between the Dutch and the Padri movement began in earnest.[144]

As a result of the war-torn situation in Tanah Datar, the Dutch garrison of Simawang was very soon persuaded by its new allies to attack the nearby Padri village of Sulit Air, a village of artisans which had shown great zeal for the revivalist cause. With this attack on 28 April 1821 began the Dutch attempt to drive the Lintau Padris over the eastern mountains and back into their valley. The main agent of the earliest Dutch conquests in Tanah Datar and Agam was Lieutenant-Colonel A.T. Raaff, a dynamic young officer who arrived in the highlands with reinforcements in December 1821 after the Batavia government had decided to support further military involvement in the area. Raaff had recieved part of his education at the French military academy of St. Cyr, and had taken part in Napoleonic campaigns in Germany before transferring to the Netherlands Indies army.[145] He was an advocate of forceful military action, and moved at once to impress the Padris that the Dutch were in earnest. In this he had the full backing of the Batavia government, which had become more fully informed of the flourishing coffee trade largely in Padri hands and was now convinced of the desirability of possessions in Minangkabau.[146]

In February 1822 a Dutch expeditionary force of approximately 400 infantry and artillery gathered in the highlands, together with certain Minangkabau forces which had agreed to serve as auxiliaries. The vast majority of these forces were from Batipuh and nearby areas, villages long linked with the royal gold trading system and to which many individuals from central Tanah Datar had fled when the Lintau incursions began. On this occasion the auxiliaries numbered between 12,000 and 15,000 men, and such numbers became common components of all subsequent Dutch military expeditions, the men returning home only at key agricultural periods. One-sixth were armed with guns of local manufacture. Before driving Tuanku Lintau back into his valley Raaff considered it necessary to take the zealously Padri villages between Mounts Merapi and Singgalang, so that Dutch troops would not be exposed to an attack from the rear as they advanced into Tanah Datar. However, opposition inside Tanah Datar was so strong that there was no time for this. Finally Tuanku Lintau gathered his forces south and southeast of Gurun for a punishing onslaught on the invaders, but in early March 1822 the Padris were worsted in a decisive battle and the *tuanku* took flight over the mountains to Lintau. By midday on 4 March 1822 the Dutch were in occupation of Pagarruyung and Suruaso, and the other main centres of south-east Tanah Datar were then taken. An expedition over the mountains in pursuit of Tuanku Lintau was regarded as too hazardous, and Raaff instead turned his attention to the Padri villages in the northern hills of Tanah Datar. In a series of encounters in May 1822 the whole area between Rao Rao and Tabatpatah was taken, and the iron smithies and gun- and sword- making establishments at Salimpaung and Sipayang destroyed. Raaff then pushed through to Tanjung Alam, from the heights of which Limapuluh Kota could be observed, and there he established his forward post against the Padris of that valley.[147]

Because Padri attacks from this side continued, Raaff decided that pursuit was the best course of action. He marched from Tanjung Alam round Mount Merapi into Agam, reaching Candung and the Kota Tua area. Realizing the danger he still ran of his Tanah Datar flank being exposed, in July 1822 Raaff turned on the villages between Mounts Merapi and Singgalang and forced the surrender of Kota Lawas, Pandai Sikat and the others. Trapped now on both sides, Padri villages on Mount Merapi such as Sungai Puar and Banuhampu also announced their surrender. But just as Raaff was still faced with the unconquered Padris of Lintau in the mountains and valleys to the east of Tanah Datar, so too in Agam he was unable to defeat the forces of Tuanku Nan Rinceh lodged in a well-nigh impregnable position north of the Empat Angkat region, where natural chasms and hills assisted fortification. Padris occupied the entire Bukit Kamang area and Tilatang and its neighbouring villages; Tilatang's main fort, Kapau, was considered unbreachable. In the hope of freeing themselves for a final onslaught on Tuanku Lintau, Dutch troops did attack Tuanku Nan Rinceh's lines in August 1822, but Kapau proved impenetrable and the Dutch retreated into Tanah Datar.

In late 1822 and early 1823 reinforcements again arrived from Java and Raaff was able to try once more to secure the Dutch position in Tanah Datar by conquering Lintau. He elaborated a grandiose plan whereby Lintau was to be taken by an attack on its fortifications on Mount Marapalam, after which Dutch troops would sweep through Limapuluh Kota, down into Agam and back to Lake Singkarak, placing all four valleys of the Minangkabau highlands in their hands. The attack began in mid-April 1823, but was a complete failure due to the strongly entrenched position of the Padris on Mount Marapalam, the only possible approach to Lintau on the Tanah Datar side. From this date Dutch zeal for expansion in Minangkabau lessened. Raaff died at Padang in April 1824, and there was nothing comparable to his highlands conquests until the 1830s, when a quite different set of circumstances prevailed.[148]

To what extent was there a lessening of Padri influence on the villages conquered by the Dutch? As far as the villages of southern and western Tanah Datar were concerned, those in the area between Sungai Jambu and Suruaso came over quite quickly in 1822, delighted to have outside help to rid themselves of a system which had never been congenial. The entire Batipuh area, right down to the shores of Lake Singkarak, for twenty years remained loyal to the ally with whom a number of villages had signed the 1821 treaty; it has been noted that many of the Dutch auxiliaries were from this area, and for many years Batipuh men were able to make careers as auxiliary soldiers, enriching themselves with booty from obstinately Padri villages. The taking of booty was not merely a random affair. *Adat* prescriptions were definite concerning the recompense to be made by a defeated village to those who had been put to the trouble of fighting, and the Minangkabau villages which sent auxiliaries to aid the Dutch invariably received a *tanda perang* (token of war), in the form of gold and buffaloes.[149] The Empat Angkat area of Agam, which under Tuanku Nan Tua had opposed the Padris for so long, also welcomed Dutch support. Just before the Dutch invasion Tuanku Nan Tua had been successful in gathering villages from Candung round to Padang Tarab into an alliance against both Bukit Kamang and Pandai Sikat-Kota Lawas, and he saw the Dutch as potential allies. By 1824 he was dead, but his family remained staunch supporters of the Dutch connection.[150]

Villages which were genuinely Padri, however, only with reluctance opened their gates to the Dutch forces, usually as a last resort to avoid burning and destruction. Pandai Sikat and Kota Lawas, for example, remained under the influence of Tuanku Mensiangan even after their submission to the Dutch, and took the first opportunity they could find to throw out their Dutch garrison. They had to be reconquered in February and March 1824 and Kota Lawas in particular, with Tuanku Mensiangan's encouragement, put up strong resistance and did not submit until many of its houses had been burnt down by the action of a Dutch howitzer. The villages of the northern Tanah Datar hills were also only reluctantly within the Dutch orbit. They had been conquered due to the apostasy of Rao Rao, which was involved in a dispute with the Padri village of Tanjung Alam further east over the disruption of the former's trade communications with Agam. Rao Rao soon regretted its accommodation with the Dutch, and all the villages in this region were quite clearly only held in check by the Dutch fort at Tanjung Alam. The villages surrounding Sulit Air, although they too had come over suddenly in 1822, from fear of vengeance of the Batipuh auxiliaries, also could barely be regarded as loyal supporters of the Dutch presence.[151]

Basically, therefore, the Dutch in 1824 held with some semblance of security only those centres such as Pagarruyung, Suruaso, Sungai Tarab, Lima Kaum and Batipuh which had been since the seventeenth century partners with the VOC at Padang in the Minangkabau gold trading network. The Kota Tua area of Agam remained a special case, brought over to the Dutch side by a long-standing dispute between the two groups of Islamic revivalists and surrounded on all sides by villages still attached to the Padri system.

Nevertheless, the Padris of Lintau, Limapuluh Kota and Bukit Kamang had reason to worry about their future. The Dutch had successfully occupied the main west coast ports and cut them off from these trading outlets, and there was always the possibility of further Dutch attacks. Raaff was succeeded as Resident and Military Commandant by Colonel H.J.J.L. de Stuers, who arrived at Padang in December 1824. Fortunately for the Padris, de Stuers was of the opinion that Dutch military conquests had been too rapid and rested on too flimsy a base; nothing more should be undertaken until the existing area under Dutch 'control' had been consolidated. He therefore occupied himself with trying to negotiate a treaty with the main Padri leaders, which would confirm the Dutch and the Padris in their respective spheres of influence. At about the same time Tuanku Nan Rinceh and Tuanku Lintau, together with the Padri leaders further east in Limapuluh Kota, seem to have decided that the founding of Singapore gave them ample scope to direct their trading ventures even more exclusively to the east, and so they were in a mood to respond to de Stuers' overtures.

The outcome of the negotiations was that both Tuanku Nan Rinceh and Tuanku Lintau sent emissaries to Padang, accompanied by Tuanku Nan Saleh of Talawi and by an emissary from Tuanku Guguk of Limapuluh Kota. Together with eight other *tuanku* and fifty-four *murid,* all dressed in white, they arrived in Padang for a stay of twenty days. The peace treaty was signed on 15 November 1825. In the discussions before the signing the Padri delegates made it clear that they wanted the Dutch to leave the interior and confine themselves to the coast, but of course there was no question of gaining agreement on this point. Short of this, they demanded that their faith should be introduced into Tanah Datar under Dutch auspices. The Dutch response was that this could only be done by good example, not by any methods savouring of coercion, and ultimately the Padri delegates reduced their demands to Dutch assistance in the gradual abolition of opium-smoking and cockfighting in Tanah Datar, indicating their continued concern with matters of personal morality and with the state of the market-places. The clauses of the treaty, however, were not so specific. The Dutch recognized the authority of the four Padri leaders over their own territories and their right to promote their religious system there, in exchange for Padri recognition of Dutch authority where it already existed. Both sides promised mutual protection of traders.[152]

The signing of the treaty coincided with the inability of the Dutch to make any further forward movements in the Minangkabau interior. The huge accumulated debt of the Netherlands Indies had resulted in the arrival at Batavia in September 1825 of a special commissioner, Count du Bus de Gisignies, with full powers to restore solvency. Although Java was the main focus of his attention, the commissioner ordered the strictest economies and retrenchments in all the 'outer islands', including Sumatra.[153] At the same time rebellion broke out in Java, a rebellion which evolved into the Java War, and all available Dutch forces were removed from Minangkabau. By September 1826 there were only 682 Dutch troops in the whole of central Sumatra, and of these less than 300 were left to occupy the interior; they garrisoned merely four forts in the highlands at Suruaso, Batu Sangkar near Pagarruyung and Tanjung Alam in Tanah Datar, and at Bukit Tinggi in Agam. All this reinforced de Stuers' inclination to consolidate the Dutch position, and the highlands experienced five years of comparative peace before the next Dutch onslaught. Not all villages were equally peaceful. Padri villages surrounded Dutch-controlled territory in a half moon, and sorties continued across the 'borders'; the worst raids took palce from Bukit Kamang into Empat Angkat and from Lintau over the mountains into the Pagarruyung-Suruaso-Padang Ganting area.[154]

During this period the Padri movement itself underwent certain changes. Its extreme puritanism simply could not be maintained for so long. Villagers in the devotedly Padri Pandai Sikat, for example, were observed in 1824 to be chewing *sirih* and smoking tobacco.[155] By 1831 such laxity was widespread, even in areas zealously attached to the Padri cause. What part women played in the revulsion from certain Padri prescriptions we do not know, but without doubt Padri regulations relating to women's dress were disliked, and ceased to be followed as soon as was possible.[156] One reason for the growing laxity in observance was the return of a new wave of *haji* to Minangkabau in the late 1820s. Although Mecca had been out of the hands of the Wahhabis for well over a decade, little attention had been paid in Minangkabau to the reports of returning pilgrims until Dutch manoeuvres made it difficult for the Padris to continue the holy war. By 1829, however, returning *haji* were gaining a hearing, especially in Limapuluh Kota, and the rigours of the original Padri system began to soften once it was established without doubt that Mecca was no longer paying attention to such matters as tobacco and silken clothing.[157]

The returning *haji* were aided by the fact that no Padri leader had ever been able to acquire unchallenged dominance over a wide area, not to speak of all Minangkabau, and there was no monolithic Padri political system to break down. Even Tuanku Lintau was confined to the few villages which made up his section of the Sinamar valley, hemmed in by the Padri leaders of Buo and Talawi to the south and south-west, and by Tuanku Halaban in the north. Some Padri leaders controlled only one village, but even they claimed the right to act and speak as they saw fit. Old disputes and rivalries between villages had risen to the surface, so that even Padri villages could be at odds with one another; a dispute between Lintau and Talawi went so far that Tuanku Lintau promoted several attacks on the life of Tuanku Nan Saleh.[158]

On some points the Padris remained adamant and exhibited a certain degree of unity. They still insisted that market-places must be cleansed of all corruption, and they refused to let any traders from Padri villages come to markets where opium-smoking and cockfighting were permitted. Both Tuanku Lintau and Tuanku Nan Saleh wrote to the Dutch on this issue, stating that cockfighting was one of the reasons they had warred so long and they could never relent in their desire to cleanse Minangkabau of such a pernicious habit.[159]

Towards the end of the Java War, despite their internal factionalism and the challenges to their doctrine, the Padris of Lintau and of Bukit Kamang seem to have been united in the opinion that the Dutch had lost their power to remain in the Minangkabau interior; they became more daring in their raids, and in June 1830 the Bukit Kamang Padris were able to cut communications between the Dutch forts at Tanjung Alam and Bukit Tinggi.[160] In March 1831, however, a new Resident, Lieutenant-Colonel C.P.J. Elout, arrived at Padang, and matters were immediately placed on another footing. Elout was a military officer very much in the mould of Raaff, and he was convinced that the Dutch would never hold even a small part of the interior without an all-out military offensive which would smash the Padris for good. In January 1831, even before he had taken up his new position, he wrote to the Governor-General of the Netherlands Indies advising: 'Your Excellency will never be confronted with so suitable an opportunity as the present to bring things in order on Sumatra.'[161]

The Governor-General in question was one of the most famous in the annals of the Netherland Indies, Johannes van den Bosch. He had commenced duty in Batavia in January 1830 possessing the inestimable advantage of personal friendship with the King of the Netherlands, Willem I. Both were men firmly dedicated to the economic resurgence of the Netherlands and to combating the widespread poverty of the Dutch lower classes who, they planned, were to be afforded 'a decent existence' by working in industries which would export to Holland's colonies. In addition, van den Bosch left for the Indies with a positive commission from the king to make the colony financially independent in the shortest possible time.[162] From this moment Batavia was firmly in control of Dutch policy on Sumatra, although initially van den Bosch devoted his entire attention to Java, and it was not until December 1830 that he found time to write to Elout outlining the policy he wished to see followed in Sumatra.[163]

Van den Bosch's earliest views on Sumatran policy reflected the way the old East India Company had conducted its affairs in the 'outer islands'. His ultimate goal he made quite plain: 'It is my aim to bring the entire Indian archipelago as far as possible under the influence of Dutch authority'.[164] But, although with the ending of the Java War he immediately dispatched troops to Padang, he disagreed with Elout that now was the time for 'an important coup' in Minangkabau.[165] Force and conquest, he felt, should not be used; far better was the method of encouraging trade and then plucking its fruits: 'It seems to me preferable to establish a principal town on each extended section of coast, and to subject to us all the other important bays and rivers where there is or could be significant trade by means of small forts; further, to establish in the interior several market-places, also defended by small forts, where the native can exchange his products for the items he needs or desires, facilitating the communication of these places with the coastal ports by improving the roads as much as possible'.[166] Actual political authority in these circumstances should extend no further than the reach of the forts' artillery. The sole concern must be the promotion of trade at the market-places, and as long as Dutch industry could provide cheaply what was wanted at these interior markets no one would bother to go right over to Singapore to get what was already under his nose, and the Dutch would acquire an advantageous share of Minangkabau trade, exchanging salt, opium and cotton piece-goods for Minangkabau agricultural produce.

Van den Bosch's plans left out of account the fact that the Minangkabau, and the Padris in particular, had shown no inclination to trade within a Dutch framework; indeed, the Padris were actively opposed to it, and tried wherever possible to use either the east coast routes, or ports on the west coast north of Tiku, outside Dutch control. Dutch commercial duties and regulations were anathema to the Padris, and to have Dutch products forced on them in the interior was hardly likely to be acceptable, particularly as it was quite clear that van den Bosch was aiming to do away with the myriad small traders who connected the interior market-places with the coasts, men who were among the most ardent adherents of the Padri cause.[167]

At the end of his December 1830 letter to Elout, van den Bosch admitted that force could not be discounted if no other means could be found to come to an acceptable settlement in central Sumatra. Elout needed no convincing. By mid-1831 Dutch forces on Sumatra had reached almost 1,500, and Elout determined that matters relating to the Padris should be 'regulated' once and for all.[168] The second Dutch conquest of the Minangkabau interior began, ironically enough with the capture of Sulit Air and surrounding villages, the first objects of Dutch attack ten years earlier. Now, as in Raaff's day, the main aim was to take Lintau. This time the Marapalam, Lintau's main bulwark, was taken in August 1831, and a Dutch force took up position on top of the mountain. The whole district of Talawi was also forced to submit. Then there was a lull, until new reinforcements arrived from Batavia and it was decided that the Dutch were strong enough to test themselves against Tuanku Nan Rinceh and the Padris of Bukit Kamang. In mid-1832 the fort of Kapau was taken, and ultimately the villages of Bukit Kamang either submitted to the Dutch or were captured outright; with the final push into Pau further north all of Padri Agam was in Dutch hands by the end of July 1832.[169]

The main Dutch force, with large numbers of Minangkabau auxiliaries, then turned for a final attack on Lintau and in July 1832 descended the Marapalam to face a Padri army 6,000 to 8,000 strong. All the Lintau villages were soon subdued, and Buo was also entered. Finally, in October 1832, the Padri line before Tanjung Alam was forced and the whole of Limapuluh Kota gave itself over with little opposition. The last major Padri area to be taken was Halaban which, after a fierce defence, was forced into submission on 24 October.[170]

All of the Minangkabau heartland was now in Dutch hands and an era seemed to have come to an end. Frightful destruction was wreaked in Lintau by the Minangkabau auxiliaries, who had mainly been recruited from Tanah Datar and had long been on the receiving end of Lintau's violence. Apart from the total destruction of houses and mosques, even coconut and fruit trees were burnt to the ground, and the entire rice crop was burnt in the fields as it stood. In 1833 it was reported that those inhabitants who had not fled had 'descended to the depths of poverty . . .'[171] Among those who did escape was Tuanku Lintau himself; he planned to make a pilgrimage to Mecca, but was murdered near Palalawan on the first stage of his journey. His death removed one of the Netherlands' chief Minangkabau opponents. In the same year death removed Tuanku Nan Rinceh from Agam, thus robbing the Padri movement in central Minangkabau of its two most prominent leaders.[172] From this the movement never recovered.

There remain to be discussed the changes the Dutch tried to introduce in Minangkabau during this early period of their direct authority, because many of these innovations paved the way for the Minangkabau rebellion of 1833. After establishing himself at Padang in 1819 the Dutch Resident, while keeping the harbour open for all foreign ships, reintroduced some of the measures familiar to the Minangkabau from East India Company days. As early as September 1819 a salt monopoly was proclaimed, together with a prohibition on the making of salt along the coast. Very soon the first patrols arrived at Tiku to destroy the salt pans. Once in the interior Dutch officials found this policy so greatly disliked that in 1825 the Resident agreed to permit salt-making along the coast, and in 1827 the salt monopoly was removed to the extent that the importation of salt was declared free, provided the salt originated from the government's salt pans on Java.[173]

Apart from the profits made from the trade in salt, each Resident had to derive other sources of income from Minangkabau to defray the costs of Dutch military operations, in addition to the customary import and export duties on all items of trade. One such source, which disgusted the Padris, was to be found in farming the sale of opium to the highest bidder, as had been done under the English regime. The opium farm was the first Dutch fiscal institution to which the uplands Minangkabau was subjected, and the provocation thereby offered the Padris was enormous.[174] Needless to say, it was Padang Chinese who were successful as bidders for the opium farm, and in late 1823 Chinese entered the highlands for the first time in connection with the sale of opium. They immediately became unpopular because of the high price of the prepared opium (*madat*) offered for sale. Moreover, Dutch policy brought these Chinese lessees into conflict with the very group which had called for Dutch assistance against the Padris. Previously the preparation and sale of *madat* from raw opium had been the province of various Tanah Datar *penghulu,* and they resented Chinese intrusion into their lucrative business. Even the ordinary opium-smoker was antagonized because the Chinese, in order to make their farm profitable, sold *madat* for more than double the price the *penghulu* had charged for it.[175]

In the search for further sources of revenue it was decided to tax the trade of the interior by the simple expedient of placing a tax on the leading market-places in the Dutch areas. On 1 April 1825 a tax was introduced on 34 *pasar* in Tanah Datar and 14 in Agam, consisting of a payment of five per cent of the market value of all goods brought for sale to the market, including foodstuffs. Again the collection of this tax was farmed out, and again Padang Chinese were the successful bidders for the farm; in 1827 the farm went to the Captain Chinese of Padang.[176] This new tax caused great annoyance among Minangkabau traders and at most markets the agents of the tax farmer, who were also Chinese, were chased away by incensed marketgoers. Even villages which had most desired the Dutch alliance, such as those around Lake Singkarak, were reported in mid-1825 to have closed their gates against the Dutch as a way of preventing the entry of the Chinese opium farmer and market tax farmer.[177] On other market-places the Chinese agent with his dear opium was either chased away or murdered, and by 1829 none of the 'Dutch-controlled' areas of Agam would admit Dutch farms, either on market-places or on opium.[178] By 1831 the opium and *pasar* farms were bringing in very little, and the Dutch Resident Elout, aware how much the Chinese were disliked, agreed to a return to the old system of retailing and preparing opium through the offices of the *penghulu* without Chinese mediation.[179] The Chinese farmers of the *pasar* tax asked in the same year to be discharged from their onerous task, and collection of this impost was also handed over to the *penghulu.*[180]

As the Dutch position in the interior began to look more permanent, attempts were made to interfere in the cultivation of Minangkabau's crops. Even before a Dutch army had entered the highlands, it had been recognized that in future the trade in coffee would provide the chief source of revenue for Dutch-controlled ports on the west coast. Although coffee did not flourish on the coastal lowlands, the very first Dutch regulations made for the Minangkabau coast in Batavia in 1821 were concerned to encourage the leading coastal *penghulu* to plant coffee and deliver it to Padang, just as they had previously been urged by the VOC to plant pepper.[181] Although these regulations were never enforced, due to the sudden Dutch entry into the interior, they foreshadowed later Dutch policy after the highlands had been pacified. During the 1820s Dutch involvement with coffee-growing in Tanah Datar and southern Agam was limited to attempts to ensure that the product flowed into Dutch, rather than foreign, hands, but even this limited interference resulted in difficulties for the coffee growers of these areas. The high differential duties on coffee exported by Americans gradually discouraged the latter from coming to Padang and so meant that the western coffee growers lost their markets; not until the rise in world prices in 1831 and 1832 did the Americans find it worthwhile to call again at Padang and the coffee growers of Tanah Datar and Agam were able to take heart at the rise in price for their product from f.10 to f.20 per *pikul* in one year.[182] By the end of 1832 the price of coffee had risen to f.25 per *pikul* and exports via Padang stood at 70,000 *pikul,* an amount greater than in any previous year, reflecting not only the price increase but also Dutch conquests in the highlands.[183]

The cultivators of other agricultural products were not so fortunate, and experienced only disadvantages from Dutch regulations. The high differential duties imposed on exports taken by foreign ships discouraged foreign traders from buying gambir and led to a decline in its export by way of Padang at the very period when Singapore was ceasing to be a good market due to competition from Riau gambir.[184] The cassia trade experienced a similar decline.[185] Dutch officials in Tanah Datar and Agam were urged to discourage the cultivation of tobacco; the policy evolved that the growing of items for internal commerce should be opposed and the Minangkabau should be encouraged to produce crops for export only, so that the Netherlands Indies government would be able to raise import duties on items needed for internal consumption and export duties on crops exported. In line with this policy, very high duties were placed on imported raw cotton, in the hope of damaging the Minangkabau domestic weaving industry and opening the way for Netherlands manufactures.[186]

While Minangkabau agriculture was beginning to experience Dutch pinpricks, the administrative system of the Minangkabau village was subject to a veritable assault. From the days of the VOC the Dutch on the coast had complained of the need to negotiate with all of a village's *penghulu* in any matter of importance, and certain officials had advocated the creation of the position of *hoofdregent* to enable one individual to represent a group of villages.[187] Very soon after the earliest conquests in Tanah Datar and Agam, plans were drawn up to introduce a system of village administration more consonant with that with which the Dutch were familiar on Java. The Dutch referred to their possessions in central Sumatra as the Residency of Sumatra's West Coast, and in late 1823 this Residency was administratively rationalized by establishing the *afdeling* (division) of the Padang Highlands, comprising all Dutch conquests in the interior. This was subdivided into two regencies, those of Tanah Datar and Agam. With the constitution of the regency of Tanah Datar arose the question of the relationship between the Netherlands Indies government and the Minangkabau royal family. It was decided that the leading signatory of the 1821 treaty, the nephew of the last Raja Alam of Minangkabau, Sultan Alam Bagagar Syah, who was a young man of thirty-four in 1823, should be appointed Regent of Tanah Datar. In September 1822 Raja Muning Syah, the Raja Alam, had sent word to Lieutenant-Colonel Raaff of his whereabouts, but when he returned to Tanah Datar in 1824 he was content to see his nephew Regent, preferring retirement on a Dutch pension. He died in August 1825 at the age of about eighty.[188]

Dutch policy thereafter was to circumscribe the position of Sultan Alam Bagagar Syah. It was announced on the Raja Alam's death that the title of Yang di Pertuan had ceased to exist,[189] the view of Resident de Stuers being that the former Minangkabau state must 'remain in that state of oblivion to which the course of history has reduced it'.[190] De Stuers considered that Alam Bagagar Syah owed his position entirely to the Dutch and the Dutch Assistant Resident of the Padang Highlands was advised to remind the Regent of Tanah Datar on all suitable occasions 'that he must consider himself entirely as a government official and never as Lord of the land, and he must carefully abstain from encouraging those ancient marks of homage from the Chiefs which were fostered by a despotic regime which was based on superstitious notions about the inviolability of the Ruler'.[191] This attitude marked the beginning of the alienation of the royal family from the Dutch, which was increased by the banning of the two Tuankus of Suruaso from the highlands on charges of misuse of authority.[192] The Regent of Tanah Datar lived in comparative poverty, supported by his salary from the Netherlands Indies government, although the Dutch did rebuild the royal residence at Pagarruyung in considerable style.[193]

In finding a Regent for that part of Agam which they held initially, the Dutch turned to the old Syattariyah Islamic establishment, unable to select a likely candidate from the bewildering assortment of *penghulu.* They chose a member of Tuanku Nan Tua's family, his nephew Tuanku Samit, who remained both a devout Muslim and a supporter of the Dutch connection.[194]

After the two regencies had been established, they were divided into districts (*laras*), twenty-three for Tanah Datar and seven for Dutch-controlled Agam, each representing an important village and its neighbouring settlements. It was in this organization of districts that the Dutch made the greatest break with Minangkabau tradition. Unable to contemplate having to deal with all the *penghulu* of one village, let alone the joint *penghulu* of several villages, it was decided that each village must be represented by a village head, to be entitled *kepala negeri.* From these village heads was to be chosen a district head, *kepala laras,* who was to be paid by the government. This new arrangement was quite at odds with the existing village political system, which gave every lineage a voice in village affairs, and much heart-burning was occasioned by the appointment of the *kepala negeri,* when candidates from every lineage but one had to be passed over. Equally the appointment of the *kepala laras* led to much inter-village hostility, newly-created 'districts' such as Sungai Tarab and Suruaso refusing to accept that they were now equal in position and prestige to any other of the twenty-three districts of Tanah Datar. In any case the Dutch authorities had considerable difficulty in finding individuals they considered suitable for these new offices, and between 1823 and 1827 there was a period of continual appointments and dismissals of both district and village heads, causing even more anxiety and distrust in village political circles.[195] After the 1832 conquests this system was extended to the rest of Agam and Limapuluh Kota, giving Agam now twenty-one districts and Limapuluh Kota fourteen. Limpuluh Kota also received its own Regent.

The very nature of the Dutch military occupation brought other changes in its wake, in particular an alteration in settlement patterns which has lasted until today. To garrison Minangkabau forts had to be speedily erected. Sometimes these were merely small affairs, no more than military posts thrown up on the heights above certain villages to observe enemy movements in the surrounding countryside, but where they were established at strategic crossroads they became foci of both political and economic significance for the surrounding population. In Tanah Datar Fort van der Capellen was built on a hill near some rocks called Batu Sangkar, across the river Selo from the old capital Pagarruyung, and this garrison place soon began to take on urban characteristics.[196] In 1825 it became the capital of the Padang Highlands *afdeling.* At Bukit Tinggi in Agam Fort de Kock was built in 1827, on a hill almost in the middle of the valley of Agam, with excellent views over the neighbouring countryside.

These burgeoning garrison settlements soon became economic magnets for nearby villages, which began to specialize in provisioning their denizens. Rice, meat and horses for military purposes were in constant demand and the garrison markets became very busy. Bukit Tinggi by 1837 possessed not only a flourishing market which attracted two hundred to three hundred people every day, in addition to thousands on the weekly market day, but the place was already becoming urbanized: ' . . . it has become a small town. Many small traders, Europeans, Koodjas and Chinese have established themselves here and carry on a profitable trade'.[197] Individuals who had been uprooted in the Padri wars moved to such settlements. At one small fort on the slopes of Mount Merapi were observed in 1824 the 'wretched huts' of people making a living by providing necessities for the army, and by serving as carriers, and this became the common pattern wherever soldiers established themselves for any length of time.[198] Skilled artisans were also in demand. Carpenters could find work not only on the forts themselves, but also on such ancillary buildings as the military hospitals. Supplying wood to the military became another important branch of the provisioning trade. In 1841 there was a report of a Minangkabau who, by provisioning the Europeans of Padang Panjang with milk, had become 'a prosperous individual . . .'[199]

Nowhere were these new developments more apparent than in Padang itself. From 1822 successive Residents set about transforming Padang from a sleepy riverside *kampung* into a European-style administrative centre, and although in appearance the port did not cease to be 'an inconsiderable place',[200] it provided new opportunities for employment. A brick-and-tile works was set up, carpenters and bricklayers were sent for to Western India, and suitable military and administrative buildings were soon on the drawing board, including a military barracks, rifle magazine, powder store, warehouse, gaol, hospital, secretariat and a house for the Resident. As a result an artisan class came into existence in Padang where previously the settlement had consisted either of traders or cultivators. A *kampung* of South Indian Muslims, *kampung kling,* was also established, the men finding employment as domestic servants and petty traders. European society began to reproduce itself. As more and more European soldiers disembarked at the port, they brought the appurtenances of European civilization with them. The ship bringing Lieutenant-Colonel Elout to Padang in early 1831 possessed a European orchestra of sixteen musicians, and the arrival of the new Resident was accompanied by parties and balls attended by 'the beau monde of Padang . . .'[201]

Dutch garrison settlements flourished also because they were provided with good roads. Almost the first Dutch undertaking in the highlands was the improvement of the roads, the need to transport heavy artillery making this imperative. Already in 1824 the villages of greatest interest to the Dutch were approached by excellent roads; it was possible to reach the Padri stronghold of Kapau, in central Agam, from the final Dutch outpost in Tanah Datar, Tanjung Alam, in seven hours on horseback along a wide, well-maintained road.[202] However, the making of these roads necessitated the imposition of compulsory labour services on certain villages, which rapidly became a further cause of disenchantment with Tanah Datar's erstwhile saviours. Dutch forces on the move also required large numbers of carriers; every three soldiers going to the highlands was accompanied by one carrier with equipment and provisions, and these carriers also had to erect huts at staging-posts and drag the artillery. Able-bodied men too often had to be requisitioned from villages, depriving rice-growing of labour reserves at a time when so many men were in any case involved in fighting as Dutch auxiliaries.[203]

The situation in the Minangkabau highlands in 1832, therefore, was not one in which the Dutch could rejoice. Although the fervour of the Padri movement had abated and the two most able Padri leaders were both dead, those Minangkabau who had not embraced Padri teachings had experienced Dutch-sponsored disruptions to their lives which in many respects were similar to those promulgated by the Padris. The stage was now set for a gradual rapprochement between Minangkabau of various persuasions in the face of foreign provocation.

NOTES TO CHAPTER IV

1 J.L. van der Toorn, 'Het Animisme bij den Minangkabauer der Padangsche Bovenlanden', *BKI,* xxxix (1890), 48-54. I have used a theoretical definition of shamanism which includes spirit possession; see I.M. Lewis, *Ecstatic Religion* (Harmondsworth, 1971), pp. 49-57.
2 Van der Toorn, 'Animisme', pp. 61-8.
3 Müller, *Berigten,* p. 12; 'Reizen van L. Horner', p. 331.
4 Van der Toorn, 'Animisme', pp. 83-91.
5 C.K. Nicholson, 'The Introduction of Islam into Sumatra and Java: A Study in Cultural Change' (Syracuse University Ph.D. thesis, 1965), pp. 17-8; R. Winstedt, *The Malays: A Cultural History* (6th edn., London, 1961), pp. 23-4.
6 Winstedt, *Malays,* p. 19; R. Goris, 'The Position of the Blacksmiths' in *Bali: Studies in Life, Thought and Ritual* (The Hague and Bandung, 1960), p. 292.
7 Van der Toorn, 'Animisme', p. 100; Couperus, 'Goudproduktie', pp. 129-31.
8 Nicholson, 'Introduction of Islam', pp. 10-12; Burger, 'Aanmerkingen', p. 201; F.M. Schnitger, *Forgotten Kingdoms in Sumatra* (Leiden, 1939), pp. 165-72.
9 Schnitger, *Forgotten Kingdoms,* p. 30; Krom, *Geschiedenis,* pp. 393-4, 413-4; Kern 'De wij-inscriptie'. p. 170.
10 Nicholson, 'Introduction of Islam', pp. 14-5; Winstedt, *Malays,* pp. 63-6; Een nota, van Zuylen van Nijevelt 102.
11 X. de Planhol, *The World of Islam* (Ithaca, 1959), pp. 3-8, 42-3.
12 Een nota, van Zuylen van Nijevelt 102.
13 Schefer, *Le Discours,* pp. 60-2, 68-9; *Pires,* i. 160-1.
14 Kroeskamp, *De Westkust,* pp. 88-9; *Best,* p. 65.
15 Stapel, 'Een verhandeling', p. 469; Marsden, *Sumatra,* p. 346; De Radicaale Beschrijving, ch. 1, par. 8, p. 14; par. 9, pp. 17-8.
16 Hamka, *Sedjarah Islam di Sumatera* (2nd edn., Medan, 1950), p. 11; I. Ja'kub, *Sedjarah Islam di Indonesia* (Jakarta, 1956), p. 22.
17 De Haan, 'Naar Midden Sumatra', pp. 345-7, 351-2; *Pires,* i. 137, 140; R.O. Winstedt, 'The Advent of Muhammadism in the Malay Peninsula and Archipelago', *JSBRAS,* lxxvii (1917), 173.
18 Winstedt, *Malays,* pp. 63-6; D.F. Lach, *Southeast Asia in the Eyes of Europe. The Sixteenth Century* (Chicago, 1968), p. 579; Westenenk, 'Opstellen. II' p. 243.
19 Een nota, van Zuylen van Nijevelt 102.
20 Westenenk, 'Opstellen. II' p. 241.
21 'Reizen van L. Horner', p. 353; Raffles, *Memoir,* i. 423-6.
22 Verkerk Pistorius, *Inlandsche Huishouding,* p. 108; for a parallel in sixteenth century France see E. Le Roy Ladurie, *The Peasants of Languedoc* (Urbana, 1974), pp. 205-6.
23 Verkerk Pistorius, *Inlandsche Huishouding,* pp. 88-9, 194-5; L.C. Westenenk, *De Minangkabausche Nagari* (3rd edn., Weltevreden, 1918), p. 55; G.D. Willinck, *Het Rechtsleven bij de Minangkabausche Maleiërs* (Leiden, 1909), pp. 295-9.
24 Nahuijs, *Brieven,* pp. 154-5.
25 Verkerk Pistorius, *Inlandsche Huishouding,* p. 81.
26 Krom, *Geschiedenis,* p. 414; Westenenk, 'Opstellen. I' p. 249.
27 M. Gilsenan, *Saint and Sufi in Modern Egypt. An Essay in the Sociology of Religion* (Oxford, 1973), p. 10.
28 Winstedt, *Malays,* pp. 20, 25; D.A. Rinkes, *Abdoerraoef van Singkel. Bijdrage tot de Kennis van de mystiek op Sumatra en Java* (Heerenveen, 1909), pp. 9-10.
29 Gilsenan, *Saint and Sufi,* pp. 4-6.
30 R.L. Archer, 'Muhammadan Mysticism in Sumatra', *JMBRAS,* xv (1937), 5.
31 ibid., p. 6; Ph.S. van Ronkel, *Rapport Betreffende de Godsdienstige Verschijnselen ter Sumatra's Westkust* (Batavia, 1916), p. 17; for Javanese parallels see S. Kartodirdjo, *Protest Movements in Rural Java* (Singapore, 1973), pp. 69-75.

32 Archer, 'Muhammadan Mysticism', p. 105; Verkerk Pistorius, *Inlandsche Huishouding*, p. 211; C. Snouck Hurgronje, 'Een en ander over het inlandsch onderwijs in de Padangsche Bovenlanden' in Snouck Hurgronje, *Verspreide Geschriften* (Bonn and Leipzig, 1924), iv. 43-4.
33 Verkerk Pistorius, *Inlandsche Huishouding*, pp. 221-2; 'De masdjid's en inlandsche godsdienstscholen in de Padangsche Bovenlanden', *IG*, x (1888), i. 325.
34 'De masdjid's', p. 321.
35 ibid., pp. 319, 324-5; Verkerk Pistorius, *Inlandsche Huishouding*, pp. 206, 219.
36 Van Ronkel, *Rapport*, p. 15.
37 ibid., p. 11; Winstedt, *Malays*, p. 42.
38 Snouck Hurgronje, 'Inlandsch onderwijs', pp. 31-4, 39, 41; idem, *The Achehnese* (Leiden, 1906), ii. 3.
39 Gilsenan, *Saint and Sufi*, pp. 129-30.
40 Verkerk Pistorius, *Inlandsche Huishouding*, p. 184; Een nota, van Zuylen van Nijevelt 102.
41 Snouck Hurgronje, 'Inlandsch onderwijs', pp. 41-2, 46.
42 Archer, 'Muhammadan Mysticism', p. 108; van Ronkel, *Rapport*, p. 14.
43 Ph.S. van Ronkel, 'Een Maleisch Getuigenis over den Weg des Islams in Sumatra', *BKI*, lxxv (1919), 365-9.
44 J.J. de Hollander (ed.), *Sjech Djilâl Eddîn: Verhaal van den Aanvang der Padri-Onlusten op Sumatra* (Leiden, 1857), pp. 15, 47; hereafter referred to as *Jalaluddin*, this is a contemporary account written c. 1824 in Malay; Hamka, *Ajahku. Riwajat Hidup Dr H. Abd. Karim Amrullah dan Perdjuangan Kaum Agama di Sumatera* (3rd edn., Jakarta, 1967), p. 23.
45 Rinkes, *Abdoerraoef*, p. 25; *Jalaluddin*, p. 5; S.A.A. Rizvi, *Muslim Revivalist Movements in Northern India in the Sixteenth and Seventeenth Centuries* (Agra, 1965), pp. 62-3.
46 Ph.S. van Ronkel, 'Het Heiligdom te Oelakan', *TBG*, lvi (1914), 281-4; Steijn Parvé, 'De Secte', pp. 264-5.
47 *Jalaluddin*, p. 6.
48 Rinkes, *Abdoerraoef*, p. 32.
49 A.H. Johns, 'Islam in Southeast Asia: Problems of Perspective', in C.D. Cowan and O.W. Wolters (ed.), *Southeast Asian History and Historiography* (Ithaca and London, 1976), pp. 317-8.
50 *Jalaluddin*, pp. 6-7.
51 Van Ronkel, 'Het Heiligdom', pp. 295-9.
52 B. Schrieke, 'Bijdrage tot de Bibliografie van de huidige godsdienstige beweging ter Sumatra's Westkust', *TBG*, lix (1920), 262-3; A.H. Johns, 'Muslim Mystics and Historical Writing' in D.G.E. Hall (ed.), *Historians of South East Asia* (London, 1961), p. 42.
53 A.H. Johns, *The Gift Addressed to the Spirit of the Prophet* (Canberra, 1965), pp. 5-8.
54 *Jalaluddin*, p. 47.
55 Schrieke, 'Godsdienstige beweging', pp. 264-5.
56 Johns, *Gift*, p. 144.
57 *Jalaluddin*, pp. 6-7.
58 Steijn Parvé, 'De Secte', p. 252; although *tuanku* on the west coast was a *penghulu* title, in the highlands it was most commonly used as an honorific for an important Islamic teacher.
59 Een nota, van Zuylen van Nijevelt 102.
60 *Jalaluddin*, pp. 7-9; von Erath and van der Stengh to Alting, 31 Jan. 1791, par. 188, KA 3853.
61 A.L. van Hasselt, *Volksbeschrijving van Midden-Sumatra* (Leiden, 1882), p. 362.
62 Nahuijs, *Brieven*, pp. 148-9; Elout to Riesz, 13 Aug. 1833, Bijl. B, van den Bosch 394. For a parallel from eighteenth century France, see O.H. Hufton, *The Poor of Eighteenth-Century France 1750-1789* (Oxford, 1974), pp. 360-2; Hufton's examples relate to ritualized violence between villages in rural areas.
63 Elout to Riesz, 13 Aug. 1833, Bijlagen B and D, van den Bosch 394.
64 M. Rodinson, *Islam and Capitalism* (Harmondsworth, 1977), pp. 14-7.
65 Gilsenan, *Saint and Sufi*, pp. 42-3; Rizvi, *Revivalist Movements*, pp. 54-6, 176-8, 202-25, 265, 301.
66 *Jalaluddin*, p. 9.

67 ibid.
68 ibid., p. 13.
69 ibid., pp. 10-11.
70 See R. Jeffrey, *The Decline of Nayar Dominance. Society and Politics in Travancore, 1847-1908* (London, 1976), pp. 152-3 for similar pressures among the Nayars of Kerala in the 1860s; the intrusion of a cash economy led to a movement for the sale or partition of matrilineal joint family land.
71 *Jalaluddin*, p. 13.
72 S.A. Wahba, *Arabian Days* (London, 1964), pp. 82-3; R.B. Winder, *Saudi Arabia in the Nineteenth Century* (London, 1965), p. 8; H.A.R. Gibb and J.H. Kramers, *Shorter Encyclopaedia of Islam* (Leiden/London, 1953), pp. 618-20; several of the major Islamic revivalist movements of the late eighteenth and early nineteenth centuries have been the subject of recent studies: see N.A. Ziadeh, *Sanūsīyah. A Study of a Revivalist Movement in Islam* (Leiden, 1958); E.E. Evans-Pritchard, *The Sanusi of Cyrenaica* (Oxford, 1949); Q. Ahmad, *The Wahabi Movement in India* (Calcutta, 1966); M.A. Khan, *History of the Fara'idi Movement in Bengal (1818-1906)* (Karachi, 1965); N.A. Smirnov, *Myuridizm na Kavkaze* (Moscow, 1963); M. Hiskett, *Sword of Truth: Life and Times of Shehu Usuman Dan Fodio* (New York, 1973).
73 J.L. Burckhardt, *Notes on the Bedouins and Wahábys* (London, 1831), ii. 109-10; J. O'Kinealy, 'History and Doctrines of the Wahhábís', *Journal of the Asiatic Society of Bengal*, i (1874), 69-70, 79.
74 O'Kinealy, 'Wahhábís', p. 73.
75 ibid., p. 69.
76 ibid., p. 75.
77 M. Abir, 'The "Arab Rebellion" of Amîr Ghālib of Mecca (1788-1813)' *Middle Eastern Studies*, vii (1971), 187-9.
78 Burckhardt, *Wahábys*, pp. 136, 147, 168-9, 176, 190-1; Winder, *Saudi Arabia*, pp. 10-1; Gibb and Kramers, *Shorter Encyclopaedia*, p. 618.
79 H.M. Lange, *Het Nederlandsch Oost-Indisch Leger ter Westkust van Sumatra (1819-1845)* ('s Hertogenbosch, 1852), i. 5; v.d.H., 'Oorsprong der Padaries', *TNI*, i (1838), 113; Korthals, *Topographische Schets*, p. 38.
80 Steijn Parvé, 'De Secte', pp. 253-4.
81 *Jalaluddin*, p. 14.
82 Steijn Parvé, 'De Secte', pp. 254-5; Moor, *Notices*, p. 133.
83 Van Ronkel, 'Het Heiligdom', p. 283.
84 Steijn Parvé, 'De Secte', pp. 254-6.
85 ibid., p. 253; *Jalaluddin*, pp. 10-1, 27.
86 H.A. Steijn Parvé, 'De Secte der Padaries in de Padangsche Bovenlanden', *IM*, i (1844), 26.
87 *Jalaluddin*, pp. 20-1, 23-5.
88 ibid., p. 25.
89 For an African comparison see J.R. Willis, '*Jihād Fī Sabīl Allāh* – its Doctrinal Basis in Islam and Some Aspects of its Evolution in Nineteenth-Century West Africa', *Journal of African History*, viii (1967), 398-9. For this and subsequent Black Africa references I am indebted to Anthony Wright.
90 Steijn Parvé, 'De Secte', pp. 271-2; de Stuers and Verploegh to van der Capellen, 30 Aug. 1825, LaE no. 20, Exh. 24 Aug. 1826, no. 41, MK 513.
91 Kartodirdjo, *Protest Movements*, pp. 122-7; J. Kathirithamby-Wells, 'Ahmad Shah Ibn Iskandar and the Late 17th Century "Holy War" in Indonesia', *JMBRAS*, xliii (1970), 50.
92 Steijn Parvé, 'De Secte', pp. 273-4; de Stuers and Verploegh to van der Capellen, 30 Aug. 1825, LaE no. 20, Exh, 24 Aug. 1826, no. 41, MK 513; Elout to Riesz, 13 Aug. 1833, Bijl. B, van den Bosch 394.
93 *Jalaluddin*, pp. 28, 33-5.
94 ibid., p. 41.
95 De Stuers and Verploegh to van der Capellen, 30 Aug. 1825, LaE no. 20, Exh. 24 Aug. 1826, no. 41, MK 513.
96 ibid.
97 *Jalaluddin*, pp. 32-6; Steijn Parvé, 'De Secte', pp. 255-6.

98 *Jalaluddin,* pp. 37-8; Steijn Parvé, 'De Secte', pp. 260-2; Een nota, van Zuylen van Nijevelt 102.
99 *Jalaluddin,* pp. 38-9; Steijn Parvé, 'De Secte', pp. 264-5. Yazid was the name of the Ummayad caliph who was the enemy and indirectly the slayer of the Prophet's grandson, Husain.
100 O'Kinealy, 'Wahhábís', pp. 70, 82.
101 *Jalaluddin,* pp. 38-40; Steijn Parvé, 'De Secte'. p. 274; Lange, *Oost-Indisch Leger,* i. 9.
102 *Jalaluddin,* p. 41.
103 ibid., pp. 47-51; Korthals, *Topographische Schets,* pp. 65-6.
104 Cochius to de Eerens, 29 Apr. 1837, no. 34/99, in E.B. Kielstra, 'Sumatra's Westkust van 1836-1840', *BKI,* xxxix (1890), 168.
105 Granpré Molière, 1844, ANHM, pp. 20-1; the population estimate appears excessive.
106 *Jalaluddin,* pp. 14-9; Steijn Parvé, 'De Secte', pp. 276-7; Korthals, *Topographische Schets,* p. 38.
107 Burger, 'Aanmerkingen', pp. 215-6.
108 Raffles, *Memoir,* i. 399-411.
109 ibid., p. 404.
110 Moor, *Notices,* p. 135; v.d.H., 'Oorsprong der Padaries', p. 127.
111 Steijn Parvé, 'De Secte', *IM,* p. 32; de Stuers and Verploegh to van der Capellen, 30 Aug. 1825, LaE no. 20, Exh. 24 Aug. 1826, no. 41, MK 513.
112 Steijn Parvé, 'De Secte', *IM,* p. 35; v.d.H. 'Oorsprong der Padaries', pp. 125-8; Lange, *Oost-Indisch Leger,* i. 20; Verkerk Pistorius, *Inlandsche Huishouding,* pp. 84-5.
113 *Malacca Observer,* Jan. 1827, in Moor, *Notices,* p. 113.
114 Raffles to Dowdeswell, 12 Aug. 1818, SFR 47; Raffles, *Memoir,* i. 421, 424; Nahuijs, *Brieven,* p. 143.
115 Steijn Parvé, 'De Secte', p. 274; Nahuijs, *Brieven,* p. 138; 'Reizen van L. Horner', p. 343.
116 Verkerk Pistorius, *Inlandsche Huishouding,* pp. 108-9, 112.
117 Müller, *Berigten,* p. 24.
118 De Stuers to Elout, 27 Sept. 1826, no. 4b, Exh. 17 Mar. 1827, no. 41, MK 547.
119 Müller, *Berigten,* p. 23.
120 ibid., pp. 33-4.
121 Korthals, *Topographische Schets,* p. 28.
122 Naamlijst der Towankos die uit den weg moeten worden geruimd, c. 1822, MK 4129.
123 Korthals, *Topographische Schets,* p. 14.
124 ibid., p. 28; de Stuers to Elout, 27 Sept. 1826, no. 4b, Exh. 17 Mar. 1827, no. 41, MK 547.
125 Korthals, *Topographische Schets,* pp. 66-7; Müller, *Berigten,* pp. 21-2; Dagboek . . . 24 Jul. 1832, Vermeulen Krieger 3.
126 Nahuijs, *Brieven,* pp. 198-9, 210; Boelhouwer, *Herinneringen,* p. 32; Burger, 'Aanmerkingen', p. 179.
127 Korthals, *Topographische Schets,* pp. 6, 28, 52, 68-9; Nahuijs, *Brieven,* p. 135.
128 Kielstra, 'Sumatra's Westkust van 1819-1825', pp. 75-6.
129 Nahuijs, *Brieven,* pp. 158, 179, 205; Boelhouwer, *Herinneringen,* pp. 20, 28-30.
130 Boelhouwer, *Herinneringen,* pp. 28-30; Nahuijs, *Brieven,* p. 199.
131 Boelhouwer, *Herinneringen,* pp. 69-70.
132 ibid., p. 96; Dagboek . . . 27 Jul. 1832, Vermeulen Krieger 3.
133 Kielstra, 'Sumatra's Westkust van 1819-1825', p. 8.
134 ibid., pp. 9-10; Raffles, *Memoir,* i. 412; J. Bastin (ed.), *The Journal of Thomas Otho Travers, 1813-20* (Singapore, 1960), p. 106.
135 J. Bastin, 'Raffles' Attempts to Extend British Power in Sumatra', in idem, *Essays on Indonesian and Malay History* (Singapore, 1961), pp. 164 *et seq.*
136 Raffles to Dowdeswell, 12 Aug. 1818, SFR 47.
137 Raffles, *Memoir,* i. 432-3.
138 Raffles to Dowdeswell, 12 Aug. 1818, SFR 47.
139 Bastin, 'Raffles' Attempts', p. 171.
140 Besluit, 6 Nov. 1819, no. 13, MK 2451; Kielstra, 'Sumatra's Westkust van 1819-1825', pp. 12, 15-6.

141 Kroeskamp, *De Westkust,* p. 111.
142 Besluit, 9 Aug. 1820, no. 17, MK 2455.
143 Besluit in Rade, 11 Sept. 1820, no. 23, MK 2773.
144 Contract gesloten tusschen den Resident van *Padang, James Du Puy* . . . en de daar toe speciaal afgevaardigde Hoofden der Landen van het gewezen ryk van *Maninkabo* . . . , 10 Feb. 1821, Exh. 24 Aug. 1826, no. 41, MK 513.
145 *Nieuw Nederlandsch Biografisch Woordenboek* (Leiden, 1912), ii. col. 1148.
146 Besluit, 30 Oct. 1822, no. 1a, MK 2467; Besluit in Rade, 8 Apr. 1823, no. 11, MK 2778.
147 Kielstra, 'Sumatra's Westkust van 1819-1825', pp. 41-2, 46-9, 52-6; H.J.J.L. de Stuers, *De Vestiging en Uitbreiding der Nederlanders ter Westkust van Sumatra* (Amsterdam, 1849-50), i. 60-7.
148 Kielstra, 'Sumatra's Westkust van 1819-1825', pp. 56-60, 72-7; de Stuers, *Vestiging,* i. 68.
149 Boelhouwer, *Herinneringen,* p. 41; Kielstra, 'Sumatra's Westkust van 1819-1825', pp. 43-4, 62.
150 Nahuijs, *Brieven,* pp. 163, 173-4; Kielstra, 'Sumatra's Westkust van 1819-1825', p. 64.
151 Nahuijs, *Brieven,* pp. 135, 165, 206, 210, 217; Kielstra, 'Sumatra's Westkust van 1819-1825', pp. 50, 62-4.
152 De Stuers to van der Capellen, 25 Nov. 1825, no. 1029, Exh. 23 Aug. 1826, no. 65, and Bijlagen LaA, LaB, LaD, MK 513; de Stuers, *Vestiging,* i. 104-6.
153 Du Bus de Gisignies to de Stuers, 18 Aug. 1826, no. 19, Exh. 17 Mar. 1827, no. 43, MK 547.
154 De Stuers to Elout, 24 Mar. 1828, no. 7, Exh. 16 June 1829, no. 132, MK 683; idem, 10 Jul. 1829, no. 1, Exh. 29 Dec. 1829, no. 53, MK 721; McGillavry to de Kock, 20 Nov. 1829, LaH, Exh. 15 Sept. 1830, no. 6/A, MK 767.
155 Nahuijs, *Brieven,* p. 214.
156 Müller, *Berigten,* pp. 22-3; Korthals, *Topographische Schets,* p. 38.
157 McGillavry to de Kock, 20 Nov. 1829, LaH, Exh. 15 Sept. 1830, no. 6/A, MK 767; McGillavry to van Gobbelschroy, 23 Apr. 1830, no. 316, Exh. 15 Sept. 1830, no. 6/A, MK 767; Elout to Clifford, 2 June 1832, no. 2/364, Exh. 26 Oct. 1832, no. 25, MK 860.
158 De Stuers to Elout, 17 May 1826, no. 4, Exh. 23 Oct. 1826, no. 48, MK 523; idem, 27 Sept. 1826, no. 4b, Exh. 17 Mar. 1827, no. 41, MK 547.
159 De Stuers to Elout, 17 May 1826, no. 4, Exh. 23 Oct. 1826, no. 48, MK 523, Bijlagen a, b and c.
160 McGillavry to Clifford, 6 Nov. 1830, no. 788, Exh. 21 Mar. 1831, no. 1/A, MK 790.
161 Elout to van den Bosch, 15 Jan. 1831, Exh. 26 Sept. 1831, no. 28, MK 810.
162 W.M.F. Mansvelt, *Geschiedenis van de Nederlandsche Handel-Maatschappij* (Haarlem, 1924), i. 262-3; J.J. Westendorp Boerma, *Een Geestdriftig Nederlander. Johannes Van den Bosch* (Amsterdam, 1950), p. 52.
163 Van den Bosch to Elout, 26 Dec. 1830 Geh., Exh. 26 Sept. 1831, no. 28, MK 810.
164 ibid.
165 Elout to van den Bosch, 15 Jan. 1831, Exh. 26 Sept. 1831, no. 28, MK 810.
166 Van den Bosch to Elout, 26 Dec. 1830 Geh., Exh. 26 Sept. 1831, no. 28, MK 810.
167 Van den Bosch to Baud, 31 Jan. 1831, Part[iculier], in J.J. Westendorp Boerma, *Briefwisseling tussen J. van den Bosch en J.C. Baud 1829-1832 en 1834-1836* (Utrecht, 1956), i. 79.
168 Elout to van den Bosch, 1 Sept. 1831, LaE, Exh. 2 Mar. 1832, no. 10/A, MK 830; idem, 28 Sept. 1831, LaFbis, Exh. 8 May 1832, no. 2/A, MK 839.
169 Elout to Clifford, 2 June 1832, no. 2/364, Exh. 26 Oct. 1832, no. 25, MK 860; idem, 15 Dec. 1832, no. 5, Exh. 28 May 1833, no. 29A, MK 881.
170 Elout to Clifford, 29 Jul. 1832, no. 4, Exh. 14 Jan. 1833, no. 12/A, MK 881; idem, 15 Dec. 1832, no. 5, Exh. 28 May 1833, no. 29A, MK 881.
171 Burger, 'Aanmerkingen', pp. 221-2.
172 Korthals, *Topographische Schets,* pp. 52-3; Lange, *Oost-Indisch Leger,* i. 2.
173 Besluit in Rade, 6 Sept. 1819, no. 3, MK 2771; de Stuers, *Vestiging,* i. 44, 113-4.
174 Besluit, 2 Oct. 1820, no. 15, MK 2456; de Stuers, *Vestiging,* i. 70.
175 Nahuijs, *Brieven,* pp. 93-5.
176 Besluit in Rade, 16 Mar. 1827, no. 22, MK 2799; de Stuers to Elout, 17 May 1826, no. 4, Exh. 23 Oct. 1826, no. 48, MK 523.

177 De Stuers to Elout, 17 May 1826, no. 4, Exh. 23 Oct. 1826, no. 48, MK 523.
178 McGillavry to de Kock, 20 Nov. 1829, L^{a}H, Exh. 15 Sept. 1830, no. 6/A, MK 767.
179 Elout to van den Bosch. 1 Sept. 1831, no. L^{a}E, Exh. 2 Mar. 1832, no. 10/A, MK 830.
180 Lange, *Oost-Indisch Leger,* i. 310-1.
181 Besluit in Rade, 3 Jan. 1821, no. 20, MK 2774.
182 Elout to Clifford, 6 May 1831, no. 1/109, Exh. 26 Sept. 1831, no. 28, MK 810; idem, 29 Jul. 1832, no. 4, Exh. 14 Jan. 1833, no. 12/A, MK 868.
183 Elout to Clifford, 15 Dec. 1832, no. 5, Exh. 28 May 1833, no. 29A, MK 881.
184 Elout to van den Bosch, 17 Dec. 1831, L^{a}I, van den Bosch 393.
185 Spengler, 1829, ANHM.
186 Besluit in Rade, 29 Aug. 1826, no. 11, MK 2795.
187 Consideratie, 22 Dec. 1789, par. 41, KA 3800.
188 Besluit in Rade, 4 Nov. 1823, no. 18, MK 2780; Kielstra, 'Sumatra's Westkust van 1819-1825', pp. 61, 108.
189 Besluit, 28 Dec. 1825, no. 5, MK 2489; the title is a common one for a ruler in the Malay world, meaning literally 'he who is made lord'.
190 Instructie voor den Adsistent Resident van de afdeeling der Padangsche Bovenlanden, Exh. 24 Aug. 1826, no. 41, MK 513.
191 ibid.
192 Besluit in Rade, 14 June 1825, no. 14, MK 2789.
193 Nahuijs, *Brieven,* pp. 141-3; Korthals, *Topographische Schets,* pp. 22-3.
194 De Stuers to Elout, 17 May 1826, no. 4, Exh. 23 Oct. 1826, no. 48, MK 523.
195 De Stuers to Elout, 15 Jan. 1827, no. 10, Exh. 29 May 1827, no. 97, MK 558.
196 'Reizen van L. Horner', p. 340.
197 Journaal . . . gehouden door . . . C.P.A. de Salis, 28 Mar. 1837, Melvill van Carnbee MSS 1, ARA.
198 Nahuijs, *Brieven,* p. 135; Lange, *Oost-Indisch Leger,* i. 405.
199 Lange, *Oost-Indisch Leger,* i. 405.
200 *The Missionary Herald,* xxxi (1835), 297.
201 Boelhouwer, *Herinneringen,* p. 16; Nahuijs, *Brieven,* p. 40.
202 Nahuijs, *Brieven,* pp. 132, 136, 156, 165, 169.
203 Kielstra, 'Sumatra's Westkust van 1819-1825', pp. 39, 56.

CHAPTER V

THE PADRI MOVEMENT IN THE NORTH, 1807-1832

The village of Bonjol, 1807-1832

The Padri movement made no impact to the south of the Minangkabau heartland. The adjoining regions of Sungai Pagu and Kerinci, although peopled by Minangkabau, were hilly, isolated and sparsely settled. To the north of Agam, however, lay two contiguous, fertile valleys which were also inhabited by Minangkabau and where Padri teachings found a ready hearing. These were the valleys of Alahan Panjang and Rao; both became famous in Minangkabau history as the virtual fiefs of two important Padri leaders, Imam Bonjol and Tuanku Rao.

Alahan Panjang was the smaller of the two. Enclosed by mountains to the west and to the east, 8,000 inhabitants won a livelihood from the valley floor which was divided in two by a river which ultimately drained into the sea on the west coast. As described in 1832, the villages of Alahan Panjang were 'surrounded by the most beautiful ricefields; everything bore witness to both prosperity and unsurpassed fertility'.[1] Cattle, fish, and fruit trees were abundant. Moreover, the hills which enclosed the valley provided excellent terrain for the cultivation of coffee, so that the area became an important producer of that crop and was described as 'covered with coffee bushes'.[2]

Politically arrangements were somewhat different from those in the heartland valleys, and resembled more the situation on the west coast. Although within the villages the lineage system and role of the *penghulu* was similar to that in central Minangkabau, there was also a form of supra-village authority. The villages were amalgamated into four loose groupings, and each of the four had as its representative a so-called *raja,* so that the valley, in a fashion similar to other outlying areas of Minangkabau, was administered by the Raja Empat Sila (the *raja* of the four seats). Like the strongly Padri areas of Bukit Kamang, north-eastern Tanah Datar and Lintau, it was a region of Bodi Caniago *laras.*[3]

In the early nineteenth century one of the Raja Empat Sila, a man with the title Datuk Bendahara, had been a student with Tuanku Nan Tua in Kota Tua before returning home to assume the lineage *gelar.* He was present in Kota Tua when Tuanku Nan Rinceh debated with the master over the meaning of the Padri teachings, and so had been exposed to both currents of Islamic revivalism. Datuk Bendahara found the teachings of Tuanku Nan Rinceh more attractive than those of his old *guru* and he joined the Padri leader in Bukit Kamang, even accompanying Haji Miskin on the latter's preaching journeys. Though so little is known of the genesis of the Padri movement in particular villages, the case of Datuk Bendahara makes it clear that lineage heads in certain economically dynamic areas were as keen to reform village institutions as were the local *malim.* On his journeys with Haji Miskin, Datuk Bendahara was accompanied by a young client of his, also from the valley of Alahan Panjang called Peto Sarif. Peto Sarif, later to become famous in Minangkabau history as Imam Bonjol, was born in 1772 in the modest hill village of Tanjung Bunga in the valley of Alahan Panjang. He was the son of an obscure *malim*, had studied under Tuanku Nan Tua and had been fortunate in gaining the patronage of a member of a powerful *penghulu* family at a time when both found themselves attracted to Padri ideas.[4]

The two converts remained for four months in Agam and then returned to their home valley hoping to propagate the Padri system. There was immediate resistance to the implementation of the new teaching, both on religious grounds and because it would give men of humble origin such as Peto Sarif a far greater say in the community. While Datuk Bendahara used all his influence to promote the abolition of cockfighting and gambling and to end the use of strong drink, opposition crystallized round the person of one of the other Raja Empat Sila, resulting in the building of a cockfighting ring right opposite the chief mosque of Alahan Panjang, and the staging of cockfights at the same time as Friday prayers. Faced with such determined opponents, the adherents of the new teaching decided that, rather than engage in a physical struggle, which might continue for months, it would be preferable to separate themselves from the rest of society and set up their own Islamic community which would be an example to the rest of the valley. It was in this way that the famous village of Bonjol was founded. The course of its founding is not clear, but it seems that initially Datuk Bendahara led his supporters – thirty families in all – out of the valley of Alahan Panjang to a spot just south of its entrance, and there built a fort for their protection. But even here they were not left in peace, another cockfighting ring was built opposite the new fortified settlement, and fighting broke out.[5]

About 1806 the reformers' cause appeared to receive a setback when Datuk Bendahara was poisoned. His uncle, who succeeded to his title, and supported the new system, was unable to carry on the affairs of the besieged community without the aid of Peto Sarif. The young *murid* had developed into a man of great firmness of character and some learning; above all he had shown a taste for fighting, leading expeditions in which he had exhibited a cool head in combat and great personal bravery, qualities which had led to the rise of the major Padri leaders in central Minangkabau.[6] He and his new patron now decided to break up the first Bonjol, which was located on a site difficult to defend and also lacked suitable agricultural land, and move back into the valley of Alahan Panjang. The eastern mountains enclosing the valley, the scene of Peto Sarif's boyhood, provided readily defensible sites, and the new Bonjol was established at the foot of Mount Terjadi in the south-eastern corner of the valley in 1807. In his memoirs Peto Sarif, now known as Imam Bonjol, applies to Bonjol – the Indonesian word for 'lump' or 'projection' – a particular symbolism, claiming that the name was intended to signify 'that this fort was erected for the maintenance of the just institutions of Islam, to oppose all evil and unlawful actions, and to recommend to everyone to practise nothing that is not fair, just and good'.[7] Even now the few families who had established a new society were not left untroubled; they were besieged by their old opponents and were only able to hold out because Tuanku Nan Rinceh came personally to their aid, with a small fighting force.[8]

The original Bonjol was only a small, square fort, inside which were built a mosque and six houses. Initially it did not exhibit the characteristics of a regular village, as it was intended to be a place only for committed Padris and their wives, and as large a number of *hulubalang* as possible to defend them. However, by about 1812 Bonjol began to attract inhabitants from other parts of Minangkabau, both to study the Padri teachings and because the village was carrying on a flourishing trade. Imam Bonjol had in common with the other major Padri leaders the desire to make his home area an important centre of trade, and he mentioned in his memoirs that soon after the settlement was established he planted rice and fruit trees, and set up a breeding place for cattle and horses.[9] He goes on to say that by about 1812 Bonjol's 'prosperity was so great due to increasing industry and trade that many people went there because of the cheapness of foodstuffs, since rice, cattle and horses were plentiful.'[10] Moreover, after the village had been properly fortified, and the inhabitants suitably armed, 'they confined themselves exclusively to trade; with the enjoyment of peace and unity the prosperity of negorij Bondjol increased more and more, and merchants came here to trade from the neighbouring places'.[11] The main trade outside the valley was the trade in coffee, which was exported overland and then downriver to Pasaman and Masang, and down to the Straits of Malacca by way of the Siak.[12] Alahan Panjang also produced a little gold, which was important in trade.[13]

With this growth in population Bonjol was bursting at the seams. As a result the fortifications were extended and a new mosque was built; room had to be made for a population of five hundred arms-bearing men and forty-three houses. The village was now protected by stone outer walls of about twelve feet high, extending to a length of 2,400 feet and a breadth of 1,200 feet, a broad, deep moat and an inner wall, in addition to small square forts placed on the adjacent mountain, dominating the settlement and the plain in front of it.[14] Gradually the other villages in the valley came to accept Padri teachings, and a mutual defence system was worked out in the building of their fortifications.[15]

Bonjol is the only Minangkabau village from which we can derive any clear information concerning the relationship between the Padri *malim* and the lineage heads. Here it is quite clear that the lineage heads survived with far greater resilience than has been imputed to them in traditional accounts of the Padri movement. Indeed, the Padri system never succeeded in displacing them. Nor was there any particular reason why it should, as prosperity and trade were in the interests of the *penghulu* as much as of anyone else. Lineage matters in the village continued to be dealt with by the *penghulu*,[16] and though the distinction between sacred and secular was hard to draw, it was made easier by the fact that Imam Bonjol quite rapidly evolved into a war leader and his attention was distracted elsewhere. To the students who flocked to Bonjol he gave training in the martial arts, and they formed his shock troops after his position in the valley became strong enough for him to declare a *jihad* on the surrounding areas. The pattern developed of annual raids on nearby regions, from which the Bonjollers always returned with considerable booty, after which they would rest and attend to the agricultural cycle for a year before engaging in another sortie. These raids were generally undertaken at the request of one or other Padri leader, and in them religious fervour and human avarice were firmly allied; there is a report that from one raid into Agam the Bonjollers brought back not only cattle, but plates, cups, pots, pans and other household goods.[17]

While Imam Bonjol was so engaged with his young men, it is not surprising that the village in all the ordinary concerns of life continued to be administered by the *penghulu.* The Imam's memoirs show that from the very start he discussed important steps, such as the fortification of the village, with the *penghulu* of the families who were living there. Even at the period of his greatest prestige he went so far as to claim that without them he could 'command nothing'.[18] More revealing still is his advice given in 1837 to the son he had chosen as his successor: 'One thing more: recognise the authority of the adat-panghoeloes, obey their rules; if these cannot be obeyed, then he is not a true panghoeloe and possesses only the title. Be as faithful as possible to the Adat, and if your knowledge is not sufficient, learn the twenty attributes of Allah'.[19]

Side by side with the *penghulu,* of course, there was an Islamic leadership group. These were the *tuanku yang berempat* (the four *tuanku*), including Imam Bonjol, whom the Imam calls in his memoirs 'judges'. In Padri fashion they used the Koran as their guide in all matters requiring their attention[20] or, as Imam Bonjol puts it, they 'followed the holy institutions of Mohammed, and all their decisions bore the mark of justice'.[21] Like Imam Bonjol himself they were men of humble birth.[22] By 1825 two of them had died, and ultimately Imam Bonjol was the only one of the original four left. However, he gradually gained other unofficial colleagues, composed of *malim* who had fled from their villages in the heartland after Dutch conquest. The chief among these was Tuanku Mensiangan, the son of the Tuanku Mensiangan who had given his support to Tuanku Nan Rinceh, a refugee in Bonjol after the fall of Kota Lawas.[23]

One of the prominent features of the Padri movement was its concern to foster the trade of Minangkabau and to confound attempts from outside to monopolize this trade. Just as the Padris of Limapuluh Kota built up their trading network on the east coast, and the Padris of Agam fostered the growth of trade in the Pariaman area before the Dutch returned, so too did the Bonjol Padris seek free and untramelled trade on the west coast, now that they were in possession of a commodity desired by the outside world. Bonjol's trade came to be conducted via the Pasaman region, an area on the west coast between Air Bangis and Tiku. During the heyday of the pepper trade Pasaman had been an important pepper-producing locality,[24] and had thus built up a tradition of independent commerce with foreign traders. Long after Pariaman and Tiku had fallen under Dutch control, Pasaman proved to be far enough north to continue to trade independently, being largely beyond the reach of cursory Dutch naval patrols. The Acehnese, well supplied with Gujarati cloths, were able to sell them on this part of the coast for many years after they had been driven away further south.[25]

When English private traders began to come into these waters the Pasaman region also supplied them with pepper, and this continued right into the late eighteenth century,[26] when it also became a rice-provisioning centre for British possessions further up the coast.[27] Pasaman also provided an export outlet for the gold of Rao, the valley immediately to the north of Alahan Panjang, which was a very ancient gold-exporting region.[28] English trade with the Pasaman area became so flourishing that in 1766 the Dutch hoisted their flag there, but they were only able to maintain themselves until 1772. Thereafter the region's ports flourished in association with the English, while Acehnese traders also came to settle in the harbours between Pasaman and the Masang river.[29] The Pasaman locality became part of a flourishing coastal trading network based on the needs of the English private trader.[30]

With this background, it is not surprising that the traders of Bonjol should have seen the advantages of building up their own trading network in this area. In any case,the valley of Alahan Panjang had historical links with the region. Just as the people of Agam made their salt and bought their fish from a particular part of the coast near Pariaman, so too were the people of Alahan Panjang accustomed to come down to the coast to the mouth of the river Masang for their own necessities. English stimulation of trade brought more and more Acehnese to the area, to settle particularly in the ports of Katiagan and Pasaman, which expanded proportionately.[31] As their own commercial activities increased, the traders of Bonjol entered into commercial relations with merchants at the coastal ports and began to participate in their trade, although unfortunately we know little of how this trade operated. We do know that by the end of the second decade of the nineteenth century Bonjol itself was regarded as controlling all the main ports between Tiku and Air Bangis and it considered the Acehnese merchants there to be Bonjol's instruments.[32] In 1826 Bonjol apparently regarded its own commercial connections as so well established that it could afford to attack the Acehnese settlements at Pasaman and Katiagan and burn them down in an effort to persuade the Acehnese to embrace Bonjol's own brand of revivalism and improve their general moral standards, particularly in relation to the use of opium.[33]

The river Masang at Katiagan provided excellent facilities for trade; vessels of the burden of 200 to 250 tuns[34] were able to be accommodated safely, whilst the river could be navigated as far inland as Binjai, a journey of between five and seven days.[35] The chief broker used by Bonjol traders at the port was a part-Acehnese called Pito Magé, who had a fortified warehouse well inland on the river. Pito Magé's own commercial position on the coast would make an interesting study, but unfortunately information is scanty. He also had an establishment at Tiku, and traded with a Padang European agency house which advanced him credit.[36] When the Dutch finally captured Katiagan and Pito Magé's warehouse, the extent of the trade carried on there was revealed in the latter's contents. Awaiting import to the highlands were one hundred large bales of cotton and many bars of iron, while for export were stored coffee, cassia, and at least one thousand *pikul* of rice. There was so much that the Dutch soldiers who took the fortified warehouse were unable to load everything into boats after a full morning's work, and at least 100 *pikul* of rice had to be burnt with the warehouse.[37]

Pito Magé also had a warehouse further north at Pasaman, and Bonjol traders operated from there too.[38] To a Dutch investigator in 1839 the merchant reported that there was a demand in the interior from Binjai to Rao for imported cotton piece-goods, tobacco, Swedish iron and English steel, all of which were bought with gold, whilst smaller items such as glassware, pottery, knives, and gold-, silver- or copper-thread were all welcome.[39] This trading network encompassed not only Padang Europeans and Acehnese ports further north, but also some Padang Chinese brokers, who maintained an entrepôt on the Batu islands after the Dutch had farmed out the islands as a monopoly concern to a Padang Chinese. Using the island entrepôt as a base, Chinese traded goods coming from Penang with the Padri ports of Katiagan and Pasaman.[40]

This burgeoning of Bonjol's trade would not have been possible without the contemporary florescence of a certain number of ports on the west coast of Aceh. Aceh and the Minangkabau coast had long been trading partners, and anything which affected Aceh was bound in the long run to have an impact on Minangkabau. The west coast of Aceh from the 1790s was experiencing an economic revival similar to that of the Minangkabau interior, though based on pepper rather than coffee. On the coastal plains of the south-west Acehnese lowlands individuals who had migrated from Great Aceh began to apply themselves to pepper cultivation, clustering for protection about certain dominant figures who were ultimately to carve out for themselves petty rajadoms, based on their control of pepper-exporting at particular ports. The pepper coast stretched for about seventy-five miles, between Trumon at 2° 50' North and Kuala Batu at 3° 50'N, and came to consist of petty port-states which had thrown off allegiance to the sultan of Aceh.[41]

That these states were able to maintain their independence was again due to Anglo-American economic activity in Sumatra. In 1751 the English East India Company established a factory at Natal, largely to serve as a port of call for the country traders operating between Bengal and Batavia, and in 1756 the British flag was also raised at Tapanuli.[42] These ports will be discussed in more detail below, in connection with the trade of the Batak country. Here it is sufficient to note that Tapanuli in particular began a successful trade with the pepper ports, and from about 1786 became the trade terminal of the pepper exporters. This trading network was expanded after 1786 with the founding of Penang, and the pepper ports gained a further trading partner when, in 1797, the first American ship arrived at Susu to buy up pepper.[43]

From 1801 Susu and the ports nearby became the leading world suppliers of pepper to the Americans. In 1803 thirty-one American vessels arrived on the so-called pepper coast and took from 30,000 to 36,000 *pikul.* In 1805 Americans took 70,000 *pikul* or seven-eighths of the crop,[44] but due to overstocking of the market prices fell from 11 Spanish dollars per *pikul* in 1804 to 5 dollars in 1809. However, after the ending of the Napoleonic wars prices rose again, and by 1819 pepper shippers were paying 11 to 12 dollars per *pikul.*[45] As well as Americans with their Spanish dollars, other traders flocked to the coast. 'In the pepper season of 1823, it has been stated that twenty-seven American ships, six country traders, and four French ships, besides the vessels belonging to the East India Company and many large junks and native vessels from Pinang, obtained cargoes on the west coast of Sumatra'.[46] American imports on this part of the coast in the official year 1821-22 amounted to about one million dollars, consisting mostly of silver, though with some Turkish opium thrown in. Pepper production continued to increase, so that by 1826 it was estimated that the pepper coast was producing 150,000 *pikul* per annum.[47] This represented the heyday of the coast, for the world market could absorb pepper in no greater amounts, and not until 1871 did pepper prices again reach the levels of 1822-23. Meanwhile, exhaustion of the soil dictated a shift in pepper cultivation from the Susu area, and about 1830 new centres were established further north.[48]

In addition to the American trade in the period 1801-1830, the whole area between Singkil and Susu prospered on account of its trade with India and Penang. Plentifully supplied with silver dollars, merchants of the port-states carried on a flourishing commerce with Bengal, Madras, Bombay, Penang and, latterly, Singapore:

. . . there were exports by free traders, French ships, Arab vessels from Mocha and Judda, Parsee vessels from Surat and Bombay, from the Maldive Islands, Rangoon, the Straits of Malacca, and English ships loading betel-nut for China; Portuguese from Macao and Goa etc., the exact amount of which is impossible to calculate.[49]

These vessels brought in Bengal and Malwa opium, cotton goods from Coromandel and Bombay, British manufactured cloth, and Chinese goods previously imported to Penang. In 1826 it was reported that ten to twelve vessels from the Coromandel coast visited the pepper ports every year, bringing numerous varieties of cloth.[50]

Among the Acehnese ports which rose to prosperity at this time, the one of greatest interest from the point of view of Bonjol's trade is Trumon. Trumon was founded by Datuk Si Ruyung, a son of the Acehnese who established the wealth of Susu by selling pepper to the British at Tapanuli from 1787. Datuk Si Ruyung's brother, Leubé Dapa, gained a considerable competence by trade at Singkil and became the port's *raja*; moving to Trumon, he stimulated pepper production there, superseded his brother and was recognized as chief of both Trumon and Singkil. After his death about 1814 his son Raja Bujang became chief of Trumon, inheriting his father's wealth and commercial connections. Two other sons of Leubé Dapa also became *raja* on the coast, one at Singkil, and so together they controlled a valuable tract of pepper country stretching over one hundred miles. By 1814 Trumon itself exported c. 10,000 *pikul* of pepper annually, and by the next decade this had increased to 40,000 *pikul*. Due to its two *rajas'* commercial sagacity, Trumon had its own ocean-going vessels. Its traders did not have merely to wait for foreign ships to come to pick up pepper, but could take cargoes to Penang and elsewhere as required.[51]

Trumon vessels traded directly with India and the ports of the Malacca Straits, and were eager to trade on the Minangkabau coast. Bonjol's commercial policies favoured such a trade, and until the death of Raja Bujang in 1832 or 1833, after which the port declined due to misgovernment,[52] Trumon found in Bonjol's ports of Katiagan, Sasak and Pasaman its main trading partners on that part of the coast. It was a relationship satisfactory to both, for Trumon, having a limited number of domestic consumers, was overwhelmed with the commercial riches of the east, and Bonjol was delighted to find a supplier who could break through the cordon the Netherlands Indies government, by its system of duties, was beginning to erect around Minangkabau. Raja Bujang himself had conceived a great enmity for the Dutch, and he came to consider Katiagan, Sasak and Pasaman as his 'factories', where in his own ships he imported large cargoes consisting of bales of cotton, cotton piece-goods, iron, steel and salt, and exported coffee and gold.[53] Guns and ammunition were also imported.[54] In this way the products of India, China and Europe were made available to Bonjol traders through the mediation of Acehnese ports.[55]

It was in this condition of flourishing commerce and zealous spiritual life that the Dutch encountered Bonjol when they returned to Padang in 1819. In addition to trading via Pasaman and Katiagan, some of Bonjol's trade also came down to Pariaman by way of Agam and the route between Mounts Merapi and Singgalang. As the Dutch commenced their reoccupation of the coast and pressed into Agam, Imam Bonjol determined on a test of strength with them, hoping at the same time to restore the Padri leader Tuanku Mensiangan to Kota Lawas. In September 1822 a Bonjol army joined with a force from Rao Rao to drive the Dutch from the villages between Mounts Merapi and Singgalang, overlooking the main route from Agam to the lowlands. Having succeeded in this, in April 1823 a Bonjol fighting force pressed down through Agam and into the lowlands behind Pariaman, but was not able to complete its task of wresting the port from the Dutch before it had to return home from fear of being cut off.[56] This defeat made it apparent that Bonjol would have to confine its coastal activities to the Pasaman region, and further Dutch advances under Raaff in the Minangkabau heartland seem to have convinced Imam Bonjol and his fellow administrators that it would be better to sue for peace while they still had the opportunity, and concentrate on building up their commercial network in the north, in a separate sphere of influence from that of the Dutch. Bonjol's broker, Pito Magé, was instructed to contact the Padang merchant A.F. van den Berg, with whom he had commercial ties, and van den Berg subsequently went to meet representatives of Bonjol at the Masang. He brought with him a draft treaty drawn up by Raaff, who was also keen for peace after the resistance he had experienced from Lintau, and the two sides signed the treaty on 22 January 1824.[57]

The nucleus of the treaty comprised an attempt to draw Bonjol firmly into the Dutch trading orbit, and it is hard to see how Bonjol, given its relations with the Pasaman area, could have taken some of the clauses seriously. The Bonjol *tuanku* promised to do all in their power to encourage their neighbours in Rao, whose gold had been important to Dutch trade in company days, to come to Padang or Pariaman to trade; to permit the free and unimpeded introduction of all articles the Dutch wished to sell in Bonjol's territory; to assist the Dutch to stop 'smuggling'; and to buy their salt from the Dutch at f.6 per *pikul.* Acceptance of these clauses can only have been intended by Imam Bonjol to give his land a breathing space in the face of Raaff's obvious military skill; the Dutch salt monopoly had always been hated, and Dutch salt was two hundred per cent more expensive than salt coming from the English possessions of Natal and Tapanuli.[58] Rao trade was operating in quite another direction, and it was hardly likely that the Dutch could offer a commercial relationship as stimulating as that conducted through the Acehnese ports. However, Bonjol could be satisfied that a period of calm had been inaugurated with the Dutch promise never to interfere with the religion or government of Bonjol's lands, and to see that Bonjol's customs were respected throughout Dutch territory on Sumatra.

As it happened, the treaty did not remain long in force. Raaff died in April 1824, and before the new Resident could arrive Dutch troops attacked the villages between Mounts Merapi and Singgalang, including Kota Lawas to which Tuanku Mensiangan had been restored. Upon the defeat of these villages, Bonjol sent the treaty back to van den Berg.[59] Subsequent Dutch attempts to renegotiate the treaty foundered on Bonjol's demand that the villages between Mounts Merapi and Singgalang be evacuated, again indicating the importance Bonjol attached to having open access to the coast. In reply to an Arab emissary sent by the Dutch Resident de Stuers to Bonjol itself, Imam Bonjol stated that the last Dutch post on the Minangkabau coast should stop at Pariaman, that the Singgalang-Merapi villages should be evacuated, and that the Dutch should recognize Bonjol's right to control the coast between the river Masang and Air Bangis. The Dutch resiled from these proposals, considering that they had a long-existing right to trade on that part of the coast, and negotiations became more acrimonious;[60] to a Minangkabau emissary sent by de Stuers to Bonjol in September 1825 Imam Bonjol gave the ultimatum that his village would not rest until all Minangkabau were brought under Bonjol's authority and 'all Europeans . . . have been driven into the sea'.[61] Finally, towards the end of 1825, the Padris of Bonjol and Rao, together with numerous other Padri bands from the fringe areas of Agam, launched a massive advance on the Dutch-occupied part of Agam, and near Kapau suffered an equally massive defeat.[62] From this date Bonjol firmly turned its eyes northwards, hoping at the same time to have turned its back on the Dutch for good.

International events decreed that this was not to be. It soon became apparent that no Dutch Resident at Padang was prepared to allow Bonjol to supply Minangkabau with goods imported through its independent west coast outlets. De Stuers was prevented from sending a garrison to Katiagan by lack of men, but he did make a ship available to cruise the waters between the river Masang and Air Bangis with the aim of driving off Acehnese trading vessels, and in this he had some success.[63] The Batavia government supported both the blockade and the proposals for a garrison, but again there was a shortage of the manpower needed to take more effective measures.[64] Nevertheless, these Dutch manoeuvres were a warning to the Bonjol Padris, who had already begun casting their eyes further north in the hope of finding equally suitable and safer commercial outlets. About 1820 they had shown signs of approaching Air Bangis, which was then in English hands, and it appeared as if their intention was to take over the port.[65]

These hopes of a successful northwards expansion were thrown into confusion when the entire situation altered as a result of treaty negotiations in Europe. Between Britain and the Netherlands several matters had been left unsettled deriving from territorial annexations during the Napoleonic Wars. With the signing of the Treaty of London in 1824, the government of the Netherlands Indies at the start of 1825 was obliged to take over three English posts to the north of the Minangkabau coast, at Air Bangis, Natal and Tapanuli, whilst a seventeenth century Dutch treaty with Barus was revived to lend support to Dutch claims to that port. Where previously Dutch possessions had stretched no further north than Tiku, Barus now became the northern limit of Dutch 'authority' on the coast, and a 'northern division' was constituted with an Assistant Resident at Tapanuli.[66] Bonjol's plans to expand its commercial network up the north coast were now confronted with the reality of the Dutch presence.

The west Sumatran coast between Air Bangis and Barus had long formed a commercial unit. The people inhabiting the mountain foothills and upland valleys behind the coastal strip were not Minangkabau but Bataks, though the ports situated at the mouths of the fast-flowing rivers tumbling down to the western shore had for centuries attracted Minangkabau traders, and there Minangkabau settlements existed side by side with Batak villages. These ports were famous as stapling places for the camphor and benjamin which grew on the mountain slopes behind the coastal lowlands. Camphor was particularly desired in China and Japan as a component of various medicines, whilst benjamin was exported to Europe and sold as incense and for use in medicine for balsam and sticking plaster. Poorer quality benjamin found markets in Arabia, Persia and India, to be burned to perfume temples and houses.[67] Barus in particular, well located with a sheltered roadstead, had stapled camphor for the Chinese market from the seventeenth century, and benjamin and camphor for Arabia from at least the ninth century.[68] The Dutch company signed a treaty there in 1668, hoping to exchange camphor and benjamin for Indian cotton piece-goods, but the VOC was never able to cut the port's links with Aceh and Indian Muslim traders from Surat and Coromandel, and it acquired only a little camphor over the years, and benjamin of the poorest quality.[69]

As the Dutch tried to monopolize the trade of Barus, other ports on the camphor and benjamin coast rose to prominence as outlets for Batak trade, where once all ports as far south as Batahan had been mere collecting points for articles shipped straight to Barus. At these ports Minangkabau traders would generally be found settled in their own villages, lying somewhat inland on the banks of a river; further back towards the mountains could be found a collection of small Batak villages, which earned a livelihood by provisioning the Minangkabau trading settlements and facilitating the transit of goods. Between Barus and the river Taru ports such as Sorkam tended to specialize in exporting benjamin, which was the chief product of this part of the coast. From the river Taru south the speciality was camphor. Here Minangkabau traders had a monopoly over camphor-exporting; they had sited their villages at all the major river mouths, at Batu Mundam, Sinkuan, Tabuyung, Kunkun, Natal and Batahan, and were supplied with camphor by the Batak villages further inland. Tabuyung was the main collection point for this section of the coast; it had a wide, deep river suited for the entry of good sized vessels, and camphor could be brought for stapling from ports to both the north and south. In 1730 it was reported to have a sizeable settlement of Minangkabau traders with their own boats, engaged both in collecting camphor from other ports, and travelling to the north of Barus to trade with the Acehnese.[70]

The three southernmost ports of the camphor-producing region, Natal, Batahan and Air Bangis, were also important because of their accessibility from the inland Minangkabau valley of Rao, which produced gold. Many traders from Rao made permanent settlements on the coast to exchange gold for supplies desired in the interior.[71] In these gold ports settlements of Acehnese traders were also in evidence. Natal was described in the late eighteenth century as

. . . a place of much commerce . . . It is inhabited by settlers there, for the convenience of trade, from the countries of *Achin, Rau,* and Menangkabau, who render it populous and rich. Gold, of very fine quality, is procured from the country . . . and there is a considerable vent for imported goods, the returns of which are chiefly made in that article and camphor.[72]

It was Dutch policy at Barus which caused the ports of the Batak coast to flourish in the eighteenth century, and so delivered them into the hands of the English and the Acehnese, who in the latter part of the century welded them into a flourishing commercial unit. In addition to introducing various monopolistic regulations at Barus, the Dutch company was not prepared to accept other than the best quality camphor and benjamin, for which alone it had a ready market, whilst the Batak sellers wished to dispose of their second-and third-grade samples at the same time. This encouraged trade at the southern ports outside the orbit of Barus. Acehnese traders and English private traders from India found their way there and were prepared to accept poorer quality camphor and benjamin because they had a wider range of markets for them.[73] From the 1740s English private traders began to discover it was worth their while to stop on this part of the coast, particularly at Natal, where all the items stapled further north were available, and gold too. Natal and nearby Tabuyung became bulking points for supplies of Indian cloth, salt and opium, which were then broken up and taken both north and south in the boats of Minangkabau traders.

Finally, as we have seen, the British flag was raised at Natal in 1751 by servants of the East India Company based on Benkulen. In an effort to outstrip the Dutch settlement of Padang, trade was declared entirely free, and the commerce of Natal received official encouragement from Madras. In the late 1750s trade was flourishing as never before; the English were prepared to pay higher prices for Rao gold than did the Dutch at Padang, they sold their cloths far cheaper, they were less particular about the quality of the camphor and benjamin they took, and they provided salt, an important item of trade in the Batak upland valleys, far cheaper than would the Dutch.[74]

In 1756 to forestall what appeared to be renewed Dutch interest in this part of the coast, the English also established a factory at Tapanuli, and it too became an important centre for the sale of opium, salt and cloth. While Natal could deliver gold in addition to camphor and benjamin, Batak districts in the highlands inland of Tapanuli were found to be producing cassia similar to that traded at Pariaman from the Agam region of Minangkabau, and the cassia trade, which was in the hands of a group of Minangkabau merchants settled on the shores of Tapanuli bay, further stimulated the trade of the area. Also in 1756 the Dutch tried to retaliate by establishing themselves at Air Bangis, but their factory tended to oscillate between accepting control from Padang and submitting to the commercial attractions emanating from the English post at Natal.[75] Competition from Tapanuli also became too much for the Dutch at Barus, and in 1774 they withdrew from the port,[76] leaving the Batak coast in a trading partnership with the English, mediated by Minangkabau brokers.

A new element was introduced into the situation by the expansion of pepper cultivation on the south-west Acehnese coast. The pepper trade for a time increased the prosperity of the benjamin and camphor coast, because initially American ships called at Tapanuli for their pepper, the first one coming in 1788, whilst from 1795 Natal was able to make arrangements for pepper deliveries with Leubé Dapa of Singkil.[77] Benjamin was also desired by the American traders, and after 1790 it became a frequent subsidiary item in the pepper trade.[78] Pepper-stapling on the coast did not last, however, as it became too easy for American ships to go to the pepper ports themselves, and Tapanuli in particular suffered a decline.[79] Natal, on the other hand, began to produce its own pepper from about 1810, and by 1823 the Natal area was exporting c. 500,000 lbs. of local pepper every year.[80]

It was within the commercial framework of these ports of the Batak country that Bonjol sought compensation for its inability to expand further south on the Minangkabau coast. To begin with it was necessary to divert trade from the European settlements on that part of the coast. This task was left in the hands of the Padris of Rao who, as will be seen below, by 1821 had practically cut off Air Bangis and Natal from the Batak population in their rear and had started to ruin the trade of these ports.[81] Bonjol's own concern was less with the landward side of the European-controlled ports, and more with keeping open the seas in the area so that its own ports, which it was encouraging at the expense of Air Bangis and Natal, could flourish.[82] From about 1820 merchants from Bonjol and its allies began to establish themselves at the most important alternative ports on the coast, at Batahan, Kunkun, Tabuyung and Sinkuan, relying on the armed ships of their Acehnese trading partners to keep the seas open. Tabuyung became their major harbour. They exported the products of the upland valleys of the Mandailing Bataks, including rice, camphor and gold, which were taken off by Acehnese ships. At Tabuyung, too, wood was available for constructing *perahu,* and Bonjol's boats used for collecting products at a variety of small coastal settlements lay safely in harbour there for repair work.[83] The possibilities of this part of the coast were such that several English agency houses together established an agent on an island off Batu Mundam, who until 1830 participated advantageously in the trade. Pito Magé's own trade was also related to goods imported by English vessels onto this island.[84]

Into this nascent commercial system now dominated by the economic dynamism of Bonjol the Dutch erupted without warning in 1825. They anticipated considerable profits from the camphor, benjamin and pepper trades at their new ports, but found instead that their trade between the years 1825 and 1830 showed an annual decline, due both to their policy of differential export duties and to Padri measures intended to do them deliberate harm; Bonjol's ports, on the other hand, flourished.[85] Not content with using commercial measures against the Dutch, Imam Bonjol had decided by 1830 to undertake a military offensive to remove them once and for all from this part of the coast, for which he had great commercial hopes. In January 1831 he himself, accompanied by his chief lieutenant Tuanku Muda and by a force of 3,000 men, marched overland to Air Bangis and blockaded the Dutch post there for four days and four nights. Such large forces were able to be raised for this and other Bonjol expeditions because, although the valley of Alahan Panjang only contained a population of 8,000, by the late 1820s virtually all agriculture was being carried out by Batak slave labour, just as Tuanku Lintau also used slaves to cultivate *sawah* in his valley and free the population for military expeditions. With the assistance of the renowned Acehnese freebooter Saidi Marah and his ships, the Bonjol force killed nearly two-thirds of the garrison before being obliged to fall back. Even more damage would have been done, had not one of Bonjol's war leaders been wounded, which was a customary signal for retreat. Two months later, in March 1831, Imam Bonjol was able to lead an army of 10,000 – Alahan Panjangers and others – overland to Natal and, again with the assistance of Saidi Marah and his armed *perahu* together with aid from Trumon, to blockade Natal from land and sea for twelve days. This time Dutch reinforcements obliged the Padris to retreat, a retreat already underway in any case because the besieging army had run out of food.[86]

These attacks represented a final act of defiance on Bonjol's part. With the assumption of the Governor-Generalship by Johannes van den Bosch, Dutch policy became one of firm assertion of the rights of the Netherlands Indies government over the west coast of Sumatra from the Sunda Strait to Barus. The first step towards the fulfillment of this policy was to be the removal of Bonjol's commercial settlements from the entire area between Padang and Natal, and the securing of Dutch control of the coast to at least two or more miles inland.[87] In July 1831 van den Bosch wrote to Resident Elout:

> I continue to be of the opinion that we must remove all our enemies from the coast by destroying their villages up to a sufficient distance to prevent their having communication by sea, and that this must even take place within the territory of Achin; subsequently we must transfer the trade of the highlands to our establishments . . .[88]

The following September the Governor-General advised Dutch forces at Padang to prepare for an attack on Katiagan and the Pasaman area,[89] and finally, in December 1831, when extra forces had been supplied from Batavia, Katiagan was stormed from both the land and the sea, and captured.[90] A Dutch naval and military expedition then sailed up the coast with the aim of ruining Bonjol's commercial outlets in the Batak lowlands as well. Batahan was taken and burnt, and in January 1832 Bonjol's main port on this part of the coast, at Tabuyung, was destroyed.[91]

Bonjol's leaders were aware that this attack on their commercial system was only part of a systematic Dutch onslaught against the remaining Padri areas in Minangkabau. Realising that other Padri regions were being threatened simultaneously, Imam Bonjol decided to turn his attention south again and try to construct an alliance with the Padri leaders of Limapuluh Kota and Lintau which would pose a serious challenge to Dutch ambitions in the highlands. Arrangements were made for a combined Padri force under the leadership of Imam Bonjol and Tuanku Muda to assemble in northern Agam and march on the lowlands near Tiku, in a massive attempt to drive the Dutch once and for all from the interior. Two Padri columns of 5,000 men in all united at Mengoppo in March 1832 and erected a fort, stacking it with rice, gunpowder, guns and other necessities, but, for some reason – probably the wounding of a major war leader, which was always regarded as too inauspicious for the continuance of hostilities – this Padri army retreated in the face of movements by Dutch troops in the area. With the collapse of the remaining Padri areas of Minangkabau to the Dutch, Bonjol was left isolated to face the foreigner's combined forces. By September 1832 Dutch troops had occupied a village only twelve hours on foot from the valley of Alahan Panjang.[92]

At this time Bonjol seems to have been gripped by a spiritual malaise. Partly this had nothing to do with Dutch advances, but reflected what was happening to Padri teachings elsewhere in Minangkabau. The return of *haji* from a Mecca which was no longer Wahhabi-dominated affected Alahan Panjang as it did other areas of Minangkabau; among those who returned to Bonjol were the nephews of some of the leading *tuanku,* including Imam Bonjol himself. These *haji* argued that many aspects of Padri puritanism, such as the bans on *sirih* and tobacco, were irrelevant to the faith of an individual, and they also condemned some of the excesses of the early *jihad.* Imam Bonjol, his commercial system in ruins and his Padri allies elsewhere in Minangkabau in flight, seems to have experienced a loss of nerve. In a Friday sermon he announced to the assembled congregation that he was prepared to admit that some of the ideas he had imbibed in his youth were now out of date. He asked to be allowed to hand over the administration of Bonjol to the assembled *penghulu,* but his request on this point was refused.[93]

Nevertheless, the result of uncertainty among the Islamic leaders of the village was that the lineage heads of Bonjol gradually acquired total control of the affairs of the settlement, and the same happened in other villages of Alahan Panjang. Even they could come to no agreement over the best strategy for confronting the European challenge, although the majority was in favour of making peace with the Dutch. In the face of *penghulu* disunity, Imam Bonjol became even more disillusioned over his own political decline. However rudderless the community might be, it was apparent that he could no longer remain at the helm, as the population was now too exhausted to continue the fight. For reasons which his memoirs do not really clarify, he decided to leave the valley and move north to Lubuk Sikaping in the adjacent valley of Rao. Dutch sources claim that there was a virtual revolt against any perpetuation of the Imam's authority inside Bonjol.[94]

Three days after his departure the three leading *penghulu* of the village offered the community's submission to the Dutch, and in September 1832 they themselves escorted Dutch troops inside Bonjol on the condition that there would be no infringements upon the religion, manners and customs of the people.[95] This was by no means the end of Imam Bonjol's career. As in other Padri areas, Dutch officialdom was not averse to giving important administrative positions to conquered Padris if they seemed more competent than other possible candidates, and it was not long before officials decided that the three leading *penghulu* of Bonjol were 'extremely lacking in judgement', whilst the other *penghulu* were 'even more wretched creatures'.[96] The Resident of Sumatra's West Coast, C.P.J. Elout, was of the opinion that the 'revolt' inside Bonjol had been 'merely a precipitate action which would certainly be followed by regret',[97] and that Imam Bonjol and his chief lieutenant-at-arms, Tuanku Muda, still exerted great influence on the population. He was able to persuade Imam Bonjol to return to the village, and to agree to a settlement whereby Tuanku Muda, who came from an important lineage, would be appointed Regent of Alahan Panjang, whilst the Imam would henceforth occupy himself with his religious duties.[98]

This settlement confirmed the apparent collapse of the Padri movement; the Dutch were now in full control of most of Minangkabau.

Padri conquest of the Batak lands

North of the valley of Alahan Panjang begins that part of the Bukit Barisan which is inhabited by the Batak people. Here, too, upland valleys are the locations most favoured for settlement but, unlike the Minangkabau in their four adjacent saucer-like valleys, the Bataks in this part of the Bukit Barisan have settled in longitudinal troughs slashed through the mountain range by rivers coursing down to both the west and east coasts. The main such trough is formed by the rivers Angkola and Gadis; the Angkola traverses two-thirds of the trough, flowing from north to south, and it joins with the Gadis, flowing from south to north, to form one river which descends into the Indian Ocean at Sinkuan. The northern part of the trough is inhabited by the Angkola Bataks, and the southern part by the Mandailing Bataks. East of the southern extremity of the Gadis valley lies another longitudinal trough, formed by the river Sumpur, which proceeds in a north-easterly direction and ultimately unites with the great Rokan river. This is the valley of Rao, adjacent to Alahan Panjang and largely inhabited by Minangkabau, though with a Batak admixture.[99] These long, narrow valleys have formed the main inland line of communication between the Minangkabau and Batak worlds, and in this part of Sumatra human contacts in a north-south direction have been easier than communication from west to east.

North of the headwaters of the river Angkola, in the region of Mount Bualbuali, the Bukit Barisan widens to form a belt of country which is known as the Batak volcanic plateau. The plateau averages 3,000 to 4,500 ft. above sea level and is covered with porous, acid volcanic soils which produce a wild, savannah-type vegetation little suited for human settlement. The main region of habitation has been in the valley of the river Taru, which forms another longitudinal trough similar to that of the Angkola-Gadis depression and provides the main avenue of approach to Lake Toba, the southern shores of which are also well suited for agriculture and settlement. The part of the plateau south-east of the lake comprises a series of highly dissected mountains, giving this region the name Dolok, the Batak word for mountain.

The eastern fringes of the Bukit Barisan at this latitude exhibit many similarities with their counterpart in the Minangkabau world, although there are also some differences. The Batak plateau slopes down gradually towards the lowlands of the east coast, but at various places many steeply graded rivers have cut deep gorges in the plateau edge. A good example is provided by the several rivers which go to make up the headwaters of the river Barumun; in the small valleys cut by these rivers, alluvial soil offers opportunities for the making of *sawah*, a development for which there is no parallel in central Minangkabau. Further eastwards, however, the lowland plain exhibits characteristics similar to those of the jungle to the south: rivers wind their tortuous way through muddy swamp-forest, ending finally in mangrove-fringed estuaries and merging into the Straits of Malacca.

The western coastal rim of the Batak highlands is similar to the Minangkabau coast further south. The entire coast between Air Bangis and Barus consists of a low shore backed by hills, with only a very narrow coastal plain. Most of the coast is exposed to the westerly monsoon and swell and offers little in the way of shelter, apart from the two bays of Air Bangis and Tapanuli. Tapanuli bay, 93 miles north of Air Bangis, is the largest indentation on the entire west coast of Sumatra, with an entrance ten miles across, broadening to fifteen miles. To the north of the bay the coast pursues its general south-east/north-west direction, with a low wooded shore and narrow, sparsely populated coastal plain, often swampy. Despite the lack of shelter there are settlements at all the river mouths, in this period all those of any significance for commerce being in Minangkabau hands. A similar pattern of Minangkabau dominance was exhibited by the settlements on the headwaters of the main rivers running east, as far north as the river Sosak. Because of this, communication between the southern Batak villages and the outside world was obstructed, and much of the trade in Batak products was in Minangkabau hands. The eruption of Padri armies into Mandailing and upper Barumun, therefore, represented merely another stage in the continuous encroachment of the Minangkabau world on that of the Bataks which had been going on for some centuries; in many respects it was similar to the encroachment of the Dutch upon Minangkabau itself.

The spearhead of the Minangkabau attack on the Bataks was the valley of Rao, which followed Alahan Panjang in its conversion to Padri principles. Rao had a long tradition of intercourse with the rest of the Minangkabau world, and its natural products had ensured its historical development along lines similar to other parts of Minangkabau. After Tanah Datar, and disregarding certain valleys further south, Rao was the most important gold-mining area in Minangkabau. The Rao gold trade was known to Indian merchants as early as the second century A.D., and from about A.D. 800 Indian settlements were made both in the valley and at a point on the upper Kampar which developed into a typical headwaters *pangkalan* for the Rao gold trade.[100] By the eighteenth century Rao gold was not exhausted and it continued to lubricate the trade of the Malacca Straits, being traded by way of Patapahan on the Siak. English observers in the straits estimated that huge amounts were exported; in 1826 the *Singapore Chronicle* placed the value of gold exports from Rao at between 130,000 and 140,000 Spanish dollars per annum, certainly an exaggeration.[101] The Rao gold merchants also traded on the west coast, bringing their gold to Natal, Air Bangis, Pasaman, and even as far south as Padang. Towards the close of the eighteenth century they were coming to Padang three or four times a year, in parties of from thirty to sixty men, each man carrying a half or one *tahil* of gold. Much more gold was in fact available for trade, but the merchants limited themselves to bringing down only an amount corresponding to the quantity of cloth and iron their carriers could take back to Rao.[102]

Not surprisingly, once Imam Bonjol had established his regime in the valley of Alahan Panjang, he turned his eyes north to his rich neighbours. The long, narrow valley beyond his own offered evidence of considerable prosperity. In the 1830s the valley of Rao was estimated to have a population of about 25,000, settled in twenty large villages and their satellite hamlets, all beautifully cared for and surrounded by ample *sawah*. Coffee was also grown.[103] The political system was similar to that of other Minangkabau fringe areas; each village was inhabited by a number of lineages each with its own *penghulu* but, in contrast to the Minangkabau heartland, a mother village and its daughter settlements also formed a sort of federation under a *raja*. The northern part of the valley, where lay the major gold mines in the vicinity of the villages of Rao and Padangmatinggi was the most thickly settled, and here the villages recognized one of the *raja* as Yang di Pertuan. For this the model appears to have been the Pagarruyung system, and the Rao Yang di Pertuan presumably had a similar origin and performed similar functions in relation to the gold trade as the Raja Alam of Pagarruyung.[104]

The leaders of the Padri community in Alahan Panjang realized that access to the gold mines of Rao could hardly fail to give an extra dimension to the trading network they were trying to create, whilst the manpower of the valley would be a welcome addition to their own. Imam Bonjol began his conquest of Rao by supervising the construction of a good road to Lubuk Sikaping, the main village in the southernmost part of the valley, and then capturing and converting this and nearby villages. The northern section of the valley remained unsubdued and unconverted, and raids were continually made from here upon the new converts to the south until, about 1820, the Bonjol leadership decided something must be done to secure the Padri position in the entire valley.[105]

It is at this point that the shadowy figure of Tuanku Rao appears on the scene. Tuanku Rao is a personality well known in Batak history, but much that has been written about him is based on early twentieth century Batak oral tradition and cannot be confirmed in any contemporary Dutch sources available to us.[106] This is surprising because letters written by Dutch officers at this time give regular space to his contemporary Tuanku Tambusai, the conqueror of the eastern Batak lands. The paucity of information can partly be explained by the fact that Tuanku Rao died in 1833, shortly after the Dutch entered Rao, and so he had no subsequent career which might have given rise to Dutch inquiries about his earlier activities. It can be accepted that Tuanku Rao was a Batak, known originally as Pongki na Ngolngolan, but the claim made in Batak oral tradition that he was a nephew of the Batak priest-king Singamangaraja X, who dominated the region Bangkara-Toba, cannot be substantiated.[107] Presumably the genealogy was elaborated to explain some of Tuanku Rao's military feats; he certainly did lead his followers on a series of extraordinary forced marches north, right into the territory of the Toba Bataks, where he encountered and ultimately killed Singamangaraja X. By considering him the dispossessed nephew of the king, Batak tradition is then able to find in revenge a plausible motive for this military encounter.

Whatever his origins, Pongki na Ngolngolan was a Batak adventurer who at some stage in his career made his way to the valley of Rao. He found a patron in a northern village, assisted this man with his daily activities, and ultimately, about 1808, was converted to Islam. Subsequently he came into contact with the teachings of the Padris further south, and appears to have felt that by gaining recognition as an exponent thereof his position as an *orang datang* or outsider in Rao society would be vastly improved.[108] Unfortunatley we have no clear picture of his relationship to Imam Bonjol, but it seems likely that when a Bonjol army of one thousand men marched from Lubuk Sikaping into northern Rao he was ready to put himself forward as a reliable collaborator and to co-operate in forcing the Yang di Pertuan into exile. As an outsider in the society, he relied for his further advancement on Imam Bonjol's support and on the maintenance of a zealously Padri regime. In return for the Imam's recognition of his authority over the Rao valley he agreed to supply Bonjol regularly with gold, buffaloes and rice, in order that Bonjol could concentrate on building up its commercial strength.[109] Like the Alahan Panjang Padris he established his own *bonjol*, fortifying an outlying part of Padangmatinggi which was very close to a mountainous region where gold was both mined and panned. His settlement was placed on a defensible hill and surrounded with strong walls, and he followed Imam Bonjol's example of encouraging young men loyal to his leadership to establish themselves there; indeed his 'capital' had more the air of a military garrison than of an ordinary village.[110]

The consolidation of Tuanku Rao's authority over the valley of Rao marks the beginning of that episode in the history of the Padri movement about which we know the least. This is the conquest of large areas inhabited by the Batak people of Sumatra, a conquest undertaken by Tuanku Rao by moving through the longitudinal troughs running south-east to north-west along the line of the Bukit Barisan, and by Tuanku Tambusai by establishing himself on the headwaters of the east coast rivers and along the foothills of the mountain spine. Some time about 1820 Padri bands from Rao crossed over the intervening hills and began to pour into the sparsely populated valley of Upper Mandailing, around the headwaters of the river Gadis. Although there was certainly religious motivation for this *jihad,* it was also dictated by economic considerations.

Like Rao, Upper Mandailing was a gold-producing region, and it already possessed important Minangkabau settlements, Minangkabau having come from as far away as Agam to work the mines. Mines were located in several places between Huta Nopan and Pakantan, but the most important ones were at the very bottom of the valley, north and south of Pakantan and therefore extremely close to Rao, and around Huta Nopan further north. The entrepreneurs who worked these mines had long-established trading connections with Air Bangis and Natal, and prior to 1820 familiarity and intermarriage with the Minangkabau commercial community of the coast had promoted the conversion to Islam of individual Bataks and their families. Rao conquest of the valley therefore possessed a certain logic quite apart from the impetus given it by the Padri movement. The results of the conquest were economically beneficial to both the Rao and Alahan Panjang Padris. Imam Bonjol himself, as Tuanku Rao's patron, is known to have been pledged the annual profits of one particular mine near Pakantan and probably of several others.[111] Control of the Upper Mandailing valley by a Padri force also advanced Imam Bonjol's plans to squeeze out European commerce on the Batak coast. The main gold-trading passes from Rao and Mandailing to the coast were now in Padri hands, and the gold trade was re-channelled down to Pasaman and to Imam Bonjol's new port of Batahan.[112]

The motivation behind Tuanku Rao's next move, down the river Gadis into Lower Mandailing, and then further north up the valleys of the river Angkola and the river Taru, is more problematical. It is likely that as Bonjol moved up the Batak coast the question of control of the mountain passes leading out of the Batak valleys grew in importance, for whoever dominated these entrances and exits controlled the landward access of traders to Bonjol's ports of Kunkun, Tabuyung and Sinkuan. Trade to rival ports could also be interfered with, and Padri control of these passes continued right through until 1832, becoming an essential part of Imam Bonjol's strategic thinking. In 1828 a trading settlement only six hours on foot east of Natal was burnt by a force coming down from Lower Mandailing,[113] and Rao domination of the passes was a vital adjunct to Bonjol's enterprises against Air Bangis and Natal in 1831. Bonjol's own ports stopped at Sinkuan, but Tuanku Rao himself seems to have followed Imam Bonjol's example and established commercial centres under his control, at Batang Taru on the main route coming down from Lake Toba to the coast, and at Sorkam on the coast north of Tapanuli, where another trade route from the Lake Toba region reached the sea.[114] As early as July 1821 English commerce at Tapanuli was being cut off from the interior by Tuanku Rao's closure of the passes leading out of the valley of the river Taru.[115]

Once in control of the mountain passes leading down to the coast, the Rao Padris were confronted by the heavily wooded slopes of the Bukit Barisan facing westwards to the Indian Ocean. The economic potential of this area produced a determination to dominate yet another ecological zone. It was on these mountain slopes that the two major natural products of the Batak lands, camphor and benjamin, grew. The camphor tree occurred naturally on the forested escarpments nearest the sea, but camphor-seeking was a laborious and time-consuming business. It was traditionally financed by Minangkabau traders in the coastal settlements, and, as often twenty to thirty trees would have to be felled before one was found containing marketable camphor, sometimes parties of men were in the forests for two to three months with little success.[116] This meant considerable expense for the Minangkabau financial backers, who had to advance the camphor-seeker and his men food and tools for a considerable period.[117] Now, by extending their control to this zone, the Rao Padris were able to ensure that only traders in Bonjol's ports of Sinkuan, Tabuyung, Kunkun and Batahan participated in the trade, squeezing out traders operating from nearly European settlements.

In the same way Padri overseers from Rao were able to channel the benjamin trade as it suited them. Unlike camphor, the benjamin tree was an object of cultivation by Batak peasants. It was grown in both forest *ladang* and in the coastal foothills of the Barisan range, and its cultivation and preparation for trade required careful supervision and organization: 'In some places, especially near the sea-coast, large plantations of it are formed, and it is said that the natives, sensible of the great advantages accruing to them from the trade, in a national point of view, oblige the proprietors, by legal regulation, to keep up the succession'.[118] To be brought into trade, the resin collected by making incisions into the tree had to be formed into cakes. Since the quality of the benjamin greatly affected its chances of sale, Minangkabau coastal traders had also long been involved in the economic life of those Batak villages which produced benjamin, and the appearance of the Rao Padris therefore represented only another order of Minangkabau penetration.[119]

Padri supervision of the camphor and benjamin trades, and of other items in circulation in the Batak country, was made easier by the operation of a regular system of markets (*onan*), similar to those of Minangkabau though distributed further apart from one another. In general markets operated in four-day cycles; those in the vicinity of Tapanuli were described by an English writer in 1772:

For the convenience of carrying on the inland-trade, there are established at the back of *Tappanuli,* which is their great mart, four stages, at which successively they hold public fairs or markets on every fourth day throughout the year; each fair, of course, lasting one day. The people in the district of the fourth stage assemble with their goods at the appointed place, to which those of the third resort in order to purchase them. The people of the third, in like manner, supply the wants of the second, and the second of the first, who dispose, on the day the market is held, of the merchandise for which they have trafficked with the Europeans and Malays.[120]

This particular cycle so described extended from Tapanuli via the river Taru to the valley of the river Angkola and then across to the valley of the Batang Onan, one of the headwaters of the river Barumun.[121]

Each region which formed part of a market cycle had its own speciality. An example is provided by the valley of Lower Mandailing, along the course of the river Gadis, which extended ten miles across and was about twenty-five in length. This valley had a comparatively dense population supported by extensive *sawah* cultivation; an American missionary estimated in 1837 that the largest village, Panyabungan, and three neighbouring large villages had together a population of about 10,000, whilst there were forty smaller villages on the plain with a total of 14,000 inhabitants, making a population of 24,000 in all.[122] This *sawah*-rich region exported its rice to Upper Mandailing, and also to the commercial settlements on the coast. The largest market in Lower Mandailing was at Panyabungan, where the gold of Upper Mandailing was exchanged for rice, the gold then being taken to the coast and exchanged for salt, iron, cotton cloths, copper thread, dried fish and other small items. Slavery was common in Batak society, and the market of Panyabungan was also a centre for the sale of slaves, and for trade in the buffaloes which were raised on the plains of the upper Barumun and which formed an important source of wealth for those purchasing them.[123] In this way the Rao Padris, once having taken the gold mines near Huta Nopan, which were the traditional suppliers of gold to the Panyabungan market, were irresistibly drawn into Lower Mandailing and its trading network, and so on up the longitudinal valleys of the Batak country, which provided food for the coastal commercial world to the west. According to Batak tradition, the Panyabungan market had in any case first been established by Minangkabau merchants from the coast,[124] and so again this penetration of a Batak valley by Minangkabau from Rao was only another in a historical series of intrusions from the Minangkabau commercial world.

The Padris pursued the Batak trading network all the way up the valleys of the Bukit Barisan; between the valley of the river Angkola and that of the river Taru an American observer in 1837 noted 'a spacious level pass, and the people are constantly seen coming and going'.[125] The valley created by the river Taru, Silindung, was about ten to twelve miles long and six miles wide, and was again covered with *sawah,* with forty to fifty small Batak villages in the plain, and about twenty in the surrounding hills.[126] A Dutch visitor in 1844 described a market in the valley, which was the resort of 3,000 to 4,000 buyers and sellers on market day. He noted articles manufactured by the Bataks themselves:

Among them my interest was aroused by some cotton cloths woven with both taste and artistry and some elegantly produced copper articles; I bought some of both the items mentioned. Among the articles from Europe there were many white cotton cloths and some coloured ones, and iron frying-pans; among the products of the Indies belonged coarse Chinese crockery and Javanese chewing-tobacco, and also all sorts of foodstuffs produced in the country itself, such as rice, chickens, sugar, coconut oil and fruit.[127]

Finally the *sawah* at the southern end of Lake Toba were reached, where the villages of Bangkara, Butar and Balige were the main markets for rice, slaves, cattle and horses. The Minangkabau village of Sorkam was the main coastal outlet for this part of the world.[128]

When the Rao Padris spilled over into Lower Mandailing, they were faced with greater difficulties than they had hitherto encountered. Whilst the sparsely populated valley of Upper Mandailing had offered virtually no resistance, Lower Mandailing attempted to rally against the invading Minangkabau. The Bataks, like the Minangkabau, lived in fortified villages (*huta*), independent of one another. These *huta* were generally much smaller than Minangkabau villages, and one lineage predominated in village affairs. The head of this lineage provided the village with its chief or *raja,* whose position was based on recognition of the fact that his lineage forebears had founded the village and he was the oldest descendant in the male line. Batak chiefs and their families over time evolved into a distinct class which intermarried and which was customarily slave-owning. Supra-village institutions were amorphous; more important than regional-dialectical divisions (Toba, Angkola, Mandailing) was the division of the inhabitants of whole areas into clans, one clan generally predominating in a particular region although branches of other clans may have settled among them and intermarried. Upper Mandailing was dominated by the Lubis clan, and Lower Mandailing by the Nasution clan, although these clans seem rarely to have evolved common institutions.[129] What supra-village institutions did exist operated somewhere below the level of the clan and above the level of the *huta.* In both Mandailing and Angkola, which were settled by Batak clans from the north over a period of several centuries, a group of villages would recognize a mother village, and the mother village would be given the title *panusunan* and acquire certain prerogatives as head of the village grouping. As in Minangkabau, inter-village jealousies and disputes were common, and village *raja* were relied upon to secure the village in time of war.[130]

When the Padris arrived in Lower Mandailing, Mandailing forces rallied around Patuan Naga, *panusunan* of Panyabungan, but he broke his leg en route to battle and the Batak army collapsed in disorder. Tuanku Rao's first raid was a lightning one, and after burning Panyabungan and taking as many slaves as possible he retreated to Rao. When signs developed that Patuan Naga was organizing another Batak army he returned, defeated the latter in two battles and laid waste several more villages.[131]

Batak accounts tend to stress the violence and confusion of the Padri period. However, Tuanku Rao did try to introduce a Padri form of administration into Batak villages, though just how this system was institutionalized, and what support it received, are virtually unanswerable questions. Some Bataks had certainly been converted to Islam before the Padri invasion; there were Muslims living in Panyabungan when it was attacked, and certain nearby villages, with trade relations with the west coast, had been Muslim for a number of years.[132] In the early period of their rule, however, the Rao invaders relied on their own manpower and appointed Minangkabau as *kadi* in Batak villages, these 'judges' basing their administration on strict obedience to the letter of the Koran. They also tried to introduce all the outward puritanism of their movement. Forced conversion was, of course, insisted upon, there was considerable killing, and the Padris were particularly zealous in destroying Batak literature, much of which was of a religious nature, wherever they could find it. At the beginning the Padri invasion was indistinguishable in character from a foreign conquest and occupation. As well as diverting Batak trade to a specified group of ports on the west coast, Tuanku Rao obliged village *raja* to provide Rao and Alahan Panjang with tribute in the form of rice, buffaloes and slaves, to pay for the upkeep of Minangkabau soldiers in their villages and to supply contingents of armed men for Padri ventures further north.[133]

It soon became clear in any case that the only way for the villages of Lower Mandailing to make good their losses was participation in Padri raids into the valleys further north where, as part of a conquering army, they could enrich themselves with booty. Conquest was made easy by the fact that so many villages were small, independent entities which did not combine to defend themselves, and by the possibility of making expeditions on horseback. The nature of the topography was such that mounted expeditions northwards up the valleys could be undertaken all the way from Tuanku Rao's home base, while horses were plentiful in certain areas and were items of considerable trade.[134] This helps account for the speed of Padri conquests in this area, the method of warfare being quite unlike the wars of attrition which had to be carried on in the Minangkabau heartland.

By 1822 the Padris were behind Tapanuli, having swept through the whole of Angkola. According to a Batak account which must be treated with great caution, Tuanku Rao appointed a certain Tuanku Lelo, a member of the Nasution clan and the son of a Batak salt trader, 'governor' of Angkola, where he built a fort at Padang Sidimpuan. From this strategic location at the crossroads of important trade paths to the coast and into Mandailing and Silindung he carried out the Padri policy of promoting trade, keeping open the trade routes, and encouraging merchants.[135]

What happened further north in the Batak country is difficult to say. The Padris had not yet entered the valley of Silindung in 1824 when the English missionaries Burton and Ward passed through,[136] but by at least 1832 they had pushed so far north that they were trading at Sorkam and threatening the commerce of Barus.[137] According to Batak oral tradition a Padri band under Tuanku Rao penetrated as far north as Butar, on the Humbang plateau, where the *tuanku* encountered the contemporary representative of the Singamangaraja dynasty of priest-kings, who lived in the rock-walled valley of Bangkara in the south-west corner of Lake Toba. Batak tradition makes Tuanku Rao the abandoned nephew of Singamangaraja in an effort to explain why the former allegedly killed the latter on the market-place at Butar, after inviting him there for a meeting.[138] More probably this murder took place because Tuanku Rao perceived in Singamangaraja X a figurehead around whom the Toba Batak clans could unite to oppose Islam, and also because the Singamangaraja had some form of commercial relationship with Barus, the threads of which the Padris were keen to break.[139] That the Padris did stay long enough in the area to institute their system of *kadi* is clear from the appearance there of a number of district chiefs bearing the title Nangkali, although Batak tradition claims that these people were appointed not by the Rao Padris, who speedily returned home, but by Padri converts from Mandailing and Angkola who came back to the region in 1827 and again in 1829, both from religious motives and in the hope of gaining booty and slaves.[140] By this time the Padri administration in Mandailing itself had come to rest on Batak converts, so many Minangkabau having had to pull out to pursue conquests further north.[141]

Tuanku Rao was not the only Padri leader to make the conversion of the Bataks his mission. On the eastern borders of the Batak world arose another leader, Tuanku Tambusai, better known than Tuanku Rao because of his frequent appearance in Dutch records. Tuanku Tambusai came from a Minangkabau-settled area on the river Sosak, one of the tributaries of the Rokan river. Both the Rokan and the more northerly Barumun were rivers with some commerce. For centuries they had been renowned for their slave markets, from where Batak slaves were distributed throughout Southeast Asia, and these markets continued well into the nineteenth century.[142] With the establishment of the English in the Straits of Malacca, a steady market was opened up for the forest products of the area adjacent to the Rokan and its tributaries. The rattans of the locality had been famous at Malacca from at least the sixteenth century, when they were used in a variety of ways in shipping, and from the 1770s they constituted a welcome cargo for English private traders, who could find markets for them in both Europe and India.[143] After the founding of Penang and Singapore they also became an important staple of the China trade, and English private traders anxious to find suitable cargoes to exchange for tea tried to emulate the collecting habits of Chinese junks in the area. The growth of the England-China tea trade did in fact cause a modest commercial florescence on both the Rokan and the Barumun because, in addition to rattans, so-called 'straits produce' was much in demand in China. Stapling points expanded or were newly established at various locations up the rivers, and here were assembled a variety of products: *damar,* resins used for lighting and caulking ship's seams; sticklac, a secretion of insects obtained from twigs and branches of trees and used as a dye or resin; dragon's blood, a red gum or resin from some of the rattan palms, used as an astringent and for colouring varnishes and lacquers; wax, and many others.[144] Minangkabau traders from these rivers also traded further north along the coast, assembling products from the Batak lands brought down to certain points on the northern rivers ready for English private traders and Chinese junks to take them away.[145]

One of the stapling points which developed as a result of this trade was Daludalu on the river Sosak. It was a Minangkabau village surrounded by a plain on which dry-field cultivation was carried out and, possessing ready access to forest products, with commerce as its main *raison d'être.*[146] This village was the home of a certain Imam Maulana Kadi, whose son, Muhammad Saleh, became known as Tuanku Tambusai after the name of the region in which Daludalu was located. Muhammad Saleh pursued his Islamic studies in the nearby valley of Rao, where he stayed for a long time, long enough to see the advance of Padri teachings in the valley and to become a zealous convert to them.[147] He returned to Daludalu, where he tried to introduce the rigour of the Padri system and where he gained a considerable number of converts, presumably among the traders in forest produce who were glad to see the introduction of a system which suited their needs.

The Tambusai area followed an institutional pattern similar to that of other Minangkabau fringe lands, with a Yang di Pertuan as a figurehead for the whole region of the upper Rokan. As the Yang di Pertuan of upper Rokan observed the success of Tuanku Tambusai in gaining followers, and as he himself was subjected to pressure from the *tuanku* to convert and support the new system, he had the Padri leader chased out of Tambusai; finally civil war erupted, as in other parts of Minangkabau, which resulted in victory for Tuanku Tambusai and his followers and the flight of the Yang di Pertuan and others.[148] Tuanku Tambusai then organized and fortified his base Daludalu on the model of Bonjol and the other fortified villages of the northern Padri leaders. It was later described by a Dutch officer as 'the most regular native fortification ever encountered on the West coast of Sumatra . . .'[149] More like a barracks than a village, its houses were laid out in completely regular rows, the whole in the form of a square and surrounded by a high, steep wall with a moat in front of it. This form of defence was twice repeated, giving the village three walls and three moats in all, with an additional small wall protecting the second moat. One side of the village lay directly on the banks of the Sosak, so that water could easily be led into the moats.[150]

Impelled by the logic of his position, Tuanku Tambusai now pursued his conquests along the upper Sosak, and also along an adjacent river, where Batak villages predominated. These villages were soon defeated and the Batak *raja* converted, leaving the Padri forces on this side facing the mountain barrier which separated the river headwaters from the valley of Lower Mandailing. Tuanku Tambusai apparently went on to assist Tuanku Rao in his conquest of Mandailing, but then, whilst the Rao forces turned their attention north-west, Tuanku Tambusai decided to concentrate on a region similar to his own, comprising the headwaters of the tributaries which flowed to make up the river Barumun. Although this was a sparsely populated territory – the whole plains area between the Sosak and the headwaters of the river Bila was estimated in 1845 to have a population of between 23,000 and 28,000[151] – it had commercial potential because of its involvement in straits trade, and the population of these plains seems to have been marked by its willingness to embrace the Padri system, village chiefs anxiously vying to gain the title of *kadi.*[152]

Most of the region subsisted from *ladang* cultivation, though in the valleys of the river Barumun around Sibuhun and of the Batang Onan around the village of the same name a denser population was supported by the availability of water for *sawah*. Commercial income derived from involvement of headwaters' villages in the straits trade in forest products, stapling points for which were provided by Sibuhun, Batang Onan, Gunung Tua and Pertibi, and in the similarly-oriented trade in slaves.[153] There were also two other sources of income. Since the 1770s the area around the Batang Onan and the Aek Hayura had been an important producer of cassia, which Minangkabau traders based on Tapanuli came regularly to buy, finding a ready market in English private trade. The village of Batang Onan had a dual advantage, acquiring income from the cassia trade to the west and also from the forest products trade to the east, and this was true of other villages in the vicinity further back towards the mountains where the cassia actually grew.[154]

Apart from the valleys of the Batang Onan and the upper Barumun, the region from the Sosak up to the river Bila was dominated by the bare, grass-covered Batak plateau, emerging out of the forest lowlands and excellently suited for cattle-raising. According to an 1845 report, before the Padri incursions this area was swarming with cattle, the village of Pertibi alone possessing between 800 and 1,000 and many nearby villages having herds of up to 3,000. The report notes: 'At that time each chief of any note had at least one hundred buffaloes, sometimes even three times that number; each smaller chief had between forty and eighty; a well-to-do commoner had twenty to forty; even each slave . . . possessed five to ten buffaloes'.[155] There was an active trade in cattle, especially with the Bataks in the mountain valleys to the west, for whom buffaloes were a major source of wealth and who had rice to exchange for them.[156]

It is possible that the regions around the headwaters of the major rivers so readily embraced the Padri system because, as links in the English private trading network, they were experiencing a modest commercial florescence from the export of their cassia and of forest products, whilst the Bataks of the western valleys, although now coping with a greater volume of trade due to the expansion of English private commerce, had not been required to make any major readjustments in their society such as would have been caused by a trade in agricultural commodities previously unknown to them. Whatever may be the case, it was only further north that Tuanku Tambusai found any real resistance, centred on the hilly region of Dolok. There was ancient hostility between the people of this region and the people of the plains. The former had few means of subsistence apart from their *ladang* and they repeatedly undertook raiding expeditions against plains villages, selling their captives as slaves. Many of those who refused to be converted to the Padri system fled to this region and, because of their repeated depredations upon the converts below, Tuanku Tambusai decided that this area must be subjugated. On the right bank of the upper reaches of the river Panai, astride a steep rock outcrop, the opponents of the Padris had built a seemingly impregnable fort at a place called Siminabun, which was a natural entry point into the whole of the Dolok region. Tuanku Tambusai was obliged to besiege this fort for a whole year before it could be taken, and his further advance into the Dolok country was so fiercely contested that, although his forces finally attained the upper reaches of the Bila river, they had become so discouraged by the difficulty of the terrain and so decimated that only one hundred men were left and there was obviously no point in going further.[157]

We know as little about the nature of Tuanku Tambusai's administrative system in the regions of the upper Rokan and Barumun as we do about that of Tuanku Rao in the western valleys. A Dutch survey written some years after Tuanku Tambusai's removal from the territory states that plunder, murder and slavery were as inseparable from the Padri conquest on this side of the island as on the other.[158] This picture might be somewhat overdrawn in relation to the areas which actually became Padri, because these localities were already in contact with the Muslim world prior to Tuanku Tambusai's incursions, and they seem from the evidence available to have been somewhat susceptible to Padri teaching; it has already been noted that chiefs in the region vied for Padri administrative titles. What is certain is that chiefs on the Panai river and the Batang Onan became rich from the intensified slave trade which was a concomitant of Padri conquests in the Batak lands in general, exporting slaves down the Bila and the Panai to Penang, and so having a pecuniary interest in supporting further Padri expansion.[159] But Tuanku Tambusai himself is described as a much milder man than Tuanku Rao, and his mildness was reinforced when he joined a number of other Padri pilgrims on the *haj* about 1829. He became conscious of the decline of the Wahhabis in Arabia and, aware of different scholars' views of the *jihad,* he returned home about 1831 to decry the use of both force and robbery in efforts at conversion. He brought with him numerous books to support his opinions, and although previously he and Imam Bonjol had been very close, now a rupture seems to have occurred between them.[160]

This mildness did not extend to Tuanku Tambusai's espousing a favourable view of the Dutch presence in Minangkabau. In September 1832, as we have seen, Dutch forces entered and occupied the valley of Alahan Panjang. Little is known of Tuanku Rao's activities at this period, but in January 1833 he was reported to be in Air Bangis trying to rally support against the Dutch, in which place he was captured with some violence, which led to his death the same month.[161] In the midst of the confusion brought about by Dutch proximity, the former Yang di Pertuan of Rao invited Dutch forces to come to his support, although this action was opposed by a number of the Rao *penghulu.* In October 1832 the Dutch Resident himself marched through the valley to Padangmatinggi, reinstated the former Yang di Pertuan, bestowed upon him the title of Regent, and erected a fort near Tuanku Rao's former capital. The valley of Mandailing was also occupied by Dutch troops moving inland from the coast and the Batak *raja* of Huta Godang, Raja Gadombang, who had assisted Dutch troops in their manoeuvres, was given the honorary title of Regent.[162]

With Padri conquests in the west apparently lost, Tuanku Tambusai, like Imam Bonjol, had to make up his own mind on how to react to the Dutch presence. He wrote to the Dutch Resident promising to respect Dutch arrangements in Rao, particularly in relation to the restoration of the Yang di Pertuan, but claimed that he had the right to continue a *jihad* against the heathen Bataks and, indeed, that he had been authorized to do so in Mecca. After sending this letter he agreed to come to Padangmatinggi to meet Resident Elout, and at this encounter made it clear that he was an implacable opponent of Dutch interference in the island of Sumatra, that his recognition of a political restoration in Rao was conditional on Dutch evacuation of the valley, and that he could only accept a Dutch presence in Sumatra on the footing that had existed in the days of the company: the Dutch should leave the entire Minangkabau interior and confine themselves to certain coastal ports, where he would ensure them a flourishing trade in the island's products.[163]

Elout refused these conditions, and Tuanku Tambusai was given three days to leave Rao and return to Daludalu.[164] The whole of central Minangkabau, with the exception of the Solok valley, was now in Dutch hands. The Padri cause appeared defeated, as did the Minangkabau people.

NOTES TO CHAPTER V

1 Boelhouwer, *Herinneringen,* p. 93.
2 Van den Bosch to Baud, 16 November 1832, Part., in Westendorp Boerma, *Briefwisseling,* i. 170; earlier Dutch reports indicate that this coffee-growing considerably predates this particular reference.
3 E. Francis, 'Korte beschrijving van het Nederlandsch grondgebied ter Westkust Sumatra. 1837'. *TNI,* ii (1839), 120; v.d.H, 'Oorsprong der Padaries', p. 118.
4 Imam Bonjol's memoirs have been reproduced in Dutch in de Stuers, *Vestiging,* ii. Bijlage B, p. 221 *et seq.* and in Ph.S. van Ronkel, 'Inlandsche getuigenissen aangaande den Padri-oorlog', *IG,* xxxvii (1915), ii. 1104 *et seq.* For my English translation of the former see C. Dobbin, 'Tuanku Imam Bonjol (1772-1864)', *Indonesia,* xiii (1972), 5-35; see also v.d.H, 'Oorsprong der Padaries', p. 119.
5 Lange, *Oost-Indisch Leger,* i. 16-7; v.d.H, 'Oorsprong der Padaries', pp. 119-21; B..d., 'De Padries op Sumatra', *IM,* ii (1845) i. 175-6.
6 Van Ronkel, 'Inlandsche getuigenissen', p. 1105; v.d.H, 'Oorsprong der Padaries', p. 122.
7 De Stuers, *Vestiging,* ii. 221-2.
8 Lange, *Oost-Indisch Leger,* i. 17-8; v.d.H, 'Oorsprong der Padaries', pp. 122-3.
9 De Stuers, *Vestiging,* ii. 221; Boelhouwer, *Herinneringen,* p. 97; v.d.H, 'Oorsprong der Padaries', p. 125.
10 De Stuers, Vestiging, ii. 222.
11 ibid., p. 223.
12 De Stuers to Elout, 17 May 1826, no. 4, Exh. 23 Oct. 1826, no. 48, MK 523; van den Bosch to Baud, 16 Nov. 1832, Part., in Westendorp Boerma, *Briefwisseling,* i. 170.
13 De Stuers to Elout, 10 July 1829, no. 1, Exh. 29 Dec. 1829, no. 53, MK 721.
14 De Stuers, *Vestiging,* ii. 222; Boelhouwer, *Herinneringen,* pp. 95-6, 98.
15 Michiels to de Eerens, 23 Jan. 1838, no. 26, van den Bosch 575.
16 De Stuers to Elout, 27 Sept. 1826, no. 4b, Exh. 17 Mar. 1827, no. 41, MK 547.
17 Van Ronkel, 'Inlandsche getuigenissen', pp. 1105-6; v.d.H, 'Oorsprong der Padaries', pp. 124-6; D.D. Madjolelo and A. Marzoeki, *Tuanku Imam Bondjol. Perintis Djalan ke Kemerdekaan* (Jakarta/Amsterdam, 1951), pp. 65-72.
18 De Stuers, *Vestiging,* ii. 227.
19 Van Ronkel, 'Inlandsche getuigenissen', p. 1116; the possibility that these words are a later interpolation in the manuscript should not be ignored.
20 Francis, 'Korte beschrijving', p. 45; v.d.H, 'Oorsprong der Padaries', p. 1.
21 De Stuers, *Vestiging,* ii. 222.
22 V.d.H., 'Oorsprong der Padaries', p. 124.
23 De Stuers, *Vestiging,* ii. 223; de Stuers to Elout, 27 Sept. 1826, no. 4b, Exh. 17 Mar. 1827, no. 41, MK 547.
24 *Best,* pp. 65-7.
25 Van Goens, 13 Mar. 1680, *GM* 4, p. 387; van Outhoorn, 11 Dec. 1692, *GM* 5, p. 539.
26 Van Riebeeck, 15 Jan. 1711, *GM* 6, p. 718; Beschrijving van Sumatras West-Custe, pp. 31-5; De Radicaale Beschrijving, ch. 1, par. 21-2, pp. 31-2.
27 Kathirithamby-Wells, *West Sumatran Presidency,* pp. 165-6; Nahuijs, *Brieven,* p. 49.
28 Consideratie, 22 Dec. 1789, par. 212, KA 3800; Nahuijs, *Brieven,* p. 49.
29 Kathirithamby-Wells, *West Sumatran Presidency,* pp. 165-6; Young, 'English East India Company', pp. 164-5; Netscher, *Padang,* p. 49.
30 Consideratie, 22 Dec. 1789, par. 243-6, KA 3800; Marsden, *Sumatra,* p. 335.
31 De Stuers to van der Capellen, 25 Nov. 1825, no. 1029, Exh. 23 Aug. 1826, no. 65, MK 513; Boelhouwer, *Herinneringen,* p. 45.
32 De Stuers to Elout, 17 May 1826, no. 4, Exh. 23 Oct. 1826, no. 48, MK 523.
33 De Stuers to Elout, 27 Sept. 1826, no. 4b, Exh. 17 Mar. 1827, no. 41, MK 547.

34 A tun is a measure of capacity common in the eighteenth century, and equivalent to 252 wine gallons.
35 Nahuijs, *Brieven,* pp. 85-6; Travel Report no. 32, M.G. van Heel, 1839, ANHM, p. 5.
36 Van Heel, 1839, ANHM, p. 7.
37 Boelhouwer, *Herinneringen,* pp. 51-2.
38 ibid., pp. 53, 64.
39 Van Heel, 1839, ANHM, p. 8.
40 McGillavry to van den Bosch, 21 Apr. 1830, Exh. 15 Sept. 1830, no. 6/A, MK 767.
41 Lee Kam Hing, 'Acheh's Relations with the British, 1760-1819' (University of Malaya, Kuala Lumpur, M.A. thesis, 1969), p. 35. I am indebted to Tony Reid for this reference.
42 Young, 'English East India Company', pp. 107-8, 119, 155-62.
43 Lee, 'Acheh's Relations', pp. 78-9, 86-7; J.W. Gould, 'Sumatra-America's Pepperpot 1784-1873. Part I: Background and Early Years to 1815', *Essex Institute Historical Collections,* xcii (1956), 102, 106-7, 114-5.
44 Gould, America's Pepperpot', pp. 132, 137.
45 Bastin, *British in West Sumatra,* pp. 135, 175.
46 Anderson, *Acheen,* p. 160.
47 ibid., pp. 161-2.
48 A. Reid, *The Contest for North Sumatra. Atjeh, the Netherlands and Britain 1858-1898* (Kuala Lumpur, 1969), pp. 14-5.
49 Anderson, *Acheen,* p. 160; betel-nut was a product of the east coast of Aceh.
50 Anderson, *Acheen,* pp. 160-2, 164.
51 E.B. Kielstra, 'Onze aanrakingen met Troemon', *IG,* x (1888) ii. 1191-5; Lee, 'Acheh's Relations', pp. 79-81, 86-7, 175-6; Reid, *Contest,* pp. 6-7.
52 Kielstra, 'Troemon', pp. 1194-5, 1203-4.
53 Intveld to Elout, 5 Mar. 1832, no. 18, Exh. 15 Aug. 1832, no. 45, MK 852; Spengler, 1829, ANHM.
54 McGillavry to de Kock, 6 Aug. 1829, no. 39/51, Exh. 26 Nov. 1829, no. 59, MK 717.
55 Rapport . . ., 21 Apr. 1830, no. 315, Exh. 15 Sept. 1830, no. 6/A, MK 767.
56 Kielstra, 'Sumatra's Westkust van 1819-1825', pp. 61-2, 83-4.
57 Besluit in Rade, 14 Feb. 1824, no. 22, MK 2781; Nahuijs, *Brieven,* pp. 190-4; the treaty is reproduced in de Stuers, *Vestiging,* i. 78-83.
58 De Stuers, *Vestiging,* i. 80; Madjolelo and Marzoeki, *Tuanku Imam Bondjol,* p. 83.
59 Besluit in Rade, 13 Jul. 1824, no. 29, MK 2783.
60 De Stuers to van der Capellen, 25 Nov. 1825, no. 1029, Exh. 23 Aug. 1826, no. 65, MK 513; de Stuers, *Vestiging,* i. 102-3.
61 De Stuers and Verploegh to van der Capellen, 30 Nov. 1825, L^{a}F no. 22, van Alphen-Engelhard MSS. 286; the letter is incorrectly dated 1826.
62 De Stuers to van der Capellen, 25 Nov. 1825, no. 1029, Exh. 23 Aug. 1826, no. 65, MK 513.
63 De Stuers and Verploegh to van der Capellen, 30 Aug. 1825, L^{a}E no. 20, Exh. 24 Aug. 1826, no. 41, MK 513; de Stuers to Elout, 17 May 1826, no. 4, Exh. 23 Oct. 1826, no. 48, MK 523.
64 Besluit in Rade, 20 Dec. 1825, no. 16, MK 2791.
65 Intveld to Elout, 5 Mar. 1832, no. 18, Exh. 15 Aug. 1832, no. 45, MK 852.
66 De Stuers to Elout, 17 May 1826, no. 4, Exh. 23 Oct. 1826, no. 48, MK 523.
67 Marsden, *Sumatra,* pp. 154-5; Nahuijs, *Brieven,* p. 71.
68 *Pires,* i. 163; Kroeskamp, *De Westkust,* p. 139.
69 Maetsuyker, 18 Oct. 1668, *GM* 3, p. 626; idem, 17 Nov. 1669, *GM* 3, p. 688; idem, 23 Nov. 1675, *GM* 4, p. 67; idem, 28 Nov. 1676, *GM* 4, p. 142; van Outhoorn, 9 Feb. 1693, *GM* 5, p. 591; idem, 8 Dec. 1693, *GM* 5, p. 630.
70 Beschrijving van Sumatras West-Custe, pp. 11-4, 17-20, 23-9.
71 De Radicaale Beschrijving, ch. 1, par. 19-20, pp. 29-31.
72 Marsden, *Sumatra,* p. 273.
73 De Radicaale Beschrijving, ch. 2, par. 55, p. 115; par. 97, p. 167.
74 ibid., ch. 2, par. 99, pp. 171-2; ch. 3, par. 10, p. 206; Kathirithamby-Wells, *West Sumatran Presidency,* pp. 159-61; Young, 'English East India Company', pp. 96, 107-8, 119, 155, 198-9.

75 Young, 'English East India Company', pp. 155-62, 169; Kathirithamby-Wells, *West Sumatran Presidency*, pp. 161-2, 166; Marsden, *Sumatra*, pp. 370-3; Netscher, *Padang*, p. 49.
76 F.W. Stapel (ed), *Corpus Diplomaticum Neerlando-Indicum, 1753-1799* (The Hague, 1955), vi. no. MXCIX.
77 Putnam, *Salem Vessels*, pp. vii, 7; Lee,'Acheh's Relations', pp. 163-6; Bastin, *British in West Sumatra*, p. 115.
78 Gould, *Americans*, pp. 17-8.
79 De Stuers to Elout, 17 May 1826, no. 4, Exh. 23 Oct. 1826, no. 48, MK 523; Bastin, *British in West Sumatra*, p. 117.
80 Nahuijs, *Brieven*, p. 21; J. Bastin, *The Native Policies of Sir Stamford Raffles in Java and Sumatra. An Economic Interpretation* (Oxford, 1957), pp. 109-10.
81 De Stuers to Elout, 17 May 1826, no. 4, Exh. 23 Oct. 1826, no. 48, MK 523; de Stuers to de Kock, 2 Jan. 1828, no. 1, Exh. 21 May 1828, no. 63, MK 618.
82 De Stuers and Verploegh to van der Capellen, 30 Nov. 1825, L^{a}F no. 22, van Alphen-Engelhard 286.
83 Elout to van den Bosch, 17 Dec. 1831, L^{a}I, van den Bosch 393; Michiels to Elout, 6 Feb. 1832, Exh. 15 Aug. 1832, no. 45, MK 852.
84 Van Heel, 1839, ANHM, pp. 21-2.
85 Rapport omtrent den staat van den handel, 21 Apr. 1830, no. 315, Exh. 15 Sept. 1830, no. 6/A, MK 767; Spengler, 1829, ANHM.
86 Rapport over de Krijgsverrigtingen te Sumatra's Westkust, pp. 269-73, MK 4136; Boelhouwer, *Herinneringen*, pp. 19-21.
87 Van den Bosch to McGillavry, 7 May 1831, Kab. no. 557, van den Bosch 231.
88 Van den Bosch to Elout, 12 Jul. 1831, Kab. no. 944, Exh. 8 May 1832, no. 2/A, MK 839.
89 Van den Bosch to Elout, 2 Sept. 1831, Geh., Exh. 8 May 1832, no. 2/A, MK 839.
90 Elout to van den Bosch, 24 Dec. 1831, L^{a}K, Exh. 15 Aug. 1832, no. 45, MK 851.
91 Michiels to Elout, 6 Feb. 1832, Exh. 15 Aug. 1832, no. 45, MK 852.
92 Elout to Clifford, 2 June 1832, no. 2/364, Exh. 26 Oct. 1832, no. 25, MK 860; Boelhouwer, *Herinneringen*, pp. 67-71.
93 Van Ronkel,'Inlandsche getuigenissen', pp. 1106-8, 1110.
94 De Stuers, *Vestiging*, ii. 226-7; Boelhouwer, *Herinneringen*, p. 94; Elout to Clifford, 15 Dec. 1832, no. 5, Exh. 28 May 1833, no. 29A, MK 881.
95 De Stuers, *Vestiging*, ii. 227.
96 C.P.J. Elout, 'Overzicht der gebeurtenissen ter Westkust van Sumatra van 1830-1834' in E.B. Kielstra, 'Sumatra's Westkust van 1826-1832', *BKI*, xxxvii (1888), 362.
97 Boelhouwer, *Herinneringen*, p. 94.
98 ibid., p. 95; de Stuers, *Vestiging*, ii. 229.
99 J. Ballot, 'Het Inlandsch Bestuur in de Onderafdeeling Loeboe Sikaping en Rau, Afdeeling Loeboe Sikaping, Residentie Padangsche Bovenlanden', *Tijdschrift voor Binnenlandsch Bestuur*, xxviii (1905), 340.
100 Krom, *Geschiedenis*, p. 132. idem, *Inleiding*, ii. 422-3; for mine locations see Nahuijs, *Brieven*, p. 76; Müller, *Reizen*, p. 151.
101 *Singapore Chronicle*, Mar. 1826, in Moor, *Notices*, p. 98; Marsden, *Sumatra*, pp. 355, 357; Anderson, *Mission*, p. 203.
102 Consideratie, 22 Dec. 1789, par. 73-4, KA 3800; Beschrijving van Sumatras West-Custe, pp. 28-30, 36; Netscher, *Padang*, p. 30.
103 Francis, 'Korte Beschrijving', p. 44; Boelhouwer, *Herinneringen*, p. 99.
104 Ballot, 'Loeboe Sikaping en Rao', pp. 340-4, 366-9.
105 Van Ronkel, 'Inlandsche getuigenissen', p. 1105; v.d.H. 'Oorsprong der Padaries', pp. 129-30.
106 The chief source used for what follows is C. Gabriel, 'Kriegszug der Bondjol unter Anführung des Tuanku Rau in die Batakländer, zusammengetragen von Guru Kenan Huta Galung und aus den Batakschen ins Deutsch übersetzt', *TBG*, lxi (1922).
107 ibid., pp. 305-9.
108 ibid., pp. 305-10.
109 V.d.H, 'Oorsprong der Padaries', pp. 129-30.
110 Gabriel, 'Tuanku Rau', p. 311; Boelhouwer, *Herinneringen*, pp. 103-7.

111 Müller, *Reizen,* pp. 143-5, 160-7, 177-9; M.O. Parlindungan, *Pongkinangolngolan Sinambela gelar Tuanku Rao. Terror Agama Islam Mazhab Hambali di Tanah Batak, 1816-1833,* n.p., n.d., pp. 74-5, 77.
112 De Stuers and Verploegh to van der Capellen, 30 Nov. 1825, LaF no. 22, van Alphen-Engelhard 286; Rapport . . . , 21 Apr. 1830, no. 315, Exh. 15 Sept. 1830, no. 6/A, MK 767.
113 De Stuers to Elout, 28 Dec. 1828, no. 10, Exh. 16 June 1829, no. 133, MK 683.
114 Michiels to Elout, 6 Feb. 1832, Exh. 15 Aug. 1832, no. 45, MK 852; Elout to van den Bosch, 6 Mar. 1832, no. 5, Exh. 15 Aug. 1832, no. 45, MK 852.
115 Prince to Raffles, n.d. Jan. 1822, SFR 49; Bastin, 'Raffles' Attempts', p. 174.
116 Marsden, *Sumatra,* p. 149; Nahuijs, *Brieven,* pp. 72-3.
117 O. von Kessel, 'Reis in de Nog Onafhankelijke Batak-Landen van Klein-Toba, op Sumatra, in 1844', *BKI,* iv (1856), 79.
118 Marsden, *Sumatra,* p. 154.
119 ibid., p. 155; Müller, *Reizen,* pp. 94-5.
120 Marsden, *Sumatra,* pp. 379-80.
121 ibid., pp. 370-2.
122 *The Missionary Herald,* xxxiv (1838), 407.
123 T.I. Willer, 'Verzameling der Battahsche Wetten en Instellingen in Mandheling en Pertibie; gevolgd van een overzigt van land en volk in die streken', *TNI,* ix (1846), 260, 373, 385-8; Willer claims that the population of Lower Mandailing had been three times greater in 1800 in comparison with 1845.
124 ibid., pp. 412-3.
125 *The Missionary Herald,* xxxiv (1838), 453.
126 'Verslag van eene Reis in het Land der Bataks in het Binnenland van Sumatra, ondernomen in het jaar 1824, door de heeren Burton en Ward, zendelingen der Baptisten', *BKI,* v (1856), 275.
127 Von Kessel, 'Onafhankelijke Batak-Landen', p. 69.
128 Müller, *Reizen,* pp. 93-4; Moor, *Notices,* p. 2.
129 Willer, 'Battahsche Wetten', pp. 113-4; L. Castles, 'Statelessness and Stateforming tendencies among the Bataks before Colonial Rule', in A. Reid and L. Castles (ed.), *Pre-Colonial State Systems in Southeast Asia* (Kuala Lumpur, 1975), pp. 68-9.
130 Castles, 'Statelessness', pp. 69-70; Marsden, *Sumatra,* pp. 374-6, 378-9; Moor, *Notices,* p. 4.
131 Willer, 'Battahsche Wetten', pp. 420-2.
132 ibid., p. 421; M. Joustra, *Batakspiegel* (2nd edn., Leiden, 1926), p. 27.
133 Willer, 'Battahsche Wetten', pp. 391, 420-3; von Kessel, 'Onafhankelijke Batak-Landen', p. 57; Boelhouwer, *Herinneringen,* p. 108.
134 Willer, 'Battahsche Wetten', p. 421; von Kessel, 'Onafhankelijke Batak-Landen', p. 62; *The Missionary Herald,* xxxiv (1838), 453; Boelhouwer, *Herinneringen,* p. 110.
135 Parlindungan, *Tuanku Rao,* pp. 78-80, 296, 312, 316.
136 'Verslag van eene Reis', pp. 275-306.
137 Elout to van den Bosch, 6 Mar. 1832, no. 5, Exh. 15 Aug. 1832, no. 45, MK 852.
138 Gabriel, 'Tuanku Rau', pp. 325-6.
139 Müller, *Reizen,* pp. 93-4; Joustra, *Batakspiegel,* p. 25.
140 Gabriel, 'Tuanku Rau', pp. 334-6.
141 Willer, Battahsche Wetten', pp. 421-2.
142 *Pires,* i. 145-9; Anderson, *Mission,* pp. 297, 330.
143 *Pires,* i. 145-9; Marsden, *Sumatra,* p. 157.
144 Cowan, 'Early Penang', pp. 112-3, 134, 170, 202; Wong, 'Trade of Singapore', pp. 14,16, 77; Anderson, *Mission,* p. 33; idem, *Acheen,* p. 173.
145 Anderson, *Mission,* pp. 27, 145, 301-2, 330.
146 Schnitger, *Forgotten Kingdoms,* pp. 71-2; J.A. van Rijn van Alkemade, 'Beschrijving eener reis van Bengkalis langs de Rokan-rivier naar Rantau Binoewang', *BKI,* xxxii (1884), 32.
147 M. Said, *Rokan. Tuanku Tambusai Berdjuang* (Padang, 1969), p. 30.
148 Schnitger, *Forgotten Kingdoms,* pp. 72-3; van Rijn van Alkemade, 'De Rokan-rivier', p. 36; van Delden, 'Dagverhaal', p. 148.
149 Lange, Oost-Indisch Leger, ii. 332.
150 ibid., pp. 335-6.

151 Willer, 'Battahsche Wetten', pp. 253-4.
152 Schnitger, *Forgotten Kingdoms*, pp. 73-4; Joustra, *Batakspiegel*, p. 29.
153 Willer, 'Battahsche Wetten', pp. 356-7, 363-4, 368; Joustra, *Batakspiegel*, pp. 98-100, 331-2, 334, 337.
154 Marsden, *Sumatra*, pp. 372-3; Joustra, *Batakspiegel*, p. 333.
155 Willer, 'Battahsche Wetten', p. 366.
156 ibid., pp. 253-5, 366-8.
157 ibid., pp. 401-2; Schnitger, *Forgotten Kingdoms*, pp. 74-6; Joustra, *Batakspiegel*, pp. 29-30.
158 Willer, 'Battahsche Wetten', pp. 402-3.
159 Schnitger, *Forgotten Kingdoms*, pp. 78-9; Joustra, *Batakspiegel*, pp. 296-7.
160 Schnitger, *Forgotten Kingdoms*, pp. 81-3; Michiels to de Eerens, 12 Feb. 1839, no. 122, van den Bosch 575; van Sevenhoven and Riesz to Clifford, 30 Nov. 1833, no. 109, Exh. 24 May 1834, no. 112^{k} Geh., MK 4233.
161 Lange, *Oost-Indisch Leger*, i. 359; Parlindungan, *Tuanku Rao*, p. 287, erroneously claims the *tuanku* was killed in 1821.
162 Elout to Vermeulen Krieger, 29 Sept. 1832, no. 176, Vermeulen Krieger 1; Lange, *Oost-Indisch Leger*, i. 227-9.
163 'Overzicht der gebeurtenissen', in Kielstra, 'Sumatra's Westkust van 1826-1832', pp. 365-6; Boelhouwer, *Herinneringen*, p. 107.
164 Lange, *Oost-Indisch Leger*, i. 229-30.

CHAPTER VI

MINANGKABAU NATIONALISM AND THE DUTCH COMMERCIAL CHALLENGE, 1833-1841

Minangkabau nationalism

On 11 January 1833 at 4 o'clock in the morning, less than four months after it had submitted to Dutch occupation, the village of Bonjol burst into rebellion against the forces of the occupiers. One hundred and thirty-nine Europeans were slaughtered, including thirty men lying sick in hospital. Other garrisons in the valley of Rao suffered the same fate. Shortly afterwards indications of plans to annihilate the Dutch in the interior of Minangkabau were discovered everywhere, and on 2 February 1833 Resident Elout wrote to Governor-General van den Bosch: 'What was once a possibility, that – once we had succeeded in destroying the power of the padries – there might arise a combination of all the natives against the Europeans, is now a reality'.[1]

To what extent are we justified in considering the rebellion of 1833 an expression of Minangkabau nationalism? Students of African history who have addressed this theme originally felt that movements of initial opposition to European occupation might be referred to as movements of 'primary resistance'; these were defined as movements of a traditionalist nature and were regarded as distinct from modern nationalist movements, organized and led by a westernized élite and inspired by western notions of national self-determination.[2] 'Primary resistance', in the words of one scholar, 'connotes the forcible, instinctual attempt of an unmodified traditional structure to extrude a foreign body'.[3] Occupying an intermediate category between primary resistance and modern nationalism is the notion of the post-pacification revolt, differing from primary resistance largely in its timing, its connection with specific grievances, and its identification with new leadership groups.[4]

More recent work, however, has challenged the validity of these separate categories, and has pointed out that many aspects of modern nationalist movements, including the geographical centres of their local support and even their demands, have been defined by long-standing traditions of resistance. In French West Africa, for example, it has been shown how several of the Islamic theocracies which opposed the French were not at all involved in reactionary, 'traditional' struggles, but were attempting reforms which modern independent governments have also been obliged to pursue; this Islamic leadership persisted throughout the colonial era, operating to give focus to mass discontent, and was able to make a fairly easy transition to notions of modern mass nationalism.[5] Much the same can be said for East and Central Africa, where both the problems with which early resistance movements tried to deal and the leadership which evolved to formulate these problems exhibit marked continuity with the ideology and leadership of the later nationalist movements.[6] What we are dealing with here, then, is the existence of what Eric Stokes has called a permanent, underlying 'ur-nationalism', manifesting its hostility to the European presence in a distinct series of historical forms.[7]

It is in this sense that the term 'Minangkabau nationalism' will be used here to describe the movement of 1833, whilst acknowledging that in this movement we are dealing with a 'primitive' rather than a 'developed' form of nationalism.[8] A striking feature of the 1833 national rebellion is the manner in which it exhibits marked continuities with both earlier and later expressions of Minangkabau nationalism. Especially pronounced is the continuity in leadership. The earliest efforts by the Minangkabau to oust the Dutch from their coast were characterized by the prominent role played by Islamic teachers and students; in coastal ports such as Pariaman and Ulakan and in lowlands villages such as Pau in the 1670s, 1680s and early 1700s *tarekat* teachers were in the forefront of all struggles to remove the Dutch from Padang.[9] Islamic teachers in the highlands also occasionally called for a holy war to expel all Christians from the region.[10] Their efforts culminated in 1784 in a mass expedition from the highlands against Padang; a certain Tuanku Arif, accompanied by 3,000 to 4,000 Minangkabau, descended from the hills and, with Acehnese support from the sea, unsuccessfully attempted to invest the port.[11]

The other source of leadership for these pre-1833 anti-Dutch movements emerged from among members of the Minangkabau royal family, some of whom appear on occasions to have tired of their trading relationship with the VOC and longed to participate in a more open commercial network. To achieve this the royal family was at times prepared to make common cause with Islamic teachers and their students. In 1713 the village of Pau and its dependent hamlets, an important locality for *surau* teaching, were able to enlist the support of a nephew of the Raja Alam of Minangkabau, the so-called Raja Suruaso, in their scheme to drive the Dutch from Padang and free the trade of the port. The *raja* brought with him down to the coast a large number of armed men from Tanah Datar, including 'five hundred divines or priests, all clothed in white and with rosaries in the right hand'.[12] This army was driven off by the Dutch garrison, but the following year another member of the Minangkabau royal house led an army in an attack on the Dutch fort at Pariaman. In 1734 yet another member of the royal family, together with a *malim,* was at the centre of a movement embracing Tapanuli, Sorkam and Barus, the aim being to drive the Dutch off this part of the coast. Even after the back of this enterprise had been broken by a Dutch expeditionary force, the *raja* remained at Sorkam and tried to disrupt Dutch trade in the area. There were two subsequent attacks on the Dutch coastal position led by members of the Minangkabau royal family, one in 1740 when Pariaman was again set upon and one in 1751 when Padang was the object of attack.[13] From the 1750s to the 1770s even the Raja Alam himself participated in these anti-Dutch movements, although he relied not on force of arms but on diplomatic negotiations with the English at Benkulen whom he hoped – in vain – could be persuaded to assist the Minangkabau to get rid of the Dutch at least at Pariaman and Tiku.[14]

Manifestations of Minangkabau national sentiment were not confined to the exhibition of hostility towards the Dutch. In the late seventeenth and early eighteenth centuries, Minangkabau settlers on the east coast of Sumatra displayed equal dislike of Johor's commercial dominance in the area. Several Minangkabau rebellions against Johor broke out in the 1680s, led by individuals who, if not in fact members of the Minangkabau royal house, considered that effective leadership required they should at least assert their claims to be so. The most successful of these revolts against Johor was that of 1718 led by Raja Kecil, who captured the Johor capital and forged a loose political tie among the east coast Minangkabau until his death in 1746.[15]

The 1833 rebellion was the last in which leadership by members of the Minangkabau royal family was a feature, for after that date the royal line gradually died out. However, despite the loss of royalty's leadership potential, subsequent resistance movements inside Minangkabau exhibit elements of continuity both with the 1833 proceedings and with those of earlier centuries. In particular the continuity of Islamic leadership is maintained. The next major Minangkabau rebellion against the Dutch after that of 1833 took place in 1908; the issue was the introduction of monetary taxation, and leadership of the anti-taxation cause was firmly in the hands of *tarekat* teachers, particularly members of Syattariyah *tarekat,* who were assisted by certain of the lineage *penghulu,* a group which had also figured prominently in the 1833 rebellion. Even geographical continuity was preserved, the focus of the anti-taxation movement being the Agam region, which from 1821 had consistently shown hostility to the Dutch; particular localities such as Bukit Kamang and Pandai Sikat, which had a long tradition of anti-Dutch activity, were in the forefront of the rebellion. Subsequently, resistance to the Dutch became an all-Indonesia movement, and here Minangkabau figured prominently. The outstanding Minangkabau leadership groups which participated in the all-Indonesia nationalist movement were either consciously Islamic or part of a Western-educated élite; in either case their representatives tended to come from the same villages in Agam which had so long struggled against the Dutch. The early regional differentiation between Agam and Tanah Datar persisted into the all-Indonesia nationalist movement and the strongest opposition to both Indonesian nationalism and Islamic reformism came from the *sawah* regions of Tanah Datar and their *penghulu* families, from villages which so many centuries before had entered into a commercial partnership with the newly arrived Europeans.[16]

The persistence of 'ur-nationalism' in Minangkabau is clear, as is the geography of that nationalism; an American commentator writing in the 1950s pointed out:

> The Minangkabau area, home of about 2.5 per cent of the total Indonesian population . . . , by very conservative estimate has produced 25 to 30 per cent of the top Indonesian intellectual leaders of this century. One small Minangkabau village alone, Kota Gedang, produced ex-Prime Minister Sjahrir and ex-Foreign Minister Hadji Agus Salim (1884-1954), and at least a dozen other notables on the national scene. The nearby city of Bukittinggi produced, among many others, ex-Vice President Hatta and ex-Prime Minister Mohammad Natsir. From the surrounding area has come a very high percentage, if not an absolute majority, of Indonesia's leading doctors and lawyers – the professionally trained men who became national revolutionary leaders . . . . Even the nation's most famous Communist, Tan Malaka (d. 1949?), was a son of the Minangkabau . . .[17]

Nor should the persistence of this 'ur-nationalism' after the achievement of Indonesian independence be forgotten, culminating as it did in the Minangkabau rebellion of 1958 against the Jakarta government.

The 1833 outburst, therefore, was a rebellion in the Minangkabau tradition, though its timing was the product of a specific historical situation. By 1833 the highland Minangkabau had experienced twelve years of Dutch involvement in their polity. This involvement had borne heaviest upon those very villages which had been most anxious for the Dutch alliance, and Dutch officials had the general impression that even in these villages Europeans were disliked and despised.[18] The attitude of the Netherlands' *soi-disant* allies was reflected in a statement by a Tanah Datar *penghulu* to a visiting Dutch official from Java in 1824: 'Oh, if we were only at peace with the Padres of Lintau, we would not need the *Orang-Hollanda* (the Dutch) here'.[19] The situation in Agam was worse still; here there was persistent hostility to Dutch administrative measures, and some formerly Padri villages on the Merapi slopes even refused to allow Dutch officials inside their walls.[20]

There were numerous causes for dissatisfaction throughout the highlands, some of which have already been mentioned. One was dislike of the market tax, which was universally resented. Another was aversion to the Dutch policy of requisitioning so-called 'coolie services'. The new, Dutch-imposed administrative divisions were expected to function as suppliers of labour, whether to assist in laying down new roads, carrying military equipment, building forts and hospitals or delivering materials. Each district was required to provide a certain number of men at regular intervals, to be put to work for a week or a fortnight at a time and supplied with both food and work tools by their home villages.[21] The administrative changes in connection with the *penghulu* system were also repugnant. Each lineage which did not acquire the position of *kepala negeri* for its representative on the village council was alienated from the system, especially if the new appointee made use of his unprecedented position to settle old scores. Those individuals who were singled out for this honour often did not remain long in the good graces of the official who had appointed them; elevation followed by dismissal became a common pattern, leading again to bitterness towards the new system on the part of those who should have been its strongest supporters.[22]

In Tanah Datar the royal family had cause to feel restive under Dutch control; the Regent of Tanah Datar was annoyed at Dutch attempts to improve his manner of attending to business and to lessen his perquisites,[23] and there was general anger in Tanah Datar when it appeared that Resident Elout had been sufficiently influenced by Padri arguments to try to limit cockfighting, which after 1832 was confined to *pasar* and subject to a small tax. To Padri villages the Dutch practice of quartering troops in mosques, the only large buildings in most settlements, was abhorrent, and all villages disliked the obligatory quartering and feeding of soldiers which was resorted to as a punishment for the refractory.[24]

There were also specifically economic grievances. It was becoming apparent that the Dutch had every intention of involving themselves in the production of coffee and the coffee trade. Under de Stuers an attempt had been made to induce certain villages in Tanah Datar to lay down regular coffee gardens on the Javanese model, and the failure of this scheme was no guarantee that it would not be tried again.[25] More irritating for the time being were Dutch efforts to improve the quality of the crop, which led to the establishment of an official post on one of the main roads from the highlands down to Pariaman, at which coffee had to be exhibited and examined for imperfections.[26] Worse appeared to be in store for Limapuluh Kota, when it became plain that the Dutch considered the export of gambir and coffee to *pangkalan* Kota Baru and the east coast as totally against their interests; soon after Limapuluh Kota's submission efforts were made to close the main trade routes to the east and reorient trade to Padang.[27]

Though every region of Minangkabau appears to have had some grievance or other against the Dutch, it was in Bonjol that the 1833 rebellion first broke out. At its start, therefore, the rebellion was quite clearly under Padri leadership. Rao duplicated Bonjol's actions, and the Padri leaders of Agam, now under the leadership of Tuanku Nan Gapau of Kamang, a district adjacent to Bukit Kamang, formulated an identical plan for the slaughter of Dutch troops and were only foiled by Resident Elout's sudden arrival in the highlands.[28] Bonjol's grievances against the Dutch were similar to those of all the recently conquered Padri districts in that part of Minangkabau: instinctive dislike of the Dutch occupation was fuelled by a series of policy decisions which gradually alienated the entire village. That part of the population which had become tired of Padri regimentation and hoped for a return to administration by the lineage heads exclusively were dismayed when Imam Bonjol's close associate, Tuanku Muda, was appointed Regent of Alahan Panjang rather than Datuk Baginda Kaleh who had been instrumental in negotiating the Dutch entry into the settlement. All land-holding families in the village were annoyed by the decision to free the large number of Batak slaves living in Bonjol; not only did men lose their concubines and the mothers of their children, but the extensive *sawah* Bonjol had been able to cultivate now faced the expectation of being denuded of labour. So serious was this prospect that Lieutenant-Colonel Elout concluded that only a certain proportion of slaves could be set free every year, to allow the villagers once again to organize their routine around the cultivation of their fields.

Furthermore, just when Bonjol was facing up to the eventual departure of its supply of labour, it came under normal Dutch requirements for 'coolie service', and many men were drafted to work on the roads, particularly that through Alahan Panjang into Rao, and to provide transport of food and materiel to Dutch troops further inland in Rao. There were other Dutch actions which produced disaffection throughout the village. One of the conditions of Bonjol's submission had been that Dutch troops would not be established inside the walls, but this was subsequently disregarded and troops were quartered both in the mosque and in private houses where their demands to be supplied with food were regarded by the inhabitants as the exaction of tribute. The market tax was also introduced straight away in both Alahan Panjang and Rao and, since it could not be farmed out, its collection was entrusted to *hulubalang,* some of whom were quite arbitrary in their exactions.[29]

And so rebellion broke out in Bonjol. Initially the outburst was confined to the contiguous, zealously Padri regions of Rao, Alahan Panjang and northern Agam. Soon, however, it became clear that wider areas of Minangkabau were involved, as were other leadership groups. The most significant addition to the revolt's Padri leadership core was the Minangkabau royal family, which staked its fortunes on the rebellion and lost. To understand the royal family's role in the events of

1833 it is necessary to look first at the contribution made by another individual of noble blood, who enters the Minangkabau world most unexpectedly at this juncture.

When Lieutenant-Colonel Elout and Dutch reinforcements arrived at Padang in 1831, the new Resident brought with him a most romantic figure. This was Ali Basa Prawirodirjo, commonly known as Sentot. Ali Basa was a relative of Diponegoro's and had been brought up in the Jogjakarta *kraton.* When the Java War broke out in 1825 he was only seventeen, but he quickly elevated himself to an important position in Diponegoro's army by his feats of bravery and daring, and by 1828 had become the army's commander-in-chief.[30] For reasons never fully explained, other than in terms of his growing conviction that Diponegoro's struggle had become hopeless, Ali Basa and his troops surrendered to the Dutch in July 1829 on most advantageous conditions. He was given the rank of lieutenant-colonel, received a salary for himself and his troops, and was allowed to maintain a *barisan* (legion) of 1,800 of his own men encamped near Batavia.[31]

Nevertheless, it was considered wise to find some employment for him and his men, and Governor-General van den Bosch conceived the idea that they could be usefully employed against the Minangkabau:

> I am very anxious that we should establish a Javanese force on Sumatra, so that we will always possess a counterweight there to the ventures of the Native populations. This force can be expanded and increased according to circumstances, by from time to time sending Javanese from here to there if it should prove necessary. With that end in view Ali Basa should be elevated to royal status; e.g., under the title of *Panum bakan*; he ought to be granted a small statelet as *vassal* of the Government, and its inhabitants must find the means to supply us with 1,500 to 2,000 men if needed.[32]

The Governor-General felt that once the Solok plain had been brought under Dutch control Ali Basa could suitably be provided there with a rice-growing district of from 5,000 to 6,000 souls, in which he could stand in the same relationship to the Netherlands Indies government as Pangeran Mangku Negoro in Surakarta.[33] Van den Bosch discounted the possibility that Ali Basa might make common cause with the Minangkabau; he felt the Javanese's own financial interests and the fact that he would be a foreigner in the eyes of the Sumatrans were sufficient safeguards against this.[34]

Once in Sumatra, Ali Basa gradually came to consider that the promise given to him of elevation to 'royal status' should imply much more than control over a mere 'statelet'. His alienation from the Dutch began when, as a practising Muslim, he came into contact with some of the Padri leaders during the pacification process of late 1832. This renewed his interest in his religion and its political connotations. He was conscious of the regard in which he was held by Resident Elout and other Dutch authorities, and was aware of the plans of van den Bosch relating to himself. Now, to his own surprise, he gained a following among many Padri *malim* in Agam when Dutch policy threw him into their company. After the murder of Dutch troops in Alahan Panjang and Rao and the pre-emption of their own revolt, the Padri leaders of northern Agam appear to have regarded Ali Basa as the most likely figure-head around whom they could rally against the Dutch.[35] Although full details of their collaboration are not known, Ali Basa persuaded Dutch military officers that, to avoid massacres such as those which had occurred in the north, his own troops should replace Dutch garrisons in the more outlying parts of Agam and Tanah Datar, and also throughout Limapuluh Kota, Halaban and Buo, enabling European manpower to concentrate on securing the Dutch position in the central regions of Agam and Tanah Datar. Once this had been done, Ali Basa seems to have felt that he was on the way to becoming the leader of an independent state in the Minangkabau highlands.[36]

By February 1833 Ali Basa was exhibiting an attitude of open contempt towards individual Dutch officers, and he was reported to be already speaking of himself as a future Raja Alam.[37] To his following among the Padris of northern Agam had been added a firm commitment to his leadership by the remaining Padris of Lintau, based on the understanding that he would use his legion to drive the Dutch from the highlands.[38] Towards the close of February 1833 he was ready to make a further move; he celebrated the end of the fasting month at Pagarruyung, the ancient royal capital, in defiance of Dutch orders, and while there sought to clarify his position *vis-à-vis* the most important families of Tanah Datar. He invited the valley's leading *penghulu* to come to him on 20 February, partake of a feast, and swear a personal oath of loyalty to him as supreme commander of the Minangkabau highlands, with the title Raja Jawa, Sultan Alam. While at Pagarruyung he talked openly of driving the Dutch from the highlands and of instigating a general rebellion if the Netherlands Indies government refused to recognize his new position.[39] Further, and of great significance in the Javanese context, he wrote to Elout addressing the Resident not with the customary 'father', but with the term 'brother', implying an equality between their two positions. Mindful of his Minangkabau supporters, he also Islamicized his name to Muhammad Ali Basa Abdul Mustafi.[40]

Unfortunately for Ali Basa, before the disunited groups of Minangkabau who were his followers could coalesce to further advance their plans against the Dutch and support him with a rebellion which would encompass both Tanah Datar and Agam, he was the object of a Dutch strategem to lure him down to Padang and put him on the first ship bound for Batavia. The pretext was the recruitment of more Javanese troops for his legion, and though once in Batavia he was made aware of the charges against him and tried desperately to clear himself, he was henceforth only an object of suspicion in Dutch eyes. He returned to Sumatra with two hundred recruits in August 1833, but to his surprise and chagrin was put off the boat, together with one hundred of his men, at the isolated settlement of Benkulen. There he remained until his death in 1854, under constant observation and never rehabilitated.[41]

Ali Basa left a political legacy in Minangkabau. The Regent of Tanah Datar, Sultan Alam Bagagar Syah, had every reason to be dissatisfied with the treatment of the royal family by the Dutch. Not only had his own actions and perquisites been subjected to rigid control, but also it was constantly made clear to him that he was a mere puppet of the Europeans. The continued existence of the royal family in Tanah Datar was now of no pressing concern to the Netherlands Indies government, which had found that it had had to come to terms with each group of villages separately, and to which by 1832 Padri leadership seemed a far more significant factor in Minangkabau society than did that of the royal remnants of another era. Neither could the royal family monopolize the society's communication with the Europeans, for they monopolized no resources which were of interest to the west, and for the Dutch they were unsuited both as political brokers and as guarantors of internal political stability.[42] Dutch recognition of the importance of certain Padri leaders prior to 1833 made it clear that the colonial power was not prepared to rely merely on one collaborating element; other clients were duly installed, producing a significant crisis in the attitude of the royal family towards the Dutch connection.

The ferocity of the Minangkabau challenge to the Dutch in the north, the apparent willingness of the Padris of northern Agam and Lintau to follow Ali Basa, and the generalized discontent with Dutch administrative measures in Tanah Datar, produced in Alam Bagagar Syah a readiness to throw in his lot with the rebellion. He himself was an opium addict and a person of limited intellectual capacities, but he was surrounded by certain old royal retainers and passed-over *penghulu* who encouraged him in the belief that, with the Dutch gone, he would be in a position to restore the Minangkabau state and extend it on the basis of Dutch administrative reforms.[43] Independently of the Padri revolt in Bonjol and of Ali Basa's manoeuvrings in the highlands he had for some months since mid-1832 been writing letters to English contacts in Singapore asking for help against the Dutch.[44] Once he became aware of the activities of other groups along these lines, he threw his support behind the plans of the northern Agam Padris led by Tuanku Nan Gapau of Kamang, and behind Ali Basa himself. For some time he carried on a secret correspondence with Tuanku Nan Gapau, and sent emissaries to covert trysts with the Padri's own emissaries. After the outburst in Bonjol he came in person to Bukit Tinggi, offering to use his influence with the population on behalf of the Dutch. He visited several villages, where he made secret contacts with potential supporters, but urged postponement of any further outbreaks until the Dutch grip on the situation loosened further.[45]

Once Ali Basa had been removed from the scene Alam Bagagar Syah allowed his own name to be used as a rallying point, and letters were written on his behalf to other parts of the highlands urging important figures to prepare for the day when all of Minangkabau would unite to drive out the Dutch.[46] Dutch interception of one of these letters led to the arrest of Alam Bagagar Syah on 2 May. Like Ali Basa he was sent to Batavia, where he was set at liberty but forced to remain until his death in 1849. One or two days after his arrest he was supposed to have taken part in a large gathering at Sumpur, on Lake Singkarak, when the date for the great revolt of Agam and Tanah Datar was to have been fixed. The arrest led to the subsequent manifestations of rebellion losing their co-ordination.[47]

The co-ordination of further plans for the rebellion was also affected for the worse because along with Ali Basa and Alam Bagagar Syah had been removed from the highlands the two major couriers of the movement, Tuanku Alam of Kota Tua and Tuanku Nan Cerdik of the coastal village of Narras near Pariaman, both of whom had been converted late in their careers to the Padri cause, had gained the confidence and favour of Elout and had manipulated this to acquire and carry information on Dutch movements between the various groups of rebels.[48] By May

1833 the Padri leaders of Agam had decided that, in view of so many arrests it would be unwise to wait longer to launch a full-scale revolt. In any case they had already initiated their movement in January to coincide with the Bonjol murders, when the Padris of Bukit Kamang, Kamang, Tilatang and Kapau began to rebuild their fortifications, which had had to be destroyed after the 1832 conquest, at the same time denying access to Dutch troops and importing as many guns as possible.[49] Further preparations were impeded by the commencement of the fasting month, though even this was broken by isolated attacks on Dutch soldiers found on the main roads or at market-places. Then, in early May, other villages on the slopes of Mount Merapi which were renowned for their sympathy to the Padri cause, such as Sungai Puar, began to show signs that they were preparing for rebellion.

The outbreak flared in the same month, when the Dutch military commandant of the highlands, Major C.J. de Quay, was attacked on the market-place of Banuhampu. Simultaneously a detachment of thirty men sent from Fort de Kock to reinforce the mountain pass down to the coast was killed to the last man near Guguk Sigandang, and the Dutch fort at Guguk Sigandang, overlooking Kota Lawas, was set alight and destroyed with the loss of its garrison. Fort de Kock and the Dutch fort at Koriri near Tilatang were surrounded, cut off from outside contacts and repeatedly attacked. It was soon clear that the southern Agam Padri villages on Mounts Merapi and Singgalang, such as Kota Lawas and Pandai Sikat, had joined the rebellion, and the revolt spread as far round Mount Merapi as Gunung, near Batipuh. From Gunung to Fort de Kock the roads were everywhere obstructed and the bridges destroyed; attempts were also made to cut the roads to the coast.[50]

Superior military force enabled the Dutch to restore their position, and after they had done so fifteen Minangkabau who had led the revolt in the southern part of Agam were executed on 28 and 29 July, largely for their part in the destruction of the Dutch fort at Guguk Sigandang. It seems clear from the names of the executed men that entire villages participated in the rebellion, and these were led by the traditional village élite, the *penghulu,* although since most of the rebel villages were strongly Padri their leaders were doubtless *penghulu* who had long supported the Padri cause in internal village politics. Three *penghulu* from Kota Lawas were executed, two from Pandai Sikat, one from Singgalang, a village near Pandai Sikat, one from Air Angkat, one from Kota Baru – both villages near Kota Lawas on Mount Merapi – and one from Gunung on Mount Merapi near Batipuh. Two other village notables – an *orang kaya tua* from Singgalang and a *hulubalang* – were also among the condemned men. The leading figure implicated was the Dutch-appointed *kepala laras* for the whole area, which was known under the name of the Enam [Six] Kota. Of the fifteen, only three were Islamic leaders: Tuanku Mensiangan of Kota Lawas and his two sons. This Tuanku Mensiangan was the son of the old ally of Tuanku Nan Rinceh, and had been an implacable opponent of the Dutch since their first entry into the highlands. As well as being responsible for the murder of Dutch soldiers in the fort at Guguk Sigandang, the executed *penghulu* were found to have fully participated in the plans centring on the person of Sultan Alam Bagagar Syah, and also to have been in touch with the Padris of northern Agam.[51]

It was partly because the Agam outbreak remained unco-ordinated with any other movement of sufficiently broad scope that Dutch forces were able to recover the situation. They took first the hill villages of southern Agam and by 29 May had reopened communications with Fort de Kock.[52] The suppression of the revolt in northern Agam was a more difficult task. Kamang and Bukit Kamang remained strongly fortified, and the major part of the inhabitants of nearby villages such as Tilatang and Kapau had left their homes and assembled there too; even Padris from as far away as Sungai Puar and Candung joined the 20,000 armed defenders of the region. Many of the leaders of the fighting were village *penghulu,* strong in the Padri cause.[53] 'In Kamang', wrote Elout in July 1833, 'the whole of Agam fought against us . . .'[54] Dutch reinforcements sent from Batavia proved too strong, however, and in July all the villages of Kamang were taken, followed by those of Bukit Kamang and finally of Pau. Many of the leading *penghulu* fled further north into Alahan Panjang.[55]

Despite the plans of Alam Bagagar Syah, Tanah Datar did not join the Agam rebellion with enough force to distract Dutch troops. One reason for this was that two key areas of Tanah Datar, Batipuh which covered the route over the Ambacang down to the lowlands, and Halaban in the extreme north-east, remained loyal to the Dutch connection. Batipuh men had done well out of providing auxiliaries for the Dutch forces, and the rebellion offered further prospects for loot from refractory villages. Halaban, which had been a devoutly Padri area under the total control of Tuanku Halaban, maintained its loyalty due to the personal influence of this *tuanku,* who had come over in 1832 and who, because of the obvious support he had from the population, was rewarded with the title of Regent and with the right to continue to maintain a Padri-style administration, which seems to have prejudiced him in Dutch favour.[56] This gave other potential rebels in the northern Tanah Datar hills around Tabatpatah and Tanjung Alam less room for manoeuvre, and, whatever plans they might have cherished, none bore fruit. The three main centres of rebellion in Tanah Datar were the hills around Lake Singkarak, a strongly Padri area, the vicinity of the former royal centre of Pagarruyung, and, not surprisingly, the valley of the Sinamar which comprised the districts of Lintau and Buo. In the region around Pagarruyung, bands of rebels led by various *penghulu* and old court retainers were able to achieve little, though they harassed Dutch troops from hiding places in chasms and rocks.[57] The Buo locality, however, sparked a movement which was potentially dangerous.

After the deportation of Sultan Alam Bagagar Syah, the so-called Raja di Buo, the representative of that branch of the Minangkabau royal family which had been left behind in the Sinamar valley when the remainder had migrated into the main Tanah Datar plain in the seventeenth century, was the senior member of the royal family remaining in the highlands. Unlike the royalty of central Tanah Datar he had been a devout Muslim and an individual of exemplary piety before the outbreak of Tuanku Lintau's revivalist movement; he was described by a Dutch officer as 'quite a different man from the wretched Regent of Tanah Datar'.[58] He was always regarded by the Padris as one of themselves, and was left undisturbed in Buo by Tuanku Lintau after the whole area became Padri.[59] With the fall of Lintau in 1832 he was persuaded by his relative Alam Bagagar Syah to come over to the Dutch and, like Tuanku Halaban further north, was rewarded with the creation of his own 'regency', which was put together administratively from Lintau, Buo and an area to the south-west called Kota Tujuh. The Padri tenor of life was left undisturbed in the region, Raja di Buo was surrounded by Padri *malim,* and the Dutch congratulated themselves on the solution of the Lintau problem.[60]

Prior to the arrest of Alam Bagagar Syah on 2 May Raja di Buo had indicated to the Dutch that the population of his regency was discontented over the new system of appointing *kepala laras* and *kepala negeri,* whereby many families felt themselves to have been humiliated.[61] However, it was not until his relative had been removed from the scene that he seems to have felt it was his mission to place himself at the head of whatever rebel forces he could command and again make an effort to revive an independent Minangkabau state. On 12 May 1833 the Dutch commandant of Buo was attacked while out on reconnaissance by a party of *hulubalang* belonging to Raja di Buo, and a plot was contrived to murder the Dutch Resident, Elout, when he visited Buo. Though the plot failed, the whole valley of the Sinamar broke into rebellion and the Dutch fort at Buo was besieged. All available Dutch troops were sent to control the outbreak. It was at this point that the Agam rebellion also started in earnest, providing clear evidence of the continued alliance between forces opposed to the Dutch in both Tanah Datar and Agam. The village of Buo and surrounding villages were finally overcome after they had put up fierce resistance and Raja di Buo, his Padri supporters and other rebels escaped across the Sinamar.[62]

Having failed on the south-eastern fringes of Tanah Datar, Raja di Buo and his followers decided that they might be able to cause trouble for the Dutch from the side of Limapuluh Kota. This valley had been marked by its almost total non-participation in the Minangkabau revolt so far. Its recent occupation meant that it had not yet been subjected to severe Dutch interference, and its ready ability to adapt to the Padri movement in the early nineteenth century indicated that a new adaptation was not beyond the temperament of its people. To this record of indifference to the rebellion there were one or two exceptions: in the Padri hill villages of the east, such as Mungkar, Arau in the mountain pass leading out of the valley and nearby Sarilamak, certain *tuanku* had been drawn into Alam Bagagar Syah's plans and already in January 1833 they were instigating attacks on Dutch soldiers on the roads and at market-places. An attempt to gain enough support for an assault on Payakumbuh in June failed, however, and Sarilamak, Arau and other refractory villages were reduced to ashes by a Dutch expeditionary force.[63]

It was in these villages, with a tradition of hostility towards the Dutch and most to lose if the trade routes to the east coast were closed, that Raja di Buo now appeared and attempted to stir up further resistance. He established himself in *pangkalan* Kota Baru and gained supporters at Arau in the mountain pass leading out of Limapuluh Kota to the *pangkalan,* but was unable to win over the recently appointed Regent of Limapuluh Kota, Tuanku Nan Cedok of Payakumbuh, another Padri who remained satisfied with his existing situation under the Dutch. In July a Dutch column aided by Payakumbuh and Taram auxiliaries drove off the *raja* and Limapuluh Kota, like Halaban, settled down to a modified form of the old Padri administration, which was reported as late as 1842 to be still acceptable to the population and suited to their needs.[64]

Even after July 1833 the Minangkabau resistance struggle smouldered on in various parts of the central highlands, despite the apparently overwhelming defeat of the rebellion. Trouble continued in the Pagarruyung area of Tanah Datar throughout the latter part of the year, led by *penghulu* who were still in contact with the exiled Alam Bagagar Syah.[65] Ultimately, however, the central plain settled down, and opposition to Dutch control was confined to the eastern hills. Raja di Buo had now established himself at Sumpur Kudus and, with his Padri supporters from Buo and Lintau, tried to cause as much trouble as possible for the Dutch. In April 1834 they unsuccessfully attacked the Dutch fort at Buo, a plot having been elaborated by a certain Haji Ismail once again to restore the Minangkabau state under Raja di Buo.[66] Haji Ismail and Raja di Buo continued to obstruct Dutch attempts to expand along the Inderagiri throughout 1835, and in 1836 Haji Ismail was reported to be in Lintau, where many devout Padris implacably opposed to the Dutch remained.[67] But by now these areas were so impoverished and sparsely populated that an adequate force could never be assembled to do significant damage to the Dutch. Raja di Buo continued to roam around the eastern borders of Minangkabau until in 1874, when he was about seventy years old, he asked Dutch permission to return home. This was refused, and he died on the fringes of the Minangkabau world in 1880, the last widely-accepted symbol of the Minangkabau royal house.[68]

It was in Agam far more than in Limapuluh Kota or Tanah Datar that the Minangkabau struggle against Dutch occupation persisted. Although anti-Dutch manifestations often centred around religious teachers, *penghulu* support was always necessary for any movement to gather momentum, and this was frequently forthcoming. In late 1834 a charismatic figure appeared among the Padris of Kamang, in a village called Batuputih; this was a saintly individual who called himself *daulat* and claimed to be inspired by God, his message being that all the *kepala laras* of Agam were betrayers of the population and deserved to be murdered because of their association with the Dutch. Unlike the earlier Padri leaders this figure reached back into the pre-Padri magical tradition of the *tarekat*; he asserted he had surrounded a Dutch officer in the highlands with evil spirits which would encompass his doom, and promised he would gradually extend this spell to all other foreigners in the interior, who would then be forced to leave Minangkabau for good. The holy man of Batuputih soon acquired a considerable number of followers in the Bukit Kamang, Kamang and Tilatang areas, including *penghulu* who had been passed over for village headships and were extremely embittered. By early 1835 the supporters of the *daulat* had begun to arm and various *penghulu* and their lineage members attacked individual Dutch soldiers; six hundred armed men were reported to be roaming the road between the Dutch forts at Bukit Tinggi and Koriri. Finally a Dutch expeditionary force was sent to Batuputih, which they reduced to ashes, driving off the rebels' champion at the same time.[69]

Agam continued to smoulder. In 1836 numerous secret gatherings were alleged to be taking place and in February of that year the whole valley was reported ripe for rebellion. Islamic leadership was still a decisive factor in all these small movements, but *penghulu* support was also crucial and was generally assured because of the great discontent still felt over Dutch administrative measures.[70] Similar plots were suspected in 1837, confined not to the traditionally Padri villages of Bukit Kamang and Mount Merapi, but expanding into regions such as Empat Angkat which in the past had been supporters of Dutch involvement in Agam.[71]

One of the reasons Agam did not again break into open rebellion was that, between August 1833 and late 1837, it was awaiting a decisive outcome to the Dutch battle against the more northerly rebels. Whilst the rebellion in central Minangkabau had been crushed by July 1833, the northern Padris under Imam Bonjol and Tuanku Tambusai were able to fight on for a number of years. This was made possible both by the difficult, hilly nature of the terrain surrounding their headquarters, which caused problems for the Dutch in the laying down of roads and bridges, and by the distances from their supply centres convoys of food and military equipment had to travel to give the Dutch army against the Padris the support it needed.[72] The well-nigh impassable chasms and mountains with which the Netherlands Indies army had to cope in its advance upon Alahan Panjang ensured that Bonjol remained for several years a beacon to Padri forces throughout Minangkabau.

All the coffee-producing areas around Lake Maninjau and further north had risen against the Dutch in January 1833, and it was not until June 1834 that Dutch troops were able to recapture Matur, a village surrounded on three sides by precipices yet dominating the main pass between Fort de Kock in Agam and the most suitable route to Bonjol. Only in April 1835, after a cessation of hostilities to give time for fruitless negotiations between the two sides, did Dutch forces cross a tributary of the river Masang which had obstructed their advance. By 11 July 1835, nearly one and a half years after the outbreak of the rebellion, they were beneath the walls of Bonjol.[73]

What followed was a siege of the fortified village which lasted, remarkably, until Bonjol's fall on 16 August 1837. During that time Bonjol for the Minangkabau became surrounded with a magical aura as a result of the length and determination of its resistance; to other Minangkabau it was a *negeri sakti,* a village endowed with supernatural powers.[74] It was also given the title *kompeni darat,* the company of the Minangkabau interior, indicating that it had proved itself a match for the Netherlands Indies government, which was commonly called 'the company' by Minangkabau in remembrance of the pre-1795 period.[75] Tuanku Muda had been killed in the January 1833 rebellion, and Imam Bonjol once again placed himself at the head of the garrison. Individuals came from all over the highlands, from as far away as Lintau, to help defend the village, and they were prepared to fight on until death. Bonjol's fortifications were excellent, and not only was the village carefully enclosed, but it was also protected by forts on Mount Terjadi which directly overlooked the besiegers. The villagers found no difficulty in going out under cover of darkness, and they were supplied with food and military necessities from further up the valley, and also from as far away as Lubuk Sikaping in Rao and from the Lake Maninjau region. These areas were still devotedly Padri, and many traders who now supplied the village had relatives living in Bonjol; in any case, trade with Bonjol was a profitable enterprise.[76]

The Netherlands Indies army was favoured by certain elements in the situation. Although it was never able completely to enclose Bonjol because of the defensive works of nearby villages, and the north of the village always remained open for inward and outward movement, in time Bonjol became cut off from all other approaches by a Dutch line which in 1837 contained twenty-five small posts.[77] This bottling up of the village was facilitated by Dutch control of the seas. All ports which could possibly be used to land supplies for Bonjol were blockaded as far north at Tapanuli, and use was also made of seapower to destroy the Bonjol saltpans between Katiagan and Air Bangis.[78] The Dutch also had access to plentiful supplies of fresh troops, in the shape of Minangkabau auxiliaries and also Bataks, and although many of these had ultimately to be allowed to go home to attend to their fields, at least 13,000 persisted in the siege to the end on a rotating basis.[79] By early 1837 the entire Dutch force in central Sumatra had been brought up to 5,230, many of whom also performed service before Bonjol. The army was also gradually able to improve its lines of communication, using forced labour, and ultimately a good military road was laid down from Fort de Kock through Matur to before Bonjol, and communications between Fort de Kock and Padang were also improved.[80]

So, despite the fact that the Dutch laboured under considerable difficulties, including the constant sickness among European troops before Bonjol, the fact that their supply lines to Padang stretched over a period of nine marching days, and the inability of their cannon to do much damage to the Bonjol walls due to the smallness of the calibre, ultimately their superior resources stretching back to a metropolitan European power won the day. By June 1837 there were only eighty armed men left in Bonjol, most of the houses had been destroyed by Dutch shells, and the remaining population lived in holes dug in the ground which were lined with stones and covered with planks.[81] Finally, making use of European sapping techniques, Dutch forces were able to get close enough to Bonjol's walls to open up a breach, and the village was entered on the night of 15-16 August 1837. For this part of Minangkabau the rebellion which had begun in January 1833 was now over. Bonjol's fortifications were destroyed and the village was rechristened Kota Generaal Cochius, after Major-General F.D. Cochius who had been responsible for the final storming of the walls. Other villages in the valley of Alahan Panjang and around the nearby Mount Talakmau immediately declared their submission to the Dutch.[82]

For Imam Bonjol himself, however, the struggle was still not over. He fled further north up the valley, and then hid in the forest with eighty companions, including members of his family. At this time he is reported to have said to the younger members of his family:

> As long as the company does not capture me there will be no peace and the fight will not end. When the time arrives, let me follow my fate, wherever it may lead me. As long as I can be buried in Alahan Pandjang, I will continue the fight against the company; my sons and I will take up this fight; may I be granted my prayer to Allah and his messenger: to die in the fight against the company.[83]

Imam Bonjol's fate was not a happy one, and he was treated more harshly than Sultan Alam Bagagar Syah. After suffering great privations in the wilderness he decided to give himself up, hoping to the last that he would be allowed to remain in Alahan Panjang as 'a free Malay'.[84] Instead he was shipped straight to Batavia, and exiled in the Priangan. In 1839 he was sent to Ambon, and in 1841 to Menado in northern Sulawesi, where it was calculated he would be as far away from Islamic influences as possible. Here he lived out the rest of his life, cultivating a small piece of ground until his death in 1864.[85]

The prostration of the Padris of Alahan Panjang was not immediately followed by the collapse of all the northern Padris. Tambusai had retained its independence even when the rest of Minangkabau had been subjugated in 1832, and while Bonjol was holding out against the Dutch between 1833 and 1837 more northerly areas under the influence of Tuanku Tambusai were doing likewise. The valley of Rao had revolted in January 1833 at the same time as Bonjol, and Tuanku Tambusai subsequently entered the valley and gained a considerable following in the villages of the southern and central part. Several forts were erected around Lubuk Sikaping, and by July 1833 large numbers of men on a war-footing were ensconced in these, including a number of *penghulu* and *malim* who had fled from Agam after the fall of Kamang and Bukit Kamang. By October the rebellion had spread to the northern part of the valley. Tuanku Tambusai established himself at Padangmatinggi, the Yang di Pertuan of Rao who had been appointed Regent by the Dutch threw in his lot with the rebels, and the Dutch garrison was forced to retreat into Mandailing.[86]

Thereafter the leadership of the Rao Padris and *penghulu* was firmly in the hands of Tuanku Tambusai, who persisted in his earlier determination that no Europeans should be allowed to establish themselves in the highlands. Delegates from Tuanku Tambusai who came to negotiate at Sasak on the coast in July 1834 insisted on this point, stating that their experience had taught them that 'too close company' with the Netherlands only exposed them to danger and mistreatment, and that the proper place for Europeans was, as in the past, on the coast.[87] Even in Mandailing Dutch posts were not secure from Tuanku Tambusai's incursions. In May and June 1834 two Dutch forts, one at Huta Nopan and one a little further south, were besieged by the *tuanku's* forces, which included a number of Muslim Bataks from the area who supported the Padri cause; only with difficulty were the Padris driven off. In the long run, however, Tuanku Tambusai's forces were too small to maintain an effective position in Mandailing for long, and in September 1834 he left the valley.[88]

All this meant that, during the siege of Bonjol, the Dutch were obliged to open up a second front against Rao and send troops into that valley from the west coast by way of the valley of Mandailing. These troops gradually pushed through into the northern part of the Rao valley and retook the major villages in May 1835. The Yang di Pertuan fled, but returned to give himself up in May 1836. Further Dutch advance down the valley to the south was hotly contested, and even the smallest villages put up fierce opposition. Lubuk Sikaping remained the major outpost of Bonjol in the valley. Like its model, it resisted a Dutch siege force and only gave in, disheartened, after the fall of Bonjol in August 1837.[89]

Even now, not all the leading representatives of the Padri movement had recognized Dutch supremacy. Tuanku Tambusai could still count on a following in the extensive area between the river Sosak and the Bila, especially in the region around Gunung Tua and Pertibi on the river Panai. He restricted his activities to this area throughout 1836, became more and more engrossed in the study of religion, and hoped to be left in peace. This was not to be. After the fall of Bonjol, he was the major target for the Netherlands Indies army in Sumatra. In November 1837 a Dutch column from Mandailing marched up the Angkola river valley, crossed into the valley of the Batang Onan, and gradually obliged Tuanku

Tambusai and his remaining forces to retreat to their base at Daludalu. All the villages along the river Panai and further south declared themselves for the Dutch.[90] Throughout 1838 Dutch forces occupied themselves with taking entrenchments around Daludalu, and finally, in December of the same year, after a siege of ten days, they entered Tuanku Tambusai's capital. On one side the village walls backed onto the river Sosak, and many of the defenders, who included Tuanku Tambusai himself, supported by refugees from Bonjol, were able to escape by a water gate and flee in *perahu*. Whether Tuanku Tambusai got very far is uncertain, and since nothing further is heard of him it seems likely that he was wounded in the escape and subsequently died.[91] With the fall of Daludalu Padri resistance to the Dutch presence in Minangkabau ended.

But Minangkabau resistance as such was not at an end, and one more major revolt broke out in the highlands before Dutch control could be said to be firmly established. As with the movements led by Sultan Alam Bagagar Syah and Raja di Buo, this was a revolt under secular leadership, and in many ways represented a continuation of the resistance offered to the Dutch by the now defunct royal family. One of the most important pillars of the Minangkabau state had been the Tuan Gedang of Batipuh, who controlled the region which straddled the major trade route out of Tanah Datar down to the coast. The leading Batipuh families had long had profitable trading relations with the Dutch at Padang, and during the Padri wars Batipuh gave succour to many individuals who had fled from Tuanku Lintau.[92] The region had been at the heart of the agreement to sign the 1821 treaty, and showed continuous zeal for the Dutch cause right up to the fall of Bonjol. In 1833, after the collapse of the Minangkabau rebellion, the Tuan Gedang of Batipuh, Kali Raja, was appointed Regent of Batipuh by Governor-General van den Bosch, with a monthly salary of f.500 in recognition of his services to the Dutch cause. Kali Raja's nephew was granted the title Pamuncak of Batipuh, nominated the Regent's successor and given a salary of f.100 a month.[93]

With the fall of Bonjol Kali Raja appears to have seen himself more and more in the role previously monopolized by Alam Bagagar Syah and Raja di Buo. He regarded himself as the leading representative of the Minangkabau state left in the highlands, and he was encouraged by his followers to think that Dutch victories would not have been possible without the support of his Batipuh auxiliaries. After the collapse of Bonjol he asked the Dutch Resident for a more distinctive title than than of Regent, but was refused. Gradually he saw himself disappointed in his hopes of obtaining Dutch support for his own elevation to a position of wider authority in the highlands, and suffered the humiliation of seeing Batipuh treated not even as a regency, but merely as one district among many in Tanah Datar. Both Kali Raja and the Pamuncak then began to cherish the notion that they could use their well-seasoned battle forces to drive out the Dutch and once again restore the Minangkabau state, of which they would be the leaders.[94]

On 22 February 1841 rebellion suddenly broke out in Batipuh. The Pamuncak ordered the murder of an Indonesian corporal, his wife and a Chinese on the main road between Batu Sangkar and Padang Panjang, and on 24 February Batipuh men burnt down nearly all the houses in Padang Panjang. Dutch forts in the vicinity were then attacked and an attempt was made to cut the road to Kayutanam and the lowlands. That a revolt on behalf of a disappointed man and a chimerical state could still arouse echoes of resistance among the old Padri villages of southern Agam was at once evident. Villages such as Sungai Puar and Banuhampu, under *penghulu* leadership, declared for the rebels, as did other more southerly villages on the slopes of Mounts Merapi and Singgalang such as Kota Lawas and Pandai Sikat. Fort de Kock was attacked. Parts of Tanah Datar which had previously been attached to the Padri cause, such as the village of Sulit Air and its neighbours near Lake Singkarak, and Tanjung Alam and nearby villages in the northern hills also declared for the rebels, and the garrison of Fort van der Capellen was forced to abandon the fort.[95]

By now, however, Dutch military forces in the Minangkabau highlands had too great a numerical preponderance and were too well equipped for the battle-weary rebels. The rebellion was over in eight days, and the Regent of Batipuh was exiled to the Priangan, where he died in 1842. His heir, the Pamuncak, did not surrender till May, and was exiled to Ambon.[96] So ended the last major rebellion in the Minangkabau highlands until 1908, a year which ushered in several decades of intense nationalist activity. By then Dutch colonial rule had had many years in which to alter the economic and political face of Minangkabau, an endeavour which began in earnest immediately after the 1833 rebellion.

Minangkabau peasant trade and Dutch commercial policy

In August 1833, after the collapse of the Minangkabau revolt in the central part of the highlands, the Governor-General of the Netherlands Indies, Johannes van den Bosch, arrived at Padang with every intention of settling the future of Minangkabau for many years to come. The conclusions van den Bosch drew about the Minangkabau situation were of great importance, because in May 1834, only a few months after he had laid down the post of Governor-General and returned home, he was appointed Minister of Colonies. Successive administrations at Padang were left in no doubt that they must follow his directions, and until his retirement in December 1839 he exercised enormous influence over the destiny of Minangkabau and its people.

The overriding Dutch interest in Minangkabau was, in the eyes of the Governor-General, the harnessing of its agricultural productivity to the needs of the Netherlands state. This in turn involved closer scrutiny of the way in which Minangkabau's commercial crops entered into trade, and of the imports Minangkabau growers might be willing to accept in return for their produce. Van den Bosch's relationship with Willem I of the Netherlands has already been touched on, as has the entry of the Nederlandsche Handel-Maatschappij into Padang trade, but certain points remain to be clarified. Willem I regarded colonies as having an important role to play in his plans for the national revival of the Netherlands, and he was determined that the British and the Americans should not dominate the trade of the Netherlands Indies a moment longer than necessary. In 1823 he was attracted by the advice of Herman Warner Muntinghe, a member of the Raad van Indië (Council of the Indies) home on leave, that the lack of capital in the hands of Netherlands merchants, capital which alone would enable them to compete successfully in the Indies, could only be made good by providing them with a means whereby they could pool their resources. Muntinghe suggested the establishment of a company for this purpose, which, without relying on monpoly, would have sufficient funds to buy up and ship considerable quantities of produce from the Indies home to the Netherlands for sale to the rest of Europe. Willem readily concurred, outlined the project in a decree published in March 1824, and opened subscriptions. On the first day subscriptions reached f.69,565,250, much of the capital being pledged by the king himself and other members of the royal family. Finally capital was fixed at f.37 million, Articles of Association were approved stating that the company would provide an import and export agency for the Netherlands throughout the world, and the Nederlandsche Handel-Maatschappij was registered on 7 February 1825.[97]

In 1826 the NHM established a factory at Padang, its only factory outside Java, and began to compete with American ships for the purchase of Minangkabau coffee. Beginning with the traditional Dutch practice of advancing goods on credit to the Minangkabau brokers of Padang, the NHM had very little success and by 1830 it was noted that the company had failed to acquire any considerable share of the exported coffee.[98] It was poorly supplied with Indian cloth, which was the speciality of the English agency houses, and had no access to American dollars, the only other item which lubricated the trade. Nor had it established adequate relationships with the Padang Chinese, who had now far outstripped the Minangkabau brokers as intermediaries in the trade with Europe and America.[99]

To formulate measures which would result in the acquisition of the Minangkabau coffee crop for the Netherlands was the task Johannes van den Bosch set himself when he arrived at Padang in 1833. Success in this enterprise he felt required the elimination of certain groups of traders operating inside Minangkabau, and in his voluminous writings from this period he made it clear that steps must be taken against three groups in particular. First of all the Minangkabau peasant traders, who made a living buying up and bulking coffee in the highlands and transporting it to the coast, were to be cut out of the coffee trade entirely, so that the Dutch could be brought into direct contact with the coffee growers themselves. Secondly, Dutch regulations were to discourage by every possible means the English agency houses at Padang, which in 1829 had seemed in a parlous state but which had recovered by 1833 because of an astute partnership with Chinese brokers in the importation and distribution of Indian cloth and cotton.[100] Finally, the American buyers of coffee, who appeared by 1830 to have been driven away by Dutch differential duties, but who had returned in force by 1833 due to the rise in world prices for coffee, were to be further disadvantaged by a new system of duties. Chinese and Minangkabau brokers on the coast van den Bosch felt could be left alone, although Chinese brokers were to be prevented for the time being from penetrating the interior, where they would doubtless provide strong competition for Dutch efforts to monopolize the coffee crop.[101]

Of all these groups, it was against the Minangkabau peasant trader, one of the mainstays of the Padri system, that van den Bosch's first efforts were directed. In fact, despite the multiplicity of intermediaries, the peasant traders provided the cheapest way of serving a market in which most consumers had low per capita incomes and were scattered due to inadequate transport facilities. But to van den Bosch, as to many administrators both colonial and bureaucratic, intermediate traders or 'middlemen' were 'Marchauntes of myschyefe that go betwixt the barke and the tree', as a Tudor document has it.[102] In the Governor-General's eyes, which disregarded the traders' distributive functions, such individuals were seen largely in relation to their role in the coffee trade. Here they were considered to be merely inflating the price of coffee sold on the coast, and depriving the grower of adequate recompense for his labour. Van den Bosch, so meticulous in his myriad calculations concerning the best interests of the Netherlands, never seems to have undertaken an analysis of the Minangkabau coffee-growing household, and he laboured under the misconception that traders in coffee formed a separate social class, distinct from the peasant grower; this class, he felt, could be eliminated without harming the planters, and he was unable to recognize that many members of planting households entered and withdrew from the coffee trade as time and circumstance demanded.

Van den Bosch's first task was to draw up a balance sheet of the losses to the Netherlands allegedly occasioned by the coffee traders. He noted that in 1833 the Minangkabau coffee producer was getting f.6 to f.8 per *pikul* for his product at the nearest large *pasar,* although coffee was selling on the coast for over twice that sum. He therefore proposed that the Dutch should erect depots at the main markets in the Minangkabau highlands, at which a so-called 'protected price' of f.9 per *pikul* should be offered for coffee, a price attractive enough to induce the peasant to sell direct to these depots, so cutting out the chain of middlemen who plied the routes to the coast.[103] This would eliminate the two main categories of coffee trader: the buyer who bought up small lots of coffee at several markets with a small amount of capital, and the bigger trader who bought from several buyers, arranged for transportation to the lowlands and sold to agents of the Chinese. To further embarrass the bigger trader who organized transportation from the main markets to the coast, his particular carrier transport system was to be subjected to competition by the setting up of a 'government transport-establishment' which would bring down the coffee to the coast and take up the articles in most demand in the highlands. Many Minangkabau who earned their living as carriers were to be deprived of it by this plan, since it was intended initially to engage coolies on contract from the Batu and Nias islands and from the Coromandel coast, and ultimately to replace manpower with carts and packhorses, after the completion of a major road improvement undertaking. Van den Bosch attached great importance to this aspect of his scheme, making detailed estimates of how much each cart could transport and elaborate calculations of how far a cart could travel and return in a day and how many relay stations would be needed.[104] By thus damaging the intermediate trader and his carriers it was also hoped to return many individuals to agriculture,[105] regardless of the fact that most carriers came from isolated hill villages where agricultural land was in short supply, and existence revolved around a combination of trade and agriculture.

To put his plans into operation, van den Bosch needed the co-operation of the NHM. Although coffee was to be sold to the Netherlands Indies government itself, the government did not wish to enter Minangkabau trade beyond this point, and so sought to enmesh the interests of the company in the undertaking. It was proposed that the company would itself establish the projected depots in the highlands, and would buy coffee and sell salt on behalf of the government, receiving a five per cent commission for its trouble; at the same time it would be in a position to trade in any other items on its own account, to sell cloth, iron, steel and other necessities and to buy up other Minangkabau agricultural products such as gambir and cassia, such products to be preferred as payment for consumer goods. In January 1834 a contract, to run provisionally for three years, was entered into between the Governor-General and the agent of the NHM at Padang, whereby the NHM undertook to establish two highlands depots at centres best suited to command the coffee trade – at Payakumbuh in Limapuluh Kota from whence coffee customarily went to the east coast and at Padang Panjang where the descent from Agam to the west coast began. Although the NHM was aware that its new depots would seem more like political outposts of the Netherlands Indies government than commercial enterprises, it too was keen to eliminate the Minangkabau intermediate trader and come into direct contact with the peasant producer.[106]

The elimination of the peasant trader did not constitute the entirety of van den Bosch's plan. Since there was to be no question of introducing the forced delivery of coffee to the new depots, measures had also to be taken which would remove from the scene both the American exporters of coffee and the English agency houses at Padang, the latter being enmeshed in the trade by virtue of their accepting American silver for the Indian cloth with which they supplied the highlands.[107] To drive away the Americans, van den Bosch increased the export duty on coffee exported to foreign harbours from f.3 to f.5 per *pikul,* a large sum compared with the f.2 per *pikul* paid by coffee exported to the Netherlands in Dutch ships.[108] The exclusion of the English agency houses was a more complex matter; since their role in the coffee trade was related to their acceptance of American dollars from Chinese brokers at Padang and Pariaman in exchange for Indian cottons, any measures against them would inevitably also affect the Chinese brokerage class. It had not been van den Bosch's stated intention to damage this class, which in many ways was useful to the Dutch, but, as far as the coffee trade was concerned, they were bound to be affected by the general policy of restricting all so-called 'private' trade in coffee.

To ensure the viability of his 'protected price', van den Bosch had to make certain that no private trader would be able to export coffee profitably and still pay the planter a price for this coffee equal to the government's f.9 'protected price'. This was to be contrived through the new device of the 'territorial duty' which was to be an imposition additional to export duty. The tax consisted of one-fifth of the worth of the coffee on export, and was imposed from 1 January 1834. The amount to be paid was fixed every month by the Resident, based on the calculation that, if the market price for a *pikul* of coffee at Padang at the end of May was f.19.50, and the territorial duty for coffee was fixed at f.4.67, the coffee would thus have a value of f.24.17. One-fifth of this value, or f.4.83, was then the territorial duty for June. Adding this to the already high export duties, total duties at Padang would amount to anything between f.7 and f.10 a *pikul,* making it impossible for the trading network of American buyer, English agency house, Chinese broker, and Minangkabau intermediate trader to operate economically enough to be able to offer the planter a price equivalent to that of the government.[109] The English agency houses in particular would, van den Bosch prophesied, experience a rapid demise.[110]

What effect did van den Bosch's new commercial policy have on the structure of Minangkabau trade? Contrary to all expectations, the peasant trader proved less easy to eliminate than van den Bosch had planned. These traders' fate depended to a considerable extent on the Americans' willingness to continue coming to Padang, and throughout most of the late 1830s profits on a consignment of coffee were still attractive enough for them to bring their silver to the Minangkabau coast.[111] As long as these customers persisted, the intermediate trader found it worth his while to remain in business. In their first two years of existence, the two depots of the NHM acquired only 3,800 *pikul* of coffee in all, although the annual export of coffee from Padang in those years was c.80,000 *pikul*. Of this total, only 624 *pikul* had been acquired at Payakumbuh.[112] Not only were broad areas of coffee-producing land excluded from the new scheme by reason of distance from the purview of the Payakumbuh and Padang Panjang depots, but Limapuluh Kota coffee traders still found the routes to the east coast *pangkalan* profitable[113] and traders in the vicinity of Padang Panjang did not have much further to go to make the journey to Pariaman and get the full coastal market price for coffee, which by 1835 was f.15.50 a *pikul.*[114] Even the raising of the 'protected price' in June 1835 did not effect much alteration in the situation, and sales to the depots continued desultory throughout 1836, the Minangkabau trader still preferring the higher coastal price, which by mid-1836 had climbed to f.19 per *pikul.*[115]

And so the intermediate trading system continued as before. It was simply not possible for individual growers to bring their coffee to such distant depots, and both small-scale buyers and larger intermediate traders pursued their livelihood undisturbed. In some ways they now enjoyed certain advantages. Dutch measures to improve the roads were of considerable benefit to them, both in the interior and on the highlands-lowlands routes. Van den Bosch's great engineering project had been the road through the solid rock of the Anai gorge, ten miles long and climbing from 450 feet above sea level at Kayutanam to 2,535 feet at its outlet near Padang Panjang, which was largely completed during 1834. It was by means of this road that van den Bosch planned to replace private traders and their carriers with a 'government transport-establishment' and bullock carts. In fact this 'transport-establishment', which had been meant to be at the service of the NHM, was very quickly overwhelmed by the needs of the army before Bonjol.[116] Army requirements continued to have priority even after 1837, and the NHM was left to fend for itself, competing on the open market for carriers and often having to pay them high wages.[117] In the meantime the new road greatly lightened the burdens of the Minangkabau trader, and it was reported in 1836 that about 2,000 people used the road daily.[118]

Consultations concerning the acquisition of Minangkabau coffee continued between Padang, Batavia and The Hague throughout 1835, 1836 and 1837. Van den Bosch in The Hague still refused to entertain the notion of forced deliveries while the pacification of Minangkabau was not complete. With Bonjol as yet unconquered, the Minister was opposed even to increasing the territorial duty in a further effort to discourage private traders. However, in a letter of March 1837 he was prepared to contemplate this prospect; after a few years of peace and consolidation he agreed that the territorial duty could be raised to such an extent that it would depress the market price of coffee and growers would be obliged to sell to the government at whatever 'protected price' was offered.[119]

In the meantime the NHM agreed in 1837 to extend its initial contract with the government, and the same agreement was reached in the following two years.[120] By this time it was convincingly apparent that the plan to eliminate the peasant trader in the interior had been a total failure. It was estimated that thousands still earned their living in the coffee trade. From the Dutch point of view they were:

. . . swindlers, who hold discussions, give advance payments, and make themselves masters of the coffee in order to sell it to the third, fourth and fifth hand before it finds its way to the lowlands; these are the individuals who run off with the profits and who by their tricks such as wetting and soaking the beans, reduce the good quality of the coffee.[121]

Between 1 September 1838 and 1 September 1839 only 18 *pikul* of coffee could be acquired by the NHM in the highlands, and in the latter year the Padang Panjang depot was closed down. By this time world coffee prices were experiencing a decline, and the concept of a 'protected price' very soon died a natural death.

The NHM now altered its buying strategy. During 1838, when low prices kept the Americans away, the company began to buy up coffee on its own account. To compete successfully it concentrated on Padang, Pariaman and Air Bangis, where its offer of f.16 to f.17 per *pikul* was competitive with the prices of Chinese brokers, some of whom gradually switched to buying for the company. In 1839 it was so successful that of 91,000 *pikul* of coffee exported in that year, the NHM acquired 60,000. In 1841 and 1842 not a single *pikul* was bought for the government.[122] This new buying strategy in no way affected the peasant trading network, and by 1841 peasant trade in Minangkabau coffee was continuing in the mould of previous decades, with merely the addition of a new buyer on the coast. The system, as described in 1844, differed little from that of earlier years:

The coffee produced in the Padang Highlands is nearly all transported to Priaman, and then subsequently transported to the more distant Padang. Thus Priaman is the stapling-place to which every year 60,000 to 70,000 picols of coffee are brought for sale; the buyers of this coffee are, in addition to Mr. van den Berg, three or four Chinese, agents of other Chinese established at Padang and Batavia who forward them for that purpose both copper money and cloth, the latter of which they always sell for cash; the coffee bought at Priaman is transported to Padang by praauw, where part of it is given in payment to the Agent of the Factory, at between f.1 and f.2 above the buying prices, and part sold to other speculators in coffee and subsequently sent to Batavia . . .[123]

It is clear from this account that the Chinese coastal brokers readily adapted to accepting the NHM as a customer for coffee. Van den Bosch's original aim of sweeping away all 'private trade' in coffee had rested on the assumption that the coastal brokers would cease to be an independent factor in the commercial equation once the NHM came into direct contact with the Minangkabau producers. That the Chinese brokerage system persisted was due not only to the continuation of the peasant trade in coffee, but also to the other activities on the NHM on the Minangkabau coast. The NHM had an interest in the Minangkabau as consumers as well as producers. One of the main purposes behind the founding of the company had been to acquire markets for the products of the Netherlands' manufacturing industry, and in particular for its cloth. As far as Padang was concerned, this meant that NHM agents were in full agreement with van den Bosch's desire to get rid of the English agency houses, which specialized in the importation of Coromandel cloth. One of the chief tasks of the NHM factory at Padang was to try to supplant the trade in Coromandel cloth with a new trade in Dutch and Belgian manufactured fabrics. To do this it would be necessary not only to drive the English firms out of business, but also to transform the Chinese and Minangkabau brokers through whom they disposed of their cloth into factors for the NHM. As early as 1829 the purpose of the NHM agency at Padang was stated to be: '. . . to make it not the sole but the leading Establishment at Padang, which, with good administration, would lead the majority of Chinese and Native merchants to commit themselves to it and so attract to it the largest part of the trade of Padang'.[124]

It was the requirements of the cloth trade which ensured that the Chinese brokerage class at Padang and Pariaman also survived in the coffee trade. Quite early the NHM agency realized that the best entrée into the cloth trade on the Minangkabau coast was by way of the Padang Chinese. The Chinese community in Padang was reported in 1837 to contain about 1,000 souls, somewhat fewer than in the previous decade.[125] Some Padang Chinese even spoke a little English: 'They are next in rank to European merchants. They do not, as in Batavia, deal in small articles; this is all left to the Malays. Most of them are wholesale merchants, very intelligent, nearly all able to read, and apparently men of wealth'.[126] From 1830 two Chinese brokers in particular – Lim Bing and Li Ma-Ch'iao, followed by the latter's brother and successor, Li Ch'iao – worked very closely with the agency and were highly trusted.[127]

Before looking more closely at the fate of these Chinese brokers, the success of the agency's cloth business should be noted. For several years efforts to sell Netherlands cloth at Padang were ineffectual, and the NHM agent there was even forced to try to persuade the European agency houses to involve themselves in the trade in Netherlands cottons, which with one exception they declined to do.[128] Gradually, however, the very real powers of the Netherlands Indies government to affect commerce, the growing cheapness of manufactured fabrics and the willingness of Dutch manufacturers to adapt to Minangkabau tastes, led to the supplanting of Coromandel cloth in the market-places of Minangkabau. After a new tariff of duties was introduced at the beginning of 1838, raising the import duty on Coromandel cloths from six per cent to twenty-five per cent, their days on the Padang market were numbered. In 1834 only f.45,000 worth of Dutch cottons were sold, but by 1838 Dutch cotton and woollen manufactures made up over twenty-five per cent of the worth of all Padang's imports. In the same year f.1,573,294 worth of Dutch textiles were imported, compared to f.371,656 worth from British India.[129] By 1844 Coromandel cloth had virtually been driven off the Minangkabau coast, and the NHM was even making a success of selling Dutch cloth from its Payakumbuh depot.[130]

In this cloth-selling enterprise the company found that it had drawn upon itself the mantles of both the old East India Company and of the English agency houses at Padang, to become the leading foreign merchant importer-exporter of Minangkabau. This could not have been achieved without the close collaboration of the local brokers, particularly of the Chinese at Padang. But in its zeal to sell Dutch manufactured cloth, the NHM unwisely involved itself in the same difficulties that the VOC had experienced on the Minangkabau coast in the 1660s. The economic position of the Chinese at Padang was based on their commercial acumen and reliability, and their ability to attract outside credits. The sudden rapid expansion of the NHM cloth trade after 1836 rested entirely on the simultaneous expansion of credit, which was soon found to have been grossly over-extended. Rather than replacing the coastal brokerage system, which it had neither the personnel nor the contacts to do, the agency vastly inflated the Padang brokerage class by following the example of the VOC in its early Padang days and granting long-term credits on easy terms to any likely individual who seemed a prospective promoter of the Dutch cloth trade. In Padang almost any Chinese was regarded as a suitable cloth broker, regardless of his means, and many former Minangkabau brokers who had been replaced by Chinese in the past decade were now also deemed to have suitable contacts for the sale of cloth, regardless of their lack of capital. At Payakumbuh the agency operated in the same way. Numerous Minangkabau small traders now set themselves up as brokers and willingly accepted credit for the sale of Dutch cloth in the highlands.[131]

In 1841 the crash came. A rush of claims on the Java Bank and the failure of a number of firms in north Java led to the revelation of the huge amount in outstanding debts at Padang; the NHM at Padang and Payakumbuh was found to have f.1,600,000 in uncollected debts, 'largely in the hands of impecunious Chinese and Malay traders'.[132] The company's agent was ordered to stop credit and collect the debts, and many of the Minangkabau brokers were particularly hard hit. Those who did not simply leave Padang or Payakumbuh were completely ruined and forced out of business; they themselves had extended credit to even more modest traders and were faced in turn with debts they could not collect. An NHM investigator in 1844 considered that even the most important Minangkabau brokers would never recover without some financial aid, and, as they were still useful in highlands trade, he recommended that this be granted to them. From the outset the company treated the leading Chinese brokers somewhat differently, especially those such as Lim Bing and Li Ch'iao who had long worked with the NHM, and granted them special terms on which to settle their debts and short credits in cloth with which to keep their businesses going.[133]

The 1841 crash again threw into relief the problems inherent in divising plans in Java or Europe to alter the social structure of Minangkabau trade. Both van den Bosch's coffee policy and the NHM's promotion of Dutch cloth were calculated to be certain to deliver the final blow to the English agency houses at Padang. Decades of expertise were, however, not to be so readily set aside. As a result of the 1841 crash, these firms experienced a new lease of life. Although we know little of their commercial histories, it seems that they now recognized the reality of Dutch control in central Sumatra and were prepared to be regarded as 'European' businesses, to the extent of cutting their ties with British India and moving into the orbit of the NHM. In the years following 1841 they adapted themselves to the position of coastal brokers for the NHM. The 'Europeanization' of these English businesses is exemplified in the metamorphosis of the firm of Townsend and Ingram. Townsend's son decided to enter into partnership with the son of the founder of the first Dutch agency house in Padang, A.F. van den Berg, and these two young men established their own firm. From 1836 they acted as brokers for the NHM cloth trade, being granted considerable credit. Their families' experience in this trade enabled them to survive the 1841 crash, and they also diversified into the coffee trade, opening up a connection with Tiku, where they bought up coffee carried down from the Lake Maninjau region.[134] By 1844 they were said to 'possess a moderate capital, have credit with the Agent and profitably engage in the cloth trade, chiefly at Priaman'.[135] By 1847 all the European firms had cut their losses in connection with the Coromandel cloth trade and were content to promote Dutch cottons. The NHM at Padang relied on them more and more, and old English firms such as W. Purvis were able to survive and continue in business by association with the NHM. Since none of these firms was adequately supplied with capital after the loosening of the Indian tie, they depended on their relationship with the company, and this was also true of one or two private Dutch enterprises which had joined the Padang scene.[136]

The Chinese coastal brokerage class took some time to restore itself and now had to take second place to the Europeans, who had staked out a claim in a field in which the Chinese had previously exercised commercial leadership. As late as 1847 it was reported that the Padang Chinese had not yet recovered from the losses of 1841, and only one Padang Chinese broker was regarded as a sound commercial risk by the NHM's agent. Nevertheless, they had the advantage of having built up contacts over the years with the European commercial firms, and they were able to continue in business trading with advances from these firms.[137] The Minangkabau coastal brokerage class also continued in existence, although it had descended even further down the commercial ladder. Its members became what an NHM official called 'subsidiary brokers'. Minangkabau petty traders bringing coffee down from the highlands never exchanged it with the Chinese directly for cloth or other goods, but acquired from them both American silver and the increasingly common and popular Dutch copper coinage, which had been introduced in 1828 to counteract the exportation of Dutch silver to Penang. This they took to a Minangkabau subsidiary broker to buy their necessities, and so the Minangkabau *pasar* of Padang and Pariaman continued to perform a useful function in the trading network.[138]

No really large-scale Minangkabau broker emerged from the class of subsidiary brokers on the coast, for the major part of the brokerage system was too firmly in foreign hands. As far as the petty traders of the highlands were concerned, however, in the late 1830s circumstances worked together to foster their activities, and the very reverse of what van den Bosch had calculated on occurred. Peasant trade was stimulated by the requirements of the Dutch cloth trade. The presence of the NHM in Payakumbuh provided a new source of credit for local traders, and even after the 1841 crash the established traders of Payakumbuh were regarded as creditworthy by the NHM and were advanced cloth and other goods to dispose of at the local *pasar,* although quick repayment was now insisted upon.[139] But even more than this, the presence of the Netherlands Indies army in the highlands promoted petty trade, as has already been noted. Provisioning the troops became a highly profitable enterprise, and was superimposed on the trade in coffee and cloth as yet another means of making additional earnings. Rice, vegetables and chickens all brought profits to the sellers. The demand for these items of daily consumption caused inflation in their prices; rice, poultry and oil were represented in 1839 as selling for three to four times as much as only a few years previously, and for the first time in many years the *sawah* villages near the main Dutch garrisons experienced economic advantage from the new regime in Minangkabau.[140]

At this point van den Bosch's economic tinkering experienced an unexpected setback. The petty trade in coffee remained structurally unscathed by his measures, but the hill coffee villages themselves found that the natural train of economic developments ensuing from the Dutch occupation hit them hard. For the first time in many years they were at a disadvantage in relation to the plains villages. Rice had become so expensive that this daily necessity could no longer be bought out of the profits of coffee cultivation and the planting of new cash crops had to be considered to bring in extra income. Often coffee beans were merely left to fall from the trees, or were left in water-pits to rot with only a few being removed to sell in small lots for certain necessities. More and more, coffee trees were not being replaced. Increasing monetarization at the main Dutch centres, which now included Payakumbuh where the NHM had erected expensive buildings and where large groups of people such as soldiers, artisans and carriers were all paid in cash, also placed the coffee growers at a disadvantage. All of this was the very reverse of what van den Bosch had hoped for; one of the basic notions behind the 'protected price' had been the incentive it was felt would be given to the expansion of coffee gardens. Instead, in certain old coffee regions, which were those nearest to the Dutch forts, the area under coffee seemed to be contracting. It was here alone that the coffee traders experienced that reverse which the policy of van den Bosch had not been able to induce, and they had to diversify to some extent, readapting themselves to trading in their villages' old staples of potatoes, cabbages and onions.[141]

Apart from this combination of economic circumstances, there was one Dutch policy measure which did hit the coffee trade hard, at least in the eastern part of central Minangkabau. This was the increasing effectiveness of attempts to ring-fence Minangkabau and cut off all its east coast trade, which it was intended to redirect westwards to Dutch ports. As early as 1825 Resident de Stuers had pointed out that, if there was to be any hope of ending the flourishing commercial relations with Penang and Singapore, access to all the headwaters of the east coast rivers rising in or near Minangkabau must be blocked by means of posts where traders should be required to pay both import and export duties.[142] Van den Bosch was also of this opinion. A special survey of the routes to the east coast *pangkalan* was made under van den Bosch's auspices after Limapuluh Kota had been taken in 1832, and it was concluded that their disruption was vital to the success of Dutch trade in that valley. Including even the rivers north of the Siak, van den Bosch drew up plans for forts to be erected at the highest navigable points on all the major tributaries of east coast rivers. These forts would operate not to raise duties, but quite simply to close the trade routes.[143]

The Netherlands Indies government thereafter pursued two parallel strategies to destroy the Minangkabau east coast trading network. The first was to establish small forts on the main routes out of Limapuluh Kota and adjacent areas, which discouraged traders from using these paths. The second was to enter into treaties with the sultans established near the mouths of the great rivers, whereby control of trade lower down the Minangkabau exit-routes would pass under Dutch 'protection'. A treaty of November 1833 with the Sultan of Jambi achieved this as far as the river Batang Hari was concerned, and in 1838 a similar treaty with the Sultan of Inderagiri had the same effect in relation to the river of the same name. Far to the north, the pursuit of Tuanku Tambusai had led to the establishment of a Dutch post on the east coast bay into which both the Bila and the Barumun emptied.[144]

The Minangkabau coffee traders who used the east coast routes were particularly affected by these measures, although it is unlikely that the bottling up of their exits drove them out of the trade; instead, they were forced to shift to trading via the west coast.[145] Those individuals of Minangkabau origin who were engaged in commerce lower down the great rivers certainly suffered a severe economic setback. By 1840 the European merchants of both Penang and Singapore were complaining that the east coast coffee trade now amounted 'to a very small part of what it did';[146] whereas in 1828 and 1829 the average monthly imports via the Kampar into Singapore alone had been nearly 1,000 *pikul*, in a twelve month period spanning 1836 and 1837 the two ports' imports of coffee from all the east coast rivers had been below a meagre 8,000 *pikul.*[147] Dutch statistics confirm this, and also the fact that far fewer British cotton fabrics were entering Minangkabau from Singapore.[148]

British complaints, which reached governmental level, were unable to alter Dutch determination in this matter, and the ring-fence imposed in the interior of Sumatra around Minangkabau stood fast. The outer ring-fence comprising the mouths of the east coast rivers was, however, forced to give way both to British pressure and, after the Batipuh revolt, to the very real financial inability of the Netherlands Indies government to support garrisons at such far-flung posts. By January 1840 another Minister had succeeded van den Bosch at the Ministry of Colonies, and a new King had succeeded Willem I in October of the same year. J.C. Baud, the new Minister, suggested to Willem II that, although van den Bosch's goal of the subjection of all of Sumatra up to the borders of Aceh must remain the final aim of Dutch Sumatran policy, it should 'no longer be considered an aim which must be pursued with every exertion'.[149] With this the King agreed, and the Governor-General of the Netherlands Indies was informed that van den Bosch's views on the subjugation of Sumatra should now be estimated to require a century to bring to fruition, rather than the original twenty-five years. In the meantime, all civil and military posts on the shores of the east coast, and all posts further inland which stood in direct connection with plans to occupy that coast, must be withdrawn.[150]

The Batang Hari, Inderagiri, Barumun and Bila posts all came under this rubric and were abandoned. As far as the Minangkabau were concerned, however, there was no relaxation of attempts to cut off their east coast trade. If anything, more determination was shown in policing the eastern borders and preventing the individual trader from getting through.[151]

NOTES TO CHAPTER VI

1 Elout to van den Bosch, 2 Feb. 1833, no. 13, van den Bosch 394.
2 J.S. Coleman, 'Nationalism in Tropical Africa', *The American Political Science Review*, xlviii (1954), 406, 409-10; idem, *Nigeria. Background to Nationalism* (Berkeley and Los Angeles, 1958), pp. 169, 172.
3 E. Stokes, 'Traditional Resistance Movements and Afro-Asian Nationalism: The Context of the 1857 Mutiny Rebellion in India', *Past and Present*, xlviii (1970), 104.
4 ibid.; Coleman, *Nigeria*, p. 172; J. Iliffe, 'The Organization of the Maji Maji Rebellion', *Journal of African History*, viii (1967), 495 *et seq.*
5 T.O. Ranger, 'Connexions between "Primary Resistance" Movements and Modern Mass Nationalism in East and Central Africa. Part I', *Journal of African History*, ix (1968), 437-9.
6 ibid., p. 453; T.O. Ranger, 'Connexions between "Primary Resistance" Movements and Modern Mass Nationalism in East and Central Africa: II', *Journal of African History*, ix (1968), 632, 634.
7 Stokes, 'Traditional Resistance Movements', p. 100.
8 For a discussion of the theoretical framework underlying this distinction, see A.D. Smith, *Theories of Nationalism* (London, 1971), pp. 171, 212-3.
9 Kathirithamby-Wells, 'Ahmad Shah Ibn Iskandar', p. 60; Kielstra, 'Onze kennis', pp. 518-20, 522.
10 De Haan, 'Naar Midden Sumatra', p. 352.
11 Netscher, *Padang*, pp. 29-30.
12 Kielstra, 'Onze kennis', p. 538; De Radicaale Beschrijving, ch. 2, par. 79, pp. 143-4.
13 De Radicaale Beschrijving, ch. 2, par. 80, pp. 144-5; par. 92, pp. 158-9; par. 94-5, pp. 162-3; par. 99, p. 173.
14 Kathirithamby-Wells, *West Sumatran Presidency*, pp. 160, 164.
15 Andaya, *Johor*, pp. 11, 112-3, 131-2, 149, 164, 250-73.
16 A. Oki, 'Social Change in the West Sumatran Village: 1908-1945' (Australian National University Ph.D. thesis, 1977), pp. 74-8, 175-90.
17 W.A. Hanna, 'The Role of the Minangkabau in Contemporary Indonesia', *American Universities Field Staff Reports*, vii (3), WAH-2-'59, 3.
18 Boelhouwer, *Herinneringen*, pp. 17-8.
19 Nahuijs, *Brieven*, p. 147.
20 Elout to van den Bosch, 24 Oct. 1831, L^{a}G, Exh. 8 May 1832, no. 2/A, MK 839.
21 Boelhouwer, *Herinneringen*, p. 79; de Stuers, *Vestiging*, i. 174; Lange, *Oost-Indisch Leger*, i. 309-10.
22 Memorie van toelichting, 11 Oct. 1833, no. 311, Exh. 9 Apr. 1834, no. 74^{k} Geh., MK 4233; van Sevenhoven to van den Bosch, 25 Dec. 1833, no. 205, Exh. 15 May 1834, no. 99^{k} Geh., MK 4233.
23 Elout to van den Bosch, 2 Feb. 1833, no. 13, van den Bosch 394.
24 Boelhouwer, *Herinneringen*, pp. 110, 151; Lange, *Oost-Indisch Leger*, i. 311.
25 De Stuers to van den Bosch, n.d. Mar. 1838, Exh. 12 Mar. 1838, L^{a}X, MK 4417.
26 Boelhouwer, *Herinneringen*, pp. 131-2.
27 Müller, *Berigten*, p. 27.
28 Elout to van den Bosch, 2 Feb. 1833, no. 13, van den Bosch 394.
29 Van Sevenhoven to van den Bosch, 25 Dec. 1833, no. 205, Exh. 15 May 1834, no. 99^{k} Geh., MK 4233; de Stuers, *Vestiging*, ii. 227, 230-1; 'Overzicht der gebeurtenissen', in Kielstra, 'Sumatra's Westkust van 1826-1832', pp. 364, 367-8.
30 Soekanto, *Sentot alias Alibasah Abdulmustopo Prawirodirdjo Senopati Diponegoro* (Jakarta, 1951), pp. 5, 12-5.
31 ibid., pp. 21, 29; de Stuers, *Vestiging*, i. 161; Kielstra, 'Sumatra's Westkust van 1826-1832', p. 353.
32 Van den Bosch to Elout, 5 June 1832, no. 1051 Kab., van den Bosch 243.

33 Van den Bosch to Elout, 24 May 1832, no. 951, in Kielstra, 'Sumatra's Westkust van 1826-1832', p. 353.
34 Van den Bosch to Elout, 5 June 1832, no. 1051 Kab., van den Bosch 243.
35 Elout to van den Bosch, 22 Feb. 1833, L^{a}C Geh., in E.B. Kielstra, 'Sumatra's Westkust van 1833-1835', *BKI*, xxxviii (1889), 166; de Stuers, *Vestiging*, i. 184.
36 Boelhouwer, *Herinneringen*, pp. 136-8; Lange, *Oost-Indisch Leger*, i. 317-8. 320-1.
37 Vermeulen Krieger to Elout, 22 Feb. 1833, no. 21, van den Bosch 394; Hendriks to Elout, 16 Mar. 1833, no. 18, van den Bosch 394.
38 Elout to van den Bosch, 23 Feb. 1833, no. 17, van den Bosch 394.
39 Besluit in Rade, 8 Mar. 1833, no. 1, MK 2846; Lange, *Oost-Indisch Leger*, i. 321-2, 324.
40 Kielstra, 'Sumatra's Westkust van 1833-1835', p. 174.
41 ibid., pp. 178-84; Lange, *Oost-Indisch Leger*, i. 323.
42 For an interesting discussion of the 'local crisis' and the traditional elite, see Stokes, 'Traditional Resistance Movements', pp. 102-3.
43 Elout to van den Bosch, 2 Feb. 1833, no. 13, van den Bosch 394; Lange, *Oost-Indisch Leger*, i. 331-2.
44 Elout to van den Bosch, 2 Mar. 1833, L^{a}E, in Kielstra, 'Sumatra's Westkust van 1833-1835', p. 173.
45 'Overzicht der gebeurtenissen', in Kielstra, 'Sumatra's Westkust van 1833-1835', p. 168.
46 De Quay to Elout, 2 Apr. 1833, van den Bosch 394; Lange, *Oost-Indisch Leger*, i. Bijl. B, pp. 474-5.
47 Kielstra, 'Sumatra's Westkust van 1833-1835', pp. 187, 189; de Stuers, *Vestiging*, i. 190-1.
48 Boelhouwer, *Herinneringen*, pp. 90-1; Lange, *Oost-Indisch Leger*, i. 326-7; de Stuers, *Vestiging*, i. 166.
49 Vermeulen Krieger to Elout, 17 Jan. 1833, no. 6, van den Bosch 394; van den Bosch to Clifford, 13 Sept. 1833, no. 253/E, Exh. 11 Feb. 1834, no. 38^{k} Geh., MK 4232.
50 Lange, *Oost-Indisch Leger*, i. 316-7, 343-7, 349-51; de Stuers, *Vestiging*, i. 197-9; 'Overzicht der gebeurtenissen', in Kielstra, 'Sumatra's Westkust van 1833-1835', p. 169.
51 Elout to Riesz, 15 Aug. 1833, in Kielstra, 'Sumatra's Westkust van 1833-1835', pp. 212-6.
52 Lange, *Oost-Indisch Leger*, i. 349-51; de Stuers, *Vestiging*, i. 197-9.
53 Riesz to van den Bosch, 10 Nov. 1833, no. 269, Exh. 9 Apr. 1834, no. 74^{k} Geh., MK 4233.
54 Elout to Riesz, 14 Jul. 1833, in Kielstra, 'Sumatra's Westkust van 1833-1835', p. 211.
55 Lange, *Oost-Indisch Leger*, i. 377-90; de Stuers, *Vestiging*, i. 204-6.
56 Müller, *Berigten*, p. 23; de Stuers, *Vestiging*, i. 200, 220.
57 Riesz to van den Bosch, 10 Nov. 1833, no. 269, Exh. 9 Apr. 1834, no. 74^{k} Geh., MK 4233.
58 Elout to van den Bosch, 3 Aug. 1832, no. 20 Geh., van den Bosch 393.
59 J.W. Ijzerman, *Dwars door Sumatra. Tocht van Padang naar Siak* (Haarlem and Batavia, 1895), p. 46.
60 Elout to van den Bosch, 3 Aug. 1832, no. 20 Geh., van den Bosch 393; de Stuers, *Vestiging*, ii. 23; Kielstra, 'Sumatra's Westkust van 1833-1835', pp. 189-90.
61 Hendriks to Elout, 16 Mar. 1833, no. 18, van den Bosch 394.
62 Lange, *Oost-Indisch Leger*, i. 335-8, 341-3; de Stuers, *Vestiging*, ii. 22-3; Kielstra, 'Sumatra's Westkust van 1833-1835', pp. 189-91, 193-4.
63 Vermeulen Krieger to Elout, 17 Jan. 1833, no. 6., van den Bosch 394; Kielstra, 'Sumatra's Westkust van 1833-1835', pp. 208-9.
64 Michiels to Merkus, 23 Mar. 1842, no. 538, in E.B. Kielstra, 'Sumatra's Westkust van 1841-1849', *BKI*, xl (1891), 136; see also Lange, *Oost-Indisch Leger*, i. 375, 385; Kielstra, 'Sumatra's Westkust van 1833-1835', p. 210.
65 Riesz to van den Bosch, 29 Oct. 1833, no. 250, van den Bosch 394; Lange, *Oost-Indisch Leger*, ii. 2-3.
66 De Stuers, *Vestiging*, ii. 22-4; Kielstra, 'Sumatra's Westkust van 1833-1835', p. 355; Rapport over de Krijgsverrigtingen, pp. 433-6, MK 4136.
67 Francis to Bauer, 10 Apr. 1835, no. 468 Geh., Exh. 1 Oct. 1835, no. 11, MK 994; Kielstra, 'Sumatra's Westkust van 1836-1840', pp. 134-5.
68 Ijzerman, *Dwars door Sumatra*, pp. 73-4.
69 Lange, *Oost-Indisch Leger*, ii. 73-4; Rapport over de Krijgsverrigtingen, pp. 455-9, MK 4136.

70 Francis to Baud, 23 Jan. 1836, no. 2, in Kielstra, 'Sumatra's Westkust van 1836-1840', pp. 138-9; see also ibid., pp. 134-5, 147.
71 Journaal . . . de Salis, 31 May 1837, Melvill van Carnbee 1.
72 Boelhouwer, *Herinneringen,* pp. 151, 161.
73 Elout to van den Bosch, 10 Sept. 1833, van den Bosch 394; Rapport over de Krijgsverrigtingen, pp. 460-1, 470, MK 4136.
74 Extract uit het Register der aanteekeningen en verrigtingen van den Resident van Sumatras Westkust, Exh. 9 Mar. 1836, no. 14, MK 1018.
75 Francis to Baud, 9 Oct. 1835, no. 102. Exh. 9 Mar. 1836, no. 14, MK 1018.
76 Bauer to Cochius, 21 Jul. 1835, no. 522, Exh. 8 Dec. 1835, no. 22, MK 1004; Francis to Baud, 24 Nov. 1835, no. 114, Exh. 31 May 1836, no. 17, MK 1031.
77 De Eerens to van den Bosch, 16 Aug. 1837, no. 154 L^{a}FF Kab., Exh. 18 Dec. 1837, Kab. L^{a}N^{6}, MK 4416.
78 Francis to Baud, 16 June 1835, no. 54, Exh. 5 Dec. 1835, no. 22, MK 1003.
79 Extract uit het Register der handelingen en aanteekeningen van den Resident van Sumatras Westkust, Exh. 16 Jan. 1836, no. 22, MK 1009; Kielstra, 'Sumatra's Westkust van 1836-1840', pp. 159-60.
80 Cochius to de Eerens, 29 Apr. 1837, no. 34/99, Exh. 23 Oct. 1837, no. 250, MK 4247.
81 Journaal . . . de Salis, 5 June 1837, Melvill van Carnbee 1.
82 Besluit, 3 Oct. 1837, no. 19, MK 2575; Michiels to de Eerens, 23 Jan. 1838, no. 26, van den Bosch 575.
83 Van Ronkel, 'Inlandsche getuigenissen', p. 1110.
84 Nota betrekkelijke de gevangen neming van den Toeanko Iman van *Bonjol,* 9 Nov. 1837, Exh. 19 Mar. 1838, no. 162 Geh., MK 4249.
85 Van Ronkel, 'Inlandsche getuigenissen', pp. 115-8, 1244-7.
86 Lange, *Oost-Indisch Leger,* i. 360, 367-8, 400; ii. 12-4, 18, 20, 30-1.
87 Extract uit het Register . . . , Exh. 4 Mar. 1835, no. 33, MK 962; Francis to van den Bosch, 23 Aug. 1834, no. 47, Exh. 28 Jan. 1835, no. 23, MK 957.
88 Rapport over de Krijgsverrigtingen, pp. 445-7, 450, MK 4136; Kielstra, 'Sumatra's Westkust van 1833-1835', pp. 467-70.
89 Bonnet to Francis, 11 May 1835, no. 138, Exh. 3 Nov. 1835, no. 9, MK 999; Cochius to Baud, 13 Oct. 1835, no. 1, Exh. 8 Mar. 1836, no. 4, MK 1017; Kielstra, 'Sumatra's Westkust van 1836-1840', pp. 157, 177.
90 Schnitger, *Forgotten Kingdoms,* pp. 79-81; Müller, *Reizen,* pp. 120-4; Lange, *Oost-Indisch Leger,* ii. 304.
91 Michiels to de Eerens, 12 Feb. 1839, no. 122, van den Bosch 575.
92 Lange, *Oost-Indisch Leger,* ii. 398-403.
93 Register der Besluiten van Zijne Excellentie den Kommissaris Generaal, 26 Sept. 1833, no. 277, van den Bosch 298; ibid., 20 Oct, 1833, no. 282, van den Bosch 298.
94 Kielstra, 'Sumatra's Westkust van 1836-1840', p. 175; Michiels to Merkus, 23 Mar. 1841, no. 445, in Kielstra, 'Sumatra's Westkust van 1841-1849', pp. 116-8.
95 Lange, *Oost-Indisch Leger,* ii. 401-3, 405, 413-5; Kielstra, 'Sumatra's Westkust van 1841-1849', pp. 107, 112.
96 Lange, *Oost-Indisch Leger,* ii. 424-5; Kielstra, 'Sumatra's Westkust van 1841-1849', pp. 110-1.
97 Mansvelt, *Nederlandsche Handel-Maatschappij,* i. 53, 64-5.
98 Rapport . . . , 21 April 1830, no. 315, Exh. 15 Sept. 1830, no. 6/A, MK 767.
99 Spengler, 1829, ANHM.
100 Granpré Molière, 1844, ANHM, p. 15.
101 Memorie van toelichting, 11 Oct. 1833, no. 311, Exh. 9 Apr. 1834, no. 74^{k} Geh., MK 4233.
102 Quoted in A.G. Hopkins, *An Economic History of West Africa* (London, 1973), p. 57.
103 Register der Besluiten van Zijne Excellentie den Kommissaris Generaal, 11 Oct. 1833, no. 310, van den Bosch 298; in 1828 the Netherlands Indies government introduced a new copper coinage into central Sumatra and f.9 silver became equivalent to f.10.80 copper. Unless otherwise noted, all prices quoted here are in silver.
104 Memorie van toelichting, 11 Oct. 1833, no. 311, Exh. 9 Apr. 1834, no. 74^{k} Geh., MK 4233.

105 Granpré Molière, 1844, ANHM, pp. 41-2.
106 Mansvelt, *Nederlandsche Handel-Maatschappij,* ii. 53-4, 61; E.B. Kielstra, 'De koffiecultuur ter Westkust van Sumatra', *IG*, x (1888), ii. 1446-7.
107 Memorie van toelichting, 11 Oct. 1833, no. 311, Exh. 9 Apr. 1834, no. 74^{k} Geh., MK 4233.
108 Kielstra, 'De koffiecultuur', p. 1438. With the Belgian revolt of 1830 Antwerp, the European port most used by the Americans, was no longer part of the Netherlands.
109 Kielstra, 'De koffiecultuur', pp. 1442-3; van den Bosch to Baud, 12 May 1835, Kab. Geh. L^{a}O/no. 2, Exh. 12 May 1835, Kab. Geh. L^{a}O/no. 2, MK 4404.
110 Memorie van toelichting, 11 Oct. 1833, no. 311, Exh. 9 Apr. 1834, no. 74^{k} Geh., MK 4233.
111 Merkus to van den Bosch, 6 Sept. 1839, van den Bosch 526.
112 Schuurmann to Baud, 9 May 1836, Exh. 1 Dec. 1836, no. 284 Geh., MK 4243; Kielstra, 'De koffiecultuur', p. 1443.
113 Plate to NHM Batavia, 23 Apr. 1835, Baud 429.
114 Francis to van den Bosch, 4 Sept. 1835, no. 90, Exh. 16 Jan. 1836, no. 22, MK 1009.
115 Francis to van den Bosch, 14 June 1836, no. 32, Exh. 18 Nov. 1836, L^{a}P^{5} Kab. Geh., MK 4410.
116 Plate to NHM Batavia, 23 Apr. 1835, Baud 429.
117 Granpré Molière, 1844, ANHM, pp. 21-2.
118 Francis to van den Bosch, 4 Oct. 1836, Exh. 16 Mar. 1837, L^{a}V^{i} Kab. Geh., MK 4412.
119 Kielstra, 'De koffiecultuur', pp. 1443-5.
120 ibid., pp. 1447-8.
121 Michiels to de Eerens, 4 Feb. 1839, no. 90, in Kielstra, 'De koffiecultuur', p. 1451.
122 Merkus to de Eerens, 23 Nov. 1839, no. 129/174, Exh. 12 May 1840, L^{a}V^{6} Kab., MK 4434; Kielstra, 'De koffiecultuur', p. 1448.
123 Granpré Molière, 1844, ANHM, p. 47.
124 Spengler, 1829, ANHM.
125 *The Missionary Herald,* xxxiv (1838), 402.
126 ibid., xxxi (1835), 297.
127 Granpré Molière, 1844, ANHM, p. 13.
128 ibid., pp. 15-6; Plate to NHM Batavia, 23 Apr. 1835, Baud 429.
129 Merkus to de Eerens, 23 Nov. 1839, no. 129/174, Exh. 12 May 1840, L^{a}V^{6} Kab., MK 4434; Mansvelt, *Nederlandsch Handel-Maatschappij,* ii. 58.
130 Granpré Molière, 1844, ANHM, pp. 15, 19-20.
131 ibid., pp. 7-9; Mansvelt, *Nederlandsche Handel-Maatschappij,* ii. 59.
132 Granpré Molière, 1844, ANHM, p. 9.
133 ibid., pp. 11-4, 17-8.
134 Travel Report no. 33, M.G. van Heel, 1842, ANHM, p. 4.
135 Granpré Molière, 1844, ANHM, p. 17.
136 Travel Report no. 39, W. Poolman, 1847, ANHM, pp. 6-7.
137 ibid.
138 Granpré Molière, 1844, ANHM, p. 49.
139 ibid., pp. 22-3.
140 Michiels to de Eerens, 4 Feb. 1839, no. 90, in Kielstra, 'De koffiecultuur', p. 1451; Mansvelt, *Nederlandsche Handel-Maatschappij,* ii. 60.
141 Merkus to van den Bosch, 6 Sept. 1839, van den Bosch 526; Granpré Molière, 1844, ANHM, pp. 38-40; Michiels to de Eerens, 4 Feb. 1839, no. 90, in Kielstra, 'De koffiecultuur', p. 1452.
142 De Stuers and Verploegh to van der Capellen, 30 Aug. 1825, L^{a}E no. 20, Exh. 24 Aug. 1826, no. 41, MK 513.
143 Van den Bosch to Elout, 26 Dec. 1830, Geh., Exh. 26 Sept. 1831, no. 28, MK 810; idem, 9 Jan. 1833, Kab. no. 16, Baud 316.
144 Lange, *Oost-Indisch Leger,* ii. 36-8, 336-7, 343-50.
145 Michiels to de Eerens, 4 Feb. 1839, no. 90, in Kielstra, 'De koffiecultuur', pp. 1449-50.
146 Anderson, *Acheen,* p. 239.
147 ibid., p. 14.
148 Baud to Buitenlandsche Zaken, 6 Apr. 1841, no. 142, in Kielstra, 'Sumatra's Westkust van 1841-1849', pp. 388-9.

149 Baud to King, 27 Aug. 1841, Zeer Geheim no. 358, Kabinet des Konings 4140.
150 Baud to Merkus, 1 Sept. 1841, no. 363/W Zeer Geheim, Kabinet des Konings 4140.
151 Baud to Rochussen, 3 Jan. 1846, L[a]A no. 3 Geh., in Kielstra, 'Sumatra's Westkust van 1841-1849', pp. 568-9.

CHAPTER VII

EPILOGUE: THE IMPERIALISM OF COFFEE, 1841-1847 AND BEYOND

In March 1822 Herman Warner Muntinghe, a member of the Raad van Indië at Batavia and the Netherlands Indies official who encouraged Willem I in the establishment of the Nederlandsche Handel-Maatschappij, wrote an extensive minute of advice to the Governor-General of the Netherlands Indies on the subject of the future of central Sumatra. Muntinghe had from 1807 held several important offices in the administration of the Netherlands Indies, and he started from a very clear premise: 'The expansion of *shipping* and of the *external* and *internal trade* of the Motherland is the chief aim and purpose of all her colonial possessions, just as it was the original cause of their establishment'.[1] The products of these possessions should in all cases, '*to the exclusion of all foreigners*',[2] be the preserve of the Netherlands' national trade and shipping, destined for direct carriage to the Netherlands and then distribution to the rest of Europe.

As far as central Sumatra was concerned, the Dutch had penetrated its interior little under a year previously, but the importance of its coffee production was already becoming known in government circles in Batavia. In Sumatra, where Netherlands merchants had not yet availed themselves of the opportunities open to them, Muntinghe's view was that 'measures should be introduced to bridle and curb foreign shipping and trade there; and, on the other hand, to foster that of the Netherlands and to place it in possession of its natural rights and advantages'.[3] In Java, where a system of free shipping and trade had followed the collapse of the VOC, Dutch merchants had been on the spot to take advantage of the benefits of such a system. The situation in central Sumatra was quite otherwise. Here the commercial successes of foreigners had meant the exclusion of both Dutch private enterprise and of the Netherlands Indies government from the profits of the coffee trade. Placed in this insupportable position, there was no other solution 'than that the Government immediately, for its own account, lays hands upon the entire trade of the *West Coast of Sumatra*'.[4]

Here we see expressed with stark clarity the thinking which so influenced both Willem I and Johannes van den Bosch in relation to the policy they pursued towards central Sumatra. The difficulties which they were to encounter were also clearly outlined by Muntinghe in his minute. Total exclusion of foreigners from the coffee trade was not, he felt, a practical possibility, any more than was a return to the old VOC monopoly system. No colony could be expected to survive for long without local incomes to defray the costs of administration and defence, and the duties paid by foreign traders at Padang were essential to the continuance of the Dutch presence in Minangkabau; monopoly was impossible because the Minangkabau, for the moment at least, had access to numerous channels outside Dutch purview through which they could export their coffee. Muntinghe's conclusion was that the Netherlands Indies government would for the time being have to rely on informal measures to gain a dominant position in the Minangkabau coffee trade. Dutch merchants at Batavia should be provided with information about Padang and encouraged to trade there; then, when Dutch shipping and trade had been stimulated, the question of interdicting foreign shipping completely could be reviewed, as also could the desirability of introducing some form of agricultural taxation into Minangkabau.

The Dutch imperial advance in Minangkabau in the nineteenth century provides a classic case of a crisis on the periphery of empire to which an imperial power was obliged to respond. In the development of this crisis, as we have seen, economic factors were present together with a considerable number of other variables. Recent research, particularly that of David Fieldhouse, has inclined to view these imperial 'crises of the periphery' as the outcome of a number of forces which were tending to create 'a disequilibrium between a "modernized" European and an unreconstructed outer world'.[5] In the case of early nineteenth century Minangkabau we should perhaps see the crisis more clearly if we thought of it in terms of a confrontation between two polities each equally intent on 'modernization' in its own terms. The Kingdom of the Netherlands was a newly-created European state with a ruler determined at all costs to industrialize and so modernize its northern half in the shortest possible time, with the state itself showing the way in many economic enterprises. The heartland of the Minangkabau world was responding to the new experience of becoming an important producer of agricultural commodities for the nascent world market economy. The transition to an agricultural export economy had imposed great strains on the polity, which had been met by the adoption of an Islamic fundamentalist ideology and an attempt to rationalize Minangkabau's commercial potential.

Islamic revivalism was Minangkabau's path to 'modernization'. Its aims were as suited to Minangkabau's needs as a newly-created commercial export sector of the world market economy as was Willem I's state-sponsored capitalism and industrialization to the position of the Netherlands in a newly-industrializing Europe. When the two societies tried to continue a relationship which had been evolved in an earlier century when both were 'unreconstructed', their basic goals were seen to be in conflict. The Netherlands could not pursue its aim of controlling economically dependent suppliers of primary agricultural products and turning them into consumers for its exports if Minangkabau was determined to sell its products on the open market, insist as far as possible on favourable terms of trade, and acquire its consumer goods likewise on the most favourable conditions. The clash between the Netherlands and Minangkabau was inevitable. In the Dutch-envisaged world division of labour which was to be a concomitant of the new world market system, the Minangkabau peasant coffee producer was actually to become, in the words of Jeffery Paige, a labourer 'who happens to control a small piece of land from which he "extracts his wages".'[6] All other functions in connection with the coffee crop were to be performed by Dutch owners of financial or industrial capital and their agents, to whom the role of processing, marketing and transporting the crop would fall.[7]

Arguing along these lines, we can agree with Fieldhouse that the economic interests of the Netherlands Indies government in Minangkabau after 1819 became politicized,[8] though not because of destabilization of the Minangkabau polity due to European pressure, but rather because the Minangkabau polity reorganized itself and presented a genuine challenge to certain European economic interests. Finally, after the development of a 'colonial sub-imperialism' based on Batavia, the home government itself stepped in to ensure that the Netherlands made the best bargain possible in her transition to formal empire in Minangkabau. We have already discussed the founding of the Nederlandsche Handel-Maatschappij and its use to strike this bargain in Sumatra. Nevertheless, by 1841 the imperial authorities were still not satisfied that they had achieved the most advantageous position open to them in this part of their empire: Minangkabau refusal to meekly hand over total control of their coffee crop to the private and public European personnel of the Netherlands Indies was a constant reminder that, after twenty years, Dutch policy was still foundering on the rock of Minangkabau's economic structure.

In 1834, very soon after the government of the Netherlands Indies began its efforts to acquire the Minangkabau coffee crop by the use of the Nederlandsche Handel-Maatschappij and the concept of the 'protected price', the Dutch Resident of Sumatra's West Coast, E. Francis, remarked in a letter to Batavia that forced deliveries of coffee were a possible solution to the apparent failure of the new scheme.[9] Both Batavia and The Hague were opposed to any such notion while the Minangkabau were not fully pacified, though it was clear by 1839 that the NHM's attempts to buy up coffee for the government in the interior had been a total failure, and the agency was forced to switch to the strategy of buying coffee on the coast on its own account, in competition with other buyers. As we have seen, the attempt to enforce a 'protected price' collapsed, the Minangkabau peasant trader flourished as before, and in 1841 and 1842 not a single *pikul* of coffee was bought for the government.

By the late 1830s Dutch authorities in Sumatra considered it was once again time to look at the whole question of acquiring Minangkabau coffee in such a way as to afford the greatest benefit to the Netherlands state. By this time practically the entire coffee-producing area of Minangkabau was in the hands of the Netherlands Indies government. The basin of the Solok plain with its surrounding hills, which had been left to itself during the wars against the Padris, was attacked and captured in February 1838. Subsequently the Minangkabau-inhabited regions to the south and east of the Solok plain were also taken over; in 1845 the gold-producing hills of Sungai Pagu behind Painan became the last major area to be forced into submission. From 1838 the Dutch Residency of West Sumatra was replaced by a Gouvernement (lit. Government), subdivided into the three Residencies of the Padang Lowlands, the Padang Highlands and, from 1842 until 1906, Tapanuli, comprising mostly Dutch conquests in the Batak lands and divided from the Minangkabau world by a line drawn near Air Bangis. The new Governor was Colonel A.V. Michiels, a man of restless determination and possessed of an unshakeable conviction concerning the rights of the Netherlands to the wealth of Sumatra.[10]

It was under this new administration that Netherlands Indies officialdom once again attempted to arrive at a solution of the coffee question more consonant with

Dutch interests. From the start of his administration Governor Michiels exhibited an almost obsessive concern with Minangkabau coffee. Putting on one side for a moment considerations relating to Dutch acquisition of the crop, as early as 1839 he began to elaborate plans to persuade the Minangkabau to grow more coffee and generally to become more productive.[11] This latter issue gave rise to a lengthy debate. Michiels was of the opinion that the government would actually have to involve itself in the process of coffee-growing if any expansion in the cultivation of this crop were to take place. His most important minute on the subject is markedly reminiscent of the VOC's efforts to turn the Minangkabau coastal brokers into supervisors of pepper cultivation in the last years of the company at Padang. Writing on 4 February 1839, he argued that to promote the cultivation of coffee the government must reach right down into the village and transform the Dutch-instituted village heads (*kepala negeri*) into 'superintendents of agriculture', with a salary of f.5 a month; further, the government should extend its involvement into the very household and, over a period of five years, require each lineage *penghulu* to be responsible for the planting of one hundred coffee trees a year by each family in his lineage, and for the delivery of the produce of these trees to the government at Padang, Pariaman or Air Bangis for a fixed price of f.12 per *pikul,* transportation to be effected at the *penghulu's* own expense.

For each *pikul* of coffee the government received from a particular lineage, the lineage *penghulu* would get half a guilder in copper for his supervision of the plucking and careful treatment of the beans, and he would also be given an advance of about half the worth of the estimated first year's crop to help bring the ground into cultivation: for example, in a lineage of thirty families, which would be required to plant 3,000 trees each year, from which in the first year of cropping 15 *pikul* of coffee worth f.180 could be expected, the lineage *penghulu* would be advanced f.90 to prepare the ground. Above the village level there would be additional supervision, to ensure that the lineage *penghulu* fulfilled their responsibilities. A *kepala laras* or district head would get a yearly payment of 20 cents for each *pikul* of coffee delivered from his district, and, at a higher level still, European government officials would carry out regular inspections to control the planting and good treatment of the coffee.

In addition to the direct involvement of the government in the economy of the Minangkabau village for the purpose of promoting coffee-growing, the other important aspect of Michiels' plan was that it represented a thorough-going attempt to implement van den Bosch's aims in connection with the private trade in coffee. In his minute Michiels proposed that private buyers be totally excluded from buying up coffee beans at coastal ports, and that the NHM once again revert to buying up coffee for the Netherlands Indies government. A final blow should also be struck at the peasant trader. The direct relationship between government officials and the lineage *penghulu,* established in the interests of increased coffee-growing, would, Michiels felt, once and for all remove from the scene this ubiquitous individual and so achieve one of the leading goals of Dutch policy.[12]

Michiels' proposals lay in abeyance because in late 1838 a Government Commissioner – P. Merkus, a member of the Raad van Indië – was appointed to investigate central Sumatran affairs. He arrived at Padang in July 1839, and very quickly joined the ranks of those who were alienated by Michiels' determined will and hearty, bibulous manner. One of his first acts was to remove the entire coffee question from the Governor's hands and place it in those of the acting Resident of the Padang Highlands, C.P.C. Steinmetz, whose views on the problem of Minangkabau coffee cultivation prevailed for the next five years. In these years the issue still revolved around the expansion of the coffee gardens, and there was inaugurated yet another period of attempted 'Javanization' of Minangkabau coffee-growing. Such a policy was almost as old as the Dutch penetration of the highlands, and it was to have a long and disastrous history. We have already seen how between 1825 and 1828 Resident de Stuers had employed two Javanese to teach certain plains villages in central Tanah Datar to lay down regular coffee gardens in the Javanese manner. The Minangkabau soon evinced their detestation of working in communal gardens and the gardens were quickly neglected and left to the ravages of decay.[13]

Yet it was upon this very system that Steinmetz looked with favour. Arguing, against the entire genius of Minangkabau coffee cultivation, that coffee grown in thick bushes around the house bore poorly and that the individual hill gardens were neglected and robbed of their fruit by wild animals, he issued regulations in January 1840 which ordered the establishment of village (*negeri*) coffee gardens, to be laid down on regular, Javanese principles. These gardens were to be organized on a district basis, using the waste land known as *tanah raja* where quarrels between villages had previously been settled by ritualized combat, and were to be under the supervision of the *kepala laras* or head of the district. Even the highlands valley bottoms were included in the scheme, although their ground and position were unsuited for coffee-growing.[14] The new system was bitterly resented by the Minangkabau and was a failure from the beginning. The fact was that, in the hills the traditional 'forest coffee' could not be bettered in terms of village resources; it made no heavy labour demands, requiring only partial clearing of the ground, and little maintenance of the closely planted trees, which could be left to themselves under natural forest shade. It also produced a good crop, if not in terms of yield per tree then certainly, due to the great number of closely growing trees, in terms of yield per garden. The 'forest gardens' also had a much longer life than did regular gardens.[15]

Minangkabau aversion to the new gardens was such that from the beginning of 1840 to the beginning of 1844 no more than 2,752,541 trees were planted in the central highlands region, representing a contribution of not more than nine trees per annum from each family. The early 1840s were bitter years for the Minangkabau. Not only were they faced with the prospect of hated work in communal coffee gardens, but in addition the price of coffee, after rising again in 1840 and 1841 to between f.15 and f.20 per *pikul,* suddenly plummetted to an unexpected low. Further, an epidemic which spanned 1842 and 1843 was estimated to have caused a staggering 80,000 deaths in the Padang and Padang Highlands Residencies. At the same time natural forces occasioned several consecutive failures of the rice crop, and the price of rice rose to unprecedented heights.[16]

Besides the continuing miscarriage of the Netherlands Indies government's labours to increase Minangkabau's coffee production, the plans relating to the trade in coffee outlined by Governor-General van den Bosch in 1833 remained unfulfilled by the mid-1840s. Both the peasant coffee trade and the competition which the NHM had to suffer from private buyers of coffee at Pariaman and Padang were unsolved problems. Authorities in The Hague, where J.C. Baud had succeeded van den Bosch as Minister of Colonies, considered that further attempts to withdraw coffee from private trade by increasing the territorial duty, a move which had been contemplated in 1837, were impractical considering the already oppressive nature of that duty.[17] And so the problem of private buyers of coffee continued. Padang Chinese brokers and their agents at Pariaman competed keenly with the NHM to buy up coffee, until their activities were checked by the 1841 crash. To the annoyance of the NHM, after 1841 a group of Batavia and Semarang Chinese entered the Minangkabau coffee market as buyers, turning the existing Padang Chinese into their agents and advancing them money to buy up both coffee and cassia. These Java Chinese competitors presented a serious challenge to the NHM because, unlike the Padang Chinese, they did not always sell the coffee they acquired direct to the Americans and were therefore not so concerned about the quality of the beans, buying up whole consignments which the NHM was unable to touch.

Moreover, the problem of foreign buyers for coffee remained unsolved. Although fewer American ships came than in the early days of the trade, they proved unwilling to stay away completely, and during the 1840s they were joined in the trade by certain French vessels. As late as 1847, at least one-third of the coffee sold at Pariaman and Padang passed into the bottoms of foreign ships and into the warehouses of ports which were not Dutch.[18]

There also remained the issue of the peasant trader. An NHM official sent to inquire into agency problems at Padang and Pariaman in 1844 estimated that 12,000 'tramps' earned their livelihood by bringing coffee down to the coast from Agam and Tanah Datar. Each trader or his carrier could cope on average with about two-thirds of a *pikul* of coffee, and each generally covered a distance of between five to six days in his downward journey, absorbing ten to twelve days of every month in one trading venture. Payment to carriers for transporting one *pikul* down to the coast was between f.6 and f.6½.[19] Using these figures as a basis for calculation, an NHM investigator in 1847 computed the share of the coffee trade which passed into the hands of the intermediate traders. At that time coffee was selling for between f.8½ and f.9 a *pikul* at Pariaman, while the grower was receiving between f.2 and f.3. Assuming that coffee exports stood at 70,000 *pikul* p.a., peasant traders and their carriers could acquire f.420,000 from the trade, compared with the growers' f.200,000 and the government's f.404,600 in export and territorial duties.[20] Transfer to the use of buffalo carts (*pedati*), although becoming more common in the upland valleys, had not taken place to the extent that peasant traders were disadvantaged, as van den Bosch had hoped. The road from Padang Panjang to the Anai gorge was still too difficult for wheeled vehicles, and there was no question at the moment of the government undertaking costly improvements.[21]

By the mid-1840s, therefore, Dutch policy in relation to Minangkabau coffee seemed to have failed on all fronts. The area under coffee cultivation had undergone little expansion, Chinese brokers and foreign buyers were still providing strong competition for the NHM at the ports, and the peasant trader had not yet been eliminated. The year 1845 marks the date when another round of intensive minuting consumed further reams of paper. It was apparent that a change of policy could be expected, and, in anticipation of this, coffee cultivation was removed from Steinmetz's hands and returned to the purview of Governor Michiels. Michiels' views were again sought by the Batavia government, and the Governor was able once more to elaborate his designs for Sumatran coffee, designs first outlined in 1839 and destined to have a tremendous impact on Minangkabau. Written with the hindsight of six years, Michiels' minutes on the subject of coffee still harked back to the need to involve the entire village administrative structure and in particular the lineage *penghulu* in the promotion of coffee cultivation; in a November 1845 minute he again set out in careful detail the number of coffee trees each lineage and each family in a lineage could be expected to plant annually.[22] In his mind, government interference was inevitable were coffee-growing to be expanded; coffee production in Sumatra had reached the heights of which it was capable 'as long as the population is left to its own, voluntary development'.[23]

As far as the intermediate trader was concerned, he too could only be removed by direct government intervention. The solution here, Michiels felt, would be found in a return to the 'protected price', reduced somewhat from the 1830s due to the lower world prices for coffee, and in the phasing out of all transport and intermediary costs by the use of unpaid forced labour (*heerendiensten*) to deliver the coffee to the coast.[24]

In addition to hearing Michiels' advice, the Batavia government consulted a number of other individuals with experience on Sumatra, including Steinmetz and employees of the NHM, several of whom had carried out investigations in Minangkabau during the 1840s. All NHM officials were at one with Michiels concerning the need for greater government involvement in coffee cultivation, and they were eager to support any scheme which would cancel the peasant trader from the commercial equation.[25] On 30 March 1847 Governor-General Rochussen gave Batavia's sanction to Michiels' views, and a new era of coffee cultivation began in Minangkabau, or more properly speaking in the Netherlands Indies Residency of the Padang Highlands. It was characterized by the payment of fixed prices to the peasant grower and the imposition on him of the requirement to compulsorily deliver his crop to the government at these prices. The *plakat panjang* or long declaration, that famous charter of Minangkabau liberties which had been issued on 25 October 1833 after Governor-General van den Bosch's visit, became a worthless scrap of paper. The new system involved the revocation of the all-important Article Five of the declaration, which had promised freedom to the peasant to sell his coffee crop to whomever he chose in the interior, or to bring it down to the coast.[26]

The remainder of the year 1847 was taken up with the framing of regulations for the new system of compulsory deliveries, which was brought into force from 1 November 1847. There were several important facets to the new system, bearing on the future of the peasant grower, the peasant trader, and the coastal broker and his foreign buyer. As far as the latter two were concerned, their persistence and expertise had proved invincible and they were allowed to pursue their existence under the incoming regulations. All coffee delivered to the government in the interior was henceforth brought down to Kayutanam and from thence, bypassing Pariaman, to Padang, there to be sold by the government itself at regular public sales. In these sales the NHM had no particular advantages, and had to compete with private buyers, who were still largely Chinese brokers, with one or two Europeans. Indeed, Michiels' aim now was to encourage foreign buyers to come to Padang, so that there would be more competition between them and coffee prices at the public sales would be driven up.[27]

Bypassing as it did the coastal buyers of coffee, it was against the intermediate traders that the new system was particularly directed. From 1 November 1847 no one in the Minangkabau interior was any longer free to buy up coffee or transport it for his own purposes. The government announced that it intended to build a number of warehouses – at least fifteen – in the main villages of the chief coffee districts, and the growers themselves were to deliver their own coffee to these locations. The grower was henceforth to be responsible for the cleansing, hulling and drying of his own beans, so that another function was removed from the intermediate trade. In a final *coup* against the peasant trader, within the highlands, and on the routes between the highlands and the coast, the government now undertook to arrange for the transportation of the coffee. For the two sectors Padang Panjang to Kayutanam, and Kayutanam to Padang, contracts were given to two well-known coastal brokers to provide transport. In December 1847 Michiels made a contract with the Padang Chinese Li Sa for the transport of coffee from Padang Panjang to Kayutanam and the transport of salt and other goods in the return direction. By now the Anai gorge road had been improved to the extent that wheeled transport could be used throughout, and it was envisaged that the contractor would use buffalo carts (*pedati*) on the route. For the lap between Kayutanam and Padang a contract was made with the European firm of W. Townsend, which also promised to use wheeled transport and outlined a tariff less than half that which had previously been paid to private carriers. Michiels was delighted with the prospect of the removal of private traders and carriers from these sectors:

> By the wheeled transportation of coffee and salt over a distance of 37 miles, approximately 500 coolies previously engaged daily in this work will now be completely released to attend to a more useful activity: agriculture, which will certainly gain by the release of so many able-bodied men, who up till now have occupied themselves with carrying loads and with swindling.[28]

By 1854 all transportation of coffee over the entire route from Padang Panjang to Padang was taking place by means of buffalo carts and horses. In the highlands a similar arrangement was gradually introduced, individuals contracting with the government to provide relays of carts and horses on a variety of sectors from the main coffee warehouses to more centralized depots such as Padang Panjang. By 1856 in the highlands too all major transportation of coffee was being done by means of carts and horses.[29] In the early years of the compulsory delivery system erstwhile coffee traders had very little success in acquiring these contracts, which largely went to *kepala laras* and *kepala negeri* who already had official connections with the government; over half of the early transport contractors in the highlands were *kepala laras.*[30] The day of the small private coffee trader was finally over.

The lynchpin of the new system was, of course, the Minangkabau coffee-growing peasant, and it is to his fate that we must now return. The system of compulsory delivery of coffee to the government was intimately bound up with Dutch administrative changes in Minangkabau, and these should be dwelt upon for a short time. After the Minangkabau rebellion of 1833 Governor-General van den Bosch had decided to retain the changes introduced in village administration during the 1820s, but he also considered that in future it would be advisable for the Netherlands Indies government to interfere as little as possible with the internal workings of the village. The tax on market-places in the interior was abolished, and the government was to rely for as much of its revenue as possible on customs duties and the new territorial duty on coffee. Van den Bosch's 1833 visit to Minangkabau was followed by the proclamation of the famous *plakat panjang* or long declaration to the people of Minangkabau which, in addition to dealing with matters relating to coffee, promised them that from then on village government would be undisturbed and that the Netherlands Indies authorities would respect *adat.*[31]

Nevertheless, it was made clear that the Dutch still required certain *penghulu* to be distinguished from others so that dealings with the village could be simplified, and these *penghulu* would continue to be paid out of government revenue. The whole tenor of Dutch policy was to create a Minangkabau 'aristocracy' which would see its fortunes bound up with Dutch interests, and the payment of salaries was regarded as a necessary step in this direction.[32] The attempt to create such an aristocracy was persisted in even after the original Dutch endeavour along these lines, the appointment of Javanese-style Regents, had quite clearly failed. By 1841 the Regents of Tanah Datar, Rao and Batipuh had been removed from the scene due to their rebellion, the Regent of Agam had died and was not replaced, it being quite clear that such a position had failed to command any support, the Regent of Limapuluh Kota was regarded as a nonentity, and the Regent of Halaban was confined to only a small district over which he had a personal influence.[33]

With the adoption of a policy of non-interference in village government the view from both Batavia and The Hague came to be that only gradually would a Minangkabau aristocracy evolve, not by further appointment of Regents, but from the families of individuals paid by the Dutch, in the process of which the lineage administrative system would decay; Baud wrote in 1841 that the rule of non-interference 'must be scrupulously followed until the *democratic* principle, which is the reigning one practically everywhere in the Padang highlands, has been supplanted by the *aristocratic* principle. This can only be the work of time . . .'[34] Indeed, the original Dutch reforms in village administration in the 1820s did lead to the ossification of the *penghulu* system. Challenges for a *penghulu* title became increasingly rare, and these titles tended to remain in the hands of those families upon whom they had been settled when the Dutch administrative reorganization began. To this extent 'Javanization' became a reality in many villages, particularly those of the plains where families of rank and title maintained their position over the decades.[35]

The new coffee system of 1847 abruptly overturned the policy of non-interference in village life, to a far greater extent than had the decision to pursue the goal of creating a village aristocracy. From 1847 it was not only the leading *penghulu* of the village or the district whose collaboration the Dutch required; to ensure the expansion of the area under coffee, the interest of the *penghulu* at every level had to be aroused and retained. To achieve this a system of incentives was elaborated. Those villages which produced considerable quantities of coffee for the government warehouses were to be rewarded by extending payment to both the lineage *penghulu* and the *kepala negeri,* as well as to the *kepala laras* of the district in which the village was located. Payments were to be made monthly, on the basis of sixty cents per *pikul*, divided in the ratio of one-third for the *kepala laras,* one-third for the *kepala negeri,* and one-third for the joint *penghulu.*[36] Such a system negated the whole genius of Minangkabau coffee cultivation. Coffee had previously been so attractive to many a village family because, once permission had been given for the alienation of land, the growers were largely removed from the administrative purview of their lineage heads, and individual enterprise and dynamism were well rewarded. Now the coffee gardens, often out of sight of the village on distant ridges and slopes, moved perforce into the orbit of the village administrative establishment.

European official interest also descended on the village. A new administrative level staffed by Europeans was created by subdividing the Residency of the Padang Highlands, itself formerly an *afdeling* or division, into *afdelingen* corresponding with the old 'Regencies' or political divisions, such as Tanah Datar, Agam, Limapuluh Kota, Rao etc. Since the Regency system had failed, it was decided that what was done on Java by the Regents would have to be done in Minangkabau by European officials, either by Assistant Residents for the *afdelingen* or by *controleurs* for one or several districts. The Dutch-staffed levels of the administration were rearranged and renamed throughout the nineteenth century, becoming larger and more complicated, whilst the Minangkabau village administration, headed by the *kepala negeri* and the *kepala laras,* remained unaltered until 1914.[37]

European officials now became directly involved in the village economy, and their duties included regular inspection of the coffee gardens. In this way both European officialdom and *penghulu* supervision intruded upon the lives of all those peasants for whom previously the planting of coffee trees had provided an escape from conventional norms. In particular the *penghulu* became agents of government coffee cultivation, and this was the major task left to them once the village administrative system began to decline during the nineteenth century. On behalf of the government, and acting on the instructions of European officials, they were obliged to interfere constantly in the peasant's cultivation of coffee. Government officials had opinions on where to plant, how to plant, what trees to use for shade and so on. This interference bore especially heavily on the hill villages, which were of course the mainstay of the coffee system. The Dutch *controleur* intruded himself at all stages of the peasant's coffee-growing activity: the grower now had to terrace the land, clear it, plant a suitable shade crop and regularly prune his trees, all to suit the particular notions of the local *controleur,* who inspected the gardens every September to observe the progress of the seedlings. Often new gardens were ordered to be established in localities where soil was unsuitable, or in places too far from the village; sometimes the trees chosen as a shade crop merely smothered the new seedlings.

The worst example of misplaced official interference was in the 1860s when, in an attempt to include the upland plains villages in the expansion of coffee-growing, orders were given to pen cattle in communal corrals and so free open grazing land for planting coffee. This resulted in an epidemic of cattle sickness which killed a large proportion of the buffalo and cattle herds of the highlands. The September visit of the *controleur* was not the end of this official's annual involvement in coffee-growing. He made another inspection visit every March, to view the new trees, count and grade them and order the removal of inferior ones. Nor was this all. In his absence, the lineage *penghulu* on their own authority were entitled – indeed obliged – to supervise the crop. Demands for quality control were particularly onerous. It became impossible for the grower simply to pick all the beans at once in a certain period of the year, sell them and turn to some other enterprise to augment his livelihood. Now he had to wait for each successive set of beans to ripen, pick them, process them and then deliver them to the coffee warehouse. According to one Dutch estimate, for each *pikul* of coffee delivered to the warehouse, a family expended some one hundred and twenty days of labour.[38]

For some years the government was satisfied with the returns from the compulsory delivery system. Exports increased markedly over earlier years, for the peasant had nowhere else to dispose of his crop and the increasing monetarization of the economy and the rising prices of basic necessities such as rice obliged him to pursue that branch of agriculture he knew best. In 1857 191,000 *pikul* were exported, although it should be noted that the Batak lands and the southern Minangkabau hills, such as the Sungai Pagu area, had a share in these exports. Coffee cultivation was introduced among the Bataks on government initiative about 1840, and after 1845 the Tapanuli Residency contributed at least 20,000 *pikul* to the annual export figures. In 1862 the government payment for coffee was increased because of the increasing dearness of rice and other daily necessities; the new prices were f.11 per *pikul* for the best quality beans, and f.5 for the lower quality.[39]

The years between 1847 and 1862 were the 'bloom period' of the compulsory delivery system. Thereafter a gradual aversion towards coffee cultivation evolved among the Minangkabau. Government prices offered at the highlands depots were well below the buying prices at Padang; in 1856, for example, the government's buying price in the interior was f.7, yet the selling price at Padang was f.30.[40] By paying the growers well below market prices, all incentive to expand coffee was removed. Not only was coffee-growing no longer considered to be a profitable activity in terms of income, but it also lost its attractiveness in terms of that social freedom which had been the lot of the coffee grower in the past. Elizabeth Graves in her work on this period has pointed out that the entire system was pervaded by coercion; all the force of government sanctions was required to keep up production statistics, and the daily registers of local Dutch and Minangkabau officials for the 1860s which she consulted show that punishments were imposed for neglect of duties associated with coffee cultivation in the same way as for failure to perform corvée tasks. Even those plains villages where coffee could not succeed did not escape the burdens associated with the successful prosecution of the system; corvée labour was required for the major building and road projects concomitant upon the compulsory delivery of coffee, and this labour was recruited largely from the plains, from villages situated near the major administrative centres of Batu Sangkar, Bukit Tinggi, Solok and Payakumbuh.[41]

By the 1870s popular revulsion towards coffee cultivation was only too apparent.[42] Writing in 1870 one Dutch official in the highlands noted the decline in coffee production in the villages on Mount Merapi and Mount Talang.

The modern traveller traversing these regions finds hardly a sign of life anywhere. Nowadays the mountain range extends as if dead and abandoned, covered as with a shroud by the drab *ilalang,* from the proud Merapi down to the still active Talang in the Southwest; and the solitary dwelling, visible in the distance due to its high roof with pointed horns, only enhances the atmosphere of desolation, of undisturbed, deathly peace which characterizes the mountains.[43]

Outlying coffee-producing areas which had been important in the Padri period now experienced a decline because of their distance from a delivery warehouse. In the 1820s and 1830s the villages of the Sumpur valley had produced much coffee and delivered it to Durian Gedang on the Inderagiri; now coffee had to be brought to the warehouse at Buo in an adjacent valley, thirty miles away. In 1885 it was noted that, whereas Durian Gedang before 1847 had exported between 800 and 1,000 *pikul* p.a., now it stapled no coffee at all:

. . . traders came here, sometimes even with sea-going vessels, to buy up coffee from people and to exchange it for trade goods. The entire region between Soempoer and Doerian Gedang, a length of 20 miles, was then well populated and prosperous; now one rides through a wilderness.[44]

In 1878 the government's response to these developments was to introduce, in addition to compulsory deliveries, compulsory cultivation of coffee in all areas where coffee had been shown to have succeeded in the past. New regulations were also introduced to effect the upgrading of gardens and to bring their layout into conformity with Javanese models. Nevertheless, despite the enforcement of penalties for neglect of coffee gardens, the interest of the Minangkabau in coffee cultivation could not be revived. By 1886 coffee exports had plummetted to 48,000 *pikul.*[45] In the following decade, with much exhausted land already out of commission, it was concluded that the administration of West Sumatra could no longer be based on profits from coffee. The Netherlands Indies government gradually worked out a system of monetary taxation for Minangkabau, and this was introduced in 1908. In the same year the system of forced delivery of coffee was brought to an end.[46]

Given that we have consumed so much space outlining the rise to prominence of the hill villages of Minangkabau in terms of their success in the coffee trade, it seems legitimate to wonder whether the gradual decay of coffee-growing brought with it the collapse of the economic and moral foundations of the hill village. Such a question is all the more justifiable because, among the hill villages' economic activities, it was not solely coffee-growing which declined. The weaving industry suffered severe blows from European imports; as early as the 1860s hill weavers were having to change over from producing cloth for everyday use to the production of a few prestige types of cloth, often of silk with gold thread, which were dear and had a limited market. As a concomitant, cotton-growing in the lowlands decayed, and indigo-growing in the hills had also virtually died out by 1880.[47] The iron-smelting industry too collapsed, in the face of cheaper imported European iron.[48]

Yet nothing could be more misleading than to see in the decline of these traditional economic activities the collapse of the long-standing economic flexibility of the Minangkabau peasant, particularly the peasant of the hill slopes. Here the work of B. Schrieke on the Minangkabau economy in the early twentieth century is open to criticism as lacking in historical perspective. Schrieke's notion of an 'agrarian revolution'[49] in Minangkabau in the second decade of the twentieth century postulates a blanket of economic stagnation enveloping the sleeping Minangkabau world prior to the magical kiss delivered by Dutch economic policy in the shape of the ending of compulsory coffee deliveries in 1908. It is from this date that Schrieke sees the Minangkabau peasant adopting an 'economic mentality'[50] and a 'growing individualism',[51] so different from anything in the past that he feels the term 'Revolution in Outlook'[52] is appropriate.

> A period of declining production, during which the people, glad, as it were, to be freed of a compulsion they loathed, discontinued cultivation, was followed by a period of unprecedented revival. Here we have to do with a revolution in spirit, similar to that of the early capitalist period in Europe, as indicated by Max Weber and Sombart. The 'economic mentality' has made its entry upon the scene.[53]

Schrieke is referring to the beginning of rubber cultivation in the Minangkabau highlands and the expansion of free coffee-growing in outlying areas. But we have already seen how these 'economic revivals' litter the pages of Minangkabau history, particularly once Minangkabau began to be drawn into the world market economy. Hundreds of Minangkabau migrated from the uplands to the coast to pursue pepper cultivation in the sixteenth and seventeenth centuries, and these coastal pepper growers where possible readily changed over to cultivating cotton when the imposition of compulsion and price fixing in pepper-growing made reliance on that crop distasteful. Two centuries later, the growers of coffee showed a similar flexibility. Although we lack research monographs on the economic history of late nineteenth century Minangkabau, it does seem quite clear that Schrieke's economic 'revolution' can be dated from the very moment a particular village began to find coffee cultivation onerous and unrewarding. In the Minangkabau heartland there were already well-tried crops which had brought prosperity to certain villages well before the coffee boom. It was to these that the Minangkabau now turned, and it is true to say that as early as 1856 coffee began to lose its quantitative lead over other crops.

The hill villages had the good fortune to be thoroughly familiar with the growing of two items important in the internal trade of central Sumatra, tobacco and sugar. In the mid-1850s tobacco began to be planted on a larger scale than ever before, particularly in the hill villages of Limapuluh Kota, in the hills around the Solok plain, and on the banks of Lake Singkarak.[54] Already in the late 1860s a Dutch official noted the villagers' growing preference for these crops over coffee.

The Malay prefers his own crops, especially tobacco cultivation, for which the ground here seems to be very well suited. This crop of the people [*volkscultuur*] is expanding more and more, and around lake Singkarah there is much land which was formerly planted with coffee and has now been transformed into tobacco fields.[55]

Gradually, with better drying and preparation, tobacco also entered external trade. The highest annual export figures for tobacco before 1880 was 682 *pikul*, but in 1897 10,000 *pikul* were exported, with an average between 1880 and 1898 of 5,500 *pikul* p.a. and a total worth over that period of f.5,500,000.[56] The cultivation of sugar for the home market also greatly increased; in 1877 'most extensive plantations between Padang-pandjang and Fort-de-Kock'[57] were reported, all in hill areas, and sugar was also growing prolifically in the hills around Batipuh.[58]

Crops which had been profitable in external trade in the late eighteenth century now also gained a new lease of life. Cassia expanded greatly after the imposition of forced coffee deliveries; prices were high in Europe, there were customers, and many new trees were planted. The crop even spread to villages which had not been traditional cassia producers, such as those in the hills around the Solok plain.[59] Cassia exports increased from 1,379 *pikul* in 1858 to 8,656 *pikul* in 1868, and then, after a period of decline, doubled during the 1880s and 1890s when prices rose markedly. The export of gambir, still a speciality of Limapuluh Kota, rose from 16 *pikul* in 1867 to 1,682 *pikul* in 1875 and 7,800 *pikul* in 1899.[60]

It was not only the hill villages of the Minangkabau interior which were finding new markets for their products. The west coast was another region which had in the past been ready to involve itself in agricultural commodity exporting. Here, particularly around Pariaman, where there was a long tradition of growing and working with coconuts, world demand for copra led to an easy transition to its production. From Padang in 1879 only f.50 worth of copra was exported, yet in 1898 copra worth f.819,000 was sent from the port, and the average exports per annum between 1880 and 1899 were worth f.400,000.[61]

One result of this movement into crops other than coffee was that the small highlands trader gradually recovered his livelihood. Excluded from the coffee trade, he simply turned his attention to trade in other agricultural commodities and resolutely defeated the planners' designs to remove him from the market-place.[62] The Netherlands Indies government-sponsored Sumatra Expedition of 1877 opened the section of its report on trade with the words: 'Everywhere in Central Sumatra an active trade is carried on; the Malay is no less a trader than a cultivator, and he exhibits in his bargaining an endless patience.'[63] The expedition's members were struck by the evidence of flourishing market-places everywhere throughout the highlands and by the bustling activity of the weekly market days.[64] The big market-places of Bukit Tinggi, Batu Sangkar, Payakumbuh and Padang Panjang, which were now urban centres, attracted more and more participants as the nineteenth century progressed, and their markets came to operate on a daily rather than merely a weekly basis. On one day in 1904 a Dutch official at Bukit Tinggi counted 29,000 individuals on nearby roads on their way to the market there, and this he considered not to be a particularly busy day. A similar count in 1879 had given a total of 15,000 to 16,000 marketgoers.[65]

Most marketing activities were still in the hands of small traders, operating with credit from a slightly larger trader or pooling capital in temporary partnerships. Very few Minangkabau developed into wholesale traders, although there were one or two exceptions at the main highlands centres.[66] These individuals were often from *penghulu* families and had generally acquired their status and capital by the early start they were able to get in the nascent transport industry, contracting with the government for the supply of buffalo carts to move government coffee. Transportation gradually became an important business, serving not only the government's needs but also those of small traders who found that to remain competitive they too needed to hire wheeled vehicles or horses to move their merchandise.[67] In 1904 the number of police-registered hire-carriages (*huurbendi*) at Bukit Tinggi was 531, compared to 125 in 1892. In the whole of Limapuluh Kota there were only 33 hire-carriages registered in 1885, a number which had risen to 1,020 in 1904.[68]

On the coast the Minangkabau brokerage class remained stunted in its potential. In the late nineteenth century the same situation prevailed there as when van den Bosch had laid his plans to drive away the major foreign coastal brokers. At Padang in 1877 there were still five European firms, including some of English origin dating from the turn of the century, and Chinese brokers still carried out important brokerage functions at the port. Well into the twentieth century Chinese brokers were handling those Minangkabau agricultural commodities which were destined for overseas markets. As van den Bosch had prophesied, once they were able fully to establish themselves in the highlands the Chinese competed successfully with the Minangkabau as wholesale traders and brokers; the tobacco trade of Payakumbuh, for example, passed completely into their hands once tobacco became a commodity in foreign trade.[69]

There was another way in which the hill villages adapted to the exigencies of Dutch rule. Just as in the long run they could not be forced to part with a crop they refused to grow, so they were exceptionally quick to see a possible way out of the bonds which sought to tie them to one particular function in the imperial world-wide division of labour. In the wider world of knowledge and education, confinement to a particular niche was not so easy to achieve. Elizabeth Graves' work on the development of an independent school system in the hill villages of Minangkabau from the 1840s offers further evidence of the ability of these villages to adapt to the norms of the *rantau,* the outside world, and to seek to master them for their own purposes, just as in the past they had become adapted to the cultivation of agricultural commodities for the world market and, before that, to the acquisition of the skills of the artisan and the craftsman. The hill villages' school network arose in response to the needs of the colonial government, which in turn evolved according to the administrative demands made by the new coffee system. Coffee deliveries necessitated the construction of government warehouses, smaller ones at the chief market centres of the main coffee-growing areas, and larger ones at administrative centres and strategic locations such as

Padang Panjang. These warehouses required personnel, who could only be recruited locally and for whom the government itself had to pay. The only European in the entire system was at the headquarters warehouse for the highlands, located at Padang Panjang. All other positions were held by Minangkabau, to whom in 1847 were thrown open five posts as district warehousemaster (*pakhuismeester*), eleven as sub-district warehousemaster and forty as clerks distributed among the various warehouses. For the first time there was revealed to Minangkabau in the highlands the possibility of a career in the service of the colonial government.[70]

It was this Minangkabau coffee adminstration personnel which came to form the nucleus of a Minangkabau bureaucracy. As coffee-growing had done in the past, a position in the coffee administration now provided the means whereby determined individuals without many assets in the village could find a wider field for their energies. The original requirements for the position of warehousemaster were literacy in Malay and a rudimentary knowledge of bookkeeping, since the warehousemaster was obliged to keep all the records for coffee production in his district. His pay was f.20 a month, which was equivalent to that of many *kepala negeri,* and in addition to this he had an ample field of patronage for relatives and friends, because each coffee delivery area gradually built up administrative teams far larger than the few original office clerks. During the nineteenth century, as the European-staffed administration of the Government of West Sumatra expanded, there were increasing opportunities for Minangkabau on the lower rungs of the civil service, as agricultural inspectors and supervisors, as office clerks and secretaries, as messengers and so on. Gradually families which specialized in civil service jobs evolved, just as previously certain families had specialized in artisan activities, trade, or teaching religion.

According to Elizabeth Graves, it was middle level socio-economic groups in the hill villages, particularly villages in coffee-cultivating regions, which grasped the opportunities offered by these new appointments. These groups already had a well-developed tradition of leaving the village for trade or to pursue a craft. They also had long encouraged their young men to leave home for study at important *surau,* which meant that they had the initial advantage of being literate in Malay. In the early 1840s, after a personal initiative by a Dutch official, certain of these villages decided to establish secular schools, from which religion as a subject would be specifically excluded, and which they would supervise and finance themselves. From the beginning Dutch involvement in these schools was minimal. By 1846, even before the warehouse system came into operation, there were eleven of these schools; five were located in regional headquarters towns in the upland plains, at Bukit Tinggi, Batu Sangkar, Payakumbuh, Solok and Sijunjung in the south, but the remainder were in important market, and later warehouse, centres for hill-country coffee districts, at Bonjol, Puar Datar in Limapuluh Kota near Suliki, Maninjau on the banks of Lake Maninjau, Sungai Puar on the slopes of Mount Merapi, Singkarak at the southern end of Lake Singkarak, and Buo. The subjects taught were those needed by government offices, particularly the copying of documents and bookkeeping. By 1846, only three years after the first schools opened, seventy-five pupils had been placed as clerks in government offices, in the offices of the *kepala laras,* or as supervisors over cultivation activities.

What is striking is the previous connection with the Padri movement of those villages which decided to support schools. Moreover, schools which opened later, in the 1850s and 1860s, were also established by hill villages where the Padri movement had taken root; Halaban is only one example. Equally striking is the fact that not one rice plains village bothered to establish its own school. Those located in administrative centres form an exception and owed their existence to the rapid urbanization of these centres from the 1830s, when towns such as Bukit Tinggi grew due to the influx of artisans, traders and so on. The Bukit Tinggi school in fact attracted pupils not from the Agam rice plain, but from villages in the nearby foothills. In general *penghulu* families, particularly in the plains, resisted such schools, and they became the preserve of those hill families which eagerly recognized an alternative to their traditional occupations, among whom families with an historic orientation towards agriculture, trade or religion were equally represented.

And so it was that civil service dynasties developed in Minangkabau. After the Dutch reorganization of education in the 1870s, families with a foothold in the civil service found that their initial investment in education had paid off handsomely. Now vistas of educational opportunities in Java and even in the Netherlands were opened to them, as were Indies-wide administrative positions and, later, secular professions such as medicine and the law. The case of Agam is particularly instructive. In the 1780s and 1790s its Islamic *surau* had responded rapidly to the problems posed by the new commerce in agricultural commodities; in the early nineteenth century its hill villages, where these commodities were grown, had attempted to reorganize their polity to cope with the effects of the new agricultural and commercial pattern; in the 1840s, with the failure of their rebellion and faced with the realities of colonial rule, certain families in these villages decided to look for advancement on the best terms available. They proved to have chosen wisely. Whereas in the past these villages had produced family clusters of traders or artisans, they now produced clusters of schoolteachers, bureaucrats, doctors or lawyers, certain families often specializing in a particular kind of 'intellectual profession' in the same way other families specialized in a particular trade. A major component of the twentieth century Indonesian élite emerged from the hill villages of Agam, and this élite proved fully equipped to deal with Dutch imperialism when the time came.[71] In this respect the hill villages of Agam continued the struggle of their Padri forebears, no longer armed with an ideology spawned by Wahhabi Arabia but rather with one which was the outcome of historical developments in Western Europe.

Does the emergence of this 'secular élite' imply a reversal in the fortunes of Minangkabau Islam? Much research still remains to be done on Islamic developments in Minangkabau after the Dutch conquest, but without doubt the emergence of a Minangkabau secular élite from formerly Padri villages should not be taken to mean that the significance of Islam in Minangkabau society was thereby negated. However, without further research it is not possible to construct a religious geography and sociology of post-1847 Minangkabau Islamic movements similar to that which has been attempted for the period prior to 1847. Available evidence indicates that the *surau* continued to play an important role in educating

Minangkabau youth throughout the nineteenth century, and both small village *surau* founded by one teacher and the major *tarekat surau* appear to have flourished. It was reported in 1869 that no reasonable sized village was without its own small *surau* where pupils learnt at least the Arabic alphabet, and many villages had two or three, often established by an individual who had returned from Mecca.

In the large *surau* belonging to the Sufi brotherhoods up to 1,000 pupils could be found at their studies at any one time. Still dominant were the *surau* established by the Naksyabandiyah and Syattariyah brotherhoods located mainly in villages with adequate *sawah* in the plains or in the foothills, and of course on the coast. In the highlands in 1869 it was estimated that there were fifteen major *surau*, and most of those had carried on a continuous existence since the eighteenth century at least. The largest ones were the Naksyabandiyah *surau* at Taram and at Cangking, each of which had 1,000 students. The Empat Angkat area persisted as an important locale for Syattariyah *surau*, and the Kota Tua *surau* there was estimated in 1869 to contain 200 to 300 students, with a similar number in a Syattariyah *surau* in a nearby village.[72]

Much of the energy of the *tarekat* leaders became reabsorbed in mutual squabbles. The period after 1847 right down to the 1890s was marked by a reflorescence of the Naksyabandiyah *tarekat* and by attacks made by its leaders on the Syattariyah as heretical. In certain villages the situation developed of members of one *tarekat* refusing to attend Friday prayers if the *imam* of the village mosque was a member of the rival *tarekat*; sometimes things went so far that a second mosque would be erected.[73] However, without further research it is impossible to determine to what extent such disputes were related to the rise of new forces in a village; much of the old fluidity of the lineage system had ossified under Dutch administrative regulations, as had the scope of debate in the village council, and it is likely that certain rising families or lineages in a village adopted alternative modes of expressing themselves, such as founding a new mosque.

We are also entitled to ask, to what extent adherence to Padri tenets did in fact decline? Many of the administrative reforms instituted by the Dutch in the Minangkabau village were similar to those for which the Padris had agitated. Where certain reforms could not be implemented by a colonial government, the Padri legacy was undoubtedly powerful enough to be revivified from Mecca on occasion. In the 1890s Minangkabau was swept by an orthodox reform movement, although, lacking adequate research on the subject, it is difficult to draw many conclusions about it. Its motivating force was Syekh Ahmad Chatib, a descendant of a Padri *kadi* and a native of the goldsmithing village of Kota Gedang near Bukit Tinggi, long noted for its important *surau*. Ahmad Chatib was a small trader in Agam who went to Mecca in 1876 and there became an influential teacher of Minangkabau students. His orthodoxy had much in common with that of the Padris; of his forty-nine books, many were devoted to attacking the Minangkabau system of matrilineal inheritance, and to abusing the *tarekat*, which he denounced as heterodox.[74]

The sociology and geography of this movement are as yet obscure. Despite its initiator's attacks on the brotherhoods, it did acquire the allegiance of a number of *tarekat* teachers, just as Tuanku Nan Tua to begin with lent his support to Padri notions of reform. The teachings of some of the supporters of the movement came very close to Padri tenets; Haji Yahya of Simabur, a village near Sungai Jambu in Tanah Datar, not only agitated gainst matrilineal inheritance but zealously preached the need to make Islamic law more widely applied in Minangkabau society, to the extent that social relations should be broken off with those who refused to be guided by it.[75] Moreover, this movement sparked off a desire in certain regions for armed resistance against the Dutch, and plans laid in 1897 for a revolt the following year only failed to materialize because of betrayal to the authorities.[76]

In the early 1900s the orthodox reform movement seems to have passed largely into the hands of Ahmad Chatib's own students, who returned to Minangkabau to live as independent religious teachers, outside the framework of the brotherhoods. The whole phenomenon of the rise of independent religious teachers in Minangkabau, who can properly be called *ulama,* also requires investigation, as does the difference between their *madrasah* and the *surau* of the brotherhoods. Certainly the number of Mecca-trained teachers increased in the late nineteenth century, and it was to them that Ahmad Chatib directed his movement. These *ulama* kept alive the orthodox movement with attacks on *tarekat* and their *surau,* and on unlawful innovations (*bid'ah*) in religious practice; further, they urged the abandonment of *taklid,* reliance on the judgements of established religious authorities, and a return to the original sources of the law, the Koran and the *hadis,* which could be construed by the use of *ijtihad* or independent judgement based on reasoning.[77] The similarities with the Padri movement are obvious.

Ahmad Chatib himself had been highly critical of the Islamic modernism of certain Muslim *ulama* in the Middle East, but ultimately, just as the Padri movement had had to abandon its extreme orthodoxy, the main branch of the orthodox reform movement tended to merge into a contemporaneous Islamic movement in Minangkabau favouring the tenets of Islamic modernism. Again we understand little of the sociology of this latter movement, but it is possible to see in it an Islamic response to the success of western-style schools in Minangkabau. In part it was also an Islamic response to the increasing urbanization of Minangkabau in the early twentieth century, and much of the activity related to Islamic modernism revolved in particular around the towns of Padang, Padang Panjang and Bukit Tinggi. The leading feature of this so-called Kaum Muda movement was the reorganization by its protagonists of the entire Islamic school system in Minangkabau, which was to be henceforth based on the two pillars of promoting orthodoxy and creating enthusiasm for secular knowledge and 'modernity'. The new, reformed schools set up by the Kaum Muda *ulama* inevitably became highly politicized and, like the secular schools, formed the basis of the Minangkabau intellectual élite's involvement in Western-style political parties.[78] As the leading student of this phenomenon has remarked, 'Minangkabau became the centre of Muslim education in Sumatra and an important source for the Islamic modernist movement elsewhere in Indonesia'.[79] Later, when sectarian conflict between the various Muslim groups abated, nationalist politics and Islamic politics for quite some time coalesced. In the final analysis, however, Islam remained an independent variable in the Minangkabau equation.

Our conclusion must be that the legacy of the Padri movement in Minangkabau was never quite erased. Nor can revivalism ever be eradicated from a religion which lays such stress on a Book and the example of an historic community. Moreover concern for reform, for rapid response to changing circumstances, remained a feature of Minangkabau life. Living high in the mountains of the Bukit Barisan, the Minangkabau retained the desire to be master of his own fate, and over a long period in his history he found in Islam the means to achieve this. More than anything his history has reflected his wish, expressed by Imam Bonjol before his capture, to be 'a free Malay'.[80]

NOTES TO CHAPTER VII

1 Muntinghe to van der Capellen, 20 Mar. 1822, KI MSS. H. 182.
2 ibid.
3 ibid.
4 ibid.; where no inaccuracies arise and Belgian interests are not involved, I have preferred to use the term 'Dutch' rather than the more awkward adjective 'Netherlands'.
5 D.K. Fieldhouse, *Economics and Empire 1830-1914* (London, 1973), p. xvi; see also pp. 77-82.
6 J.M. Paige, *Agrarian Revolution. Social Movements and Export Agriculture in the Underdeveloped World* (New York and London, 1975), p. 14.
7 cf. I. Wallerstein, *The Modern World-System. Capitalist Agriculture and the Origins of the European World-Economy in the Sixteenth Century* (New York and London, 1974), pp. 349-50.
8 Fieldhouse, *Economics and Empire*, pp. 475-6.
9 Baud to van den Bosch, 22 Dec. 1834, no. 446, Exh. 16 May 1835, no. 26, MK 974.
10 See, for example, A.V. Michiels, *De Toestand van Sumatra's Westkust in 1848* ('s Hertogenbosch, 1851). The capital of the Padang Highlands Residency was moved from Batu Sangkar to Bukit Tinggi.
11 Van den Bosch was also concerned about this; see van den Bosch to King, 22 Oct. 1838, L^{a}S^{7}, Exh. 22 Oct. 1838, L^{a}S^{7} Kab., MK 4419.
12 Michiels to de Eerens, 4 Feb. 1839, no. 90, in Kielstra, 'Koffiecultuur' p. 1452.
13 De Stuers to van den Bosch, n.d. March 1838, Exh. 12 Mar. 1838, L^{a}X, MK 4417.
14 Besluit, 21 Jan. 1840, no. 108/154, in Kielstra, 'Koffiecultuur', pp. 1456-7.
15 C. Lulofs, 'Koffiecultuur en Belasting ter Sumatra's Westkust', *IG*, xxvi (1904), ii. 1638-9.
16 Kielstra, 'Koffiecultuur', pp. 1459-60, 1470.
17 Baud to Merkus, 5 Sept. 1843, no. 4/514, in Kielstra, 'Koffiecultuur', pp. 1445-6.
18 Van Heel, 1842, NHM, p. 3; Granpré Molière, 1844, NHM, pp. 47-9.
19 Granpré Molière, 1844, NHM, pp. 43-4.
20 Poolman, 1847, NHM, pp. 19-21.
21 Granpré Molière, 1844, NHM, p. 42.
22 Michiels to Steinmetz, 13 Nov. 1845, no. 2254, in Kielstra, 'Koffiecultuur', pp. 1462-3.
23 Michiels to Rochussen, 23 Sept. 1846, no. 1568, in Kielstra, 'Koffiecultuur', p. 1466.
24 ibid., pp. 1465-8.
25 Mansvelt, *Nederlandsche Handel-Maatschappij,* ii. 62; Poolman, 1847, NHM, pp. 19-20.
26 Kielstra, 'Koffiecultuur', pp. 1473, 1478-80. Prices were based on a selling price of f.11 at Padang and were to be f.7 per *pikul* for first grade coffee, f.6 for second grade and f.5 for third grade. After the first six months of the opening of coffee delivery warehouses, third grade coffee would no longer be accepted.
27 Mansvelt, *Nederlandsche Handel-Maatschappij,* ii. 62; Kielstra, 'Koffiecultuur', p. 1477.
28 Michiels to Rochussen, 26 Oct. 1847, no. 2188, in Kielstra, 'Koffiecultuur', p. 1476.
29 Kielstra, 'Koffiecultuur', pp. 1489, 1617, 1624.
30 Graves, 'Ever-Victorious Buffalo', p. 166.
31 Register der Besluiten van Zijne Excellentie den Kommissaris Generaal, 11 Oct. 1833, no. 310, van den Bosch 298; van Sevenhoven and Riesz to Clifford, 11 Nov. 1833, no. 68, Bijl. E, Exh. 9 Apr. 1834, no. 74K Geh., MK 4233.
32 Van den Bosch to de Eerens, 17 Apr. 1839, L^{a}A^{5} Kab. Zeer Geh., Exh. idem, MK 4423.
33 Kielstra, 'Sumatra's Westkust van 1836-1840', pp. 320-2.
34 Baud to Merkus, 1 Sept. 1841, no. 363/W Zeer Geh., Kabinet des Konings 4140.
35 Graves, 'Ever-Victorious Buffalo', pp. 164-6.
36 Kielstra, 'Koffiecultuur', p. 1484.
37 Kielstra, 'Sumatra's Westkust van 1836-1840', pp. 320-3; Graves, 'Ever-Victorious Buffalo', pp. 157-8, 169.

38 Kielstra, 'Koffiecultuur', pp. 1480-2; Lulofs, 'Koffiecultuur', pp. 1642-3; Graves, 'Ever-Victorious Buffalo', pp. 167-8, 210-2, 214-5.
39 Kielstra, 'Koffiecultuur', pp. 1464, 1612-3, 1623, 1633-4, 1643.
40 ibid., pp. 1621, 1624.
41 ibid., p. 1475; Graves, 'Ever-Victorious Buffalo', pp. 215, 219-21.
42 Kroesen, 'Het grondbezit', p. 1.
43 Verkerk Pistorius, *Inlandsche Huishouding,* p. 127.
44 M.C.E. Stakman, 'De Afdeelingen Lintau en Boea (Padangsche Bovenlanden) en Toelang Bawang (Lampongsche Districten)', *IG,* vii (1885), ii. 88.
45 Kielstra, 'Koffiecultuur', pp. 1660-1, 1665-8, 1674; Lulofs, 'Koffiecultuur', p. 1655.
46 Lulofs, 'Koffiecultuur', p. 1649.
47 Van Hasselt, *Volksbeschrijving,* pp. 343-4, 346, 386-7; Verkerk Pistorius, *Inlandsche Huishouding,* pp. 37, 151.
48 'Reizen van L. Horner', p. 371.
49 Schrieke, *Indonesian Sociological Studies,* i. 108.
50 ibid., p. 99.
51 ibid., p. 114.
52 ibid., p. 99.
53 ibid.; C. Geertz, *Agricultural Involution* (Berkeley and Los Angeles, 1968), pp. 116-22, has accepted these arguments of Schrieke.
54 Couperus, 'Landbouwkundige nijverheid', pp. 306-7; A.L. van Hasselt and J.F. Snelleman, *Reizen in Midden-Sumatra, 1877-1879* (Leiden, 1881), p. 39.
55 Verkerk Pistorius, *Inlandsche Huishouding,* p. 179.
56 Lulofs, 'Koffiecultuur', pp. 1630-1. These figures only relate to tobacco exported from Padang to the Straits. There was also a considerable increase in tobacco exports overland to the east coast, and to Java.
57 Van Hasselt, *Volksbeschrijving,* p. 347.
58 ibid., p. 408.
59 Couperus, 'Landbouwkundige nijverheid', p. 311.
60 Lulofs, 'Koffiecultuur', pp. 1630-1; van Hasselt, *Volksbeschrijving,* p. 363.
61 Lulofs, 'Koffiecultuur', pp. 1630-1.
62 Kielstra, 'Koffiecultuur', pp. 1614-6, 1630.
63 Van Hasselt, *Volksbeschrijving,* p. 360.
64 ibid., p. 361; van Hasselt and Snelleman, *Reizen,* pp. 99, 104-6, 197-8.
65 Lulofs, 'Koffiecultuur', pp. 1632-3.
66 Van Hasselt, *Volksbeschrijving,* p. 360.
67 Graves, 'Ever-Victorious Buffalo', pp. 221-4, 296-7. Whether these families deserve Graves' epithet of 'merchant dynasties' with 'great wealth' requires further research.
68 Lulofs, 'Koffiecultuur', pp. 1632-3.
69 Van Hasselt, *Volksbeschrijving,* pp. 360-1; W.J. Cator, *The Economic Position of the Chinese in the Netherlands Indies* (Oxford, 1936), pp. 235, 244.
70 Kielstra, 'Koffiecultuur', pp. 1483, 1485.
71 Graves, 'Ever-Victorious Buffalo', pp. 171-2, 235-7, 248, 250-9, 278, 282, 290-6, 319, 322-4, 334-44, 357-9, 378, 389, 391.
72 Verkerk Pistorius, *Inlandsche Huishouding,* pp. 188 *et seq.,* especially pp. 204-5, 220-3.
73 Schrieke, 'Godsdienstige beweging', pp. 263-5.
74 ibid., pp. 268-9, 272-3; van Ronkel, *Rapport,* pp. 19-20; D. Noer, *The Modernist Muslim Movement in Indonesia 1900-1942* (Kuala Lumpur, 1973), pp. 31-3.
75 Schrieke, 'Godsdienstige beweging', pp. 274-5.
76 Oki, 'West Sumatran Village', pp. 71-3.
77 Van Ronkel, *Rapport,* pp. 22-5; T. Abdullah, 'Modernization in the Minangkabau World: West Sumatra in the Early Decades of the Twentieth Century' in C. Holt (ed.), *Culture and Politics in Indonesia* (Ithaca and London, 1972), pp. 225-6; idem, *Schools and Politics: The Kaum Muda Movement in West Sumatra (1927-1933)* (Ithaca, 1971), pp. 45-6.

78 Noer, *Modernist Muslim Movement,* p. 32; Abdullah, *Kaum Muda,* pp. 35-40, 46-7; idem, 'Modernization', p. 235.
79 Abdullah, *Kaum Muda,* p. 54.
80 See Braudel, *Mediterranean,* i. 38-41, the section headed 'Mountain freedom'.

APPENDIX

Exports of Coffee from Padang, 1819-1899, in *pikul*

1819	4,500	1846	66,973	1873	108,505
1820	16,500	1847	58,224	1874	131,474
1821	14,500	1848	56,101	1875	145,014
1822	24,500	1849	52,833	1876	102,891
1823	26,500	1850	71,118	1877	175,034
1824	28,500	1851	81,976	1878	82,351
1825	32,500	1852	122,903	1879	112,030
1826	48,500	1853	137,679	1880	123,347
1827	39,500	1854	131,322	1881	109,985
1828	29,371	1855	127,547	1882	98,309
1829	39,703	1856	128,259	1883	150,127
1830	27,697	1857	190,947	1884	89,660
1831	40,200	1858	129,121	1885	102,268
1832	60,794	1859	120,259	1886	48,211
1833	80,753	1860	150,057	1887	83,627
1834	78,581	1861	150,000	1888	99,125
1835	78,837	1862	144,000	1889	48,336
1836	84,823	1863	131,954	1890	65,050
1837	59,920	1864	187,323	1891	44,834
1838	56,295	1865	124,057	1892	59,766
1839	96,181	1866	165,138	1893	56,724
1840	90,961	1867	157,982	1894	26,038
1841	93,919	1868	142,767	1895	40,895
1842	83,080	1869	141,962	1896	47,045
1843	100,584	1870	182,869	1897	33,387
1844	74,697	1871	155,548	1898	40,342
1845	81,941	1872	90,819	1899	48,555

Source: C. Lulofs, 'Koffiecultuur en Belasting ter Sumatra's Westkust', *IG*, xxvi (1904), ii. 1658-61.

Some of these figures do not correspond exactly with figures given in the body of the text, which were taken direct from MSS. sources.

Note: These figures reveal little about total Minangkabau coffee exports in the period 1819-1840, as much coffee was exported by alternative ports to Padang. After 1845 Batak coffee is included in the figures.

GLOSSARY

Abbreviations: A = Arabic; B = Batak; D = Dutch. Otherwise all words are spelt in their Bahasa Indonesia form.

adat : custom; tradition
afdeling (D) : division; administrative unit of the Netherlands Indies
alam Minangkabau : the universe or world of the Minangkabau people
alang-alang : *Imperata cylindrica*; a type of tall grass
anak murid : pupil
anau : sugar palm; commonly called *aren* in Java
arak : arrack; spirituous liquor distilled from the coconut palm or from rice and sugar
atap : roofing thatch, generally of palm leaves
aur-aur : *Commelina nudiflora*; a type of thorny bamboo
bahar : a measure of weight, varying between 360 and 600 lbs
balai : council hall; meeting place for the *penghulu* council in a Minangkabau village
barisan : (1) line; row (2) troops
bendahara : Minangkabau title, deriving from the Sanskrit title First Lord of the Treasury or Prime Minister
benteng : small fort or stockade, constructed of turf or tree trunks
beras : hulled rice
bertuah : endowed with magic powers
bid'ah : innovation, novelty; a view or mode of action which has not formerly existed or been practised, and therefore the exact opposite of *sunnah*
Bodi Caniago : one of the two politico-legal traditions in Minangkabau, particularly prevalent in villages with no royal connections
bonjol : projection outward; hence, fort
controleur (D) : European official in the Netherlands Indies administration
damar : resin
dār al-ḥarb (A) : abode of war; that part of the world which is not under Muslim rule and which is therefore a potential sphere of war for Muslims until it is turned into *dār al-Islām* or 'abode of Islam'
darat : the central portion of the Minangkabau highlands; the heartland and original home of the Minangkabau people
datuk : (1) title of address for a *penghulu* (2) village headman in Minangkabau east coast villages
daulat : term applied to individuals who, usually through saintliness, are believed able to work miracles
dikir : chanting of religious phrases, performed communally as a devotional exercise by members of an Islamic brotherhood
fikh : the study of Islamic law, the *syariat*
gelanggang : cockfighting ring
gelar : title; on taking office, a *penghulu* and other hereditary officials in a lineage would assume a particular title handed down in the lineage

guru : spiritual guide, teacher; secondary to the *syekh* in a large *surau,* though he might also run a small establishment of his own
hadis : 'statement'; the short narratives told by one of the Prophet's Companions, in which form the *sunnah* of the Prophet was handed down
haj : pilgrimage to Mecca
haji : title given to one who has performed the *haj*
harimau yang delapan : eight tigers
harta pencarian : goods and wealth acquired by an individual's own labours during his lifetime
harta pusaka : inherited property: the goods and wealth belonging in common to one matrilineal family
heerendiensten (D) : forced labour required from the local population by the Netherlands Indies government, to complete public works, provide transport etc.
hoofd (D) : head, chief; prefixed to a number of Dutch titles
hulubalang : professional soldier; in Minangkabau each lineage possessed its own *hulubalang* whose title was hereditary and whose role was to serve the lineage *penghulu*
huta (B) : fortified village
huurbendi (D) : hire-carriage
ibadat : religion; lit., performance of religious obligations
ijtihad : the forming of one's own opinion by applying analogy to the Koran and the *sunnah*
ilmu : knowledge, learning; in connection with the knowledge purveyed by a *syekh,* the connotations are of secret or esoteric knowledge
ilmu alat : the study of the Arabic language
ilmu hakikat : study of the truths of revealed religion; in mysticism, a higher wisdom which engenders a sense of confidence in the mystic
ilmu mantik maana : the study of the logical exposition of the meaning of the Koran
ilmu tafsir : the study of Koranic commentary
imam : leader of the congregation in a mosque; also used in the sense of 'leader of the people'
imam besar : chief *imam*
jamā'āt (A) : assembly for prayer
jihad : holy war; the duty of Muslims to spread Islam, by arms if necessary
kaba : Minangkabau story told in a kind of rhythmic prose
kadi : Muslim judge
kampung : technically a neighbourhood; often used in the sense of 'village'
kasumba : flower of the *Carthamus Tinctorius,* which produces a saffron dye
kaum : (1) branch family (2) group
Kaum Muda : Young Group, i.e., progressives
kepala laras : *laras* head; a Dutch-created position, to which was appointed a single *penghulu* to represent all the *negeri* in a *laras*
kepala negeri : village head; a Dutch-created position, to which was appointed one lineage *penghulu* in each *negeri*
kepala tambang : entrepreneur who opens and sees to the working of a mine
keranjang : container
kerbau yang tiga kandang : waterbuffaloes of the three stables (term of contempt)
keris : creese; a dagger
kitab : book; generally refers to religious or learned works
kompeni : popular term for the Dutch East India Company, and by extension for the Netherlands Indies government

kota : original nucleus of a Minangkabau village settlement, usually fortified
Koto Piliang : one of the two politico-legal traditions in Minangkabau, associated in particular with the royal family and the gold trade
koyan : a measure of weight, varying between 27 and 40 *pikul*
kraton : Javanese royal palace
kuli : coolie; labourer
ladang : dry field (not irrigated)
lapau : small inn or shop
laras : (1) word for the two politico-legal traditions in Minangkabau, Bodi Caniago and Koto Piliang (2) Dutch-created administrative unit, above the *negeri* and below the *afdeling*
lombong : rice barn; granary
madat : opium prepared for smoking
madrasah : Islamic school, usually connected with a mosque
mahasenapati : supreme commander of the army
malim : (1) designation given to an individual learned in Islamic subjects (2) title of Minangkabau lineage religious functionary
mamak : maternal uncle; also used to mean guardian and leader of a lineage or family group
martabat tujuh : mystic doctrine of the seven phases of emanation of the Absolute
merantau : to go to the *rantau*; the custom of young men leaving their native villages to seek their fortune elsewhere
mu'min : believer, i.e. a Muslim
murid : pupil; student
nakoda : captain of a ship; extended to include the leader of a production team
negeri : the basic unit of settlement in Minangkabau, comprising the *kota* or original village and dependent out-settlements; under the Dutch it became the lowest unit of administration
NHM : Nederlandsche Handel-Maatschappij; Netherlands Trading Company
onan (B) : market
opperhoofd (D) : head of a VOC mercantile establishment, such as Padang
orang bangsat : vagabond, tramp; colloquial term for a carrier in a trading party
orang datang : immigrant; newcomer to a village
orang galas : pedlar
orang kaya : an important personage in society, as distinguished from the *orang banyak*, the populace
orang putih : white people, the term used in Minangkabau for the Padris; the original connotation was moral and did not refer to the wearing of white garments
pagar kopi : hedge coffee; coffee bushes grown close together around a family compound to form a thick hedge
pakhuismeester (D) : warehousemaster
pandita : title of pre-Islamic religious functionary in Minangkabau
pangkalan : stapling-post; depot
panglima : (1) title given to Acehnese governors on the Minangkabau coast (2) title used by leading west coast *penghulu*
panusunan (B) : title of the leading *raja* of a group of Batak villages
pasar : market; market-place
patih : ruler's chief minister
pawang : village shaman; expert in any art believed to need the use of magic
pedati : buffalo cart

pekan : market; week
penghulu kecil : head of a branch family
perahu : boat; prow
pikul : measurement of weight, equivalent to 133 lbs
pinang : areca nut
plakat panjang : Long Declaration; charter of Minangkabau liberties proclaimed by Dutch authorities on 25 October 1833
puasa : Muslim fasting period
pucuk : title given to village headman in Minangkabau east coast villages
pusaka : heirloom; family property
Raad van Indië (D) : Council of the Indies; highest administrative and legislative body in the Netherlands Indies
raja : originally 'king', but used in many titles, both royal and non-royal, as an honorific
Raja Adat : King of Tradition; one of the three positions held by members of the Minangkabau royal family
Raja Alam : King of the World; title of the supreme ruler of Minangkabau
Raja Empat Sila : Rulers of the Four Seats; titles of the four leading *penghulu* of the valley of Alahan Panjang
Raja Ibadat : King of Religion; one of the three positions held by members of the Minangkabau royal family
rameh : China grass, used for making string
ranjau : pointed stakes, generally fashioned from bamboo
rantau : fringe areas outside the four central Minangkabau valleys; also the non-Minangkabau world in general
rapat : council
Regent (D) : title granted to Indonesian chiefs and princes by the Dutch East India Company and, in the early nineteenth century, by its successor
rijksdaalder : coin equivalent to f.2.50 or, in the eighteenth century, to 3s.8d. sterling
rumah gedang : large Minangkabau family house
sakti : supernatural power
saudagar : merchant
sawah : wet-rice field
sebuah perut : family; lit., one womb
semangat : soul; spirit of life
sembahyang : prayer
sirih : a quid consisting of betel leaf, areca nut, gambir and lime
Spanish dollar : silver coin much used in trade with Indonesia from the seventeenth to the early nineteenth century; its contemporary value was between 4s.6d. and 5s. sterling
suku : matrilineage
sunnah : the custom of the Islamic community handed down by oral transmission, as distinct from the *kitab*, the written Book
surau : (1) dormitory for unmarried men (2) lineage or village Koranic school (3) centre for Islamic studies run by teachers of a religious brotherhood
syariat : Islamic law, based on religious revelation, in contrast to law based on custom
syekh : chief instructor at one of the major centres of Islamic studies founded by a religious brotherhood
tahil : a measure of weight for gold equivalent to 1 1/3 oz. avoirdupois

taklid : uncritical acceptance of the judgements of established religious authorities
tambang : mine
tambo : traditional Minangkabau chronicles
tanah raja : waste land between villages, used for inter-village combat
tandah perang : token of war; tributary payment from a conquered village to its conquerors
tarekat : Islamic brotherhood or religious order, members of which follow a *ṭarīḳa* with mystical connotations
ṭarīḳa (A) : path, way; the particular 'way' to God followed by members of an Islamic brotherhood
tasauf : devotion to the mystic life; becoming a Sufi
tua : old
tua galas : leader of a party of traders
tua tambang : entrepreneur who opens and sees to the working of a mine
tuak : palm wine
tuanku : (1) title given to important Islamic teachers (2) honorific title used by leading west coast *penghulu*
tumanggung : official of very high rank in a Malayo-Javanese state
ulama : Muslim scholar (used in both singular and plural)
ummat : the community of Muslim believers
VOC : Verenigde Oostindische Compagnie; United East India Company
wakil : deputy; representative
Yang di Pertuan : he who is made lord; the highest title given a Malay ruler

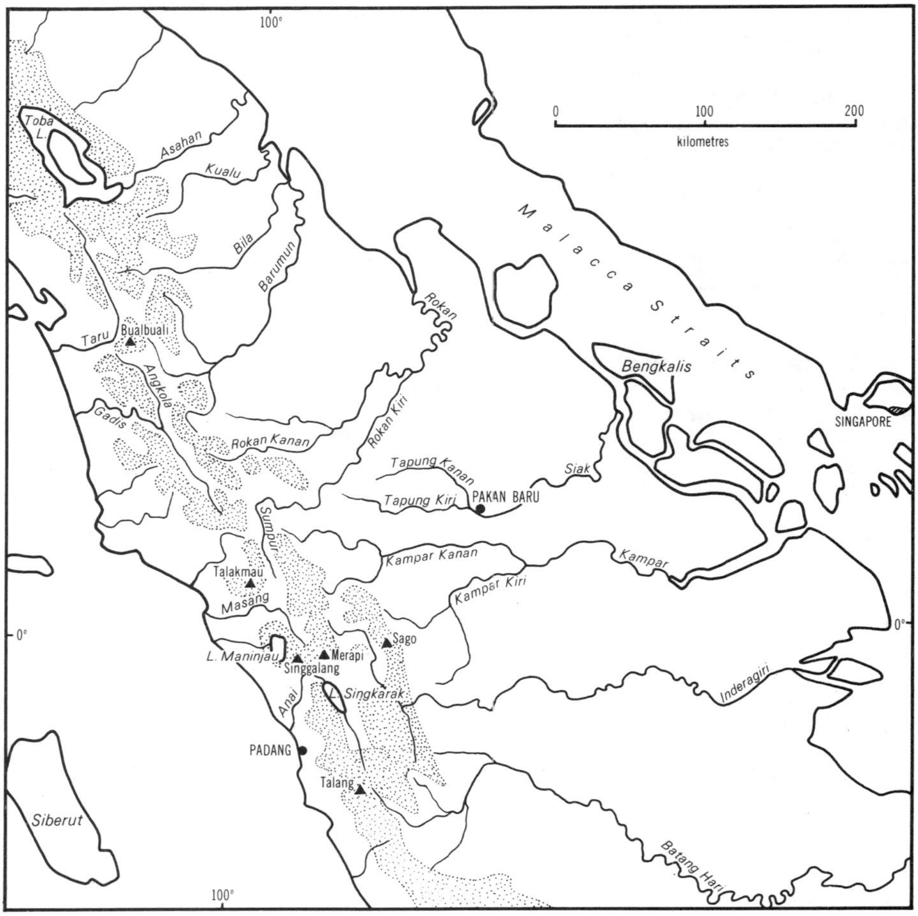

Map A: Physical Features of Central Sumatra

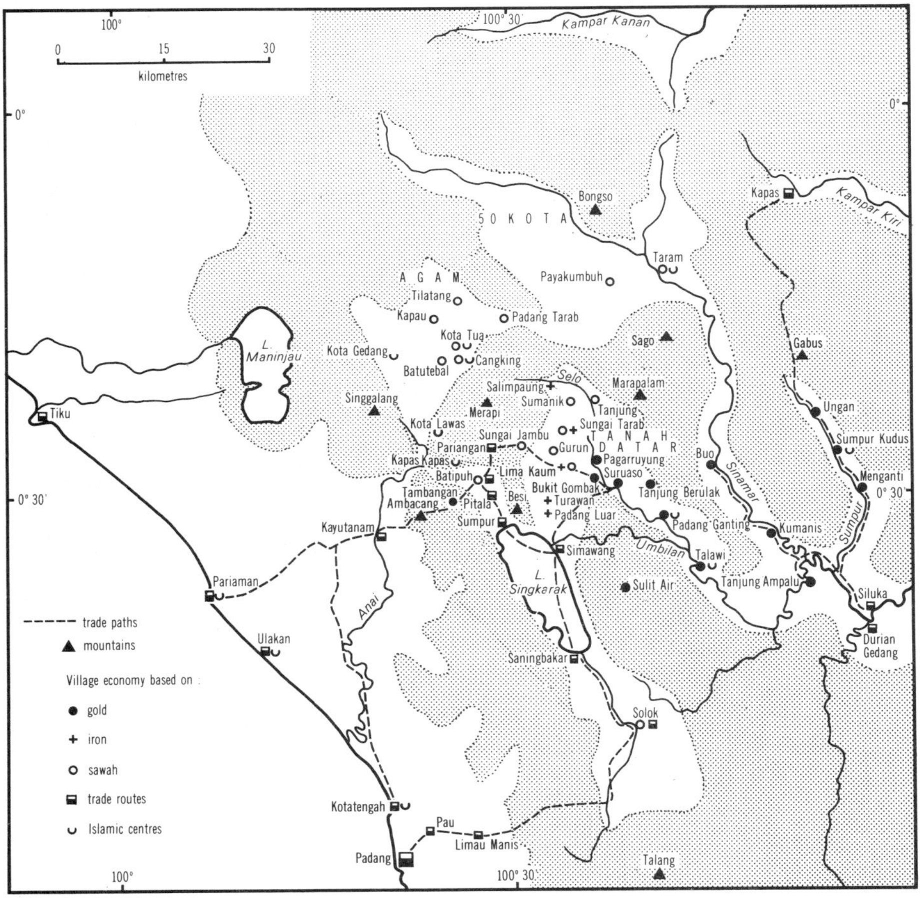

Map B: Villages of the Minangkabau Valleys: their economy before 1803

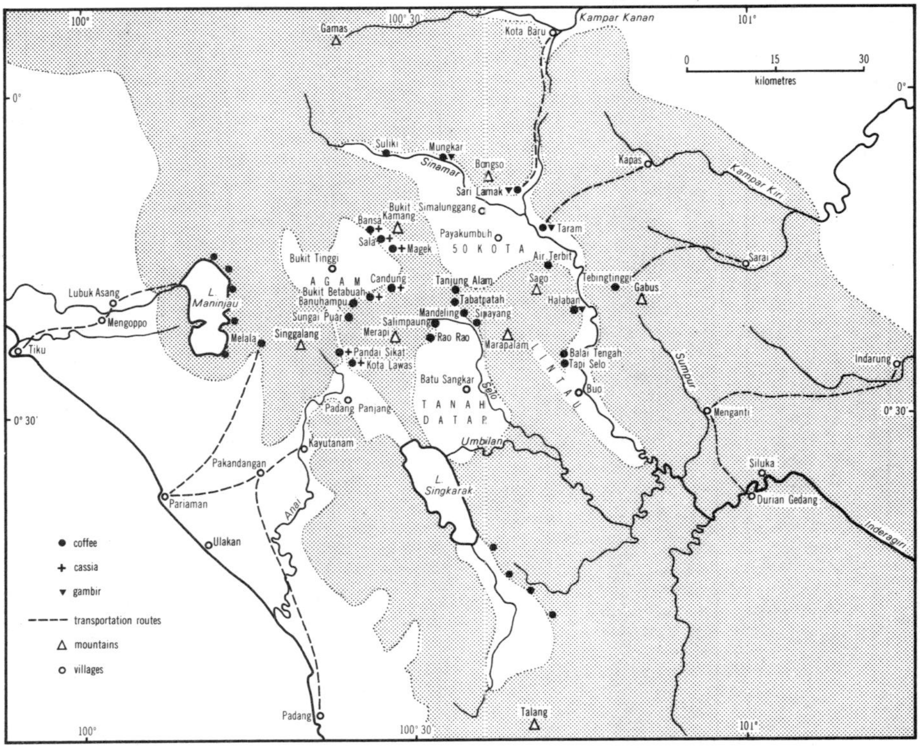

Map C: Villages of the Minangkabau Hills: export crops, 1784-1838

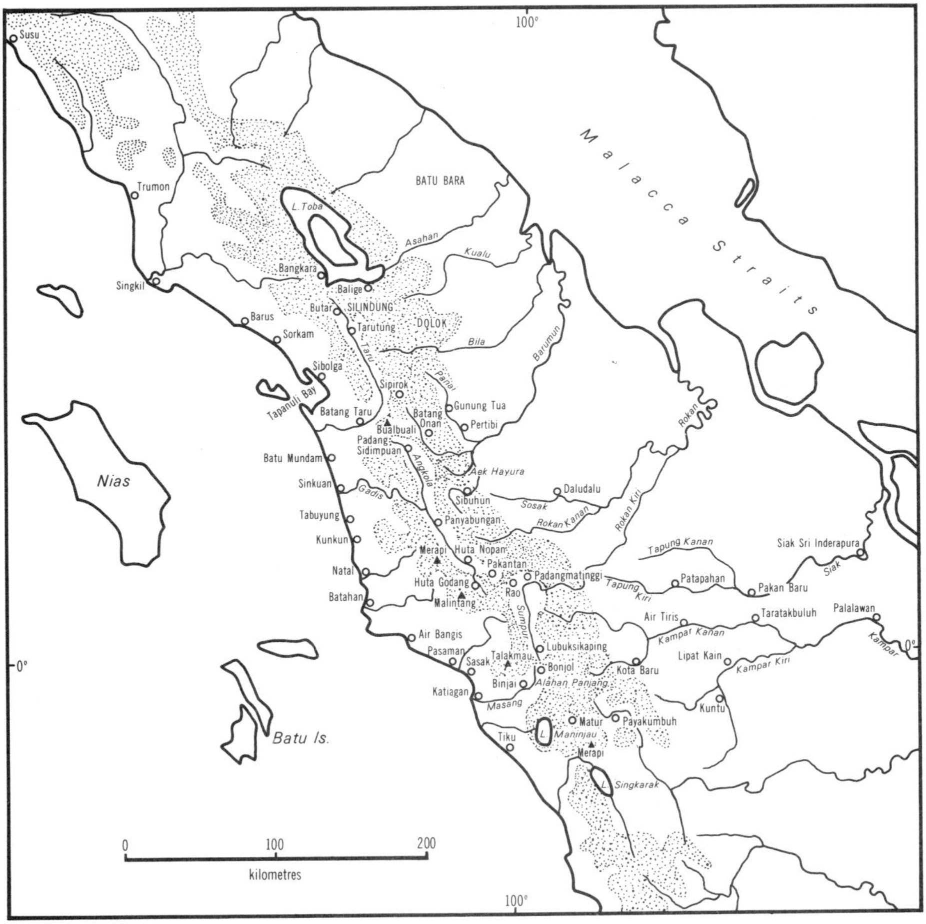

Map D: Northern Minangkabau and the Batak Lands, 1807-1847

BIBLIOGRAPHY

I Manuscript Sources

A. Algemeen Rijksarchief, The Hague

1. Koloniaal Archief

This archive contains the records of the United East India Company. The series used consists of letters from VOC out-stations to the Governor-General at Batavia, and is entitled Bataviasche Inkomende Brieven, Overgekomen. For Padang the following items were consulted:

3752 Inkomend Briefboek en Bylagen van Sumatra's Westkust Overgekomen 1790
3800 Inkomend Briefboek en Bylagen van Sumatra's Westkust Overgekomen 1791
3853 Inkomend Briefboek en Bylagen van Sumatra's Westkust Overgekomen 1793
3876 Inkomend Briefboek en Bylagen van Sumatra's Westkust Overgekomen 1794

2. Archief van het Ministerie van Koloniën

The major documents generated by the Ministry of Colonies in the period 1814-1849 are filed in one of three Verbalen (minutes) – Openbare (public), Geheim (secret) and Kabinets. All three categories were used for this work. Each Verbaal consists of a numbered series of dossiers, and each of these dossiers contains a series of Exhibitum, which are filed by date. Access to material on central Sumatra is by way of indexes, from which it is necessary to extract both the number of a particular dossier and the date of the relevant Exhibitum. In addition there were used for this study the volumes of Besluiten (resolutions) of the Governor-General of the Netherlands Indies, and certain other miscellaneous documents.

The following dossiers were consulted:

Openbare Verbaal
1826 513, 515, 519, 523
1827 547, 551, 558, 567, 568, 574, 582, 583, 591
1828 595, 618, 625, 626, 652
1829 683, 717, 718, 721
1830 745, 767, 776
1831 790, 810, 812, 820
1832 830, 839, 849, 852, 860
1833 868, 876, 881
1835 956, 957, 962, 969, 971, 974, 994, 999, 1003, 1004
1836 1008, 1009, 1014, 1017, 1018, 1019, 1024, 1031, 1032, 1033, 1037, 1049, 1063, 1065
1837 1100
1838 1140

Geheim Verbaal
1833 4230
1834 4232, 4233, 4234
1836 4243
1837 4247
1838 4249

Kabinets Verbaal
1835 4403, 4404
1836 4409, 4410, 4411
1837 4412, 4414, 4415, 4416
1838 4417, 4418, 4419, 4420, 4421
1839 4423, 4424, 4425
1840 4431, 4434

Register der Handelingen en Besluiten van den Gouverneur-Generaal over Nederlandsch Indie, in en buiten Rade

1819	2451, 2771
1820	2453, 2455, 2456
1821	2462, 2774, 2775
1822	2467, 2776
1823	2470, 2471, 2473, 2778, 2779, 2780
1824	2476, 2477, 2781, 2782, 2783, 2785
1825	2480, 2484, 2489, 2789, 2791
1826	2498, 2792, 2795
1827	2507, 2799, 2803, 2804
1828	2516
1830	2835, 2836
1832	2842, 2843
1833	2550, 2846, 2847
1834	2554, 2556, 2853
1835	2557, 2560
1836	2561, 2562
1837	2566, 2571, 2575
1838	2578, 2582
1840	2607

Miscellaneous dossiers

3070, 4129, 4131, 4136, 4137, 4497

3. Kabinet des Konings

1841 4140

4. Private Collections

Name of Collection	Inventory Numbers of Items Consulted
D.F. van Alphen – N. Engelhard	286
J.C. Baud	78, 128, 316, 331, 429, 480, 493, 494, 600
J. van den Bosch	216, 231, 243, 244, 245, 247, 259, 260, 263, 296, 298, 304, 393, 394, 526, 570, 572, 575, 576, 578
L.P.J. du Bus de Gisignies	163
H.M. de Kock	168
P. Melvill van Carnbee	1
W.J.M. van Schmid	15
G.J.C. Schneither	119
P.F. Vermeulen Krieger	1, 3, 4
P.J. van Zuylen van Nijevelt	102

B. Algemeen Rijksarchief Hulpdepot, Schaarsbergen, Archief van de Nederlandsche Handel-Maatschappij

Reisverslagen (Travel Reports), 1826-1840 nos. 13, 32, 33, 38, 39

C. Koninklijk Instituut voor Taal-, Land- en Volkenkunde, Leiden

The following Western Manuscripts were consulted:

H.166 Beschrijving van Sumatras West-Custe. 1730
H.167 De Radicaale Beschrijving van Sumatra's West Cust. 1761
H.182 H.W. Muntinghe, Rapport betreffende Sumatra's Westkust, 20 Mar. 1822
H.803 Collectie L.C. Westenenk

D. The India Office Library, London

Straits Settlements Factory Records

vols. 1-6 Bengal Consultations Relative to Prince of Wales Island, 1786-1795

vol. 9 Prince of Wales Island, Letters, June 1808-Jan. 1823

vols. 13-14 Prince of Wales Island Public Consultations, Mar. 1806-Oct. 1806.

Sumatra Factory Records

vols. 45-47 Letters from Fort Marlborough to the Court, 1793-1819

vol. 49 Original Letters from Fort Marlborough to the Court, 1 Jan. 1822-4 Jul. 1825

vol. 50 Original Letters from Sir Stamford Raffles to the Secretary, East India Company, 3 Oct. 1819-12 Dec. 1821

II Printed Sources

A. Primary Sources

Anderson, J., *Acheen, and the Ports on the North and East Coasts of Sumatra.* London, 1840.

——, *Mission to the East Coast of Sumatra, in MDCCCXXIII.* Edinburgh and London, 1826.

Anon, 'Het Inlandsch bestuur ter Westkust van Sumatra', *TNI,* ii (1839), i.

B..d., 'De Padries op Sumatra', *IM,* ii (1845), i.

Bastin, J., *The British in West Sumatra (1685-1825).* Kuala Lumpur, 1965.

——, (ed.), *The Journal of Thomas Otho Travers, 1813-20.* Singapore, 1960.

'Beschrijuingh van de Westcust van Sumatra [in ± 1630]', *BKI,* iii (1855).

'Bezoek ter hoofdplaatse van het Djambische rijk op Sumatra in 1834, door den toenmaligen resident van Palembang J.W. Boers', *TNI,* xii (1850), ii.

'Bijdrage tot de kennis van het grondbezit op Sumatra', *TNI,* xiv (1852), i.

Boelhouwer, J.C., *Herinneringen van Mijn Verblijf op Sumatra's Westkust, Gedurende de Jaren 1831-1834.* The Hague, 1841.

Burckhardt, J.L., *Notes on the Bedouins and Wahābys.* 2 vols. London, 1831.

Burger, H., 'Aanmerkingen Gehouden op eene Reize door Eenige Districten der Padangsche Bovenlanden', *VBG,* xvi (1836).

Coolhaas, W.Ph. (ed.), *Generale Missiven van Gouverneurs-Generaal en Raden aan Heren XVII der Verenigde Oostindische Compagnie.* vols. 1-6. The Hague, 1960-1976.

Cortesão, A. (ed.), *The Suma Oriental of Tomé Pires.* 2 vols. The Hakluyt Society, Series II, vols. lxxxix, xc. London, 1944.

Couperus, P. Th., 'Aanteekeningen omtrent de landbouwkundige nijverheid in de residentie Padangsche Bovenlanden', *TBG,* v (1856).

——, 'Eenige Aanteekeningen Betreffende de Goudproduktie in de Padangsche Bovenlanden', *TBG,* v (1856).

——, 'De Instellingen der Maleijers in de Padangsche Bovenlanden', *TBG,* iv (1855).

——, 'De Residentie Tapanoeli (Sumatra's Westkust) in 1852', *TBG,* iv (1855).

Crichton, A., *History of Arabia and Its People.* London, 1852.

Delden, E.Th. van, 'Dagverhaal van eene Reis naar Gloegoer VI Kota', *TBG,* xxvii (1882).

——, 'Verslag over den Toestand van het Landschap Gloegoer VI Kota', *TBG,* xxvii (1882).

'De denkbeelden van den Generaal van den Bosch over het Nederlandsch gezag op Sumatra', *TNI,* xxix (1867), i.

Dion, M., 'Sumatra Through Portuguese Eyes: Excerpts from Joâo de Barros' *Decadas da Asia', Indonesia,* ix (1970).

E.S., 'Het rijk Pasaman op Sumatra's Westkust', *TNI,* xxvii (1865), i.
'Eenige berigten omtrent Indragiri op de Oostkust van Sumatra', *TNI,* iv (1841), i.
Faes, J., 'Het Rijk Pelalawan', *TBG,* xxvii (1882).
Foster, W. (ed.), *The Voyage of Sir Thomas Best to the East Indies 1612-14.* The Hakluyt Society, Series II, vol. lxxv. London, 1934.
——, *The Voyages of Sir James Lancaster to Brazil and the East Indies 1591-1603.* The Hakluyt Society, Series II, vol. lxxxv. London, 1940.
Francis, E., *Herinneringen uit den Levensloop van een' Indisch' Ambtenaar van 1815 tot 1851. Medegedeeld in Brieven.* 3 vols. Batavia, 1856-59.
——, 'Korte beschrijving van het Nederlandsch grondgebied ter Westkust Sumatra 1837', *TNI,* ii (1839), i.
Gabriel, C., 'Kriegszug der Bondjol unter Anführung des Tuanku Rau in die Batakländer, zusammengetragen von Guru Kenan Huta Galung und aus den Batakschen ins Deutsche übersetzt', *TBG,* lxi (1922).
Gerretson, F.C. and Coolhaas, W.Ph. (eds.), *Particuliere Briefwisseling tussen J. van den Bosch en D.J. de Eerens 1834-1840.* Groningen, 1960.
Godon, A.P., 'De assistent-residentie Mandaheling en Ankola, op Sumatra's Westkust, van 1847 tot 1857', *TNI,* xxiv (1862), i.
H., v.d., 'Oorsprong der Padaries', *TNI,* i (1838), ii.
Haan, F. de, 'Naar Midden Sumatra in 1684', *TBG,* xxxix (1897).
Hamka, *Ajahku. Riwajat Hidup Dr H. Abd. Karim Amrullah dan Perdjuangan Kaum Agama di Sumatera.* 3rd edn. Jakarta, 1967.
Hasselt, A.L. van, *Volksbeschrijving van Midden-Sumatra.* Leiden, 1882.
——, and Snelleman, J.F., *Reizen in Midden-Sumatra, 1877-1879.* Leiden, 1881.
Hesse, E., *Gold-Bergwerke in Sumatra 1680-1683.* The Hague, 1931.
Hollander, J.J. de (ed.), *Sjech Djilâl Eddîn: Verhaal van den Aanvang der Padri-Onlusten op Sumatra.* Leiden, 1857.
Ijzerman, J.W., *Dwars door Sumatra. Tocht van Padang naar Siak.* Haarlem and Batavia, 1895.
Johns, A.H., *The Gift Addressed to the Spirit of the Prophet.* Canberra, 1965.
——, *Rantjak diLabueh: A Minangkabau Kaba.* Ithaca, 1958.
Kemp, P.H. van der, 'Eene Bijdrage tot E.B. Kielstra's Opstellen over Sumatra's Westkust', *BKI,* xlvi (1894).
Kern, H., 'Nog iets over 't opschrift van Pagarruyung in Menangkabau', in Kern, *Verspreide Geschriften,* vi. The Hague, 1917.
——, 'Het Sanskrit-inschrift op den grafsteen van Vorst Ādityawarman te Kubur Raja (Menangkabau; ± 1300 Çāka)', in Kern, *Verspreide Geschriften,* vii. The Hague, 1917.
——, 'De wij-inscriptie op het Amoghapāça-beeld van Padang Candi (Midden-Sumatra); 1269 Çāka', in Kern, *Verspreide Geschriften,* vii. The Hague, 1917.
——, 'Het zoogenaamde rotsinschrift van "Batu Beragung" in Menangkabau (1269 en 1297 Çāka', in Kern, *Verspreide Geschriften,* vi. The Hague, 1917.
Kessel, O. von, 'Herinneringen aan Sumatra', *BKI,* iv (1856).
——, 'Reis in de Nog Onafhankelijke Batak-Landen van Klein-Toba, op Sumatra, in 1844', *BKI,* iv (1856).
Kielstra, E.B., 'De koffiecultuur ter Westkust van Sumatra', *IG,* x (1888), ii.
——, 'Onze kennis van Sumatra's Westkust omstreeks de helft der achttiende eeuw', *BKI,* xxxvi (1887).
——, 'Sumatra's Westkust van 1819-1825', *BKI,* xxxvi (1887).
——, 'Sumatra's Westkust van 1826-1832', *BKI,* xxxvii (1888).

Kielstra, E.B., 'Sumatra's Westkust van 1833-1835', *BKI,* xxxviii (1889).
——, 'Sumatra's Westkust van 1836-1840', *BKI,* xxxix (1890).
——, 'Sumatra's Westkust van 1841-1849', *BKI,* xl (1891).
Korthals, P.W., 'Aanteekeningen over de Vijftig Kottas in de Padangsche Bovenlanden op Sumatra', *TNGP* (1835), ii.
——, *Topographische Schets van een Gedeelte van Sumatra.* Leiden, 1847.
Kroesen, Th. A.L., 'Het grondbezit ter Sumatra's Westkust', *TNI,* xxxvi (1874), ii.
Lange, H.M., *Het Nederlandsch Oost-Indisch Leger ter Westkust van Sumatra (1819-1845).* 2 vols. 's Hertogenbosch, 1852.
Linden, J. van der, 'Het Inlandsch Bestuur in het Gouvernement van Sumatra's Westkust', *TBG,* iv (1855).
Lulofs, C., 'Koffiecultuur en Belasting ter Sumatra's Westkust', *IG,* xxvi (1904), ii.
'Malacca in the Eighteenth Century. Two Dutch Governors' Reports'. Translated by B. Harrison. *JMBRAS,* xxvii (1954).
Marsden, W., *The History of Sumatra.* 3rd edn. London, 1811.
'De masdjid's en inlandsche godsdienstscholen in de Padangsche Bovenlanden', *IG,* x (1888), i.
Michiels, A.V., *Neêrlands Souvereiniteit over de schoonste en rijkste gewesten van Sumatra.* Amsterdam, 1846.
——, *De Toestand van Sumatra's Westkust in 1848.* 's Hertogenbosch, 1851.
Milburn, W., *Oriental Commerce.* 2 vols. London, 1813-1825.
The Missionary Herald, xxxi-xxxiv. Boston, 1835-1838.
Moor, J.H., *Notices of the Indian Archipelago, and Adjacent Countries.* Singapore, 1837.
Müller, S., *Berigten over Sumatra.* Amsterdam, 1837.
——, *Bijdragen tot de Kennis van Sumatra.* Leiden, 1846.
——, 'Over Eenige Oudheden van Java en Sumatra', *BKI,* iv (1856).
——, *Reizen en Onderzoekingen in Sumatra, gedaan op last der Nederlandsche Indische Regering, tusschen de jaren 1833 en 1838.* The Hague, 1855.
Nahuijs, H.G., *Brieven over Bencoolen, Padang, het Rijk van Menangkabau, Rhiouw, Sincapoera, en Poelo-Pinang.* Breda, 1826.
Netscher, E., *Padang in het laatst der XVIIIe eeuw. VBG,* xli. Batavia and The Hague, 1881.
Nieuwenhuijzen, F.N., 'Het rijk Siak Sri Indrapoera', *TBG,* vii (1858).
O'Kinealy, J., 'History and Doctrines of the Wahhábís', *Journal of the Asiatic Society of Bengal,* i (1874).
Ophuijsen, J.A.W. van, 'Over het Grondbezit en de Onderscheiding der Gronden in de XIII Kota's (Sumatra's Westkust). Verzameld en uit het Maleisch Overgebragt', *TBG,* iii (1855).
Raffles, S. (ed.), *Memoir of the Life and Public Services of Sir Thomas Stamford Raffles.* 2 vols. London, 1835.
Rehatsek, E., 'The History of the Wahhábys in Arabia and in India', *Journal of the Bombay Branch of the Royal Asiatic Society,* xiv (1878-1880).
'Reizen Over Sumatra. Uittreksel uit het Dagboek van Wijlen L. Horner', *TBG,* x (1860).
'Report of Governor Balthasar Bort on Malacca 1678'. Translated by M.J. Bremner. *JMBRAS,* v (1927).
Rijn van Alkemade, J.A. van, 'Beschrijving eener reis van Bengkalis langs de Rokanrivier naar Rantau Binoewang', *BKI,* xxxii (1884).
Ronkel, Ph.S. van, 'Inlandsche getuigenissen aangaande den Padri-oorlog', *IG,* xxxvii (1915), ii.

Ronkel, Ph.S. van, 'Een Maleisch Getuigenis over den Weg des Islams in Sumatra', *BKI*, lxxv (1919).

——, *Rapport Betreffende de Godsdienstige Verschijnselen ter Sumatra's Westkust.* Batavia, 1916.

Scheemaker, L. de, 'Nota Betreffende het Landschap Batoebarah', *TBG*, xvii (1869).

Schefer, Ch. (ed.), *Le Discours de la Navigation de Jean et Raoul Parmentier de Dieppe.* Paris, 1883.

'Schets van de Bereiding der Gambier te Paija Komba (Padangsche Bovenlanden)', *TNNI*, iii (1852).

Schrieke, B.J.O., 'Bijdrage tot de Bibliografie van de huidige godsdienstige beweging ter Sumatra's Westkust', *TBG*, lix (1920).

——, *Indonesian Sociological Studies.* Part I. The Hague, 1966.

Snouck Hurgronje, C., *The Achehnese.* Translated by A.W.S. O'Sullivan. 2 vols. Leiden, 1906.

——, 'Een en ander over het inlandsch onderwijs in de Padangsche Bovenlanden', in Snouck Hurgronje, *Verspreide Geschriften*, iv. Bonn and Leipzig, 1924.

——, *Mekka in the Latter Part of the 19th Century.* Translated by J.H. Monahan. Leiden and London, 1931.

Stakman, M.C.E., 'De Afdeelingen Lintau en Boea (Padangsche Bovenlanden) en Toelang Bawang (Lamponsche Districten)', *IG*, vii (1885), ii.

Stapel, F.W. (ed.), *Corpus Diplomaticum Neerlando-Indicum.* vi. 1753-1799. The Hague, 1955.

——, 'Een verhandeling over het ontstaan van het Menangkabausche rijk en zijn Adat', *BKI*, xcii (1935).

Steijn Parvé, H.A., 'De Secte der Padaries in de Padangsche Bovenlanden', *IM*, i (1844), i.

——, 'De Secte der Padaries (Padries) in de Bovenlanden van Sumatra', *TBG*, iii (1855).

Stuers, H.J.J.L. de, *De Vestiging en Uitbreiding der Nederlanders ter Westkust van Sumatra.* 2 vols. Amsterdam, 1849-1850.

Swieten, J. van, 'Over het Grondbezit ter Sumatra's Westkust', *TNI*, xxv (1863), i.

Toorn, J.L. van der, 'Het Animisme bij den Minangkabauer der Padangsche Bovenlanden', *BKI*, xxxix (1890).

'Trade in the Straits of Malacca in 1785. A Memorandum by P.G. de Bruijn, Governor of Malacca'. Translated by B. Harrison. *JMBRAS*, xxvi (1953).

'Uittreksels van een verslag over Sumatra's Westkust. 1829', *IM*, ii (1845), ii.

Verkerk Pistorius, A.W.P., *Studien over de Inlandsche Huishouding in de Padangsche Bovenlanden.* Zaltbommel, 1871.

'Verslag van eene Reis in het Land der Bataks in het Binnenland van Sumatra, ondernomen in het jaar 1824, door de heeren Burton en Ward, zendelingen der Baptisten', *BKI*, v (1856).

Westendorp Boerma, J.J. (ed.), *Briefwisseling tussen J. van den Bosch en J.C. Baud 1829-1832 en 1834-1836.* 2 vols. Utrecht, 1956.

Willer, T.I., 'Verzameling der Battahsche Wetten en Instellingen in Mandheling en Pertibie; gevolgd van een overzigt van land en volk in die streken', *TNI*, ix (1846), ii.

B. Secondary Sources

Abdullah, T., 'Adat and Islam: An Examination of Conflict in Minangkabau', *Indonesia,* ii (1966).

——, 'Modernization in the Minangkabau World; West Sumatra in the Early Decades of the Twentieth Century', in C. Holt (ed.), *Culture and Politics in Indonesia.* Ithaca and London, 1972.

——, *Schools and Politics: The Kaum Muda Movement in West Sumatra (1927-1933).* Ithaca, 1971.

Abir, M., 'The 'Arab Rebellion' of Amīr Ghālib of Mecca (1788-1813)', *Middle Eastern Studies,* vii (1971).

Abun-Nasr, J.M., *The Tijaniyya. A Sufi Order in the Modern World.* London, 1965.

Ahmad, A., *An Intellectual History of Islam in India.* Edinburgh, 1969.

Ahmad, Q., *The Wahabi Movement in India.* Calcutta, 1966.

Ahmat, S., 'Some Problems of the Rhode Island Traders in Java, 1799-1836', *JSAH,* vi (1965).

Andaya, L.Y., *The Kingdom of Johor 1641-1728.* Kuala Lumpur, 1975.

Archer, R.L., 'Muhammadan Mysticism in Sumatra', *JMBRAS,* xv (1937).

Attas, S.M.N. al-, *Rānīrī and the Wujūdiyyah of 17th Century Acheh.* Singapore, 1966.

——, *Some Aspects of Sūfism As Understood and Practised Among the Malays.* Singapore, 1963.

Bachtiar, H.W., '*Negeri* Taram: A Minangkabau Village Community', in Koentjaraningrat (ed.), *Villages in Indonesia.* Ithaca, 1967.

Ballot, J., 'Het Inlandsch Bestuur in de Onderafdeeling Loeboe Sikaping en Rau, Afdeeling Loeboe Sikaping, Residentie Padangsche Bovenlanden', *Tijdschrift voor Binnenlandsch Bestuur,* xxviii (1905).

Barratt Brown, M., *The Economics of Imperialism.* Harmondsworth, 1974.

Bastin, J., 'The British in West Sumatra', in Bastin, *Essays on Indonesian and Malayan History.* Singapore, 1961.

——, 'The Changing Balance of the Southeast Asian Pepper Trade', in Bastin, *Essays on Indonesian and Malayan History.* Singapore, 1961.

——, *The Native Policies of Sir Stamford Raffles in Java and Sumatra. An Economic Interpretation.* Oxford, 1957.

——, 'Raffles' Attempts to Extend British Power in Sumatra', in Bastin, *Essays on Indonesian and Malayan History.* Singapore, 1961.

Batuah, A.Dt. and Madjoindo, A.Dt., *Tambo Minangkabau dan Adatnja.* Jakarta, 1965.

Belshaw, C.S., *Traditional Exchange and Modern Markets.* Englewood Cliffs, 1965.

Bernstein, H., *Underdevelopment and Development.* Harmondsworth, 1973.

Bhagat, G., *Americans in India 1784-1860.* New York, 1970.

Boeke, J.H., *Economics and Economic Policy of Dual Societies.* New York, 1953.

Bouman, H., *Enige beschouwingen over de ontwikkeling van het Indonesisch Nationalisme op Sumatra's Westkust.* Groningen and Batavia, 1949.

Braudel, F., *The Mediterranean and the Mediterranean World in the Age of Philip II.* 2 vols. London, 1975.

Castles, L., 'Statelessness and Stateforming tendencies among the Bataks before Colonial Rule', in A. Reid and L. Castles (eds.), *Pre-Colonial State Systems in Southeast Asia.* Kuala Lumpur, 1975.

Cator, W.J., *The Economic Position of the Chinese in the Netherlands Indies.* Oxford, 1936.

Coedès, G., *The Indianized States of Southeast Asia.* Canberra, 1968.
Coleman, J.S., 'Nationalism in Tropical Africa', *The American Political Science Review,* xlviii (1954).
——, *Nigeria. Background to Nationalism.* Berkeley and Los Angeles, 1958.
Coulson, N.J., *Succession in the Muslim Family.* Cambridge, 1971.
Cowan, C.D., 'Early Penang and the Rise of Singapore 1805-1832', *JMBRAS,* xxiii (1950).
Cuisinier, J., 'La guerre des Padri (1803-1838-1845)', *Archives de Sociologie des Religions,* vii (1959).
Dekmejian, R.H. and Wyszomirski, M.J., 'Charismatic Leadership in Islam: The Mahdi of the Sudan', *Comparative Studies in Society and History,* xiv (1972).
Dewey, A.G., *Peasant Marketing in Java.* New York, 1962.
Dobbin, C., 'Economic Change in Minangkabau as a Factor in the Rise of the Padri Movement, 1784-1830', *Indonesia,* xxiii (1977).
——, 'The Exercise of Authority in Minangkabau in the Late Eighteenth Century', in A. Reid and L. Castles (eds.), *Pre-Colonial State Systems in Southeast Asia.* Kuala Lumpur, 1975.
——, 'Islamic Revivalism in Minangkabau at the Turn of the Nineteenth Century', *Modern Asian Studies,* viii (1974).
——, 'Tuanku Imam Bondjol (1772-1864), *Indonesia,* xiii (1972).
Dobby, E.H.G., *Southeast Asia.* London, 1950.
Drewes, G.W.J., 'De Herkomst van Nuruddin ar-Raniri', *BKI,* cxi (1955).
Dumont, R., *Types of Rural Economy. Studies in World Agriculture.* London, 1957.
Elkan, W., *An Introduction to Development Economics.* Harmondsworth, 1973.
Evans-Pritchard, E.E., *The Sanusi of Cyrenaica.* Oxford, 1949.
Evers, H-D., 'Changing Patterns of Minangkabau Urban Landownership', *BKI,* cxxxi (1975).
Fieldhouse, D.K., *The Colonial Empires. A Comparative Survey from the Eighteenth Century.* London, 1966.
——, *Economics and Empire 1830-1914.* London, 1973.
——, *The Theory of Capitalist Imperialism.* New York, 1967.
Firth, R., *Malay Fishermen, their Peasant Economy.* London, 1946.
Firth, R. and Yamey, B.S., *Capital, Saving and Credit in Peasant Societies.* London, 1964.
Fisher, C.A., *South-East Asia. A Social, Economic and Political Geography.* London, 1964.
Furnivall, J.S., *Netherlands India: A Study of Plural Economy.* Cambridge, 1944.
Geertz, C., *Agricultural Involution.* Berkeley and Los Angeles, 1968.
——, *Islam Observed. Religious Development in Morocco and Indonesia.* New Haven and London, 1968.
——, *The Religion of Java.* New York, 1960.
Geyl, P., 'The Dutch in India', in *The Cambridge History of India,* v. Delhi, 1968.
Gibb, H.A.R. and Kramers, J.H., *Shorter Encyclopaedia of Islam.* Leiden and London, 1953.
Gilsenan, M., *Saint and Sufi in Modern Egypt. An Essay in the Sociology of Religion.* Oxford, 1973.
Glamann, K., *Dutch-Asiatic Trade 1620-1740.* Copenhagen and The Hague, 1958.
Glassburner, B. (ed.), *The Economy of Indonesia.* Ithaca and London, 1971.
Goris, R., 'The Position of the Blacksmiths', in *Bali. Studies in Life, Thought and Ritual.* The Hague and Bandung, 1960.

Gorkom, K.W. van, *De Oost-Indische Cultures, in Betrekking tot Handel en Nijverheid.* 3 vols. 2nd edn. Amsterdam, 1884.

Gould, J.W., *Americans in Sumatra.* The Hague, 1961.

——, 'Sumatra-America's Pepperpot 1784-1873. Part I: Background and Early Years to 1815', *Essex Institute Historical Collections,* xcii (1956).

Gourou, P., *The Tropical World.* 3rd edn. London, 1961.

Great Britain. Geographical Handbook Series. Naval Intelligence Division, *Netherlands East Indies.* 2 vols. London, 1944.

Hall, D.G.E., *A History of South-East Asia.* 2nd edn. London, 1966.

Hamka, *Sedjarah Islam di Sumatera.* 2nd edn. Medan, 1950.

Hanna, W.A., 'The Role of the Minangkabau in Contemporary Indonesia', *American Universities Field Staff Reports,* vii (3), WAH-2-'59.

Hiskett, M., *Sword of Truth: Life and Times of Shehu Usuman Dan Fodio.* New York, 1973.

Hobsbawm, E.J., *The Age of Revolution. Europe 1789-1848.* London, 1962.

Hoffman, B.G., *The Structure of Traditional Moroccan Rural Society.* The Hague, 1967.

Hooyer, G.B., *De Krijgsgeschiedenis van Nederlandsch-Indië van 1811 tot 1894.* 3 vols. The Hague and Batavia, 1895.

Hopkins, A.G., *An Economic History of West Africa.* London, 1973.

Hufton, O.H., *The Poor of Eighteenth-Century France 1750-1789.* Oxford, 1974.

Ibrahim, A., *Islamic Law in Malaya.* Singapore, 1965.

Iliffe, J., 'The Organization of the Maji Maji Rebellion', *Journal of African History,* viii (1967).

Indonesian Economics. The Concepts of Dualism in Theory and Policy. The Hague, 1966.

Ja'kub, I., *Sedjarah Islam di Indonesia.* Jakarta, 1956.

Jeffrey, R., *The Decline of Nayar Dominance. Society and Politics in Travancore, 1847-1908.* London, 1976.

Johns, A.H., 'Islam in Southeast Asia: Problems of Perspective', in C.D. Cowan and O.W. Wolters (eds.), *Southeast Asian History and Historiography.* London and Ithaca, 1976.

——, 'Malay Sufism as illustrated in an anonymous collection of 17th century tracts', *JMBRAS,* xxx (1957).

——, 'Muslim Mystics and Historical Writing', in D.G.E. Hall (ed.), *Historians of South East Asia.* London, 1961.

Josselin de Jong, P.E. de, *Minangkabau and Negri Sembilan. Socio-Political Structure in Indonesia.* The Hague, 1952.

Joustra, M., *Batakspiegel.* 2nd edn. Leiden, 1926.

——, *Litteratuuroverzicht der Bataklanden.* Leiden, 1907.

——, *Minangkabau. Overzicht van Land, Geschiedenis en Volk.* The Hague, 1923.

—— and Tideman, J., *Overzicht der Litteratuur Betreffende Minangkabau.* 2 vols. Amsterdam, 1924-1937.

Kahn, J., 'Economic Scale and the Cycle of Petty Commodity Production in West Sumatra', in M. Bloch (ed.), *Marxist Analyses and Social Anthropology.* London, 1975.

——, 'Imperialism and the Reproduction of Capitalism: Towards a definition of the Indonesian Social Formation', *Critique of Anthropology,* ii (1974).

——, ' "Tradition", Matriliny and Change Among the Minangkabau of Indonesia', *BKI,* cxxxii (1976).

Kartodirdjo, S., *Protest Movements in Rural Java.* Singapore, 1973.

Kathirithamby-Wells, J., 'Achehnese Control over West Sumatra up to the Treaty of Painan of 1663', *JSAH,* x (1969).
——, 'Ahmad Shah Ibn Iskandar and the Late 17th Century "Holy War" in Indonesia', *JMBRAS,* xliii (1970).
——, *The British West Sumatran Presidency (1760-85): Problems of Early Colonial Enterprise.* Kuala Lumpur, 1977.
——, 'The Inderapura Sultanate: The Foundations of its Rise and Decline, From the Sixteenth to the Eighteenth Centuries', *Indonesia,* xxi (1976).
Kedourie, E., *Nationalism.* 3rd edn. London, 1966.
Khan, M.A., *History of the Fara'idi Movement in Bengal (1818-1906).* Karachi, 1965.
Kielstra, E.B., 'Het Ontstaan van den Padrie-Oorlog', *Indisch Militair Tijdschrift* (1887), ii.
——, 'Onze aanrakingen met Troeman', *IG,* x (1888), ii.
Klein, M.A., *Islam and Imperialism in Senegal: Sine-Saloum, 1847-1914.* Stanford, 1968.
Kroeskamp, H., *De Westkust en Minangkabau (1665-1668).* Utrecht, 1931.
Krom, N.J., *Hindoe-Javaansche Geschiedenis.* 2nd edn. The Hague, 1931.
——, *Inleiding tot de Hindoe-Javaansche Kunst.* 2 vols. 2nd edn. The Hague, 1923.
La Gort Dillié, P.M., *Bijdrage tot de Kennis der Oorlogvoering in de Nederlandsch Oost-Indische Gewesten.* Semarang, 1863.
Lach, D.F., *Southeast Asia in the Eyes of Europe. The Sixteenth Century.* Chicago, 1968.
Landon, K.P., *Southeast Asia. Crossroads of Religions.* Chicago, 1949.
Landsberger, H.A., *Rural Protest: Peasant Movements and Social Change.* London, 1974.
Le Roy Ladurie, E., *The Peasants of Languedoc.* Urbana, 1974.
Leeuw, W.J.A. de, *Het Painansch Contract.* Amsterdam, 1926.
Levy, R., *The Social Structure of Islam.* Cambridge, 1969.
Lewis, I.M., *Ecstatic Religion.* Harmondsworth, 1971.
Leyds, W.J., 'Larassen in Minangkabau', *Koloniale Studiën,* x (1926).
Lichtheim, G., *Imperialism.* Harmondsworth, 1974.
Loeb, E.M., *Sumatra. Its History and People.* Vienna, 1935.
Lombard, D., *Le Sultanat d'Atjêh au Temps d'Iskandar Muda 1607-1636.* Paris, 1967.
MacLeod, N., 'De Oost-Indische Compagnie op Sumatra in de 17e eeuw. IV.', *IG,* xxvi (1904), ii.
——, 'De Oost-Indische Compagnie op Sumatra in de 17e eeuw. IV (Vervolg)', *IG,* xxvii (1905), i.
——, 'De Oost-Indische Compagnie op Sumatra in de 17e eeuw. V.', *IG,* xxvii (1905), ii.
Madjolelo, D. Dt. and Marzoeki, A., *Tuanku Imam Bondjol. Perintis Djalan ke Kemerdekaan.* Jakarta and Amsterdam, 1951.
Mansoer, M.D. *et al., Sedjarah Minangkabau.* Jakarta, 1970.
Mansvelt, W.M.F., *Geschiedenis van de Nederlandsche Handel-Maatschappij.* 2 vols. Haarlem, 1924.
Marks, H.J., *The First Contest for Singapore 1819-1824.* The Hague, 1959.
Marrison, G.E., 'The Coming of Islam to the East Indies', *JMBRAS,* xxiv (1951).
Meilink-Roelofsz, M.A.P., *Asian Trade and European Influence in the Indonesian Archipelago between 1500 and about 1630.* The Hague, 1962.

Meillassoux, C., *The Development of Indigenous Trade and Markets in West Africa.* Oxford, 1971.
Meulen, W.J. van der, 'Ptolemy's Geography of Mainland Southeast Asia and Borneo', *Indonesia,* xix (1975).
——, 'Suvarṇadvîpa and the Chrysê Chersonêsos', *Indonesia,* xviii (1974).
Migdal, J.S., *Peasants, Politics, and Revolution. Pressures toward Political and Social Change in the Third World.* Princeton, 1974.
Minattur, J., 'Some Notes on Indian Influence on Malay Customary Law', in D.C. Buxbaum (ed.), *Family Law and Customary Law in Asia: A Contemporary Legal Perspective.* The Hague, 1968.
Myint, H., *The Economics of Developing Countries.* 2nd edn. London, 1965.
Naim, M., *Merantau: Causes and Effects of Minangkabau Voluntary Migration.* Occasional Paper No. 5, Institute of Southeast Asian Studies, Singapore, 1971.
——, 'Merantau: Reasons and Patterns of Minangkabau Voluntary Migration', *Sumatra Research Bulletin,* i (1971).
Nieuw Nederlandsch Biografisch Woordenboek. vols. 1-10. Leiden, 1911-1937.
Nieuwenhuijze, C.A.O. van, 'Nur Al-Dîn al-Ranîrî als bestrijder der Wugudîya', *BKI,* civ (1947-1948).
——, *Samsu-l-dîn van Pasai. Bijdrage tot de Kennis der Sumatraansche Mystiek.* Leiden, 1945.
Noer, D., *The Modernist Muslim Movement in Indonesia 1900-1942.* Kuala Lumpur, 1973.
Paige, J.M., *Agrarian Revolution. Social Movements and Export Agriculture in the Underdeveloped World.* New York and London, 1975.
Parlindungan, M.O., *Pongkinangolngolan Sinambela gelar Tuanku Rao. Terror Agama Islam Mazhab Hambali Di Tanah Batak. 1816-1833* n.p., n.d.
Pillai, E.P.N.K., *Studies in Kerala History.* Kottayam, 1970.
Planhol, X. de, *Les Fondements Géographiques de l'Histoire de l'Islam.* Paris, 1968.
——, *The World of Islam.* Ithaca, 1959.
Polanyi, K., Arensberg, C.M. and Pearson, H.W., *Trade and Markets in the Early Empires.* Glencoe, 1957.
Putnam, G.G., *Salem Vessels and Their Voyages. A History of the Pepper Trade with the Island of Sumatra.* Series I. Salem, 1924.
Radjab, M., *Perang Paderi di Sumatera Barat (1803-1838).* Jakarta, 1954.
Ranger, T.O., 'Connexions between "Primary Resistance" Movements and Modern Mass Nationalism in East and Central Africa. Parts I and II', *Journal of African History,* ix (1968).
Redfield, R., *Peasant Society and Culture. An Anthropological Approach to Civilization.* Chicago, 1956.
Reid, A., *The Contest for North Sumatra. Atjeh, the Netherlands and Britain 1858-1898.* Kuala Lumpur, 1969.
——, 'Sixteenth Century Turkish Influence in Western Indonesia', *JSAH,* x (1969).
Richards, D.S. (ed.), *Islam and the Trade of Asia. A Colloquium.* Oxford, 1970.
Rinkes, D.A., *Abdoerraoef van Singkel. Bijdrage tot de kennis van de mystiek op Sumatra en Java.* Heerenveen, 1909.
Rizvi, S.A.A., *Muslim Revivalist Movements in Northern India in the Sixteenth and Seventeenth Centuries.* Agra, 1965.
Robequain, C., *Malaya, Indonesia, Borneo and the Philippines.* London, 1954.
Rodinson, M., *Islam and Capitalism.* Harmondsworth, 1977.
Ronkel, Ph.S. van, 'Het Heiligdom te Oelakan', *TBG,* lvi (1914).
Sabean, D., 'Markets, Uprisings and Leadership in Peasant Societies: Western Europe 1381-1789', *Peasant Studies Newsletter,* ii (1973).

Safwan, M., *Sultan Alam Bagagar Syah (1789-1849)*. Jakarta, 1975.
Said, M., *Rokan. Tuanku Tambusai Berdjuang*. Padang, 1969.
Schmitz, Y., *Willem I, Koning van Noord en Zuid*. Hasselt, 1966.
Schnitger, F.M., *Forgotten Kingdoms in Sumatra*. Leiden, 1939.
Scott, J.C., *The Moral Economy of the Peasant. Rebellion and Subsistence in Southeast Asia*. New Haven and London, 1976.
Seton-Watson, H., *The Russian Empire 1801-1917*. Oxford, 1967.
Shanin, T., *Peasants and Peasant Societies*. Harmondsworth, 1971.
Siegel, J.T., *The Rope of God*. Berkeley and Los Angeles, 1969.
Simon, G., *The Progress and Arrest of Islam in Sumatra*. London/Edinburgh/New York, 1912.
Sjafiroeddin, D.S., 'Kubueng Tigo Baleh Lubuek Nan Tigo', *Sumatra Research Bulletin*, iv (1975).
——, 'Pre-Islamic Minangkabau', *Sumatra Research Bulletin*, iv (1974).
Smith, A.D., *Theories of Nationalism*. London, 1971.
Smith, W.C., *Islam in Modern History*. New York, 1957.
Soekanto, *Sentot alias Alibasah Abdulmustopo Prawirodirdjo Senopati Diponegoro*. Jakarta, 1951.
Stavenhagen, R., *Social Classes in Agrarian Societies*. Garden City, 1975.
Steensgaard, N., *The Asian Trade Revolution of the Seventeenth Century*. Chicago and London, 1974.
Stokes, E., 'Late Nineteenth-Century Colonial Expansion and the Attack on the Theory of Economic Imperialism: A Case of Mistaken Identity?', *The Historical Journal*, xii (1969).
——, 'Traditional Resistance Movements and Afro-Asian Nationalism: The Context of the 1857 Mutiny Rebellion in India', *Past and Present*, xlviii (1970).
Tarling, N., *Anglo-Dutch Rivalry in the Malay World 1780-1824*. Sydney, 1962.
Tay, J.S., 'The Attempts of Raffles to Establish a British Base in South-East Asia, 1818-1819', *JSAH*, i (1960).
Terpstra, H., *Buitenlandse Getuigen van Onze Koloniale Expansie*. Amsterdam, 1944.
Thoman, R.S., Conkling, E.C. and Yeates, M.H., *The Geography of Economic Activity*. 2nd edn. New York, 1968.
Thorner, D., Kerblay, B. and Smith, R.E.F. (eds.), *A.V. Chayanov on The Theory of Peasant Economy*. Homewood, 1966.
Trimingham, J.S., *The Sufi Orders in Islam*. Oxford, 1971.
Trouton, R., *Peasant Renaissance in Yugoslavia 1900-1950*. London, 1952.
Turnbull, C.M., *The Straits Settlements 1826-67*. London, 1972.
Turner, B.S., *Weber and Islam. A critical study*. London, 1974.
Utrecht, E., 'Political Mobilisations of Peasants in Indonesia', *Journal of Contemporary Asia*, vi (1976).
Voorhoeve, P., *Twee Maleise Geschriften van Nūruddīn ar-Rānīrī*. Leiden, 1955.
Wahba, S.H., *Arabian Days*. London, 1964.
Waldman, M.R., 'The Fulani *Jihād*: A Reassessment', *Journal of African History*, vi (1965).
Wallerstein, I., *The Modern World-System. Capitalist Agriculture and the Origins of the European World-Economy in the Sixteenth Century*. New York and London, 1974.
Weber, M., *The City*. Glencoe, 1958.
Westendorp Boerma, J.J., *Een Geestdriftig Nederlander. Johannes Van den Bosch*. Amsterdam, 1950.

Westenenk, L.C., *De Minangkabausche Nagari.* 3rd edn. Weltevreden, 1918.
——, 'Opstellen over Minangkabau. I.', *TBG,* lv (1913).
——, 'Opstellen over Minangkabau. II.', *TBG,* lvii (1916).
Willinck, G.D., *Het Rechtsleven bij de Minangkabausche Maleiërs.* Leiden, 1909.
Willis, J.R., '*Jihād Fī Sabīl Allāh* – its Doctrinal Basis in Islam and Some Aspects of its Evolution in Nineteenth-Century West Africa'. *Journal of African History,* viii (1967).
Winder, R.B., *Saudi Arabia in the Nineteenth Century.* London, 1965.
Winstedt, R.O., 'The Advent of Muhammadism in the Malay Peninsula and Archipelago', *JSBRAS,* lxxvii (1917).
——, 'The Early Muhammadan Missionaries', *JSBRAS,* lxxxi (1920).
——, *The Malays: A Cultural History.* 6th edn. London, 1961.
Wolf, E.R., *Peasants.* Englewood Cliffs, 1966.
Wong, L.K., 'The Trade of Singapore, 1819-69', *JMBRAS,* xxxiii (1960).
Worsley, P., 'Social class in emergent countries; bourgeoisie and petty bourgeoisie', in A. Béteille (ed.), *Social Inequality.* Harmondsworth, 1969.
Wright, H.R.C., *East-Indian Economic Problems of the Age of Cornwallis and Raffles.* London, 1961.
——, *Free Trade and Protection in the Netherlands 1816-30. A Study of the First Benelux.* Cambridge, 1955.
Young, M. de, *Man and Land in the Haitian Economy.* Gainesville, 1958.
Zenkovsky, S.A., *Pan-Turkism and Islam in Russia.* Cambridge. Mass., 1960.
Ziadeh, N.A., *Sanūsīyah. A Study of a Revivalist Movement in Islam.* Leiden, 1958.

C. Unpublished Theses

Graves, E.E., 'The Ever-Victorious Buffalo: How the Minangkabau of Indonesia Solved their "Colonial Question".' Ph.D., University of Wisconsin, 1971.
Lee, K.H., 'Acheh's Relations with the British, 1760-1819'. M.A., University of Malaya, 1969.
Lewis, D., 'The Dutch East India Company and the Straits of Malacca, 1700-1784; Trade and Politics in the Eighteenth Century.' Ph.D., Australian National University, 1970.
Nicholson, C.K., 'The Introduction of Islam into Sumatra and Java: a Study in Cultural Change'. Ph.D., Syracuse University, 1965.
Oki, A., 'Social Change in the West Sumatran Village: 1908-1945'. Ph.D., Australian National University, 1977.
Penders, C.L.M., 'The Expansion of Dutch Control on the Central West- and East-Coasts of Sumatra: 1816-1873'. M.A., Australian National University, 1962.
Young, R.J., 'The English East India Company and Trade on the West Coast of Sumatra, 1730-1760.' Ph.D., University of Pennsylvania, 1970.

PLATES

Patterns of Settlement

1 *Padang and surroundings, 1828.* F marks the entry to the harbour, E represents the Dutch customs' house, and A the old Dutch fort. The Minangkabau *pasar* is located near the bend in the Padang river.

2 *View of Bukit Padang, c. 1828.* The hill lies on the left bank of the Padang river where it enters the sea. Note the houses typical of the west coast, and the covered *perahu.*

3 *Bonjol and other villages in the valley of Alahan Panjang, 1837.* All the villages are walled, while the cross-hatching indicates rice fields. Roman numerals represent Dutch encampments and batteries used in the siege of Bonjol, whilst small Latin letters on Bukit Terjadi indicate Bonjol's defences. Three breaches have been shot in Bonjol's fortifications. The two buildings marked by diagonal crosses inside and outside of Bonjol's walls are the village mosques. Imam Bonjol's birthplace, Tanjung Bunga, is on the extreme right.

4 *The Dutch Fort de Kock, Bukit Tinggi, 1826.* On the right is a Padri carrying a matchlock on his shoulder, and wearing a copy of the Koran – or part thereof – around his neck.

5 *Fortified village of Daludalu, 1838.* The numerals represent: (1) high ramparts, (2) deep moats, (3) Tuanku Tambusai's house, (4) watch towers, (5) main gates, (6) mosque.

The Village

6 *Houses.* The upper drawing is of a house in the Minangkabau heartland. On the right is a structure protecting the village drum, and on the extreme right a building used for cooking. The lower drawing is of a house in a *rantau* settlement on one of the routes from the Minangkabau heartland to the headwaters of an east coast river. Beneath the house is a pen for cattle. River stones facilitate access to the house in the rainy season.

7 *Rice barns.* The upper drawing is of a barn from the Minangkabau heartland, and shows the harmony between barn and house styles. The lower barns are from the *rantau.*

8 *Mosque of the Padri period.* The walls are of wood, the roof-covering of palm fibre, and there is a glittering tin spire. The door is at right, and usually two large stones serve as steps. On the left is an extension which provides a small room for the *imam.*

The People

9 *Penghulu from the Lake Singkarak region, c. 1825.* Both the robe and head-covering are dark blue, the latter being decorated with gold ornaments. The woven cloth over the left shoulder is of red, blue and gold, and in the right hand the *penghulu* holds a staff tipped with silver.

10 *Minangkabau women, c. 1825.* A variety of form of adaptation to Padri tenets is shown. The woman second from the left has covered her face completely, while the woman on the right has apparently made few concessions.

11 *A petty trader.* The trader's load is lashed to a bamboo frame, on the side of which are a gourd for water and a bag for personal necessities. He wears a *keris* in his waistband and carries in his right hand a knife for cutting through undergrowth.

12 *A Padri, allegedly Imam Bonjol.* The white garb is modelled on Arab dress, and the left hand holds prayer beads.

The Economy

13 *Waterwheel for irrigation.* The hub of the wheel turns on an axle which rests on a forked stake fixed into the ground. Bamboo tubes fill with water as the wheel moves round, emptying into a trough from which the water passes into a conduit, firmly tied to a tree.

14 *Gold mine south of Padang, c. 1680.* This is a mine laid down under VOC auspices on an existing Minangkabau site. Letters B and D represent the original Minangkabau shafts, and S and T the main new shafts. At the top left, L marks the Dutch fort, N the slaves' quarters and M the quarters of European mine-workers imported from Saxony.

15 *Iron implements of Minangkabau workmanship.* (1) matchlock, made in Sirukam; (2) (3) lances, made in Sipayang; (4) rope sling, used with stones; (5) long *keris* with scabbard; (6) short *keris* with scabbard; the blade was made in Sungai Puar, Agam, and the weapon completed in Sipayang; (7) (8) knife with scabbard; (9) sword with scabbard; (10) dart, made in Sipayang and used in a blow-pipe; (11) (12) knives used for cutting wood, etc.; (13) horn for gunpowder.

16 *Loom from Silungkang.* The loom is placed under the house, and is similar to one described in Chapter II, part 2. Figure 2 is an enlargement of b, the shuttle comb.

17 *Gambir-making.* On the right, the gambir leaves are boiled in a large iron pan over a clay oven fuelled by wood. Figure 1 at the bottom of the picture illustrates the wooden mortar into which small quantities of the boiled leaves are placed, to be pounded with a wooden pestle. The major illustration is of the press. A basket of pounded leaves is placed on the wooden disk (b) and secured by a wooden block (c). The leaves are pressed by manipulating the wooden beam (f), the liquid being conducted into a trough (e) and subsequently scooped into smaller troughs (m) for hardening.

Acknowledgements

The plates in this book are drawn from:

H.J.J.L. de Stuers, *De Vestiging en Uitbreiding der Nederlanders ter Westkust van Sumatra.* 2 vols. Amsterdam, 1849-1850. Plates 1, 2, 4, 5, 9, 10, 12.

G.B. Hooyer, *De Krijgsgeschiedenis van Nederlandsch-Indië van 1811 tot 1894.* 3 vols. The Hague and Batavia, 1895. Plate 3.

A.L. van Hasselt, *Ethnographische Atlas van Midden-Sumatra, met Verklarenden Tekst.* Leiden, 1881. Plates 6, 7, 8, 11, 13, 15, 16, 17.

E. Hesse, *Gold-Bergwerke in Sumatra 1680-1683.* The Hague, 1931. Plate 14.

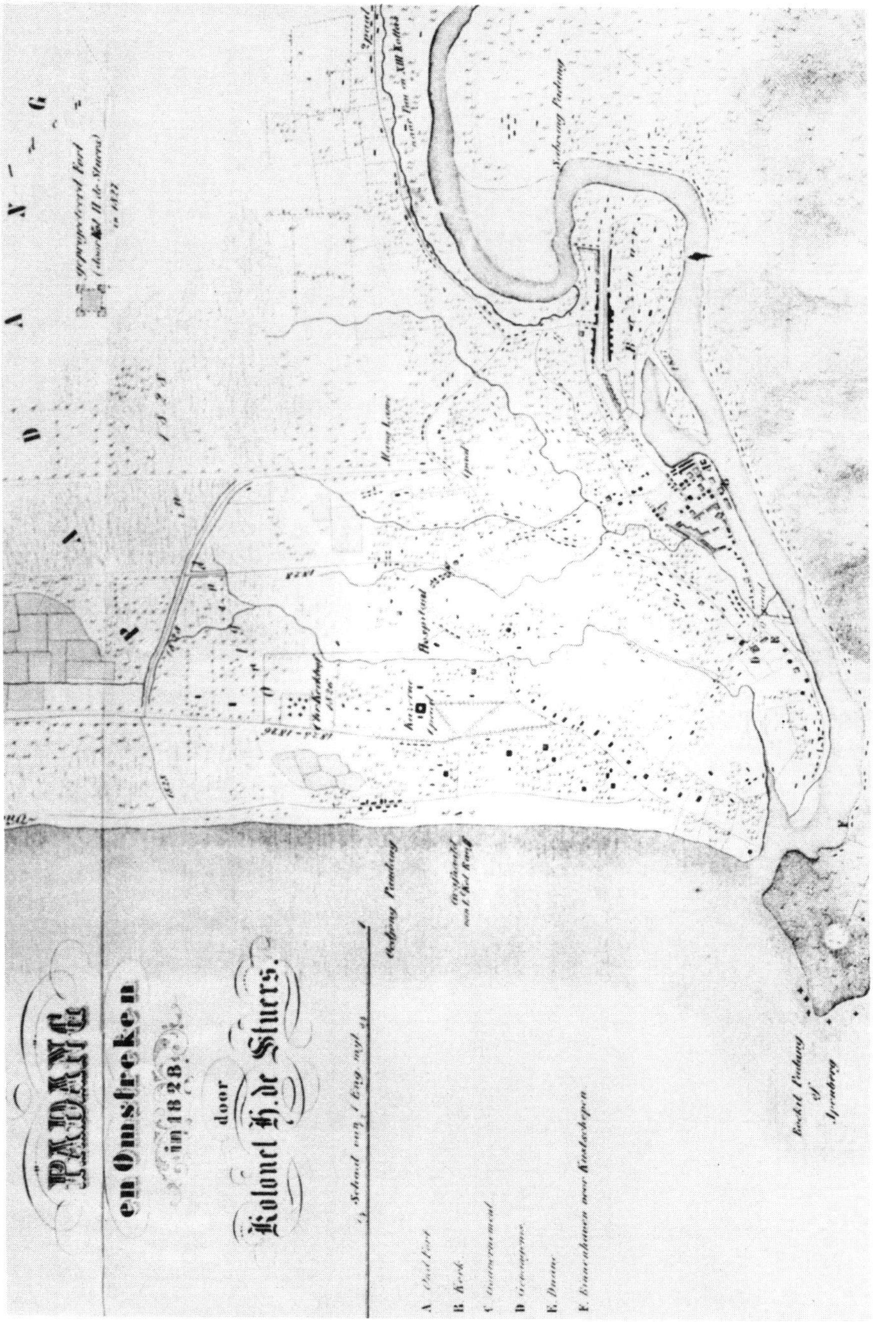
PADANG
en Omstreken
in 1828
door
Kolonel H. de Stuers.
B Kerk
E Douane
F Binnenhaven voor Kustschepen
Apenberg

1

2

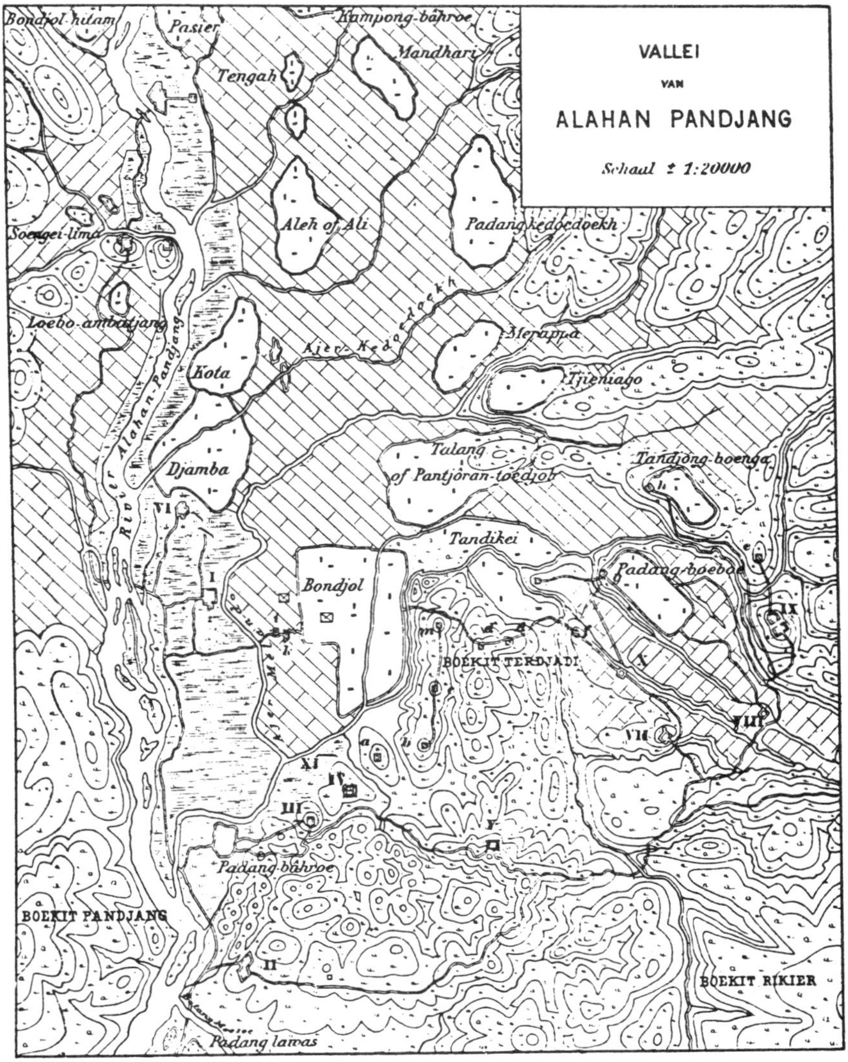
VALLEI
VAN
ALAHAN PANDJANG
Schaal 1:20000
Pasier
Kampong-bahroe
Mandhari
Tengah
Aleh of Ali
Padang kedoedoekh
Soengei-lima
Loebo-ambatjang
Kota
Ajer Kedoedoekh
Merappa
Tjieniago
River Alahan-Pandjang
Djamba
Talang
of Pantjoran-toedjoh
Tandjong-boenga
Tandikei
Bondjol
Padang-boeboe
BOEKIT TERDJADI
Padang-bahroe
BOEKIT PANDJANG
BOEKIT RIKIER
Padang lawas

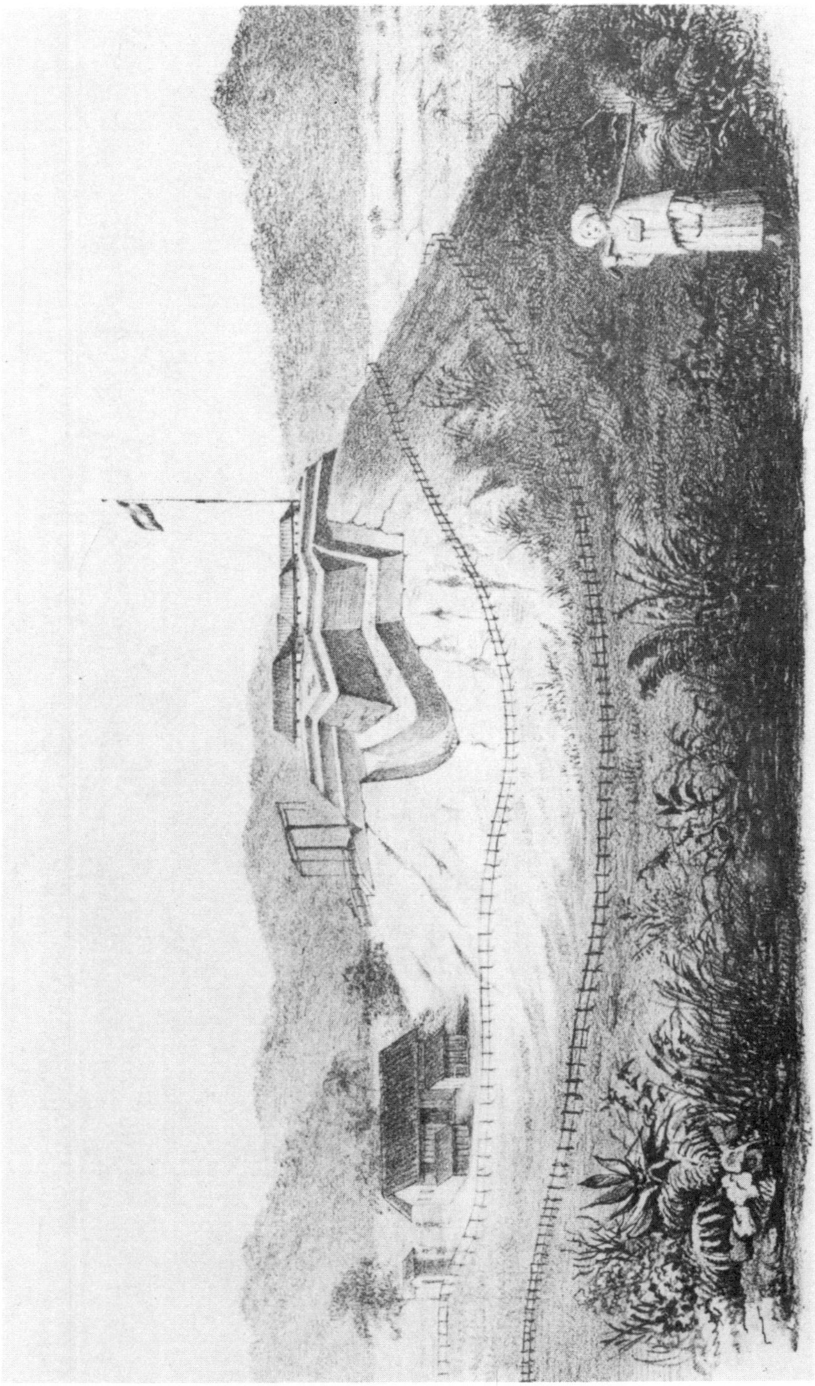

4

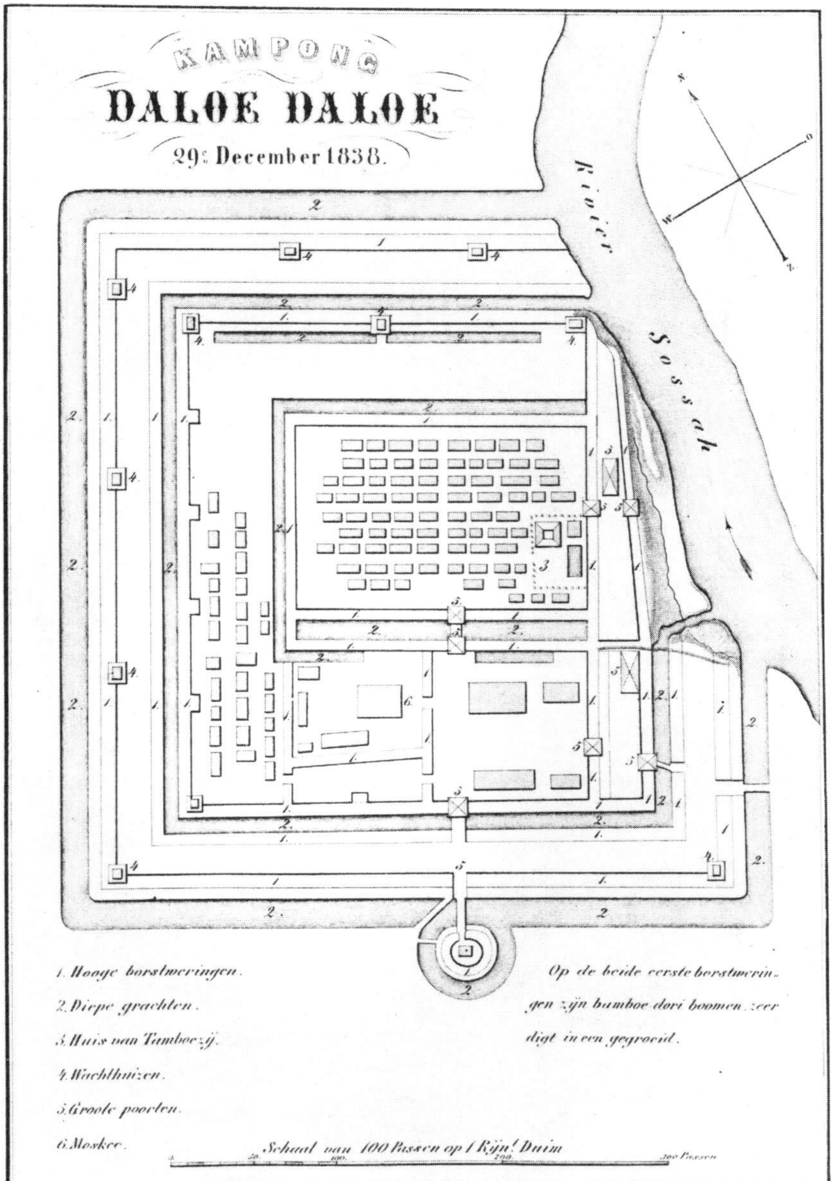
KAMPONG
DALOE DALOE
29e December 1838.
Rivier Sossah
1. Hooge borstweringen.
2. Diepe grachten.
3. Huis van Tamboezij.
4. Wachthuizen.
5. Groote poorten.
6. Moskee.
Op de beide eerste borstweringen zijn bamboe dori boomen zeer digt in een gegroeid.
Schaal van 100 Passen op 1 Rijnl. Duim

5

6

1* $\frac{1}{50}$
2. $\frac{1}{50}$

8

9

10

11

12

13

14

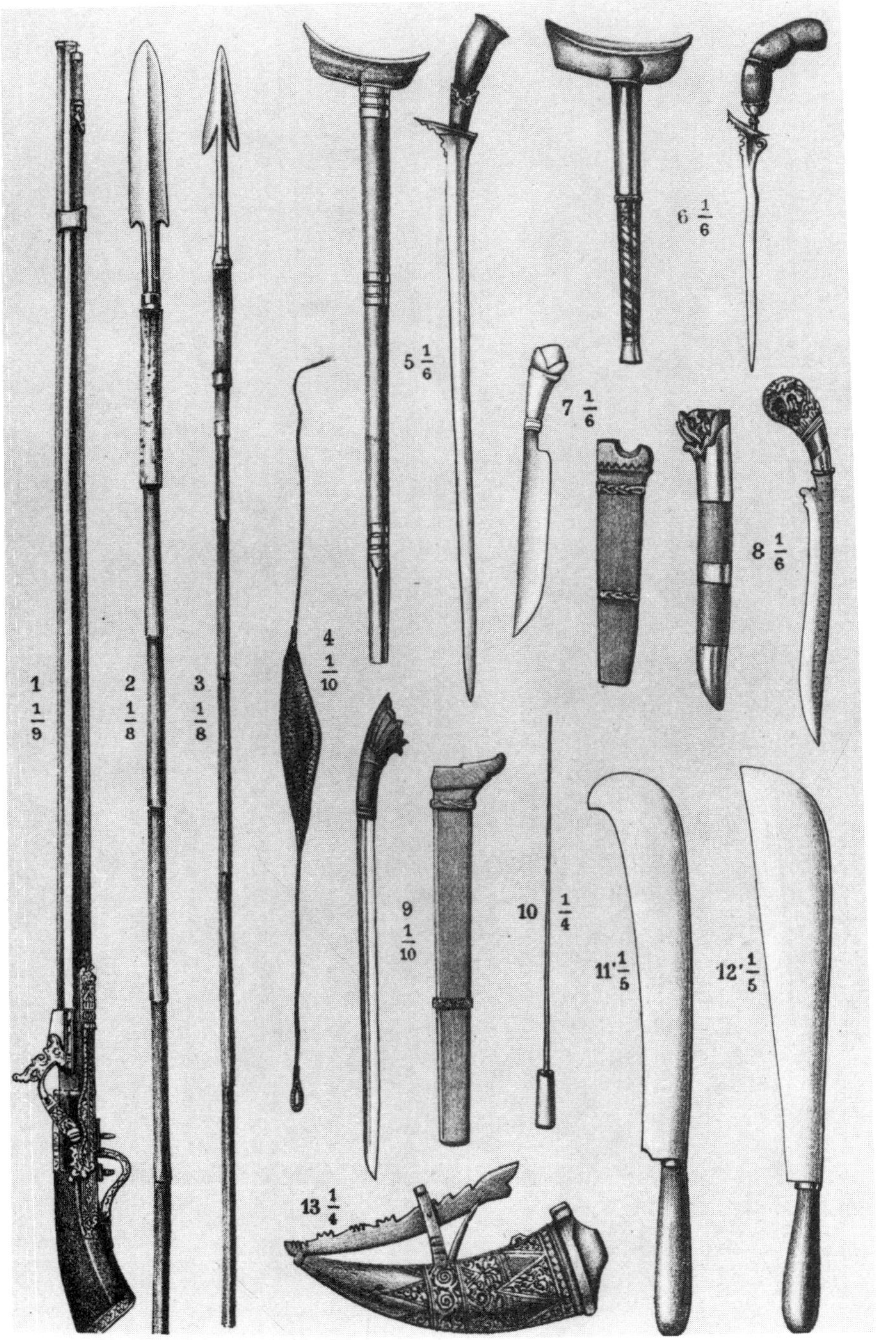

15

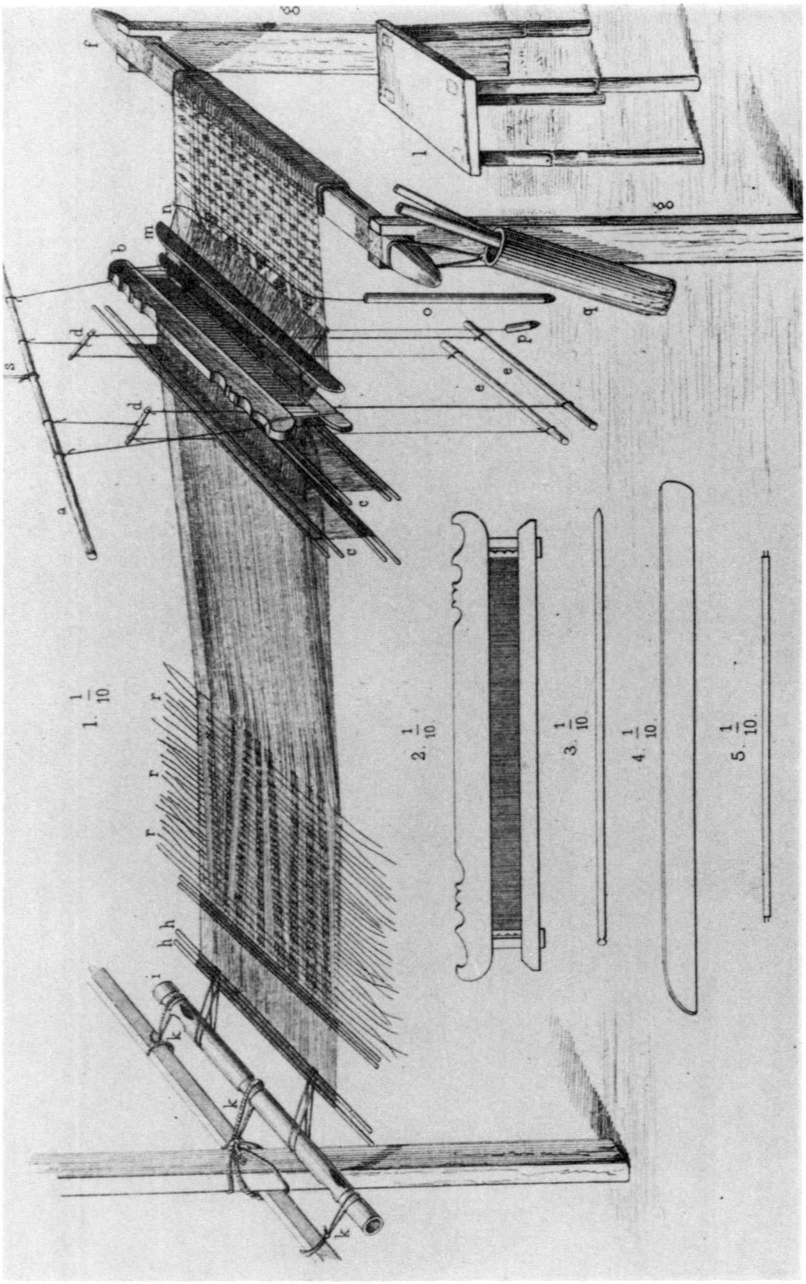

16

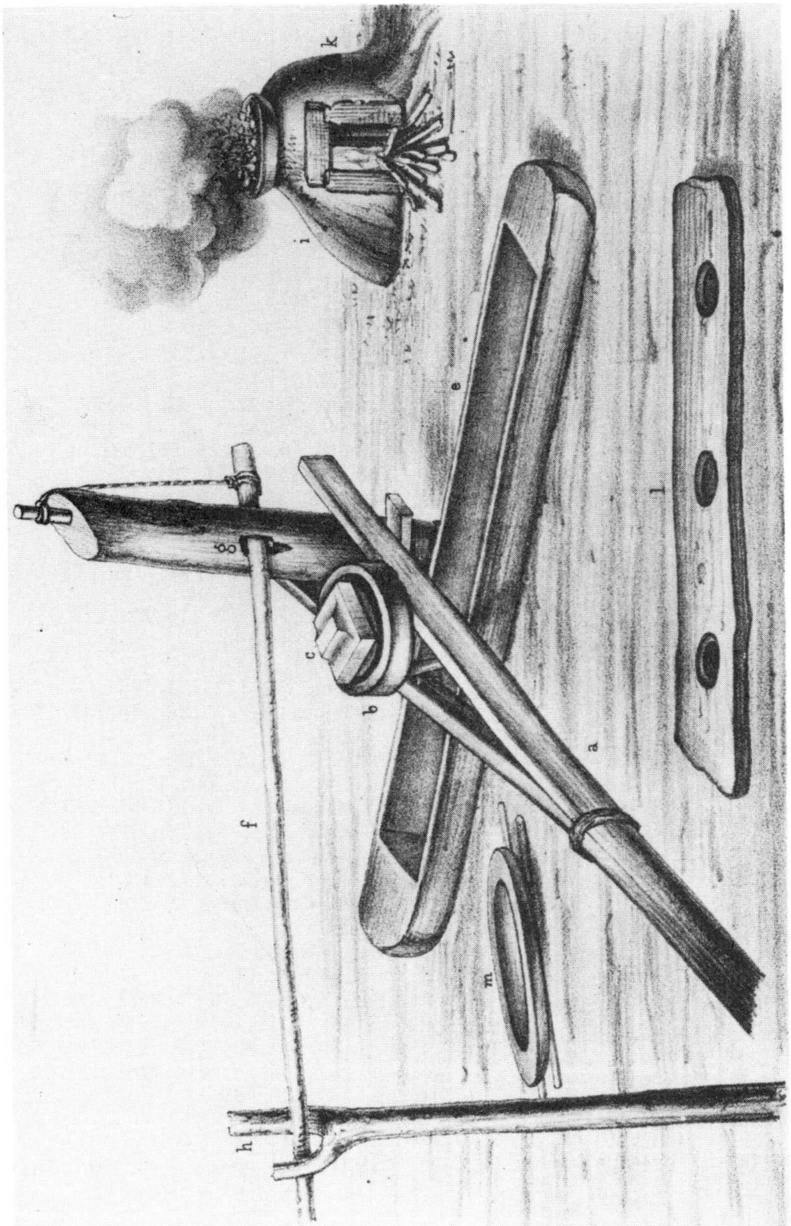

17

INDEX